Date Due

	MAY 1 3 1993	
MAR 05 1986		JAN 2 1 1995
3/19/86		NOV 2 9 1995
1/2/86		FEB 0 1 1996
MAR 07 1987		
FEB 2 4 1988		FEB 1 7 2004
FEB 2 1 1989		
FEB 2 0 1990		JAN 1 2 2005
FEB 2 0 1990		
FEB 2 0 1991		FEB 0 8 2005
MAR 0 6 1991		
MAR 2 2 1991		FEB 1 9 2005
APR 0 1 1992		SEP 2 6 2009
FEB 1 2 1993		
APR 2 6 1993		

BRODART, INC. Cat. No. 23 233 Printed in U.S.A.

Great Negroes, PAST AND PRESENT

Great Negroes

PAST AND PRESENT

THIRD EDITION

by **Russell L. Adams**

Illustrated by **Eugene Winslow**

Edited by **David P. Ross, Jr.**

AFRO-AM PUBLISHING COMPANY, INC.
Chicago, Illinois, 1969

Standard Book Number 910030-07-3

Library of Congress Catalog Card Number 72-87924

THIRD EDITION

TABLE OF CONTENTS

v

TABLE OF CONTENTS

TABLE OF CONTENTS

TABLE OF CONTENTS

PREFACE

Since the release of the first edition of this title in 1963 there has been a national awakening to the realization that historical and cultural contributions of African-Americans have been omitted from our textbooks. This blind spot in our educational system has created problems of great magnitude in the schools across the nation. Educators have been hard pressed by the demands of Negro students to implement the teaching of "Black History."

In December of 1966 the National Educational Association held a national conference in Washington, D.C. and conducted workshops with leading educators and textbook publishers in an effort to resolve some of the basic problems involved in creating a realistic multi-ethnic curriculum. One of the major concerns was that of securing adequate teaching materials needed to implement changes in the courses of study. The scarcity of materials was acknowledged to be the prime obstacle in the path of immediate changes in the curriculum. Until this time only a very few of the producers of text materials had anticipated the social changes which were taking place, nor did they realize the urgent need for black history teaching tools.

This meeting was followed in January of 1967, by a meeting of the American Federation of Teachers in Washington, D.C. The subject of its conference was "Integrated Education." Here, more attention was devoted to the social aspects of the problem than to the solution of the curriculum needs. The historical significance of "Black Pride" was emphasized and related to integrated education. It was concluded that the total teaching system must reflect the multi-ethnic composition of the country.

Since that time, state and municipal governments have made the teaching of black history mandatory. The mandate required teaching tools for implementation, and teachers trained in the use of the tools. The lack of adequate tools and trained teachers in the subject area has stymied the progress of initiating the subject in many of the school systems.

The format of GREAT NEGROES, *Past and Present* has made it one of the most adaptable supplementary texts for the primary and secondary grades. In order to more fully broaden its use as a supplementary text, this third edition has been revised, updated and expanded to give it a greater depth and wealth of information. As publishers engaged exclusively in the publication of African-American history and culture, we are striving to develop materials which can be integrated into the existing curriculum with the minimum of orientation on the part of the teacher. With this in mind, a guide has been written which correlates this text with standard United States history textbooks.

DAVID P. ROSS, JR.
Editor

ACKNOWLEDGEMENTS

I wish to thank the individuals and institutions contributing to this book. I am grateful for the assistance of Dr. Metz T. P. Lochard, W. Louis Davis, Mrs. Geraldine Scott and Miss Julia Davis. I am indebted to Consolidated Book Publishers of Chicago, the George Cleveland Hall Branch of the Chicago Public Library, and to the staff of the James E. Shepard Library at North Carolina College. I deeply appreciate the job of research done by my associate, Eugene Winslow, which also contributed to the authentic illustrations that enhance the text. Finally, I wish to thank my wife, Eleanor, for her assistance and encouragement.

This third edition has been strengthened as a result of many suggestions and criticisms received from readers of the second edition throughout the nation.

Grateful acknowledgments are made to:

Alfred A. Knopf, Inc. for permission to quote lines from "The Negro Speaks of Rivers" in *The Big Sea* by Langston Hughes (Alfred A. Knopf, 1940)

Dodd, Mead & Company for permission to quote lines from "Little Brown Baby" and "Ode to Ethiopia" in *The Collected Poems of Paul Laurence Dunbar* (Dodd, Mead & Company, 1954)

Harper & Row, Inc. for permission to quote lines from "Heritage" in *Color* by Countee Cullen (Harper & Brothers, 1925); from "Black Majesty" in *On These I Stand* by Countee Cullen (Harper & Brothers, 1947); from "The Ghosts at the Quincy Club" in *The Bean Eaters* by Gwendolyn Brooks (Harper & Brothers, 1960)

Twayne Publishers, Inc. for permission to quote lines from "If We Must Die" in *The Selected Poems of Claude McKay* (Bookman Associates, 1953)

The volumes of *The Journal of Negro History, The Negro History Bulletin, The Dictionary of American Biography, Current Biography, Ebony* and *Negro Digest* were of inestimable value to this writer.

RUSSELL L. ADAMS

CHICAGO, ILLINOIS
APRIL, 1969

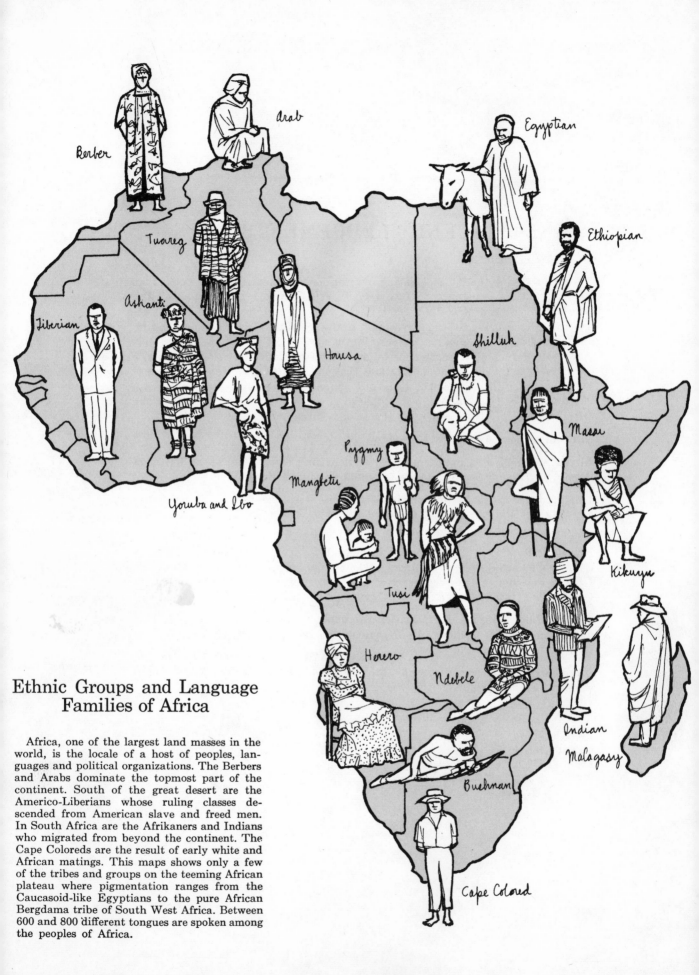

Ethnic Groups and Language Families of Africa

Africa, one of the largest land masses in the world, is the locale of a host of peoples, languages and political organizations. The Berbers and Arabs dominate the topmost part of the continent. South of the great desert are the Americo-Liberians whose ruling classes descended from American slave and freed men. In South Africa are the Afrikaners and Indians who migrated from beyond the continent. The Cape Coloreds are the result of early white and African matings. This maps shows only a few of the tribes and groups on the teeming African plateau where pigmentation ranges from the Caucasoid-like Egyptians to the pure African Bergdama tribe of South West Africa. Between 600 and 800 different tongues are spoken among the peoples of Africa.

Berber
Arab
Egyptian
Tuareg
Ethiopian
Liberian
Ashanti
Shilluk
Housa
Masai
Yoruba and Ibo
Pygmy
Mangbetu
Kikuyu
Tusi
Herero
Ndebele
Indian
Malagasy
Bushman
Cape Colored

I OUR AFRICAN HERITAGE

Out of the Mists of Time... a New Song

The history of the black man is the oldest but the least known of all mankind. The continuing study of the past by anthropologists and archaeologists indicates that central Africa bears evidence of being the land of the first human life. It is on the continent of Africa that the oldest human-like fossils have been found.

In the northeastern part of Tanganyika, Dr. L. S. B. Leakey, the famed archaeologist, has unearthed human remains nearly two million years old. At Olduvai Gorge, Dr. Leakey and his associates have been able to trace the evolution of man from the beginning of the Old Stone Age of Africa. Other evidence of man has been uncovered at Broken Hill, North Rhodesia. There, hand axes, picks and even anvils at least fifty thousand years old have been discovered. In central Nigeria, stone tools at least 39,000 years old have been dug from the earth. In the Congo, crude calculating devices dating back six thousand years have been retrieved. On the fringe of the Sahara Desert exist rock paintings of and by black men. The sensitive and realistic works have survived three thousand years of time.

Black men sat on the throne of Egypt at least three thousand years before Christ. Around 2500 B.C., masses of black men were serving in Egyptian armies. The Nubians, a black people, gained positions of power and honor in the land of the Pharaohs around 2000 B.C. During the early years of Egyptian greatness, Ra Nahesi, a Nubian sat on the throne. Following the Hyksos invasion of 1703 B.C., African influence in Egypt was even more pronounced. With the retreat of the Egyptians to the region of the Upper Nile at this time, the Pharaohs—Amenophis II, Amenophis III and Amenophis IV—all showed definite Negroid strains in their features. Amenophis IV is better known as Akhenaton, the first man to insist on the existence of one living God. His mother, Queen Tiyi, has been described as a "coal black" woman.

During the first millennium B.C., the Ethiopians of the Sudan gained control of Egypt. In 751 B.C., the Kushite warrior, Pianky, again subdued the country and started a hundred-year reign of black rulers. Through Egypt, the land of Kush controlled territory from the Mediterranean to the edge of modern Ethiopia. Perhaps the greatest of these black rulers was Taharka who assumed supreme power in the "cradle of civilization" in 688 B.C. His control of Egypt was so complete that Taharka styled himself "Emperor of the World." In 670 B.C., the Ethiopians were driven from the land and retired to the black capitals of Napata and Meroe. Napata was a famous Kushite center for the worship of the sun god, Amun, while Meroe was the first known commercial iron-producing settlement in history. One of the most outstanding rulers in the area of Napata and Meroe was Metekamane, who built great monuments to himself and his queen, Amanetari, along the western side of the Nile and on Argo Island.

The African presence in Egypt is still quite noticeable in the statuary which stare unblinkingly across the centuries. The Sphinx and many other sculptured monuments have the broad nose and full lips of the Africans. Not only did many Africans supply much of the manual labor for the building of the pyramids and the statues of the country, but also many of the architects and designers of these structures. One of the most skilled was Sehmut, the architect of Queen Hatshepsut's exquisitely beautiful temple, Deir-al-Bahari.

The blacks of Africa did more than help construct tombs and monuments. They pioneered, along with the Hittites, in the making of iron, the working of gold and silver, and in the use of oil-bearing plants for medicinal and dietary purposes, especially palm oil. They developed basic cereals, including several kinds of millet and rice. They took the wild plant *Gossypium herbaceum* and evolved it into the world's first cotton cloth, and from its fibers developed the art of weaving. The blacks of Africa are believed to have been the world's first farmers, producing wheat, groundnuts, gourds, kola, and possibly coffee and cress, as well as yams, watermelons and peanuts. A few writers assert that painting and sculpture reached Greece and Europe via Egypt and the Sudan, particularly work in bronze, brass, ivory, quartz and granite.

The Greek historian, Herodotus, mentioned the presence of Africans in the armies of Xerxes (480 B.C.) and wrote of them as "black and curly-haired." Blacks have been portrayed in the work of Greek sculptors and potters. It is difficult to evaluate the role of blacks in ancient Greece, although there is evidence supporting the view that Aesop, the moralist, was an African slave living in Greece. The Greeks were, of course, aware of the color contrast between white and black racial types, but there is little to suggest that they were particularly concerned with color as such. There is also ample evidence that considerable contact existed between Rome and Africa. Kush itself became one of the provinces of Rome in the fourth century A.D. Under Roman rule, Kush continued to be a link between the peoples of eastern Europe and the Arab tribes on the eastern side of the Red Sea.

In addition to Napata and Meroe, several other African states existed in the centuries before and after the birth of Christ. Ethiopia, then known as Axum, began its growth nearly 500 years before Christ. Axum was known to the Persians, especially during the reign of Cambyses in the sixth century B.C., and was deeply engaged in trade up and down the African coast and with Arabia, India and Ceylon. But, the entire region south and southwest of Egypt was often termed Ethiopia, and persons living there, Ethiopians.

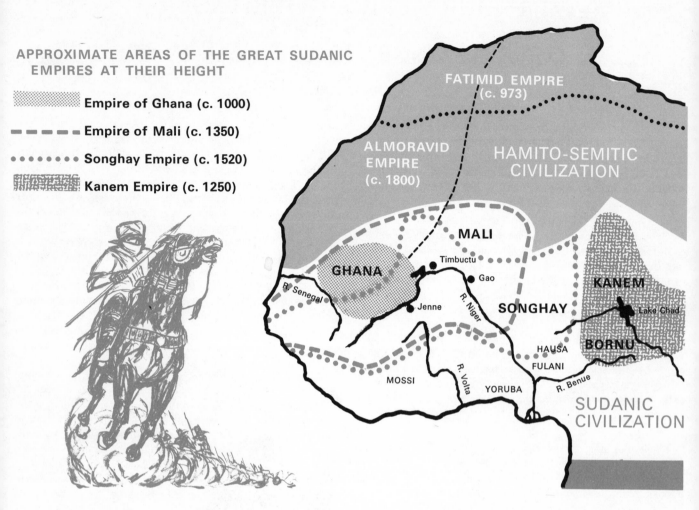

APPROXIMATE AREAS OF THE GREAT SUDANIC
EMPIRES AT THEIR HEIGHT

Empire of Ghana (c. 1000)

Empire of Mali (c. 1350)

Songhay Empire (c. 1520)

Kanem Empire (c. 1250)

FATIMID EMPIRE
(c. 973)

ALMORAVID
EMPIRE
(c. 1800)

HAMITO-SEMITIC
CIVILIZATION

MALI

Timbuctu

GHANA

Gao

KANEM

R. Senegal

Jenne

R. Niger

SONGHAY

Lake Chad

HAUSA

BORNU

FULANI

MOSSI

R. Volta

YORUBA

R. Benue

SUDANIC
CIVILIZATION

During the period when Europe entered the Dark Ages, several major African states rose to prominence. Ancient Ghana was the oldest of these states where, as early as 300 A.D., at least forty-four kings had ruled the country. In 1000 A.D., Ghana was an empire that reached from the Senegal River to the region of the upper Niger River. El Bakri wrote that, in 1066, Tenhamenin, the ruler of Ghana, could place 200,000 warriors in the field. The wealth of ancient Ghana rested on trade. Its twin capitals were located between the salt deposits of the north and the gold mines of the south, and the kings of Ghana exacted a tax on all salt and gold passing through the kingdom. Ghana also imported wheat, fruit, textiles, and brass and exported leather goods and household and personal wares made from gold and silver. Just how large were the towns of ancient Ghana is unknown, but, in 1951, excavators uncovered a walled city capable of holding at least 30,000 individuals.

As Ghana was going into a decline around 1000 A.D., the state of ancient Mali was rising to eminence with gold as one of its major trade items. In 1050 A.D., it burst into prominence when one of its kings, Baramendana Keita, made a spectacular pilgrimage to Mecca. A number of African states envied the wealth of Mali, and in 1224 the king of Soso staged a successful attack on Mali and ruled

it for a decade. Finally the people of Mali revolted and regained control of their country. In addition, they completed the destruction of ancient Ghana. Mali reached the zenith of its glory under the leadership of Mansa Musa who reigned from 1307 to 1332, out-doing all former kings in building up Mali. He was an excellent administrator. The country's ample finances were well managed. Trained lawyers and judges filled its courts. His army was under firm control. Commercial relations were established in Morocco to the north and greatly expanded with Arabian countries to the east. At Mansa Musa's death in 1332, Mali stretched from the Atlantic Ocean on the west to the region of modern Nigeria on the east.

Songhay was the third of the great African states which flourished during Europe's feudal period. It began to expand during the middle part of the 14th century, although it had existed for nearly 500 years prior to this time. In 1488, the rulers of Songhay conquered much of Mali, including the fabled city of Timbuktu, the site of the University of Sankore, a center of learning to which hundreds of black and white scholars journeyed. Trade which had passed through ancient Ghana now came to Timbuktu. When Songhay began to decline near the end of the 16th century, it had nearly a thousand years of history behind it.

To the south and east of Songhay was the land of Monomotapa, located in what is now South Rhodesia. In this African society was the rather intriguing Zimbabwe culture. The Portuguese were familiar with Zimbabwe in the 15th century, although Monomotapa and its capital, Zimbabwe, were "lost" to history until shortly after the Civil War in America. When Zimbabwe was "rediscovered" in 1868 by Adam Renders, archaeologists and historians attributed it to Caucasoid peoples. Later study convinced scholars that Zimbabwe and the land of Monomotapa were the sites of a black civilization developed by the Africans themselves. The ruins at Zimbabwe include remnants of elaborate stone buildings and a great stone wall constructed in an oval shape rising to a height of thirty feet, and encompassing an area more than 800 feet in circumference. Standing for nearly 500 years at the least, this wall and other stone structures were erected without the aid of cement or mortar. The earth around Zimbabwe was riddled with tunnels, some of them 150 feet below the surface. Experts have estimated that these tunnels, over the centuries have produced gold with a value of at least $350,000,000.

Located near the Indian Ocean, the peoples of Monomotapa were great traders. They exchanged gold and slaves for textiles from India and porcelain from China. There exists solid evidence that from the 15th century, the African coastal settlements all along the eastern shores of Mozambique, Tanganyika, Kenya and Somalia had a long and profitable trade with the Orient. However, Zimbabwe suffered much from rebellions and civil strife within its borders, and by the 17th century this outstanding culture began to disintegrate. Only its mute stones and silent tunnels give witness to a major black civilization that once thrived among the hills and valleys now bearing the name of South Rhodesia.

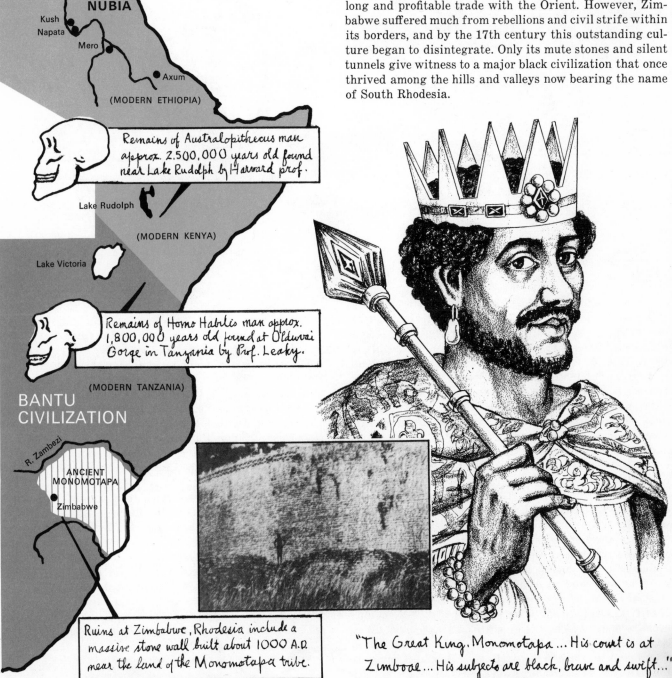

NUBIA

Kush
Napata
Mero

Axum

(MODERN ETHIOPIA)

Remains of Australopithecus man approx. 2,500,000 years old found near Lake Rudolph by Harvard prof.

Lake Rudolph

(MODERN KENYA)

Lake Victoria

Remains of Homo Habilis man approx. 1,800,000 years old found at Olduvai Gorge in Tanzania by Prof. Leakey.

(MODERN TANZANIA)

BANTU CIVILIZATION

R. Zambezi

ANCIENT MONOMOTAPA

Zimbabwe

Ruins at Zimbabwe, Rhodesia include a massive stone wall built about 1000 A.D. near the land of the Monomotapa tribe.

"The Great King. Monomotapa ... His court is at Zimboae ... His subjects are black, brave and swift ..."

OUR AFRICAN HERITAGE *(Continued)*

Touré, first pres. of Republic of Guinea (1958)

William Tubman, pres. of Liberia (1943)

Nkrumah, pres. Republic of Ghana (1960)

Kenyatta, first African prime minister of Kenya (1963)

Haile Selassie, king of Ethiopia (1928)

SOME LEADERS OF MODERN AFRICA

Although Europeans had known of Africa since the days of Homer, they were not interested in or able to penetrate the continent itself. Until the American Civil War, Europe was barely able to maintain a series of tiny coastal stations along the western fringes of the continent. The millions of slaves that Africa afforded the Europeans were generally taken from areas near the oceans. Only with the coming of motor-driven boats and steam-powered ships were Europeans able to make a little headway up the few rivers leading to the high plateau which is Africa. When slavery began to decline as a result of humanitarian impulses and the development of the steam engine, Europeans decided to gain control of the continent itself. In November, 1884, Great Britain, Germany, France, Portugal, Spain, Belgium and the United States met to divide the entire continent, Ethiopia excepted.

Africa then fell victim to the rise and expansion of European civilization and technology, both of which were rather stagnant during the epochs of African glory, and by the end of the 19th century many places in Africa carried European names. From this time until after World War II, the results of the partitioning of Africa could be seen in maps which listed such places as French West Africa, Portuguese East Africa, the German and British Cameroons, Spanish West Africa, the Belgian Congo and the like. The interaction between the Europeans and the original inhabitants of these different parts of the African continent produced the usual problems of foreign rule and local resentment. The resentment and eventual resistance to foreign control generated a thirst for self-rule and independence, and, like corks popping to the surface of the water, the once submerged African societies, beginning with Ghana in 1957, started regaining their independence. In 1968 the only major remaining enclaves of white domination were in the Republic of South Africa, the two Rhodesias, Spanish Sahara, Angola and Mozambique.

In summary, the history of the black man is just beginning to emerge from the dim past. Scholars are now beginning to give the same attention to reconstructing the history of Africa as was given to unveiling the ancient record of Egypt, Greece and Rome. The half-dreamed accounts of African grandeur are now being proven through the work of archaeologists and anthropologists. As the winds of change continue to blow away the mists of time, the historical record of the African past should become the common knowledge of mankind.

Grace H. Beardsley, *The Negro in Greek and Roman Civilization* (New York, 1967), pp. 1-12, 78, 115-118; Henry Barth, *Travels and Discoveries in North and Central Africa, 1849-1855*, Vol. III (New York, 1959), pp. 281-294; Basil Davidson, *The Lost Cities of Africa* (Boston, 1957), pp. 44-49, 218-219; Basil Davidson, *Black Mother: The Years of the African Slave Trade* (Boston, 1961), pp. 23-30; John Hope Franklin, *From Slavery to Freedom*, 2nd edition (New York, 1957), pp. 5-22; David Weidner, *A History of Africa South of the Sahara* (New York, Vintage Book edition, 1962), pp. 167-178.

Piankhy (720 B.C.)
CONQUEROR OF EGYPT

Standing on a wharf and shaded by huge umbrellas held aloft by slaves, Piankhy, the black king of Nubia, seethed with rage and frustration as he watched ships, loaded with casks of gold, scores of slaves, and bands of fighting men, float down the Nile en route to Osorkin III, king of Egypt. For 1800 years other Nubian kings had witnessed the same sight, the payment of tribute to the Egyptians who dominated the Fertile Crescent. But, unlike others, Piankhy decided that he would make war on the Egyptians and put an end to the ceaseless and annoying greed of his powerful neighbor.

For years Piankhy plotted, watched, and waited, but sent his yearly tribute to Egypt. All the while he planned his strategy and built his army. Smug in their domination of the subjected countries and lulled into carelessness by the steady payment of tribute, the Egyptians paid no attention to Piankhy.

Finally, Piankhy decided that the time was ripe to make war on Egypt. Again the sleepy Nile was loaded with ships headed for Egypt. This time, however, instead of tribute, they carried soldiers and warriors. With disciplined skill, Piankhy's soldiers captured town after town until at last they arrived at the first large Egyptian fortress of Hermopolis and laid siege to it. With crushing power, Piankhy defeated Namlot, the Egyptian commander. Prostrating himself before Piankhy, Namlot begged for mercy, explaining that he was one of the king's slaves, paying duty into the treasury.

Piankhy pressed on, capturing one city after another until he came to the great city of Memphis, which was at that time the capital of Egypt. Memphis was surrounded by a high wall, the western wall being higher than the eastern one which faced the open sea.

Word of Piankhy's victories had preceded him and the Egyptians at Memphis planned their defense. They expected to defeat this Nubian who was placing much of their country under his rule. But Piankhy did the unexpected. Strategically deploying his fleet, he soon had control of the harbor and then the eastern sea wall which, as he suspected, had been neglected.

Before the western defenders of Memphis could come to the aid of the seaward side of the city, the Nubians had scaled the sea walls from their ships and were soon in control of the city. Tefnakhte, the commander of Memphis, meekly surrendered. With Memphis conquered, Piankhy continued his triumphal march toward Heliopolis where King Osorkin waited. The king had grown fat and indolent from years of ruling and had no desire to fight. He gave up without resistance and Piankhy became master of Egypt.

Following the adage of "to the victor belong the spoils," Piankhy sailed for home. Again hundreds of ships covered the Nile laden with treasures of gold and silver. This time, however, they were bound for the vaults of Egypt's new master, the mighty Piankhy.

J. A. Rogers, *World's Great Men of Color—3000 B.C. to 1946 A.D.*, (New York, 1947), pp. 36-38; *Encyclopædia Britannica*, 1957 Edition (vol XVI) p. 586.

Antar (615 A.D.)
AFRO-ARABIAN POET-STORY TELLER

Africa and the land of Arabia blend into one another, separated mainly by the desert. Peoples of Africa and the desert are unlike in many ways; yet they also have much in common. The love of story-telling and poetry and the love of personal adventure are only two of a host of things they share.

One of Arabia's greatest story-tellers and warriors was the legendary Antarah Ibn Shaddad in whose veins flowed both African and Arabian blood.

Antarah Ibn Shaddad, known to history simply as Antar, wrote many poems based on the great love he had for his high-born wife, Abla. No one knows just how many poems were composed by Antar, for most of his compositions were handed down through the generations by oral tradition. In 1889 some thirty-two volumes of *The Romance of Antar* were published at Cairo, Egypt. A few years later, ten volumes were published at Beirut, Lebanon.

Antar was born of an African slave, Zabuba, and an Arabian prince and warrior, Shaddad. He soon grew into a very intelligent and sensitive young man of great physical strength. Other chieftains competed for the ownership of this strangely dark youth who had killed a wolf when he was ten years old.

Herding sheep, tending camels, and doing a variety of things left for slaves alone, Antar met the love of his life, Abla, the hauntingly beautiful daughter of his father's brother. Smitten beyond caring, Antar began composing odes to Abla's beauty to express his love for her. Abla, herself a princess, slowly developed a kindred but carefully guarded affection for Antar, the slave boy. Antar's skill and bravery in combat and skill in verse won his freedom and the hand of Abla. His love for her inspired many of his finest odes.

Antar's poems were regarded as models of Arabic style. Inscribed in gold and hung high in the Kaabah at Mecca is one of his poems. At Aleppo, Baghdad or Constantinople his poems are still recited in coffeehouses and around glowing fires. Arabian poetry lovers have an adage which claims that *The Thousand and One Nights* is for the amusement of women and children. Antar's is a book for men."

In the verses of Antar, the Arabian may find reflected virtues he admires: personal courage, pride, fierce love, and the grand gesture. Antar himself embodied many of these virtues. He died in battle in A.D. 615, but his poems live on in *The Romance of Antar*.

J. A. Rogers, *World's Great Men of Color—3000 B.C. to 1946 A.D.*, vol I, (New York, 1947), pp. 70-73; A. O. Stafford, "Antar, The Great Arabian-Negro Warrior", *Journal of Negro History*, vol. I (January, 1916), pp. 151-162.

Sonni Ali (-1492)

WARRIOR-KING OF SONGHAY

Sonni Ali, a native of Songhay, whose birthdate is unknown, was the eighteenth ruler in a line of kings dating back to A.D. 1010. At the time Sonni became king of Gao and its nearby Songhay lands in A.D. 1464, Mali was becoming weak, and many of its peoples were claiming their independence. Sonni Ali, an ambitious and skillful warrior, planned to unite the Mali territories into Songhay dependencies through his army and a river navy which would subdue kingdoms along the Niger River. In the early years of his reign he was constantly engaged in battles. He began by fighting off the Mossi, the Dogon, and the Fulani. In 1469 he drove the Tuareg out of Timbuktu, which they had held since 1433.

Aware of the tremendous wealth sent to the Arabian city of Mecca by the Muslim Mansa Musa, Sonni broke the grip of the Islamic faith on the empire by bringing the priestly class under his authority and by exercising more direct control over the University of Sankore, the gathering place for Sudanese and Arabian scholars.

Sonni Ali then turned his attention to Jenne, a beautiful city made into a formidable fortress by the treacherous swamps and floodwaters which surrounded it. This vital market center had never before fallen to an invader. Using his amphibious troops, Sonni Ali besieged Jenne for more than seven years before the courageous people were finally starved into submission in 1473. Sonni Ali consolidated his victories by encouraging intermarriage between the people of Mali and Songhay. He himself married the queen mother of the young king of conquered Jenne. By 1476 the entire lake region west of Timbuktu was in his hands. In 1480 he repulsed the raids of the Mossi from the south, and later did the same with all the peoples who envied the wealth of their northern neighbor.

Sonni Ali has been called "one of the born soldiers of the world"; his empire covered more territory than Napoleon's during his apex. But he was more than a fearless soldier; he made significant improvements in government. A tremendous canal-building project was left uncompleted by his death in November 1492. His son, Sonni Baru, ruled Songhay for fourteen months before being deposed by the powerful rebel, Askia the Great.

Enshrouded in myth and legend, the ancient African empires of Ghana, Mali, and Songhay (Songhai) are little known to the world today. Yet between the eleventh and sixteenth centuries, they rivalled Europe in both size and sophistication. Their major cities of Jenne, Gao, and Timbuktu (Timbuctu) were centers of trade, commerce, and learning. Of all the Mellestine and Songhaese rulers, Sonni Ali, in the words of W. E. B. Du Bois, was among the "last and greatest." Beginning his career as a soldier, by 1480 Sonni Ali found himself master of the most powerful state in the Sudan of his time.

W. E. B. Du Bois, *Black Folk: Then and Now* (New York, 1937), p. 47; Anna Melissa Graves, *Africa: The Wonder and the Glory* (Baltimore, 1961), pp. 35-36; Basil Davidson, *A History of West Africa to the Nineteenth Century* (New York, Doubleday & Company, Anchor Books, 1966) pp. 119-122; Roland Oliver and J. D. Fage, *A Short History of Africa*, 2nd ed. (Baltimore, Penguin Books, 1966), pp. 89-90.

Askia the Great (1444?-1538)

BUILDER OF SONGHAY

Askia the Great was the ruler who built Songhay into one of the most powerful African countries in the Sudan. A pure-blooded black, Askia was born around 1444 on a small island in the Niger, a short distance below Sinder. When Sonni Ali, the king of Songhay, was alive, Askia was known as Muhammad Abou Bekr Et-Toui. After emerging victorious from the three-year struggle for the throne left vacant by Ali, Muhammad Abou Bakr adopted the name Askia which meant usurper or thief, the appellation hurled at him by disgruntled descendants of Sonni Ali. And, because of Askia's tremendous contributions to the growth of Songhay, historians dubbed him "Askia the Great."

When he came to power, he was already over fifty years of age. All of his life, he had been first and foremost a military man. However, in 1495 he went to Egypt and remained there for two years to study the art of government, taxation, rules of trade, uniform weights and measures, governmental administration and questions of religious toleration. On his return to Songhay in 1497, he set about applying his new knowledge to the affairs of his nation, re-organizing the army, and setting up a competent civil service. One of the highest accolades a public official could receive was that "he was appointed by Askia."

Under Askia the Great, the country was divided into four major sections, each with its governor. Special attention was given to the fair and efficient collection of taxes and to honesty in trade and commerce. The banking and credit system was placed on such a sound footing that traders and businessmen from Songhay had no trouble in their dealings from one end of the Sudan to the other. Much support was given to education, particularly at the University of Sankore, where literature, law and science were the main subjects of instruction. Located in the fabled city of Timbuktu, this institution attracted students from all the surrounding African states as well as from the East.

Askia engaged in many battles with surrounding nations in an attempt to maintain the independence and power of Songhay. Finally he brought the valuable salt mines of Tegazza to the north and the territory of the Fulani to the south under his sway. In 1501, Askia defeated the kingdom of Mali; in 1513, he reduced the Hausa states of Katema, Zaria, Zamfara, Kane and Gober to subjection. He also conquered Aghaaz, a white settlement to the north of Songhay, and required it to pay the equivalent of $150,000 annually. Toward the end of his reign, Askia lost his eyesight. Supplanted in 1528, he managed to mastermind the successful efforts of one of his sons to take over the throne. Askia the Great died in 1538, after having ruled Songhay for a total of 36 years.

Basil Davidson, *The Lost Cities of Africa* (Boston, 1959), pp. 71-81; J. A. Rogers, *World's Great Men of Color* 3000 B.C. to 1946 A.D. (New York, 1947), pp. 134-137; Flora L. Shaw, *A Tropical Dependency: An Outline of the Ancient History of the Western Soudan with an Account of the Modern Settlement of North Nigeria* (London, 1905), Chaps. 22-23.

Abram Hannibal (1697-1782)
SOLDIER, COMMANDER IN RUSSIA

Captured in Africa at the age of eight and sold to a Russian nobleman in Constantinople, Abram Hannibal was given as a slave to Tsar Peter the Great of Russia. Peter grew fond of Abram, and he soon became a court favorite. The young black captive was brought up in the Russian Orthodox Church, where he was baptized Abram Hannibal.

When Abram completed his early schooling in 1716, the Tsar sent him to Paris to study military engineering with the expectation of his joining the Tsar's army. In Paris, Abram repeated his earlier social success by becoming a preferred intimate of the Duc d'Orléans, then Regent. A strikingly handsome young Hannibal was permitted to join the French Army and soon attained the rank of commander. After seven years, to the regret of the Duc, he returned to Russia and joined the Tsar's own guard regiment as an engineer lieutenant.

He became a good military man and grew very fond of Russia. When his brother in Africa learned of his whereabouts and offered the Tsar a rather generous ransom for his return, Hannibal turned it down, saying "Convey my thanks to my brother. May God bless his good intention on my behalf. But tell him that I am happy here in the land of my adoption. I will remain here."

For a time Hannibal enjoyed favor and esteem in his adopted country. However, at the death of Peter the Great, Hannibal discovered that Queen Catherine was not so interested in him. Peter II was even less fond of Abram and, with the connivance of Abram's enemies, sent him to Siberia where he suffered greatly. Abram managed to escape but was eventually captured and returned to Siberia.

By 1741, under still another ruler, Abram was forgiven and reinstated in the Russian army, and made many military contributions to the Tsar. Honors began to come his way. In a border conflict between Russia and Sweden, Abram was commissioned to fix the disputed boundary line. After this, he was appointed a member of the Logoda Canal Commission and a member of the inspection staff of the Russian Forts. His crowning honor was his appointment as commandant of the city of Reval and major in the garrison at Tomesk where he had been held captive many years before.

Abram Hannibal married a German girl who gave him five sons; one of these sons became the father of Russia's greatest poet, Alexander Pushkin.

Albert Parry, "Abram Hannibal, the Favorite of Peter the Great", *Journal of Negro History*, VII (October, 1923), pp. 359-366; Beatrice Fleming and Marion Pryde, *Distinguished Negroes Abroad* (Washington, 1946), pp 166-170.

Chaka (1787-1828)
18TH CENTURY ZULU KING AND WARRIOR

Out of a chance encounter between an African warrior prince and a beautiful commoner was born Chaka. Being an outcast from birth, Chaka developed a drive for power and revenge which carried him to the head of the Zulus.

As a solitary, brooding youth, he was ridiculed by his fellows because of his illegitimate birth. He saw his father, Zenzangakona, drive his mother, Nandi, and himself into exile where he grew up with a rival tribe. But, instead of being crushed by the hardships he and his mother endured, Chaka sharpened his native intelligence and conditioned his body to win recognition and acceptance as a warrior. It is upon his military skill and leadership that his fame rests.

Dingiswayo, leader of Chaka's tribe and his father's rival, quickly took note of Chaka's unusual courage and intelligence and groomed him to become a leader of the Mtetwas, a small tribe numbering between two and three thousand people. In this part of Natal, South Africa, different chiefs, sub-chiefs, and plotters were usually engaged in a daily round of wars and assassinations, and the Mtetwas were no exception. Dingiswayo successfully plotted the death of Chaka's father. Then Zwide, who was another aspirant for power, tricked Dingiswayo causing his early death. Chaka ascended to leadership of the Mtetwas and set out to destroy Zwide. Chaka met and defeated Zwide's army. Zwide escaped but was later assassinated.

Under Chaka, the Mtetwas began a series of conquests which brought most of Natal under their control. His armies used a special kind of stabbing knife known as an assegai, instead of the spear. It enabled them to subdue many times their number. He also employed tactics of the old Greek and Roman phalanxes in battle.

In 1824 Chaka saw his first white men. Among them was H. F. Fynn, a Britisher who was exploring this section of Natal. Fynn successfully treated Chaka for a battle wound. In gratitude, he made a grant of Port Natal to Fynn and his companion, Farewell.

Chaka brought together many tribes of his region and they learned to live together in harmony. However, he was not without enemies, for in 1828 he was assassinated but left a proud people in their unity.

E. A. Ritter. *Shaka Zulu* (New York, 1955).

Gustavus Vassa (1745-1801)
SEA-FARER, COLONIZER

On March 21, 1788, Her Royal Highness, Charlotte, Queen of England received a petition containing among other things, these words:

"I presume . . . your gracious Queen, to implore your interposition with that of your royal consort (King George III) in favor of the wretched Africans, that by your Majesty's benevolent influence, a period may now be put to their misery; and that they may be raised from the condition of brutes to which they are at present degraded to the rights and situation of free men . . ."

The petitioner was Gustavus Vassa who had risen from the rank of kidnapped slave to that of "commissary of the government," superintending part of a plan to return Africans to their native lands.

Born in the Essaka Valley of Guinea, he was kidnapped and hustled aboard a slave ship headed for the Barbadoes, British West Indies. After a fearful Middle Passage, Vassa only eleven years old, was sold at a slave auction and became the property of a Virginia planter. This worthy gentleman sold Vassa to a sea captain, one Pascal, who commanded a ship called the *Industrious Bee.* Aboard the ship was a young American who taught Vassa the rudiments of the English language.

After two years, Captain Pascal sent his little slave to England to be the household servant of two pious ladies who insisted that he learn to read the Bible. Over the next few years, Vassa changed hands as owners saw fit and again he found himself at sea. Shipped again to the West Indies, Vassa fell into the hands of a Quaker merchant from Philadelphia who permitted him to earn extra money to purchase his freedom. Within a few years, Vassa was a free man.

Gustavus Vassa desired to go to England where he had spent the best years of his life, and after much voyaging reached London only to find it impossible for him to complete his haphazard education without funds. In 1773 Vassa joined an expedition seeking a northwest passage to India and wound up on the coast of Greenland. Still deeply addicted to the sea, Vassa traveled to Spain and India and made occasional journeys to the United States.

In 1785, the Crown was trying to return Africans to their native land. Vassa was appointed to a post with the government and was placed in charge of the commissary which supplied the Africans with clothing and other items deemed necessary for the voyage home. Vassa reported the dishonesty and the thievery among his English co-workers who wasted little time securing his dismissal from his post. Vassa continued to work for the emancipation of his fellow Africans and made his famous appeal to Queen Charlotte.

In 1789, Vassa published his autobiography, *The Interesting Narrative of the Life of Olaudah Equiana or Gustavus Vassa.* This was the first and, to us, the fullest account of the life of a free Negro during this period. The book was so popular that it went through eight editions in five years.

Benjamin Brawley. *Early Negro American Writers* (Chapel Hill, 1935), p. 56.

Jacques Eliza Jean Captein

(1745-   )

ORATOR, PHILOSOPHER

Jacques Eliza Jean Captein holds a curious place in the history of the Negro. At a time when the Dutch were getting an increased share of the African slave trade, it was by chance Captein who was used to prove that the African was capable of understanding the tenets of Christianity and, hence, had a soul to save. Slavery, through the Dutch, would be one-method of "saving these heathens from hell-fire."

When Captein was bought at the age of eight by a fellow African, little did he realize that he would be a guinea pig to "prove" to the Dutch populace that a human being stood behind the dark skin of men greedy business entrepreneurs saw as a source of great profits. Captein found himself in the hands of a Dutch captain who, for amusement, began teaching him the rudiments of his native language and was startled at the brilliance of his little pupil. Soon Captein was given books to pore over and, in short order, he became familiar with their contents. His owner was convinced that he had made a most unusual purchase. This conviction was reinforced when one day he chanced upon his dusky scholar holding a small painting which he had done without any instruction.

Convinced that he would profit even more from systematic training, Captein was sent to the Hague where he was placed under a teacher familiar with languages. Greek, Hebrew, Latin, and Chaldean he soon learned to read. By now Captein was a young man and his patron made it possible for him to enter the University of Leyden where he took a degree in theology.

News of his proficiency and brilliance spread and Captein, upon graduation, was sent back to Elmina, on the Gold Coast, to work among his people as a missionary. However, it was soon apparent that the natives of Elmina had not heard of the great experiment, for Captein was much less successful as a missionary than as a scholar. He soon returned to Holland where he made a name for himself, first as a curiosity and still later for what he had to say about Christianity and the institution of slavery.

Strictly a brilliant product of his training and the designs of his master and teacher, Captein was misled to use his intellect in a defense of the institution of slavery, arguing that slavery was one way for his fellow Africans to save their immortal souls. He was unable to see the deeper design of the Dutch, which was to provide a rationale for pursuing the slave trade with ever-increasing vigor.

In addition to his prose work, Captein wrote poems in Latin which have endured much better than his defense of the peculiar institution of slavery. Misguided though he was, his intelligence as pure brain power would have made him conspicuous anywhere.

Beatrice Fleming and Marion Pryde, *Distinguished Negroes Abroad* (Washington, 1946), pp. 141-146.

Joseph Cinque (1811-1879)

AFRICAN PRINCE AND REVOLUTIONIST

Few stories of heroism and bravery hold greater interest than that of Joseph Cinque, an African prince kidnapped and sold into slavery in Havana, Cuba. It is a story of mutiny and revolt, a story of court room drama and freedom. It really began in 1839 in Havana.

After being prodded, poked, and pinched by Spaniards who were buying slaves, Cinque and thirty-eight other hapless people were packed into the hold of a 120-ton schooner called the *Amistad* whose destination was the Island of Principe. Two days out of Havana, a raging storm hit the ship. The regular crew fought to keep the ship moving against the elements until they fell into a deep sleep near midnight. Stuffed in the hold below, Cinque and his fellow slaves plotted their escape. Cinque dominated this group as he had dominated nearly every other. He gave the instructions. The others listened carefully, feeling that a man as self-confident as Cinque must be fully aware of what he was planning.

On board the *Amistad* were machetes and knives, placed out of reach of the chained slaves. Yet Cinque and the slaves got free of their irons. Peering up toward the deck, they could see no one but a solitary helmsman trying to keep the ship on its proper course. Silently spreading out, Cinque and his men fell upon all the whites at once. Senor Don Jose Ruiz and Senor Don Pedro Montez, their owners, were spared; the rest, including the Captain and the crew, were slain.

Cinque was now in complete control of the ship but knew nothing about navigation. Using Ruiz and Montez as helmsmen and navigators, Cinque directed them to steer the schooner eastward toward Africa, the land of his fathers, the land where his wife and three children were still mourning his absence.

The two Spaniards had not amassed the wealth to buy almost forty slaves by being dull-witted. During the day, they kept the ship going in an easterly direction, but at night they slowly headed the *Amistad* in a northwest direction. Days passed. Cinque and the others did not have the slightest idea of the ruse being pulled on them by Ruiz and Montez. By steering a cleverly zig-zagged course, the wily Spaniards worked the *Amistad* all the way from the Caribbean to Long Island, New York.

A sensation was created when Ruiz and Montez told of the revolt and of the killings on board the ship. Never had a slave been so brazen as Cinque who promptly sat down to negotiate with the Americans for passage to Africa. But he and all of the Africans were taken prisoner. The Abolitionist fever was running high. Quickly a committee was formed to defend the legal rights of the slaves. The U. S. District attorney for New York moved that the rebels be turned over to the Spanish government.

Through a maze of claims and arguments, the case of the *Amistad* revolt began its tortuous journey up through the courts, with each succeeding court deciding that Cinque and his cohorts were free men. The U. S. Justice Department fought this view all the way up to the United States Supreme Court where John Quincy Adams, now an old man, defended the *Amistad* revolt, basing his argument on the inherent right of every human being to be free, regardless of legal arrangements to keep him in fetters. The U. S. Supreme Court ruled in favor of Cinque and the other Africans, declaring them free to return to Africa, their native land.

William Owens, *Slave Mutiny: The Revolt on the Schooner Amistad* (New York, 1953).

Menelik II (1844-1913)
FOUNDER OF MODERN ETHIOPIA

Ethiopia, for more than two thousand years, has been a symbol as well as a place. Of all the African countries, it is the only one with a record of continuous independence, unbroken except for the Italian occupation in 1935-1940. No monarchy on earth can match that of Ethiopia in tenure, for it is said to have begun with the Queen of Sheba and her son, Menelik I. Although Ethiopia is a part of the African continent, one does not think of the country as really a part of Africa. In reality, this country is neither black nor white, nor even yellow. It is in part Semitic and in part Arabic, with a very strong Negroid mixture. For hundreds of years, the rest of the world has thought of Ethiopia as some sort of exotic jewel, shining on the east coast of Africa. Little does the world realize that until the 19th century Ethiopia was not a united country, but a collection of tribes from the same racial stock under the name of Ethiopia. The Gallo, the Tigre, the Shoa, and the Harar tribes embraced a great mass of the people. Serious conflict and rivalry existed among these tribes, aggravated by the Madhists and Somalis to the south and east, and other tribes and countries. Internal strife and chaos were the rule until the advent of one man, Menelik II.

During his early years, Sahala Mariem, or Menelik, as he later called himself, aspired to be the Negus Negusti, the King of Kings, leader of all the tribes in the land. Brought up in splendor befitting a prince of a Shoa king, Sahala was made a prisoner in 1855 of one Kassai, the governor of Shoa. Kassai then seized power over all the tribes. After a rather debauched five-year reign Kassai died in 1868. Sahala Mariem (Menelik), by this time a young, ambitious, extremely energetic and intelligent man of 24 years, once more tried to succeed to the high throne of Negus Negusti, but again was unsuccessful. Instead, the Ras (King) of Tigre emerged victorious in the struggle for supreme power, taking the name of John IV. Sahala then decided on a more subtle tactic. He married his daughter, Zaudith, to John IV's son, the Ras Area. This move caused Sahala to be regarded as a remote claimant to the throne, but few people had any idea that within three years Sahala would be the emperor. In a campaign against the Madhi, a stray bullet ended the life of John IV, and with the help of the colony-minded Italians, Sahala at last ascended to the throne.

With the ascension of Menelik, as Sahala called himself, the tribes began to close ranks. Unwittingly helping to unify the country were the Italians, joined by the British and the French, each seeking some type of concession.

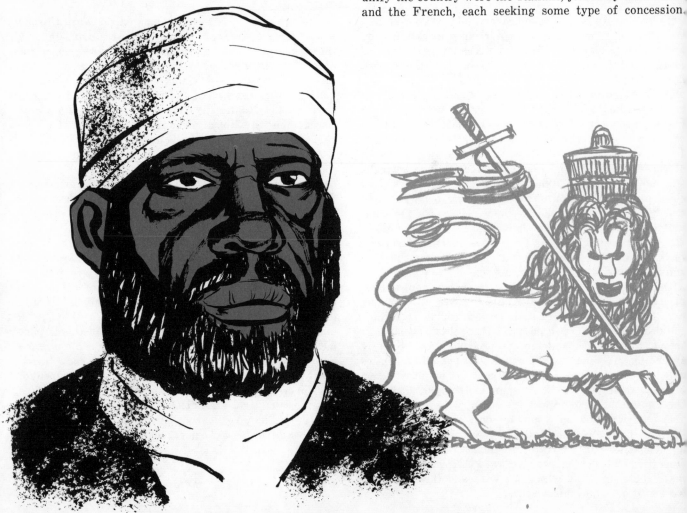

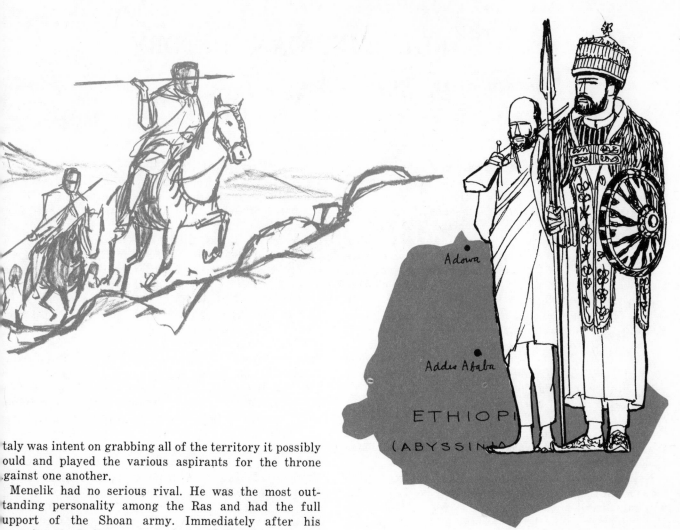

taly was intent on grabbing all of the territory it possibly
ould and played the various aspirants for the throne
gainst one another.

Menelik had no serious rival. He was the most out-
tanding personality among the Ras and had the full
upport of the Shoan army. Immediately after his
scension, the Italians rushed to have him sign the Treaty
f Ucialli, a treaty which was the seed of much trouble
or both Ethiopia and Italy. The terms of the treaty, in
he Italian view, gave Italy complete control over the
ountry's relations with foreign powers, in effect, making
he country subservient to Italy. Menelik viewed the
reaty differently, claiming that it left full control and
overeignty with himself. As a part of the treaty settle-
ent, the Italians gave Menelik 38,000 rifles and twenty-
ight cannons, and loaned him 4,000,000 francs with the
Iarar province as collateral. The first thing Menelik did
vas to repay the loan, but the question of Ethiopia's
overeignty continued to fester. Meanwhile, the Italians
ot a foothold in the north-eastern part of the country
nd christened the area Eritrea.

Menelik, ever alert to the question of his country's
ndependence, began to rally the populace behind him.
Ie slowly added arms and equipment to his arsenal. He
aade peace with most troublesome of the minor Ras.
Iowever, Italy also started moving men and material
ito the country. Finally in 1896, 14,500 Italian officers
nd soldiers moved toward Adowa, the Ethiopian holy
ity. With over-extended lines, unreliable maps and a false
stimate of Menelik's strength, the Italians were attacked
nd routed on the plains of Adowa. They left behind some
2,000 killed and over a thousand prisoners. Finally, in
•ctober, 1896, the Italians sued for peace.

Menelik had startled the world, for never before had
an African nation so decisively defeated a would-be col-
onizer. There were no further questions of sovereignty.
Britain, France, Turkey, and Russia sought concessions
and monopolies in the country. The French built a railroad
and tried to turn control of it over to the British until
Menelik stopped them. During all of these transactions,
Menelik had two goals uppermost in his mind: the continued sovereignty of the government and the extension
and consolidation of borders within and without the
territory. He used the greed of the foreigners to his and
his country's advantage. With one major exception, most
of the border disputes were settled. The exception led to
the Italo-Ethiopian War of 1935.

Up to 1906, Menelik rode herd on the Ras, tribes,
provinces, and the host of foreigners in the country and
succeeded in bringing Ethiopia into a more or less unified
whole. In this year and in 1908, Menelik suffered strokes
and gave active control of the country to others. In 1913,
worn out by his strenuous labors, he died, paving the way
for Haile Selassie some seventeen years later.

A. H. M. Jones and Elizabeth Monroe, *A History of Ethiopia* (Oxford, 1955).

II EARLY AMERICAN HISTORY

Heralds of a New Day

From the very beginning Negroes have been part and parcel of American history. They were present during the exploration of the American continent. They took part in the American Revolution, in the abolitionist movement, and in the agitation preceding the Civil War.

Doubtful legend has it that a Negro, Alonzo di Pietro, was a pilot on one of Columbus' ships. Historians are agreed that, since 1501, Negroes have been present in the New World. In 1513, thirty blacks, including Nuflio de Olan, were with Balboa when he discovered the Pacific Ocean. They helped him build the first ships made on the Pacific Coast. Cortez, the explorer of Mexico, was accompanied by Negroes. Three Negroes accompanied the explorer, Velas, in 1520. Negroes were with Alvarez when he went to Quito, the oldest city in the New World. They were with Pizarro when he went to Peru in 1541.

The best known of black pioneers in the Americas was Estavanico, or Estevanillo—one of the four men to live through the expedition of Narvarez. Little Stephen, as Estavanico was called, explored for Spain the land which is now Arizona and New Mexico in 1527.

Negroes were present when the French explorers wandered in the Canadian wilds. Jean Baptiste Pointe De Sable was only one of hundreds of Negroes who settled in the Mississippi Valley in the eighteenth century. By the end of the eighteenth century, approximately 500,000 Negroes were living on the North American continent. Virtually all of them were slaves, although here and there were to be found free men of color.

Five thousand Negroes participated in the American Revolution. Some of them served on the navy's galleys and brigs; others fought with the Continental army. A Negro from Connecticut, known simply as George, was active on a brig, the *Defense Colony Service*, in the spring of 1776. In that same year the galley *Trumbull* carried three Negroes known only as Peter, Brittain and Daniel. The *Aurora*, captained by the famous David Porter, carried black seamen. One Cato Blackney served on three Massachusetts brigs, the *Hazard*, the *Deane* and the *Prospect* during 1778 and 1779.

A large number of these early black seamen were pilots as indicated by a letter written by George Washington on July 26, 1779, wherein he stated that, "I have granted a Warrant of 1,000 dollars promised the Negro pilots." The Virginia legislature bought the freedom of a slave, known only as Caesar, because he had "entered early into the service of his country, and continued to pilot the armed vessels of this state during the late war."

As the colonists became more desperate for able-bodied men, even slaves were accepted for military duty. Many slaves received their freedom as a result of their service during the Revolution.

Caesar Ferrit and his son, John, as well as Samuel Craft Peter Salem, Pomp Blackman, and Lemuel Haynes were a the battles of Lexington and Concord in April of 1775. A the battle of Bunker Hill, Caesar Brown lost his life i action. Peter Salem fired the shot that killed Major Pit cairn, leader of the British troops during this battle Lemuel Haynes, Primas Black, and Epheram Blackma took part in the battle of Ticonderoga. Prince Whipple wa with George Washington when he crossed the Delawar on Christmas Day, 1776. Tack Sissons was one of th raiders who captured the British General, Richard Pres cott, at Newport, Rhode Island on July 9, 1777.

During the course of the War for Independence, Negroe fought in all of the major battles, including Brandywine Boonesborough, Yorktown, White Plains, Saratoga, Tren ton, and Monmouth. Almost all of the colonies supplie Negroes who took part in the war. Vermont, New Hamp shire, Rhode Island, New York and Connecticut ha especially heavy enlistments.

After the War for Independence ended, Negroes bega taking part in the general development of the country Prince Hall organized the first Masonic Lodge amon Negroes in this country in 1787.

In 1791 the St. Thomas Episcopal Church was organize by Absalom Jones. Andrew Bryan was preaching to congregation of two hundred persons in Savannah Georgia in the late 1780's. Fifty of his communicants wer able to read. Benjamin Banneker was publishing hi Almanac between the years 1792 and 1803. James Derham was beginning to practice medicine as the first Negr physician in America.

In the abolitionist movement were men such as Willian Still in Philadelphia; Stephen Myers in Albany, Ne York; J. W. Loguen in Syracuse, New York; and Marti R. Delany in Pittsburgh, Pennsylvania. In the year im mediately preceding the Civil War, black writers an orators were expressing themselves on such matters a colonization of Negroes, the institution of slavery, and th progress of the Negro as a group. Negro conventions de voted to these subjects were meeting in different part of the North.

The early history of the Negro shows him as an explorer a settler, a slave and as a patriot, beginning his vigorou pursuit of freedom, liberty, and equality. In these day he saw himself as an American. As the nation develope and expanded, the Negro developed into an ardent sup porter of the nation's highest ideals.

Benjamin Brawley, *A Short History of the American Negro* (New Yor 1931), pp. 2-3; John Hope Franklin, *From Slavery to Freedom* (New Yor 1956), pp. 44-45; Herbert Aptheker, *The Negro in the American Revolu tion* (New York, 1940), pp. 27-41.

Estavanico (? -1539)

ARIZONA'S AFRICAN DISCOVERER

...Black skin, bushy beard, feathered regalia with two greyhounds at his side.

The survivors were promptly enslaved by the Indians as they entered Galveston Bay. Within a year only four were left, among them Estavanico. Those durable four discovered they could "heal" afflicted Indians by a touch, and they used their mysterious talents to secure their freedom. For nearly a decade they wandered among the Indians who showered gifts upon them and called them "Children of the Sun." Finally Estavanico and his companions reached the Sinola River near the Gulf of California where they met other Spanish explorers. They were taken before the Spanish Viceroy in Culiacan, Mexico, Don Antonio de Menduzo, who listened to their almost unbelievable recital and wanted to send them northward in search of the legendary "Seven Cities of Gold." But the Spaniards declined.

The viceroy then leased the servant Estavanico from his master, Dorantes, and made him guide to a special party to locate the Seven Cities. Retracing some of his earlier routes, Estavanico led the group up to the present day Fairbank, Arizona. Each band of Indians they met along the way told them in increasingly vivid terms of the Seven Cities farther north. Estavanico and his fellow explorers were positive they had located the cities when, just outside of the village of Hawikuh, they were informed that "there are seven very large cities, all under one Lord, with houses of stone . . ."

Estavanico left the party behind in the Sonora Valley. His instructions had been to send back, by Indian runner, crosses varying in size to indicate the relative importance of the things he saw. Within four days, the runners appeared before the main party with a cross nearly six feet long. This was taken to mean that the "Seven Cities of Gold" had been located, and one of the friars in the main party immediately took off with the runners to join Estavanico. But three days before reaching the area where Estavanico was supposed to be, the friar learned that Estavanico had been killed by the Indians. A cloud of mystery surrounds the circumstances of his death. The fabled "Seven Cities of Gold" turned out to be only a pueblo settlement of adobe structures. To this day no gold has been found, but a memory of Estavanico still lingers in the Indian legends of a black "Mexican" who travelled among the Indians over 400 years ago.

Estavanico was the best known of the hundreds of African slaves who accompanied the Spaniards on their explorations of the Americas, from Florida to Mexico, Colorado and Arizona. Born in the village of Azamer, near the Moroccan coast, Estavanico was the servant of Andres Dorantes de Carranze who joined the 600-man expedition of Panfilo de Narvaez to the New World seeking land and gold.

When the expedition reached Santo Domingo, 143 men deserted. Going on to Cuba more men were lost in hurricanes. By the time they reached Florida only 400 remained. Finding no gold there, the Spaniards worked their way west, passing Mobile Bay, New Orleans and landing at Galveston, Texas in the summer of 1528. Death by starvation, shipwreck and Indian arrows had reduced the group to only eighty men.

Morris Bishop, *The Odyssey of Cabeza de Vaca* (New York, 1933), chap. 8. John B. Brebner, *The Explorers of North America*, 1492-1806 (New York, 1937), pp. 83-88; Florence Laughlin, "Estavanico and the Cities of Gold," *Negro Digest* (August 1963), pp. 19-22.

Toussaint L'Ouverture
Jacques Dessalines
Henri Christophe

Toussaints' victories earned him the name "The Opener" among the blacks.

La Citadel, looming high above Cap Haitien like some hand-carved Gibraltar, is a monument to the lives of three men and a slave revolution. Still piled row after row are twelve-pound cannon balls and hundreds of huge cannons scattered about the ramparts of La Citadel as though waiting for the return of Henri Christophe, its builder.

Before Toussaint L'Ouverture, Jacques Dessalines and Henri Christophe, the history of Haiti, then called Saint Domingue, could be summed up in one word: slavery. African slaves were first brought to Saint Domingue by the Spaniards in 1512 and at the turn of the 17th century they out-numbered their masters.

In 1630 the French came to the island and took control of the western side of Saint Domingue. With the sweat of the blacks they made their territory the richest European colonial possession, sending to France a steady stream of sugar, cotton, and indigo. By the end of the seventeenth century, some 20,000 Frenchmen, 50,000 mulattoes and 2,000,000 blacks lived there in an uneasy balance. Caste and class separated the three groups. Complicating these divisions was the presence of the Spanish rule on the eastern half of the island. High, well-nigh impassable mountains sliced Saint Domingue in two parts.

While France itself was astir with talk of the rights of man and of freedom, equality, and fraternity, autocratic governors-general held absolute sway over thousands of slaves who produced the wealth of Saint Domingue and over dissatisfied mulattoes who could own land, but had no political or social standing. When the Bastille fell in 1789, the island trembled as though in anticipation of some dreaded catastrophe. In this same year the mulattoes revolted. France then loosened its rule a bit and allowed the mulattoes to have seats in the new colonial assembly.

Warned of the plot by a native maid, Dessalines escaped by leaping through the window.

But the enslavement of the blacks continued, harsh and cruel as ever. As the revolution in France gained momentum, the far away island of Saint Domingue became increasingly restless. The blacks became fired with the desire for freedom and deep in the forest at night they gathered and plotted. The tom-tom language of the Africans told the blacks of the planned uprising.

On August 1, 1789, in the late night hours Boukmann, a voodoo priest, whose name and reputed deeds struck terror in the hearts of slaves, held a meeting of leaders. Among them was Pierre Dominique Toussaint, known for his wisdom and respected for his learning. That night the conspirators plotted their revolt.

Eight days later, the entire 2,000 miles of French territory reverberated to the rhythm of hundreds of drums. The whites were terrified. With a mad sweep the blacks moved from village to village, putting the torch to everything that would burn and killing every white encountered. For weeks the sky glowed with the flames. More than 6000 coffee plantations and 200 sugar refineries went up in smoke. The French rallied their forces and finally routed the slaves. Boukmann, leader of the revolt, was captured at Cap François and his head was impaled on a pole to put fear in the hearts of the slaves.

Toussaint succeeded Boukmann as leader of the slaves and sought an honorable peace for the blacks, who had taken refuge in the forests. At the same time, across the ocean, France had declared war on Spain and England. Thus the French and Spanish halves of Saint Domingue were at war. Following the Arab dictum that "he who is the enemy of my enemy is my friend," Toussaint collected his forces and joined the Spaniards to war against the French army.

Second in command to Toussaint was Jacques Dessalines, a homely African who had been brought to the island as a young slave but was virtually free because his master feared him.

The Spaniards equipped the slave rebels, and they began attacking the French from the northern and eastern portion of the island. Aided by the Spanish, Toussaint drove the French forces from the area. France sent 3,000 soldiers to subdue Toussaint and his black Spartans, but they were soon overcome by the forces of Toussaint or the fever which spread throughout the island. Recognizing that it was helpless to control the revolt, France proclaimed an end to slavery.

Toussaint was not satisfied with the proclamation. He abandoned his Spanish allies and fought his way through the French territory, routing the enemy in town after town. His victories won for him the nickname of L'Ouverture (the Opener) and the title of "General of Saint Domingue" for life. All of the blacks praised him and when he conquered Cap François, called him the "Deliverer." It was here that he was joined by Henri Christophe, a slave who was born in Grenada in 1767. As a mere boy Henri worked as a mason and later was bought by a Negro master who operated an inn where Christophe served as a waiter. In the army of L'Ouverture, Henri used his native ability to promote himself to the rank of Sergeant in short order.

After conquering all of the French territory, Toussaint established himself as governor-general of Saint Domingue. Dessalines, his comrade in arms, was made governor of the province. Christophe had been elevated to the rank of general by this time and was made governor of Cap François and the surrounding region. To the south of the island, a region predominately inhabited by the mulattoes, Alexander Sabes Petïon ruled the prosperous peninsula.

Toussaint turned his attention to the tasks of peace, developed the island's natural resources and foreign trade. The island began to prosper. Trade with France was begun, for the revolt as seen by Toussaint, was not directed so much against the French as against the institution of slavery. Proving his lack of blind hatred for France, he sent his two sons to study in Paris.

Under Emperor Napoleon, France was conquering all Europe. Napoleon held a very low opinion of the black rulers of the former colony. He was determined to regain France's former rich possession. He saw the blacks as only savages whose numbers made their rule of the island possible. To reconquer the island, Napoleon ordered eighty-six ships built to carry 22,000 fighting men.

With Captain-General LeClerc in command, the mighty armada arrived in the waters of Saint Domingue in February, 1802. Its main force was directed at Cap François; other ships were stationed around the island to await the attack. LeClerc sent word to Christophe, governor of Cap François, to prepare for his formal reception. Not having the approval of Toussaint, Christophe refused his entry.

The French forces attacked. Henri's veterans put up a valiant but fruitless fight. The peasants did not support the resistance, having been made indolent by the successes of their armies. Christophe, determined to leave Cap François a smoldering ruin, signalled the burning of the the city by first putting a torch to his own fabulous palace. He then fled with his troops to the hills. LeClerc, taking command of the Cap, decreed that all plantations be returned to their former French owners and that slavery be re-instituted for all blacks. The latter decree jolted the peasants out of their indifference and they rushed to join Christophe.

Sensing that his military success was meaningless without the blacks, LeClerc declared all blacks free forever. He also offered Christophe and Dessalines generalships in the French army and they accepted. The aged Toussaint L'Ouverture was retired with honor. But LeClerc was insincere. On the pretext of having Toussaint meet with the French to discuss the final disposal of his troops, LeClerc had him captured and taken to France where in 1803 he died in prison.

Then LeClerc planned to destroy Dessalines, but the plan failed when a maid learned of the plot and warned Dessalines, telling him of the plot in African sign language in the presence of his enemies.

News of the attempt on the life of Dessalines set off a new revolt. Saint Domingue was again the scene of burnings and killings. This time the mulattoes joined the blacks and drove the French into the sea. Saint Domingue was proclaimed a Republic and given the Indian name of Haiti. Dessalines had himself named governor of Haiti for life and his first act was to have all Frenchmen on the island put to death.

The blacks had no idea that Dessalines could be almost as cruel to them as he had been to the French. In short

He resumed construction on La Citadel which was started by Dessalines.

order, his cruelty and tyranny proved too much for his own people and resulted in his assassination in 1806.

Henri Christophe became the new ruler of Haiti. He found himself the head of a poor war-torn country virtually prostrate with strife and aimlessly floundering ex slaves. Christophe negotiated with the United States an several European powers and offered them opportunitie for commerce and trade. Declaring all green gourds th property of the state, Henri converted them into a mediur of exchange. Before the end of 1807 the Gourds had bee replaced by metal coins, which until this day are calle Gourds.

Convinced that Haiti would gain more respect if it ha a king, the assembly named Christophe, King Henri I i 1811. Moving ahead with his plans to rebuild and stabiliz the kingdom, he created ranks of nobility and based th retention of titles on the productivity of the individua Every boy over ten years of age was compelled to lear a trade. The state furnished the tools and technician Every facet of the economy was under central contro

Haiti prospered and within one year the new kingdo produced ten million pounds of sugar, twenty millio pounds of coffee and five million pounds of cotton. Thes goods were exchanged with foreign powers for gold an stabilized the economy of Haiti. Christophe built a sma merchant fleet to transport the nation's produce.

Henri I was a master builder and within a short tim seven of his palaces were built on his vast person property. The most elaborate was Sans Souci. He resume construction on La Citadel which was started by Des salines. La Citadel was constructed on the highest mour tain in the region of Cap Haitien some 300 feet abov sea-level. This great fortress was built in the shape of a irregular square, with walls between 20 to 30 feet thicl towering skyward 130 feet. Three hundred and sixty-fiv bronze cannons capable of firing 12-pound balls surrounde the ramparts of La Citadel. The huge fortress was capabl of accommodating 10,000 soldiers. To provide water, a enormous underground cistern was built and rain fallin on the structure was collected in it.

Into the palace of San Souci went the most elegan furnishings and art treasures available from around th

hristophe imitated Napolean in manner and dress...

orld. Although King Henri learned only to sign his name,
e placed great importance on education.

With the fields glistening with abundant crops and
laces shining in the sun, Haiti again could be called the
earl of the Antilles." Beneath the outward show and
tivity, however, was dissatisfaction and resentment.
enri could not understand why every Haitian did not
ork as hard as he did. His increasing pressure for pro-
uction (and penalties for the lack of it), was resented by
any. In addition, it was rumored that the King was
otivated by ambition for personal gain. As before,
oups of malcontents plotted the death of Henri I.

Gaffie, Henri's chief executioner, beheaded so many of
e plotters that he became adept to the point that he
uld remove the head of the condemned without soiling
s shirt. Haitians swore that Henri was drunk with power
d neither the bloody sword of Gaffie nor the high walls
La Citadel would stop the resistance.

King Henri I, while earning a grudging respect from
her nations, had alienated himself from his own subjects,
d his drive had taken its toll on him. In 1820 his body
llapsed and he suffered a stroke which paralyzed his
wer limbs. Rumors of his illness swept the island. At
int Marc, Henri's army officers on hearing the news of
s illness felt themselves no longer bound by their oath
allegiance. Most islanders rejoiced that the King was
sabled. The royal guards deserted their post at La
itadel on Cape François.

Christophe sensed that the end was near. He got his
ife and daughters out of danger, but his son, Prince
ictoire, was captured and murdered to put an end to the
yal line of inheritance. On October 8, 1820 Henri had
s worn-out body placed on a stretcher and secretly
rried to La Citadel. Here, virtually alone, he put a pistol
his head and fired a silver bullet into his brain.

Toussaint L'Ouverture, Jacques Dessalines and Henri
hristophe, all extraordinary men, loom like a triple-
eaked mountain in the history of Haiti. La Citadel
ands today as a monument to those champions of free-
m and independence.

hn W. Vandercook. *Black Majesty* (New York, 1928).

Crispus Attucks (-1770)

FIRST TO DIE FOR INDEPENDENC[E]

Crispus Attucks shed the first blood in the struggle for American independence. "The first to defy and the first to die," Attucks has been described as the "leader and voice" when, in 1770, he fell before the bullets of the British on old King Street. Years later, John Adams wrote, "On that night the foundation of American independence was laid."

The occasion of the death of Attucks and several other colonists became known as the Boston Massacre. Little is known, however, about the first black patriot prior to that fateful night except that he was born in Framingham, Massachusetts, had escaped from his master some twenty years earlier, and secured work as a seaman. An account of his burial in the *Gazette and Country Journal* refers to him as a "stranger." He is described by the same newspaper as being "6 feet two inches high, short curl'd hair, his knees nearer together than common" and was known to the townspeople as the "mulatto."

The Boston Massacre marked the turning point in the relations between England and the thirteen colonies. The smoldering resentment of the late 1760's was to turn into open hostility and conflict. George III and his minions understood little of frontier America and failed to see that it was not an English borough but a budding nation. In the manner of all tyrants, they dispatched troops to qu[ell] the rebellious colonists. Soon Boston and other cities we[re] filled with British troops, and tension began to mount. T[he] winter of 1770 was marked by street brawls and tave[rn] fights.

At approximately nine o'clock on the night of March [5,] 1770, as a result of a call for help from a beleaguered Br[it]ish sentry, seven soldiers representing the might of Ki[ng] George III paraded toward the Commons with bayon[ets] fixed. Crispus Attucks and forty or fifty patriots wait[ed] at the head of the street armed with clubs and sticks. [As] the soldiers drew near, Attucks yelled, "The way to get r[id] of these troops is to attack the main guard."

The Americans let loose a shower of sticks and ston[es.] "Do not be afraid," they shouted. "They dare not fir[e."] The soldiers fell back. Suddenly there was the crackle [of] rifle fire. Tall, distinguishable by his color, and in the fro[nt] ranks, Attucks was the first to fall.

As a symbol of resistance to tyranny, Attuck's dea[th] placed him among the immortals. Today his name to[...] the names of the five carved in the monument of grani[te] and bronze erected to commemorate that historic nig[ht] in the Boston Common.

City of Boston, *A Memorial of Crispus Attucks, Samuel Maverick, Jam[es] Caldwell, Samuel Gray and Patrick Carr* (Boston, 1889), pp. 77-83; Benjam[in] Quarles, *The Negro in the American Revolution* (Chapel Hill, N.C., 196[ ]) pp. 3-7; "The Story of Crispus Attucks," *Negro Digest* (July 1, 1963), [pp.] 46-49.

Peter Salem (1750-1816)

BLACK HERO OF BUNKER HILL

The April battles of Lexington and Concord in 1775 marked the end of the talking and the beginning of the fighting for American independence from Great Britain. The colonists girded their loins for a showdown. The city of Boston and its environs were the focus of the spreading conflict between the settlers and the British Redcoats, and on June 17, 1775, the colonists and Redcoats squared off at Bunker Hill. More than a score of blacks stood shoulder to shoulder with the white American rebels. Among them were Prince Hall, destined to be the founder of the first Negro Masonic Lodge in America; Seymour Burr, Pomp Fisk, Salem Poor, Barzillai Lew, Cuff Whittemore and Peter Salem.

Peter Salem was a member of the First Massachusetts Regiment, one of the better disciplined units gathered on the hill. A native of Framingham, Massachusetts, Salem had been freed by his master to fight in the war. He had already given a good account of himself in the earlier skirmishes at Lexington and Concord. When the Redcoats launched their attack on Breed's Hill, he was in the thick of the fight. During the advance of the British, the colonial officers rode back and forth in front of their troops, urging the colonials, "Don't fire 'til you see the whites of their eyes!" The British made a number of sorties against the colonials, and conspicuous among them was Major John Pitcairn. It was during one of these assaults that Pitcairn fell mortally wounded, with a colonial bullet in his chest. Peter Salem is credited with having fired the fatal shot. The colonials were finally pushed from Breed's Hill, but not before the British learned that the raw American troops were willing and able soldiers.

Peter Salem remained in the Continental army for seven years. He took part in the critical battle of Saratoga in 1777. When the hostilities ended with America victorious in 1783, Peter Salem left the army. He later married and settled in Leicester, Massachusetts for a time. He earned his livelihood as a basketweaver. Eventually he returned to his native city where he died on August 16, 1816. In 1882, the city of Framingham placed a memorial over his grave. The Daughters of the American Revolution purchased the land on which his home once stood in Leicester, and erected an inscription which read, "Here lived Peter Salem, a Negro soldier of the Revolution." John Trumbull's famous painting of the battle of Bunker Hill shows, in the lower right hand section, Lt. Grosvenor with Peter Salem just after wounding Major Pitcairn. In many reproductions of this painting, the right side of the picture is cropped off. In 1968 the federal government's commemorative stamp for John Trumbull used the small section which included Peter Salem, the black hero of Bunker Hill.

Benjamin Quarles, *The Negro in the American Revolution* (Chapel Hill, N.C., 1961), pp. 10-11; *Black Heroes of the American Revolution*, 1775-1783, New York, N.A.A.C.P. publication, n.d. p. 9.

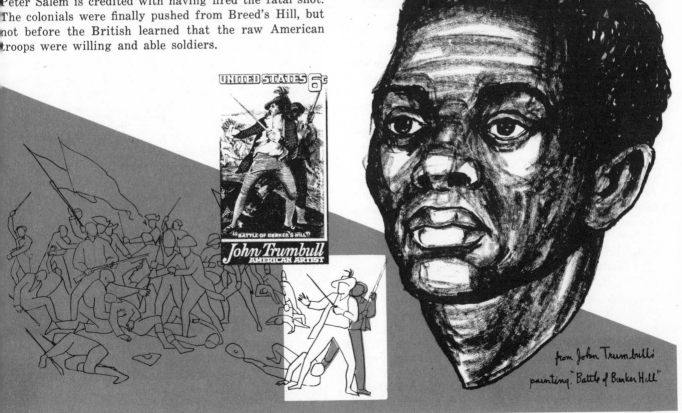

from John Trumbull's painting "Battle of Bunker Hill"

Oliver Cromwell (1753-1853)

WITH WASHINGTON AT DELAWARE

After a frustrating year of trying to build an army, George Washington in 1776 declared in effect that not only were his soldiers hard to organize and discipline but also that they "leave you at the last critical moment."

However, there were many black soldiers under his command to whom this did not apply. One of them was Oliver Cromwell who crossed the Delaware River with Washington on the cold, windy night of December 25, 1776. The purpose of the crossing was to attempt capture of the British garrison located at Trenton. A victory was needed to bolster the wavering spirits of the band of patriots whose ardor had been cooled by the realities of battle and the coming of winter.

Oliver Cromwell was among the 2,400 hand-picked troops whose daring caught the unsuspecting mercenaries of the British unawares. The gamble was a complete success. The Hessians were routed; the victory did much to lift the spirit of the colonists. Only two colonial soldiers lost their lives, not in battle, but due to the cold waters of the Delaware. Three men were wounded, one of them being James Monroe, a future president of the United States. Oliver Cromwell was in the thick of this particular fight and came out unscratched.

Oliver Cromwell was also in the battles of Princeton and Brandywine in 1776, the battle of Monmouth in 1778, and the battle of Yorktown in 1781. These battles were among the most important of the entire war. The Delaware crossing resulted in the capture of the British garrison at Trenton. The battle of Princeton removed British troops from western New Jersey and slowed their advance toward Philadelphia. And, the battle of Yorktown was the closing battle of the entire war. It was at Yorktown, Cromwell later declared, that he saw the last direct casualty of the American Revolution fall.

Oliver Cromwell was born in Burlington County, New Jersey on May 24, 1753. Whether or not he was ever a slave is not known. He joined the Second New Jersey Regiment at the onset of hostilities and, in the beginning under the command of a Colonel Israel Shreve. In the words of William Cooper Nell, Cromwell then served for "six years and nine months under the immediate command of George Washington." After the war, Cromwell received a pension of ninety dollars annually. A farmer by occupation, Cromwell retired and reared a family on a small farm which he purchased with his pension funds. He had a total of fourteen children and survived all but six. He lived to see the beginning of the end of American slavery. Oliver Cromwell died in 1853 and was interred in the burial grounds of Broadstreet Methodist Church, Columbus, New Jersey.

William C. Nell, *The Colored Patriots of the American Revolution* (Boston, 1855), pp. 61-62.

Benjamin Banneker (1731-1806)
MATHEMATICAL WIZARD
AND INVENTOR

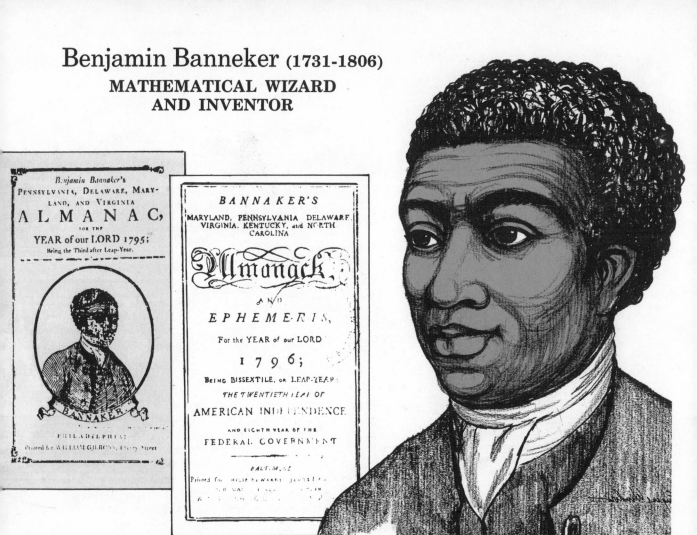

Banneker, a free-born Negro, was an essayist, inventor, mathematician and lay astronomer and, because of his intellect, was called a "sable genius." Born on November 9, 1731 in Ellicott, Maryland, Benjamin Banneker was a self-taught mathematician and astronomer. While still a youth, he made a wooden clock which kept accurate time until he died. This clock is believed to be the first clock wholly made in America. In his forties, with the aid of books lent to him by the Ellicotts of Maryland, he became a proficient mathematician, able to solve any problems which were submitted to him. Deeply interested in natural phenomena, Banneker started publishing an almanac in 1791 and continued its publication until 1802. He published a treatise on bees, did a mathematical study of the cycle of the 17-year locust and became a pamphleteer for the peace movement.

His style of life was unusual. By night Banneker could be found wrapped in a cloak, studying the stars until dawn; by day he slept or worked on mathematical problems and received the curious, who came from near and far to see this strange genius. He never married but was always a most charming host, receiving one and all in his full suit of drab cloth and wearing his beaver hat and carrying his cane while showing visitors about his large farm which he subsequently sold in order to devote all of his time to his scientific pursuits.

Banneker was aware of slavery and its evils. In 1791, he wrote his famous letter to Thomas Jefferson in which he declared that if Jefferson's reputed liberalism were true, "I apprehend you will embrace every opportunity to eradicate that train of absurd and false ideas and opinions which so generally prevail with respect to us (Negroes); and that your sentiments are concurrent with mine which are: that one universal Father hath given being to us all; that He not only made us all of one flesh, but that He hath also without partiality afforded us all with the same faculties and that, however variable we may be in society or religion, however diversified in situation or color, we are all the same family and stand in the same relation to Him."

The intellect, insight, and ability of this untrained and unschooled genius caused Jefferson, as they had others, to spread the name of Banneker across the seas. Banneker died in 1806, with the shadow of slavery deepening across the land. The significance of Banneker's life lay in its dramatization to a slave-holding nation that Negroes are a part of the human family. This sable genius's life did not end slavery, but it did indicate to even the most skeptical the possibilities within the Negro when left free and unfettered.

Benjamin Brawley, *Negro American Writers* (Chapel Hill, 1935), pp. 74-77; Sauran Morris, "A Sketch of the Life of Benjamin Banneker", *Proceedings of the Maryland Historical Society*, 1854 (Baltimore, 1854).

Jean Baptiste Pointe De Sable (1745-1818)

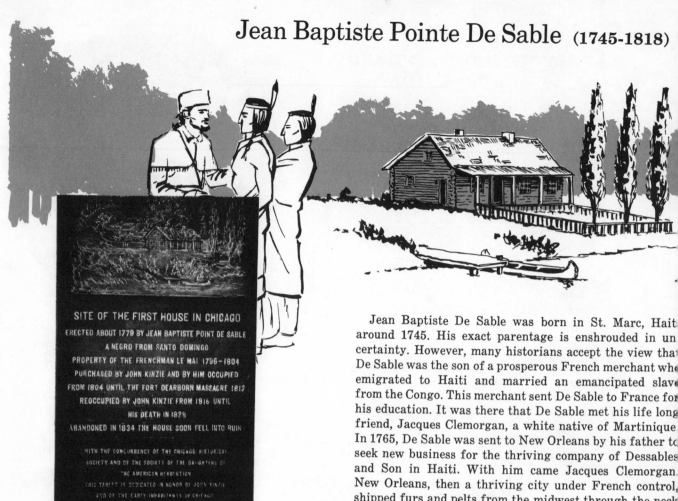

SITE OF THE FIRST HOUSE IN CHICAGO
ERECTED ABOUT 1779 BY JEAN BAPTISTE POINT DE SABLE
A NEGRO FROM SANTO DOMINGO
PROPERTY OF THE FRENCHMAN LE MAI 1796-1804
PURCHASED BY JOHN KINZIE AND BY HIM OCCUPIED
FROM 1804 UNTIL THE FORT DEARBORN MASSACRE 1812
REOCCUPIED BY JOHN KINZIE FROM 1816 UNTIL
HIS DEATH IN 1828
ABANDONED IN 1834 THE HOUSE SOON FELL INTO RUIN

WITH THE CONCURRENCE OF THE CHICAGO HISTORICAL
SOCIETY AND OF THE SOCIETY OF THE DAUGHTERS OF
THE AMERICAN REVOLUTION
THIS TABLET IS DEDICATED IN HONOR OF JOHN KINZIE
AND OF THE EARLY INHABITANTS OF CHICAGO
IN THE CENTENARY OF THE FORT DEARBORN MASSACRE

A black man from Haiti founded the city of Chicago, yet 150 years after his death, the second largest city in the United States had done little to commemorate its first settler. On a downtown building in the heart of the city's richest real estate, there was once a plaque which read in part, "Site of the first house in Chicago, erected about 1779 by Jean Baptiste Point De Sable, a Negro from Santo Domingo . . ." The plaque was removed in 1927 and never replaced.

Records indicate that in 1772, on the north bank of what is now the Chicago River, Jean Baptiste Pointe Dessables (French spelling) erected a large cabin to which he later brought his wife and a small band of Indians from Peoria. De Sable continued to build other structures such as barns and storehouses, the Indians built their homes, and soon the settlement of Eschikagou was firmly established.

Popular legend has it that Chicago was founded by John Kinzie, a ne'er-do-well trader and speculator from Detroit. Historical evidence, however, contradicts this legend. John Kinzie enters the true story of the founding of Chicago in 1800, when he served as a witness for De Sable who was selling his buildings and holdings in Chicago. De Sable then moved to Peoria, Illinois and later to St. Charles, Missouri.

Jean Baptiste De Sable was born in St. Marc, Haiti around 1745. His exact parentage is enshrouded in uncertainty. However, many historians accept the view that De Sable was the son of a prosperous French merchant who emigrated to Haiti and married an emancipated slave from the Congo. This merchant sent De Sable to France for his education. It was there that De Sable met his life long friend, Jacques Clemorgan, a white native of Martinique. In 1765, De Sable was sent to New Orleans by his father to seek new business for the thriving company of Dessables and Son in Haiti. With him came Jacques Clemorgan. New Orleans, then a thriving city under French control, shipped furs and pelts from the midwest through the neck of the Mississippi and on abroad. Shortly after De Sable landed, the fortunes of war shifted New Orleans to Spanish control. De Sable immediately left the city for St. Louis, another French controlled settlement up the Mississippi. At St. Louis, De Sable developed a bustling business with the Indians, but in 1767, a British take-over of the city led De Sable to move still further north, near Peoria. Here he settled among the Peoria and Potowatomi Indians. Here he took an Indian wife whose name was Chikiwata, and came to know the great Indian chief, Pontiac.

In 1769, De Sable travelled to Canada, following the water routes of the Illinois River and Lake Michigan. The main portage point was a place bearing the Indian name Eschikagou where De Sable would stop in his travels to and from Canada. In 1772, he decided that this point, in spite of its odorous marshes, would be an advantageous spot for his trading cabin. In 1774, after finishing and furnishing the cabin, he brought his family, along with a band of Indians from Peoria, to Point De Sable at Eschikagou on the river bank near Lake Michigan . . . and so Chicago was born. And, it was here that De Sable's daughter, Suzanne, Chicago's first child was born.

The little settlement continued to grow, and De Sable's home became the stopping place of virtually all traders coming to the area. French fur traders passed through on their way back and forth between St. Louis and Canada; Indian canoes and French bateaux skirted the rim of Lake Michigan. De Sable himself had immense influence on the Indians, the British and the French. But the British, fearing his influence on the Indians and suspicious of his ties

CHICAGO'S FIRST SETTLER

with the French, arrested him in 1778 on the unfounded belief that he was a spy for the French. He was held in custody at Fort Mackinac for nearly a year before being released. Upon regaining his liberty, De Sable resumed his trading. Many of the business transactions De Sable had were entered on various account books of different merchants in Detroit between the years of 1780 and 1784.

De Sable lived in a house rather than a hut or cabin as mentioned in most accounts of Chicago's first settler. This dwelling measured twenty-two feet by forty feet, an unusually large structure for this part of the country in the 1790's. In addition to his home, De Sable also built a bake house, a dairy, a poultry house, a smoke house for curing meat, a stable, a workshop and a horse mill. He had some relatively up-to-date farm tools, including a plank saw, a large rip saw, a seven-foot cross-cut saw, and one complete plow with spare parts. A further listing of De Sable possessions gives an indication of the style of life led by this immigrant from Haiti who was living at least two miles from the nearest major settlement.

The contents of his home have been inventoried as follows: one large cabinet with glass doors, one bureau, four tables, seven chairs, one large feather bed, one couch, a stove, a score of large wooden dishes, four tin face basins and three pewter basins, a churn, one iron coffee mill, one pair of scales with weights, eleven copper bottles, two copper bells, one tin lantern, one leather and one metal wire rack, one toasting iron, two mirrors, and two pictures, one hatchet and four planes, plus a bag of carpenter's tools. De Sable supplemented with hunted game the domesticated animals maintained by him: thirty head of cattle, thirty-eight hogs, over forty chickens, two mules and one horse.

In 1800 De Sable sold most of his holdings to one Jean Lalime. The alleged founder of Chicago, John Kinzie, was a witness to the sale and carried the bill of sale to St. Joseph, Michigan which contained the articles referred to above. In this same year, John Kinzie married a resident of St. Joseph and in 1804 moved to Chicago to live. De Sable, dissatisfied with the land policies followed by the United States in disposing of the Northwest Territory, then abandoned the settlement at Chicago and, with his wife, returned to Peoria.

Following the death of his wife in 1809, De Sable moved southward to St. Charles, Missouri, where the next year he purchased his last home from one Pierre Rodin, another black man. This house subsequently became the residence of Alexander McNair, the first governor of Missouri.

De Sable always took a keen interest in the plight of the slaves, many of whom he purchased and set free. In gratitude, these emancipated blacks composed songs exalting his virtues. But when Jean Baptiste Pointe De Sable died on August 28, 1818, he was buried in an unmarked grave in the St. Boromeo cemetery alongside Louis Blanchette, the founder of St. Charles. On October 25, 1968, in a ceremony marking the grave with granite stone, the state of Illinois and the city of Chicago recognized De Sable as the founder of Chicago, now one of the greatest cities of the world.

Documents supplied by Fritz Etienne, a direct descendant of De Sable; Edna McElhiney Olson (comp.), *Historical Saint Charles, Missouri* (St. Louis, Mo., 1967); Rev. Thomas A. Meehan, "Jean Baptist Point Du Saible," *Negro Heritage*, vol. 7, #3, pp. 27-46; Altai Margit (pseudonym), "The Father of Chicago . . .", *Hyde Park-Kenwood Voices* (August, 1968), pp. 1, 6.

Prince Hall (1735-1807)
FRATERNAL LEADER

Prince Hall was the founder of the oldest social organization among Negroes in America. Today's Prince Hall Masonic order goes back to the seedtime of the Republic. While almost all Negroes are acquainted with the Prince Hall Masons and their social and charitable activities, very little is known about Prince Hall.

Prince Hall, the founder of the first Masonic Lodge, came from Barbadoes, British West Indies. Born in 1735, he was the son of an English father and a free Negro woman. At the age of twelve, he was apprenticed to a leather merchant. After a few years, Hall gave up his apprenticeship and, after working at a variety of jobs, finally came to Boston, Massachusetts in 1765. Working in and around Boston, he saved enough money to buy property and to become a voter. During his spare time he educated himself.

In 1774, Prince Hall joined the Methodist church and eventually became a minister and the leader of the small Negro community then in Boston. When the American Revolution reached the shooting stage, he petitioned John Hancock of the Committee of Safety for the Colonies to allow him to join the Continental Army. This petition was approved by George Washington himself.

On March 6, 1775, at Hall's initiative, he and fourteen other Negroes were inducted into a British Chartered Lodge of Freemasons at Boston Harbor. After the Revolutionary War in 1787, Prince Hall and his fellow Masons were chartered as African Lodge No. 459. Four years later, an African Grand Lodge was formed and Prince Hall elected Master. In 1797, Hall organized African Lodges in Philadelphia and Rhode Island. After Hall's death in 1807, Negro Masons decided to change the name of their organization from the African Grand Lodge to the Prince Hall Grand Lodge.

Hall's interests were not restricted to Lodge activities. He took a deep interest in the general status of Negroes in Boston and elsewhere. As early as 1776 he urged the Massachusetts legislature to support the cause of emancipation. He successfully prodded the city of Boston to provide schools for free Negro children in 1797.

The hundreds of Lodges throughout the country may be seen as a monument to Prince Hall who adopted America as his home.

Harold van Voorhis, *Negro Masonry in the United States* (New York, 1940) pp. 7-13; Harry E. Davis, "Documents Relating to Negro Masonry in America", *Journal of Negro History*, **XXI** (October, 1936), pp. 411-432.

Paul Cuffe (1759-1817)

EARLY BUSINESSMAN AND COLONIZER

Paul Cuffe was one of the most unusual of all the men from New Bedford, Massachusetts who went down to the sea in ships. Unlike most Negroes who sailed in those days, Cuffe was no mere deck-hand or roustabout, but a shipowner and businessman. He owned several ships and made his living hauling cargo to different parts of the world.

Starting with a small boat built with his own hands, Cuffe became the owner of sloops, schooners, brigs, and several other ships of various sizes, the largest being the 268-ton *Alpha* which, in 1806, he and a crew of nine Negroes sailed from Wilmington, Delaware, to Savannah, Georgia, and thence to Gothenburg, Sweden. Six years before this, Paul Cuffe had sailed the 162-ton *Hero* around the Cape of Good Hope.

Fearless, capable, and energetic, Paul Cuffe at one point owned one regular ship, two brigs, and several parcels of land. After spending considerable sums of money on various projects, Cuffe was able to leave an estate of over $20,000.

However, Cuffe was not solely interested in making money. As a free Negro whose father had been a slave, the status of Negroes in New Bedford and elsewhere was of paramount concern to him. One of Cuffe's earliest acts was to have the family name, Slocum, changed to Cuffe, for Slocum was the name of his father's master. At this time Cuffe was seventeen years of age. Two years later he and a brother, John Cuffe, sued in the Massachusetts courts for the right to vote. The suit was unsuccessful but it did help make possible legislation to achieve the same end several years later.

Going to sea at the age of sixteen, Paul Cuffe was able to purchase a $3500 farm in 1797 for himself and his Indian wife, Alice Pequit. While granting the vote by this time, New Bedford still had no schools for the offspring of free Negroes. At his own expense Paul Cuffe built a school on his farm and, with money out of his own pocket, hired a teacher for free Negro children.

A Quaker and a Negro, Paul Cuffe had a double interest in the freedom of the Negro. Enlightened opinion at this time generally favored colonization as the answer to the incipient racial problem. In 1811 Paul Cuffe sailed one of his ships, the *Traveller*, from Westport, Massachusetts to Sierra Leone, Africa where he founded the Friendly Society for the emigration of free Negroes from America. The War of 1812 interrupted his colonization plans, but in 1815 he took thirty-eight Negroes to Sierra Leone at a cost of $4,000 from his personal funds.

Cuffe planned many more trips with black colonists but his health failed and he died in 1817.

H. N. Sherwood, "Paul Cuffe", *Journal of Negro History*, VIII (April, 1923), pp. 153-229.

James Forten (1766-1842)

FORGOTTEN ABOLITIONIST

A powder boy in the infant American navy at fifteen, foreman in a sail loft at twenty, James Forten was one of the vigorous opponents of colonization and slavery during the early years of the nineteenth century. He was one of the driving forces behind the Negro Convention movement which gave voice to the opinions and ideas of free Negroes in the North long before Frederick Douglass.

James Forten's opposition to slavery and colonization was implacable and unbending. Within twenty years after being made the foreman in the sail loft, Forten was its owner, employing forty men, white and Negro. Amassing over $100,000 from his business, he threw his great energy and shrewdness into the struggle for the rights of free Negroes. His loyalty to the United States was unquestioned, for during the War of 1812, he personally recruited 2,500 Negroes to help guard Philadelphia when the city appeared threatened by the British. In 1813 he wrote "A Series of Letters by a Man of Color" opposing proposed legislation requiring the registration of all Negroes in Philadelphia.

When William Lloyd Garrison, the abolitionist, started his newspaper, *The Liberator*, James Forten solicited many of its 1700 Negro subscribers. Although Richard Allen's name appears as Chairman on the record of the first Negro Convention (held in Philadelphia in 1830), Forten was one of the prime movers making the convention possible.

On several occasions James Forten used Richard Allen's church, Bethel, to address the city's Negroes on issues of the day, including proposals made by the American Colonization Society which was trying to interest free Negroes in returning to Africa. Over and over he drove home the idea that America was now the home of the Negro.

Although uneducated in a formal sense, his writings reveal a vigorous mind and his deeds show him as he was —an uncompromising advocate of freedom and equality for men of color. Due to his influence, anti-slavery groups had a clear idea of what most Negroes of his era desired: the right to live as truly free men in America.

Roy Allen Billington, "James Forten: Forgotten Abolitionist," *Negro History Bulletin* (November 1949), pp. 1-6; Benjamin Brawley, *A Short History of the Negro in America* (New York, 1931); Esther M. Douty, *Forten the Sailmaker* (Chicago, 1968).

Has the God who made the white man and the black left any record declaring us a different species? Are we not sustained by the same power supported by the same food, hurt by the same wounds, wounded by the same wrongs, pleased with the same delights, and propagated by the same means? And should we not then enjoy the same liberty, and be protected by the same laws?

THE LIBERATOR.

VOL. III.   WILLIAM LLOYD GARRISON AND ISAAC KNAPP, PUBLISHERS   NO. 33.

BOSTON, MASSACHUSETTS.   OUR COUNTRY IS THE WORLD—OUR COUNTRYMEN, ALL MANKIND   [SATURDAY, AUGUST 17, 1833.

Denmark Vesey (1767-1822)
ANTI-SLAVERY INSURRECTIONIST

Telemarque—known to history as Denmark Vesey—is one of those leaders who made history because of his hopes and not because of his deeds. Denmark Vesey is popularly known as a leader of a slave "revolt" in Charleston, South Carolina—a "revolt" which never got beyond the planning stage. For his plan and ideas, Telemarque and thirty-four other Negroes were hanged.

Telemarque's life was filled with melancholy irony. As a slave, for over twenty years he sailed with his master, one Captain Vesey, to the Virgin Islands and Haiti, which was then ruled by free black men. Telemarque was Captain Vesey's property but moved about the streets of Charleston like a free man. He secured his own freedom by winning a $1,500 lottery, $600 of which he used to buy himself from his master. He tried to purchase his children but was unable to do so.

Born in 1767, Telemarque was sold at an early age by Captain Vesey but later was re-purchased because he suffered from epilepsy. As Captain Vesey's constant companion, Telemarque learned much about the nature of freedom and of business. When he became free, he applied his experience and knowledge to his own business ventures and soon prospered.

Telemarque wanted more than anything to secure the freedom of his people. Partly because of his ability to read and write, and partly because the church was the one place where one could speak to large numbers of Negroes without questioning by the whites, Telemarque became a Methodist minister. In short order his home was made a regular meeting place. Money was collected to buy arms. Telemarque had a blacksmith make a large number of daggers and bayonets. A white barber sympathetic to his plans was engaged to fashion wigs and whiskers out of European hair, so that his mulatto conspirators could penetrate the heart of the city and seize control when the time came. Zero hour was set for the second Sunday in July of 1822.

Everything was in readiness, when suddenly the whole scheme had to be advanced to June 16. The plans which were two years in the making had been revealed to the whites by a Negro whom Telemarque had felt he could trust. In a twinkling, Charleston was an armed camp. The whites rounded up hundreds of Negroes believed to be involved in the plot. Telemarque went into hiding, but after two days was discovered and taken captive.

A local tribunal, operating as judge and jury, heard condemning testimony from scores of witnesses. Telemarque had a good lawyer and during the trial showed himself adept at cross-examining witnesses, but there was no doubt that he was planning the overthrow of the city. For this he was sentenced to be hanged along with thirty-four other Negroes. Four whites who had aided them were merely fined and imprisoned.

Two days before Independence Day, 1822, Telemarque—Denmark Vesey—died on the gallows.

Herbert Aptheker, *American Negro Slave Revolts* (New York, 1943), pp. 268-272.

David Walker (1785-1830)
"APPEAL TO THE SLAVES"

WALKER'S
APPEAL,
IN FOUR ARTICLES
TOGETHER WITH
A PREAMBLE
TO THE
COLORED CITIZENS OF THE WORLD
BUT IN PARTICULAR AND VERY EXPRESSLY TO THOSE OF THE
UNITED STATES OF AMERICA

In 1829, David Walker published his first edition of *Appeal*. In it he proclaimed to the slaves, ". . . it is no more harm for you to kill the man who is trying to kill you, than it is for you to take a drink of water."

The *Appeal* exploded with shattering force in the North and in the South. Anti-slavery leaders of both races rejected the violence advocated in Walker's publication and he was forced to circulate it at his own risk and expense. In the South its circulation was deemed a capital offense but this did not stop it. The governor of Massachusetts, the state in which Walker lived, was asked to suppress it, but refused. A reward was then offered for Walker; $1,000 dead, or $10,000 delivered alive.

"I will stand my ground. Somebody must die in this cause. I may be doomed to the stake and the fire or to the scaffold tree, but it is not in me to falter if I can promote the work of emancipation." Thus spoke David Walker in answer to the pleas of his wife and friends who urged him to go to Canada to escape the wrath brought upon himself by his stirring publication.

His courage and determination had deep roots. David was born in Wilmington, North Carolina, a border state, in 1785 while the Revolutionary War phrases of "liberty" and "pursuit of happiness" were still echoing faintly in the air. His mother was free, which entitled him to the status of free-born, but his father, Merel Walker, was a slave. Young David hated slavery with all his heart. He finally left home and wandered to Boston where he became a permanent resident and, in 1827, opened a second-hand clothing store.

David Walker was self-taught, and read extensively the literature on human slavery, concentrating on the history of resistance to oppression. *Appeal* became one of the most widely read and circulated books written by a Negro. Following its third edition in 1830, Walker died and foul play was suspected. The *Appeal* was the only work produced by Walker, but up to that time it was the boldest attack by a Negro writer against slavery in America.

Herbert Aptheker, *A Documentary History of the Negro People in the United States* (New York, 1962), Paperback, pp. 90, 93-97; Richard Bardolph, *The Negro Vanguard* (New York, 1961), pp. 41, 55.

Nat Turner (1800-1831)

ANTI-SLAVERY REVOLUTIONIST

From the early 1600's slaves had made many attempts to gain the same liberty that other groups had found in America. The first major revolt against slavery in North America occurred during August of 1831 in Southampton County, Virginia. It was led by Nathaniel Turner, the Black Prophet, a short, slightly plump "black Negro of the pure African type," who, then 31 years old, had felt destined for great deeds from his childhood.

Born a slave in Virginia on October 2, 1800, Nat Turner showed evidence of outstanding intellect at an early age. Learning to read, he could quote long passages from the Bible, knew enough about science and mechanics to be an expert repairman and to experiment in the making of gun powder, paper and pottery. His various masters—four in all—were proud to own such a brilliant and model slave. His reputation as being a slave minister was well known throughout the country.

His fellow slaves sensed that he was no ordinary man and regarded him with a mixture of respect and awe. His account of visions and prophecies increased this sense of difference. He reported visions of blacks and whites struggling in the heavens; the outstretched hands of Christ; and voices telling him he was too wise to be a slave. In 1823 Turner decided that these signs meant that he was to lead a black army of liberation against the slaveholders.

For two years Turner brewed over the mission he felt had been given him. In February, 1831, he confided his decision to four trusted companions and an insurrection was set for the fourth of July. Because Turner became ill the revolt was postponed. On August 13, 1831, a contemporary historian records that the sun rose "pale green, later turning to cerulean blue, and then to silver white." People all over Virginia were frightened and bewildered. But Nat Turner took this strange event as his signal, saying, "As the black spot passed over the sun, so shall the blacks pass over the earth." August 21st was set as the day of deliverance.

Starting with a half-dozen men, soon to number nearly sixty, Turner and his group moved from one house of whites to another, killing everyone in sight. For forty-eight hours they roamed the plantations of Southampton County leaving fifty-five dead in the wake of their fury. Turner then set out to capture Jerusalem, the county seat, in order to get guns and ammunition. En route there, they were met by a posse of aroused whites who dispersed them. Turner regrouped his men, but again was routed. He and a few survivors fled to the great Dismal Swamp where he was captured six weeks later.

Southampton was enraged and terror stricken. Many slaves were suspect; hundreds were shot at random. Of the accused insurrectionists, four free blacks were discharged for lack of evidence; twenty were acquitted; twelve were convicted and sent out of the state; and seventeen, including Nat Turner, were hanged.

Rayford Logan, "Nat Turner, Fiend or Martyr," *Opportunity*, IX (1931). William Sidney Drewry, *Slave Insurrection in Virginia, 1830-1865* (Washington, 1900).

William Still (1821-1902)
UNDERGROUND RAILROAD LEADER

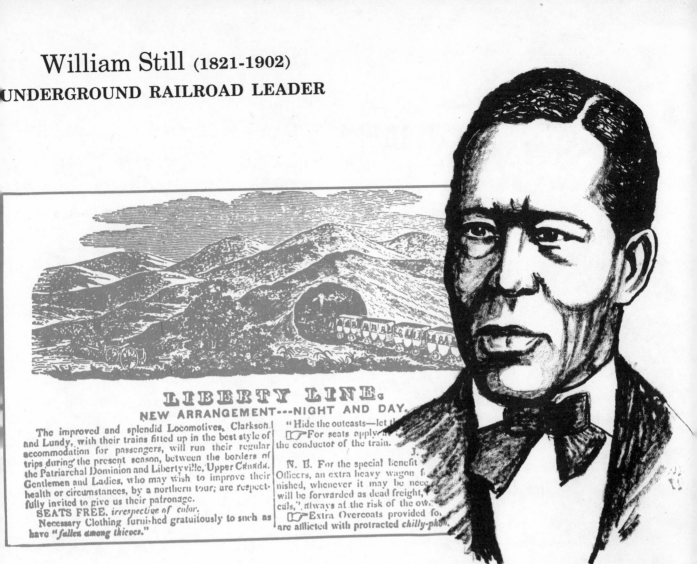

LIBERTY LINE.
NEW ARRANGEMENT---NIGHT AND DAY.

The improved and splendid Locomotives, Clarkson and Lundy, with their trains fitted up in the best style of accommodation for passengers, will run their regular trips during the present season, between the borders of the Patriarchal Dominion and Libertyville, Upper Canada. Gentlemen and Ladies, who may wish to improve their health or circumstances, by a northern tour, are respectfully invited to give us their patronage.

SEATS FREE, *irrespective of color.*

Necessary Clothing furnished gratuitously to such as have "*fallen among thieves.*"

"Hide the outcasts—let th
☞ For seats apply
the conductor of the train.
J.

N. B. For the special benefit
Officers, an extra heavy wagon f
nished, whenever it may be nece
will be forwarded as dead freight,
cals," always at the risk of the ow
☞ Extra Overcoats provided fo.
are afflicted with protracted *chilly-ph*

Of all the Underground Railroad stations dotting the North, perhaps the busiest and most efficient was run by William Still, secretary of the Pennsylvania Society for the Abolition of Slavery. During his fourteen years as an official of the Society, William Still was awakened hundreds of times in the middle of the night to give refuge to escaping slaves. He kept his big house stocked with food and clothing for the runaways bound for freedom.

Because secrecy was an absolute necessity, information is vague and imprecise regarding the extent of the underground railroad. However, Still kept meticulous records of the fugitives so that relatives and friends might locate them. For a time these records were hidden in a cemetery and later published in a book, *The Underground Railroad.* By his own count, he aided 649 slaves to freedom.

Extremely able and vigorous, William was the last of eighteen children of slaves, Levin and Sidney Steel. Levin bought his own freedom and left his native Maryland for New Jersey. His wife, Sidney, escaped and, on joining her husband, changed the family name to Still and her given name to Charity. She left two young children in bondage during her escape.

This family experience made a deep impression on William. In the year 1844 he left the family farm in New Jersey and went to Philadelphia, arriving with no friends and only five dollars in his pocket. He taught himself to read and write. Three years after arriving, he was named secretary of the Pennsylvania Abolition Society, then a very small group of whites. In order to offer practical aid to the slaves, the Society needed someone who knew the Negro community well. Still performed his chores so well that the Society elected him chairman in 1851 and he served for ten years.

Acting as a conductor of the Underground Railroad was only part of Still's activities. He helped organize and finance a "social, civil and statistical association" to collect data on the Negro. Through his efforts an orphanage for the offspring of colored soldiers and sailors was set up in Philadelphia. The energetic Mr. William Still was one of the organizers of the first Y.M.C.A. for his people in America.

In 1860 after retiring from the chairmanship of the Abolition Society, he went into the stove business with great success. Later he branched out into the coal business as a retailer in 1865 and earned a modest fortune. An indication of financial and business acumen is evident in the fact that he was elected to the Board of Trade in Philadelphia. He remained active until his death in 1902.

"William Still," *Dictionary of American Biography,* XVIII (1935), p. 22; William Still. *The Underground Railroad* (Philadelphia, 1872).

Harriet Tubman (1826-1913)

"BLACK MOSES OF HER RACE"

Strong as a man, brave as a lion, cunning as a fox was Harriet Tubman who, unable to read or write, made nineteen journeys into the Deep South and spirited over 300 slaves to freedom. Harriet Tubman, a medium-sized, smiling woman, was the leading "conductor" of the Underground Railroad over which countless thousands of nameless slaves fled from bondage. The Underground Railroad was neither a railroad nor underground, but a system for helping slaves to escape. By moving from one friendly hand to the next, from house to house, from church to church, on foot, by horseback, wagons, trains, passing through slave state after slave state they reached the freedom of Ohio, New England, or Canada. By day and by night, summer and winter, escaping slaves took the Underground Railroad to the North.

It was dangerous for anyone to help the slaves as most states had severe penalties for aiding "property" to escape. It was doubly dangerous for a Negro female to go South and lead slaves North, for she could lose her own freedom and herself become enslaved. To the dauntless Harriet Tubman, these considerations were as nothing. Every possible trick and disguise were used by her to help the slaves. On several occasions, at gun-point, Harriet forced wavering slaves onward. "You'll be free or die," she quietly commanded.

Slaveowners and their agents looked high and low for her but she always managed to elude them. Once on a train she was almost caught but, pretending to read a newspaper and hoping that she held it right side up, Harriet Tubman was overlooked, for her pursuers knew she could not read. Her luck held and she remained free.

Born in Maryland in 1826, Harriet Tubman herself escaped from her master and went to New York. In her own words, she described her first taste of liberty: "I was free and I couldn't believe it. There was such a glory all around and the sun was shining through the trees and on the hills. I was free!"

During the Civil War, Harriet Tubman served both as a nurse and a spy for the Union. When she died in 1913 she was buried in Ohio with military honors.

Sarah Bradford, *Harriet Tubman: The Moses of Her People* (New York, 1961).

Sojourner Truth (1797-1883)

"A PILGRIM OF FREEDOM"

PROCLAIM LIBERTY T̶ ̶ ̶ ̶HE
LAND UNTO ALL THE I̶ ̶ ̶ ̶ ̶EOF

She began life as Isabella but lived it as Sojourner Truth. She was the first Negro woman orator to speak out against slavery. Although unable to read or write, she traveled through Connecticut, Massachusetts, through Ohio, Indiana, Illinois, and Kansas, speaking to tens, hundreds, and thousands of people, both Negro and white. Sojourner felt herself a "Pilgrim of God" whose one mission was to free her people from slavery.

At a time when oratory was a fine art, Sojourner Truth, through her strong character and acid intelligence, was among the best and most famous anti-slavery speakers of her day. She met most of the outstanding white abolitionists such as Gerit Smith, Parker Pillsbury, Lyman and Harriet Beecher Stowe, and she was received by Abraham Lincoln at the White House. Only Frederick Douglass outshone her in eloquence.

She began life as a slave and, after running away to freedom, worked as a domestic. Not until 1843 did she feel an overpowering urge to speak out against slavery. Already deeply religious, Sojourner, in the spring of that year, suddenly felt reborn. In her own words she declared, "I felt so tall within—I felt as if the power of the nation was with me." Isabella then renamed herself Soujourner Truth, and, on foot, set out to "gather in the flock," speaking out against slavery and for women's suffrage. Her deep, bass voice, her fierce intelligence, sense of drama, and the utter sincerity of her speeches quickly spread her fame throughout the North and astounded an unbelieving South.

Frequently efforts were made to silence her. She was beaten and stoned but nothing could stop her. Sleeping where she could, working only enough to keep soul and body together, Sojourner thundered against slavery from countless rostrums. She wore across her chest, a satin banner bearing the words, "Proclaim liberty throughout the land unto all the inhabitants thereof." Because of her daring, strength, and almost hypnotic control over an audience, some doubted her, the mother of five children, to be a woman. Once when a heckler, in the middle of one of Sojourner's speeches, dared her to prove that she was a woman, Sojourner ripped her blouse to the waist and declared that it was to his shame, not hers, that such a question should be raised. Deeply compelled to wander from state to state, Sojourner lived up to her new name, staying in one place only long enough to proclaim the truth and move on.

Hertha Pauli, *God's Faithful Pilgrim* (New York, 1958); Saunders Redding, *The Lonesome Road* (New York, 1958), pp. 65-74.

Frederick A. Douglass (1817-1895)

GOLDEN TROMBONE OF ABOLITION

The first day of 1863 was bitter cold. The three thousand abolitionists and free Negroes gathered in Boston's Tremont Temple were excited and waiting impatiently for news from Washington, D.C. They had gathered early and passed the time with oratory and singing. Among them were people whose lives had been dedicated to bringing about this moment—Harriet Beecher Stowe, William Wells Brown, and Frederick Augustus Douglass, the greatest orator of them all.

Finally, into the hall burst a man shouting, "It is coming, it's on the wires, the telegram is coming in!" The telegram was news of the Emancipation Proclamation, now taking effect. The crowd quickly translated the telegram into song:

> Sound loud the timbrel o'er Egypt's dark sea
> Jehovah has triumphed: His people are free!

Four million black men and women would soon be free. Not all of them and not all at the same time, but inevitably, all one day would be free.

For Frederick Douglass, already a free man, this night was the high point of his life. From Tremont Temple, Douglass could look back on a life which had begun in slavery and obscurity. Rising like some bronze Phoenix, Douglass for years had been the golden trombone of abolition, ever pressing for the freedom of his fellow Negroes. No one knows just how this ex-slave, ship caulker, wood cutter, coal handler and odd job man, almost overnight, became the spokesman of his race.

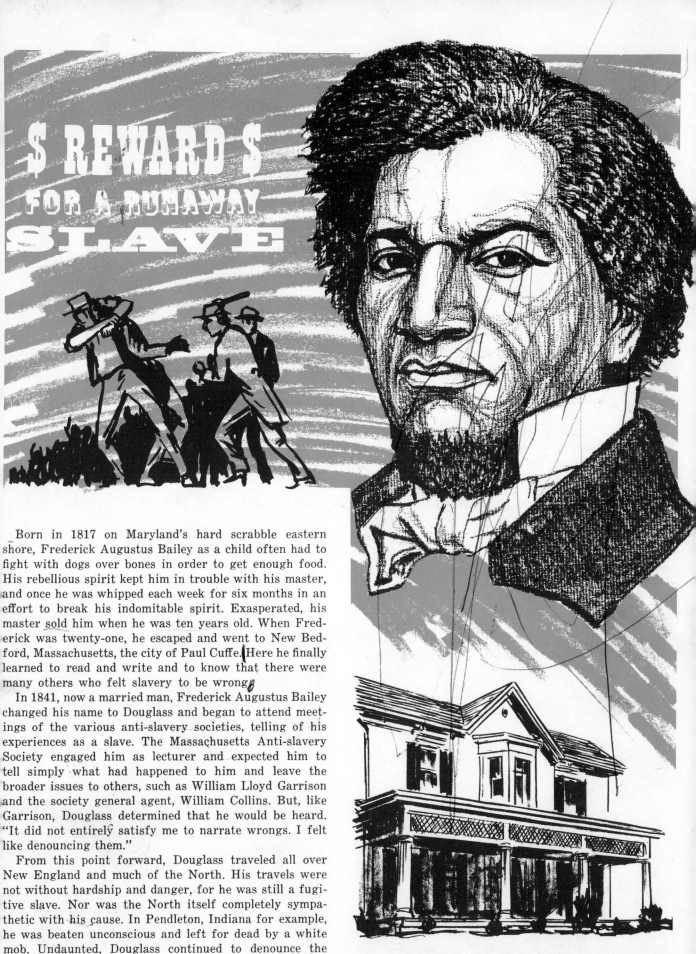

$ REWARD $
FOR A RUNAWAY
SLAVE

Born in 1817 on Maryland's hard scrabble eastern shore, Frederick Augustus Bailey as a child often had to fight with dogs over bones in order to get enough food. His rebellious spirit kept him in trouble with his master, and once he was whipped each week for six months in an effort to break his indomitable spirit. Exasperated, his master sold him when he was ten years old. When Frederick was twenty-one, he escaped and went to New Bedford, Massachusetts, the city of Paul Cuffe. Here he finally learned to read and write and to know that there were many others who felt slavery to be wrong.

In 1841, now a married man, Frederick Augustus Bailey changed his name to Douglass and began to attend meetings of the various anti-slavery societies, telling of his experiences as a slave. The Massachusetts Anti-slavery Society engaged him as lecturer and expected him to tell simply what had happened to him and leave the broader issues to others, such as William Lloyd Garrison and the society general agent, William Collins. But, like Garrison, Douglass determined that he would be heard. "It did not entirely satisfy me to narrate wrongs. I felt like denouncing them."

From this point forward, Douglass traveled all over New England and much of the North. His travels were not without hardship and danger, for he was still a fugitive slave. Nor was the North itself completely sympathetic with his cause. In Pendleton, Indiana for example, he was beaten unconscious and left for dead by a white mob. Undaunted, Douglass continued to denounce the evils of slavery.

Home of Frederick Douglass in Washington, D.C.

35

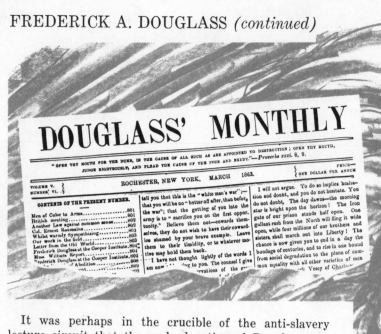

It was perhaps in the crucible of the anti-slavery lecture circuit that the real education of Douglass was earned. So great was Douglass's skill as an orator, his fame soon overshadowed that of other able Negro spokesmen such as Charles Remond and Henry Highland Garnett, and even caused tension between himself and some of his white colleagues. Three things contributed to his success as a spokesman: the inherent justice of his cause in a North growing increasingly doubtful of the wisdom of slavery, the vigor of his oratory, and the drama of his person. A powerfully-built, strong-featured mulatto with a huge leonine head, Douglass's bearing was nobility itself. James Russell Lowell said that "the very look of Douglass was an irresistible logic against the oppression of his race."

In 1845 against the advice of his friends, Douglass decided to write an account of his life, fully aware of the possibility that this would mark him as the "Bailey, runaway slave of Thomas Auld." When his *Narrative of the Life and Times of Frederick Douglass* appeared in this same year, Douglass went to England and continued to speak out against slavery. English friends raised money to secure his formal freedom from his old master and two years later Douglass returned to America to start a newspaper, first called *The North Star*, and later *Frederick Douglass' Paper*. In his own words, Douglass managed "to keep my anti-slavery banner steadily flying during all the [slavery] conflict from the autumn of 1847 till the Union of the states was assured and Emancipation was a fact accomplished."

Shifting slowly from the spoken to the printed word, Douglass now moved even closer to direct action. In 1848 he joined the short-lived Liberty Party. During the early winter of 1850, he met with John Brown before his raid on Harper's Ferry and cautioned the latter, declaring that "from insurrection nothing can be expected but imprisonment and death." Douglass's prediction came true and Douglass himself had to live in Canada for a while.

When the impending crisis finally erupted in outright war, Frederick Douglass urged Lincoln to free the slaves and arm Negroes. He also recruited Negroes for the Union armies, among them his own sons.

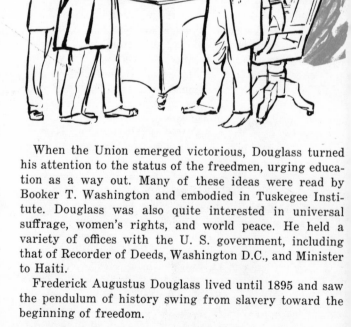

When the Union emerged victorious, Douglass turned his attention to the status of the freedmen, urging education as a way out. Many of these ideas were read by Booker T. Washington and embodied in Tuskegee Institute. Douglass was also quite interested in universal suffrage, women's rights, and world peace. He held a variety of offices with the U. S. government, including that of Recorder of Deeds, Washington D.C., and Minister to Haiti.

Frederick Augustus Douglass lived until 1895 and saw the pendulum of history swing from slavery toward the beginning of freedom.

Frederick Douglass, *Narrative of the Life of Frederick Douglass, An American Slave* (Boston, 1845); Frederick Douglass, *Life and Times of Frederick Douglass* (Hartford, 1887).

III FROM THE CIVIL WAR FORWARD
They Lift Their Heads High

When the Civil War began, Frederick Douglass boldly voiced the sentiments of many free Negroes and slaves. He declared that "never since the world began was a better chance offered to a long-enslaved and oppressed people. The opportunity is given to us to be men." Douglass went further to urge that "colored troops from the North be enlisted and permitted to share the danger and honor of upholding the government."

In less than a year the First South Carolina Regiment was organized by Major General David Hunter in May of 1862, and later made a memorable record under the leadership of Thomas Wentworth Higginson. This regiment was composed of ex-slaves. The Fifty-Fourth Massachusetts Regiment, composed of free Negro volunteers under the command of Colonel Robert Gould Shaw, is mentioned in all accounts of the Civil War because of the exceptional valor of its personnel. Serving with the Fifty-Fourth Massachusetts was Sergeant William H. Carney, a standard bearer who kept the Union flag from touching the ground during the furious attack on Fort Wagner. In the Union attack on Fort Hudson in Mississippi, the eight Negro regiments involved were conspicuous by their bravery. Here another standard bearer, Anselmas Plancianois, made his famous remark: "Colonel, I will bring these colors to you in honor or report to God the reason why."

The black troops were not all standard bearers. They performed a variety of tasks. Many of them were spies who knew the Southern terrain better than their white counterparts. Some of them built fortifications. Tens of thousands of Negroes fought as soldiers not only at Fort Wagner in South Carolina, and Fort Hudson but also at Petersburg, Virginia, Milliken's Bend in Louisiana, Fort Pillow in Tennessee and many other places.

The consequences of the Negro's participation in the Civil War went far beyond combat. The black soldier learned military discipline. He became accustomed to giving and executing orders. Many learned to read for the first time. For many, also, the military banks, which served as depositories for their pay, gave them their first opportunities for systematic saving.

Nearly 200,000 Negroes served in the Union Army; three-fourths of them were ex-slaves. As a group they were competent soldiers. Abraham Lincoln's appraisal of their effectiveness, made on December 8, 1863, has been borne out in the reviews of later historians: "So far as tested, it is difficult to say they are not as good soldiers as any." Ulysses S. Grant was enthusiastic in his praise of the courage and bravery of these troops. Over thirty-six thousand Negro soldiers gave their lives in the fight for the abolition of slavery and the salvation of the Union.

The Northern victory in the Civil War was the end of slavery in America and the beginning of freedom for the Negro. Representing the aspirations of the four million ex-slaves were hundreds of Negroes who rose to positions of leadership during the Reconstruction era. Most of them were ministers. Many of them had been soldiers. Some had been school teachers; others had been employees of the Freedmen's Bureau. Some were ex-slaves as in the case of Robert Smalls of South Carolina. They were all concerned with the situation of the black man and the future of the South.

At the national level, several Negroes, notably Henry Highland Garnet, Frederick Douglass, John Smythe and Ebenezer D. Bassett represented the United States abroad. Two able Negroes, James Matthews and James Trotter, were Recorders of Deeds in Washington, D.C.

Twenty-two Negroes were elected to Congress from the South. In addition to those treated in this book, Jeremiah Haralson, Henry P. Cheatham, Robert C. DeLarge, John A. Hyman, Alonzo J. Ransier, Thomas E. Miller, Charles E. Nash, James O'Hara, Joseph T. Rainey, Benjamin S. Turner, Joseph T. Walls, George H. White, and George W. Murray sat in the nation's highest legislative body. (Brief biographical sketches of these men may be found in the comprehensive *Biographical Directory of the American Congress: 1774-1961*.)

The belief that the Negro dominated Southern politics after the Civil War has been more of a myth than a reality. Only in the state of South Carolina did the Negro approach anything resembling control. The state's first legislature following the Civil War consisted of eighty-seven Negroes and forty whites. Two Negroes were lieutenant governors —Alonzo Ransier in 1870 and Richard H. Graves in 1874. Francis L. Cardozo was successively secretary of state and state treasurer. Jonathan J. Wright was an associate justice of the state supreme court for seven years. Six Negroes went to Congress from South Carolina.

On the other hand, in the state of Mississippi where the Negroes were a majority of the population, there were forty Negro lawmakers in a state legislature of 115 men. In Louisiana three Negroes served as lieutenant governor: Oscar J. Dunn, P. S. B. Pinchback and C. C. Antoine. W. G. Brown was superintendent of public instruction, and Antoine Dubuclet was state treasurer.

Most of the Negroes who came to public notice already had some experience in civic affairs. Many of them had been members of constitutional conventions in states seeking re-admission to the Union. Others had been state senators, representatives, sheriffs and tax assessors. As a group they did yeoman service in a chaotic South. Northern neglect and Southern hostility drove them from public life by the end of the nineteenth century. Speaking of the Negro's performance during these early years of freedom, James G. Blaine declared that "the colored men who took seats in both the Senate and the House did not appear to be ignorant or helpless. They were as a rule studious, earnest, ambitious men, whose public conduct . . . would be honorable to any race."

Dudley Taylor Cornish, *The Sable Arm* (New York, 1956), pp. 27, 285-291; John Hope Franklin, *Reconstruction—After the Civil War* (Chicago, 1961), pp. 84-103, 127-173; John Hope Franklin, *From Slavery to Freedom* 2nd Ed. (New York, 1961), pp. 267-275, 286-290.

James P. Beckwourth (1798-1867)

WESTERN FRONTIERSMAN

One of the most famous mountain men was James P. Beckwourth (sometimes Beckwith), a Virginia-born mulatto blacksmith, who, in 1823, joined General William H. Ashley's Rocky Mountain Fur Company in St. Louis Missouri. Leaving the expedition in 1825, he lived with the Crow Indians for six years where he acquired a third wife and a reputation as a warrior and a horse thief. He was eventually made a chief. In a short time Beckwourth's exploits rivaled those of the famous Kit Carson, one of his associates, although historians ignored his detailed life story published in 1856. In 1844 he had joined Kearny's forces in California, had participated in the Mexican War (1846-1848), joined the Colorado gold rush in 1859, and had fought in the Cheyenne wars of 1864. He died in 1867 near Denver while on a peace mission for the government. It was said that he had been poisoned by members of his adopted people.

The average black westerners were ex-slaves who had come to Texas with their masters, and, when the Civil War freed them, settled there or moved north to Colorado and Wyoming, helping in large cattle drives. When gold was discovered in the Black Hills, hundreds flocked to the Dakota territories to become miners. In the campaign against the Indians, Negroes could be found on both sides: as guerrillas, warriors or scouts for the Comanches, Sioux, Seminoles and Creeks, or as infantrymen and cavalrymen in the four Negro regiments established by Congress in 1866.

While much of the period has become the myth adapted to movies and television, the neglected but indisputable fact is that black men and women were an integral part of the winning of the west.

America's westward expansion, its most colorful saga, has traditionally excluded black pioneers and adventurers. Now, historians are admitting that thousands of Negro men and women played various roles in the exploration and settlement of lands west of the Mississippi. There were more than 5,000 Negroes among the cowboys who rode the ranges from Texas to Montana. Most were ropers like Bill Pickett, the "Dusky Demon from Texas," while others were horsebreakers, wranglers, cooks and trail bosses. Some became law enforcers like Major William Brady, hotel proprietors like Cheyenne's B. M. Ford, and even swindlers like Dodge City's Ben Hodge, or outlaws like Texas Cherokee Bill. But many were heroic frontiersmen, ranging the Rocky Mountains and plains as hunters, trappers and pony express riders.

Dobie, J. Frank, *The Mustangs* (Boston, Little, Brown & Co., 1952); Beckwourth, J. P., *The Life and Adventures of James P. Beckwourth* (DeVoto, New York, 1931); Durham, Philip and Everett L. Jones, *The Negro Cowboys* (New York; Dodd, Mead & Co., 1965).

Alexander Crummell (1819-1898)

WRITER, ADVOCATE OF EQUALITY, MINISTER

Alexander Crummell was one of the few African-American leaders whose influence was felt before and after the Civil War and on both sides of the Atlantic Ocean. Minister, missionary, orator, publicist, Crummell's career began in 1844 with his ordination as an Episcopal bishop in Boston, Massachusetts, and came to a close with his establishment of the American Negro Academy in 1897. Born in New York City in the year 1819, Alexander Crummell was a contemporary and schoolmate of Henry Highland Garnet, James McCune Smith, and Ira Aldridge.

A leading black New York minister, Peter Williams, encouraged Crummell to study for the Episcopalian ministry. Crummell began his studies at Oneida Institute of New York State. He attempted to enter the General Theological Seminary of that state but was rebuffed because of his race. He had to go to Boston in order to complete his education and receive ordination. From 1844 to 1847 Crummell tried to establish the Episcopal denomination among blacks. Having little success, he decided to go to England to solicit funds for this work. With the help of friends such as John Jay, he traveled to London and while there decided instead to continue his studies at Queen's College, Cambridge. Graduating in 1853, Crummell went to Africa both for reasons of health and for missionary activity. For twenty years, he labored in Monrovia, Liberia as a missionary and teacher of theology.

Returning to the United States in 1873, Alexander Crummell was appointed rector of St. Luke's Episcopal Church, Washington, D.C. and held this post until his retirement in 1894. He continued his writing and lecturing. In 1897 Crummell founded the American Negro Academy which was devoted to the promotion of literature, art, and science and the defense of blacks against racist propaganda. Both as a minister and an organizer of black intellectuals, Crummell wielded great influence.

Alexander Crummell's writings include *The Man, the Hero, the Christian: A Eulogy on the Life and Character of Thomas Clarkson* (1846). Clarkson was one of the early fighters against chattel slavery. The next major work was *The Duty of a Rising Christian State to Contribute to the World's Well-Being and Civilization* (1855). This speech was delivered in Monrovia, Liberia, and it encouraged transplanted blacks to feel the equal of any race as they went about developing Liberia. One of his more noted works was *The Future of Africa* (1862). Two others which received wide attention, *The Greatness of Christ and Other Sermons* (1882) and *Africa and America* (1891), were collections of sermons and essays. "The Black Woman of the South: Her Neglects and Her Needs" was an address delivered before the Freedmen's Aid Society of the Methodist Episcopal Church in 1882, which was distributed in 500,000 copies to meet the demands of the public.

W. E. B. Du Bois, *The Souls of Black Folk* (New York 1961), pp. 157-161; William J. Simmons, *Men of Mark* (Cleveland, 1887), pp. 530-535; Vernon Loggins, *The Negro Author* (Port Washington, N.Y., 1931), pp. 197-209.

Robert Smalls (1839-1915)

The *Planter*, a dispatch and transport vessel of the Confederacy, lay at anchor in Charleston Harbor. Its captain and officers, weary from a full day of hauling guns from Cole's Island to James Island, had gone ashore to relax amid the merriment occasioned by the outbreak of war between the North and South. Captain Ripley left Robert Smalls and eight members of the crew on board the *Planter*. Smalls and his fellow crewmen were slaves, pressed into service as deckhands and laborers aboard ships of the Southern fleet. Robert Smalls knew well the treacherous waters between Morris Island and Fort Royal where the vessels of the infant Southern fleet operated. As soon as the captain left the decks, Smalls began to put into operation a plan which had long been fermenting in his active mind.

He waited until four A.M. during which time his wife and two children were smuggled aboard. Putting the crew to work, Robert Smalls got the *Planter* underway. He was sure that if any errors were made in any portion of his plans, certain death was the only possible outcome. His plan was simple: deliver a vessel to the Union fleet and he would have his freedom. The odds were high, but so were the possible rewards. Fort Sumter was heavily armed. Successfully running a gauntlet of cannons was no guarantee that he would safely reach the blockading Northern fleet. Between him and the nearest Yankee vessels stood the guns of Fort Sumter and Morris Island.

Even if Smalls succeeded in getting the vessel past these two obstacles, there was the chance that the ship would be mistaken for a hostile Southern vessel and be fired upon. This was a chance he chose to take.

As the ship neared the Fort, cannons could be seen, silhouetted against the night. The night watch idly glanced at the passing vessel. No one could mistake the huge straw hat worn by Captain Ripley or the manner in which he leaned out the window of the pilot house with his arms folded. On the other hand, no one on the Fort had the slightest idea that, under the hat, was not the *Planter's* captain but an audacious slave of twenty-two, stealing one of their most valuable ships from under their very noses. When it became clear that Captain Ripley was not on the ship, the Fort frantically signalled Morris Island to intercept the *Planter*, but by this time, the ship was beyond the reach of shells. As the *Planter*, with its slave captain and crew, neared the Federal squadron, Robert Smalls ran up a small white truce flag and drew near enough to explain his mission.

The *Planter* was thus turned over to the Northern forces. Smalls was taken aboard another ship, the *Crusader*, where a few months later, at Simmons Bluff, he served as pilot. Subsequently both the *Planter* and the *Crusader* engaged in a sharp battle with Confederate artillery and infantry and the Southerners were completely routed.

NAVIGATOR, SLAVE-HERO, CONGRESSMAN

The capture of the *Planter* itself was the war's most daring exploit up to this point. The ship was invaluable to the North. It was in good condition and worth over $60,000. Flag Officer Dupont said of Robert Smalls, "This man Robert Smalls is superior to any who have come into our lines—intelligent as many of them have been." The *Dictionary of American Biography* states: "This daring exploit gave him national fame. He was made a pilot in the U.S. Navy and given a share of the prize money."

Smalls continued to pilot both the *Planter* and the *Crusader*. When the *Planter* was sailing through heavy Confederate fire, the Captain panicked and deserted the ship. Pilot Smalls calmly took command of the vessel and carried it out of danger. For this particular feat, Smalls was promoted to Captain and served on the *Planter* until the end of the war.

Robert Smalls was born in slavery in Beaufort, S. C. on April 5, 1839. He was moved to Charleston by his master in 1851 and became quite familiar with every brink and shoal in Charleston harbor. Weathering many engagements, Robert Smalls served out the war as blockading pilot of the Union Navy.

Not only did this brave and intelligent man serve with distinction during the war itself, but he also went on to achieve fame as a legislator. Although meagerly educated by an indulgent master, Robert Smalls "was good humored, intelligent, fluent and self-possessed." He was a delegate to the South Carolina Constitutional Convention in 1868 and from that year to 1870 he was in the South Carolina House of Representatives. From 1870 to 1874 he served in the South Carolina State Senate.

Robert Smalls took his seat in the United States House of Representatives in 1875 and served until 1887. The ex-slave and former pilot was a good orator, eloquently speaking out against dishonest election tactics of the southern Democrats and for bills to provide equal accommodations for Negroes in interstate conveyances. His major legislative accomplishment was his introduction and support of the immediate post-Civil War Civil Rights bills, making clear the right of the freedmen to make contracts, to hold property, and to enjoy full protection of the laws.

Robert Smalls was active in behalf of the Negroes during the remaining years of his life. His last major public effort to alleviate the conditions of the freedmen was as a delegate to the South Carolina Constitutional Convention in 1895 where he made a gallant but futile attempt to prevent the disfranchisement of Negroes in the state. From that time on, he lived quietly in Beaufort, giving counsel and advice to whites and Negroes alike until his death in 1915.

Dorothy Sterling, *Captain of the Planter; The Story of Robert Smalls* (New York, 1958); *Biographical Directory of the American Congress: 1774-1961* (Washington, D.C., 1961), p. 1611.

John Mercer Langston (1829-1897)

U. S. CONGRESSMAN FROM VIRGINIA

In 1855 at a meeting of the American Anti-slavery Society gathered in New York City, a slim, debonair mulatto went to the speaker's rostrum and uttered these words:

"A nation may lose its liberties and be a century in finding it out. Where is the American liberty? . . . In its far-reaching and broad sweep, slavery has stricken down the freedom of us all . . ."

The speaker was John Mercer Langston, the first Negro elected to public office in the United States. The young lawyer whose remarks were quoted throughout the anti-slavery press was destined to be among the last Negroes elected to Congress during the nineteenth century.

The road from the plantation of his master and father Ralph Quarles of Virginia, to the United States House of Representatives was long and arduous, yet it was filled with significant achievement. John Mercer Langston was at various times a member of the city council of Brown helm, Ohio (1855-1860); member of the Oberlin, Ohio Board of Education (1867-1868); school inspector general of the Freedmen's Bureau (1868-1869); dean of the Law School at Howard University (1869-1876); an able and successful minister-resident to Haiti (1877-1885); and president of Virginia Normal and Collegiate Institute (1885-1888). John Mercer Langston was elected to the U. S. Congress as a representative from Virginia in 1889 and served until 1891.

John Mercer Langston was also very active in the various movements and organizations devoted to enlarging the area of freedom for the American Negro. He opposed the objectives of the emigration movement of the 1850's; he was a prime mover in the various Negro Conventions which met in different parts of the country. In 1865 he was president of the National Equal Rights League; in 1870 Langston became a guiding spirit of the Negro National Labor Union which sought to grapple with the economic problems facing the freedman.

After his congressional career came to an end, John Mercer Langston became a very popular lecturer. He maintained his interest in political and economic affairs until his death in 1897.

Williams J. Simmons, *Men of Mark* (Cleveland, 1887), p. 515; *Biographical Directory of the American Congress: 1774-1961* (Washington, D.C., 1961), p. 1191.

Blanche K. Bruce (1841-1897)

SENATOR FROM MISSISSIPPI

The time: March 4, 1875. The place: the Senate of the United States of America. The occasion: swearing-in ceremonies of new Senators for the Forty-fourth Congress. The roll call of states had been going on for some time. The new Senators were escorted to and from the rostrum by the senior Senators from their states. The roll call and marching to-and-fro finally reached Mississippi. All eyes turned to Blanche K. Bruce, a light-skinned, 36-year-old Negro, who had been elected to the U. S. Senate from the sovereign state of Mississippi. As he started his proud march towards the rostrum, expectant eyes shifted from him to Mr. Alcorn, the white senior Senator from Mississippi. Mr. Alcorn was terribly busy with his newspaper and did not look up. Walking alone as though Mr. Alcorn did not exist, Bruce was half way up the aisle when Roscoe Conkling, Senator from New York stepped up and said, "Excuse me, Mr. Bruce. I did not until this moment see that you were without escort. Permit me. My name is Conkling." Together the two Senators completed the round trip. Thus began a career in the Senate which lasted longer than that of any other of the twenty-two Negroes who served in Congress during the last thirty years of the nineteenth century.

Bruce was born in slavery in Farmville, Prince Edward County, Virginia on March 1, 1841, the natural son of his master and a slave woman. Young Bruce was made the body servant of his white half-brother and was schooled along with him. When his half-brother joined the Confederate army, Bruce escaped from him and went to Missouri where he started a small school for blacks. He later heard of Oberlin College and eventually completed his formal education there.

After the Civil War ended, Blanche K. Bruce moved to Mississippi and settled in the town of Floreyville to become a planter. He began his life of public service as a sergeant-at-arms in the Mississippi state senate. Following this, he was appointed tax assessor in Bolivar County, Mississippi and served two terms. In 1873, Bruce was urged to run for the Senate of the United States where two senatorships were at stake: one for a full term and one for a year. The last was the incompleted portion of Jefferson Davis' term. Bruce was elected for the full term. Bruce's term ended in 1881, but he later was appointed Register of the Treasury and twice Recorder of Deeds in Washington D.C.

Robert B. Elliott (1842-1884)

U. S. CONGRESSMAN
FROM SOUTH CAROLINA

As a Congressman, most of his energies were spent in trying to stem the flood of anti-Negro legislation advocated by the Southern states. One memorable encounter between Elliott and his Southern foes concerned the Civil Right bills. Elliott naturally supported the bills which were designed to put teeth into the Fourteenth Amendment. Many Southern Senators, including Alexander Stephens of Georgia, opposed them. To this unrepentant racist, Elliott had this to say:

"I meet him only as an adversary, nor shall age or any other consideration restrain *me* from saying that he now offers this government, which he has done his utmost to destroy, a very poor return for its magnanimous treatment, to come here to seek to continue, by the assertion of doctrines obnoxious to the true principles of our government, the burdens and oppressions which rest upon five million of his countrymen, who never fail to live their earnest prayers for the success of this government, when the gentleman was seeking to break up the Union of their states and to blot the American Republic from the galaxy of nations."

Following his resignation from the House of Representatives, Elliott, in 1876, made an unsuccessful bid for the position of attorney general of South Carolina. He subsequently moved to New Orleans and resumed the practice of law until his death on August 9, 1884.

William J. Simmons, *Men of Mark* (Cleveland, 1887), p. 468; *Biographical Directory of the American Congress: 1774-1961* (Washington, D.C., 1961) p. 856.

Few men, black or white, in the Forty-second and Forty-third Congresses were able to match the polish and brilliance of Robert B. Elliott, who represented the state of South Carolina from 1871 to 1874. Elliott was not an ex-slave, but a free-born Boston-bred Negro so dark of complexion that his law partner once affectionately called him "an undoubted African." His parents were of West Indian extraction.

Elliott's education was obtained at private schools in Boston and in the British West Indies, at Highbon Academy in London, and at Eton where he graduated with high rank in 1853. In 1868, he was a member of the State Constitutional Convention. After the adoption of South Carolina's new constitution, Elliott was elected to the lower house of the South Carolina state legislature and served from 1868 to 1870. Elliott was then elected to the Forty-second and Forty-third Congresses.

Richard H. Cain (1825-1887)

U. S. CONGRESSMAN FROM SOUTH CAROLINA

Another outstanding individual from South Carolina was Richard H. Cain, who served two terms in the U. S. House of Representatives. He was also one of the outstanding Methodist ministers and church organizers of his time. It has been estimated that under his influence roughly 100,000 people joined the Methodist Church in South Carolina.

A free-born Negro, Richard H. Cain was licensed to preach in 1844 at the age of 19, was ordained a deacon in 1859, and then entered Wilberforce (now Central State College) at the age of 35. After two years at Wilberforce he left Ohio for New York where he began the real labors of his career. After heading several churches in New York, he was sent to South Carolina in 1865 to minister to the newly freed slaves there. Using his Charleston church of 10,000 members as a base, Cain covered the state in a manner reminiscent of the great founder of Methodism, John Wesley.

When the Constitutional Convention met in Charleston in 1868, Cain, like Elliott, was elected to the South Carolina House of Representatives after serving in the State Senate for four years. During his political career, he served two terms in Congress, one term lasting from 1873 to 1875, and the other from 1877 to 1879.

Richard H. Cain has been described as an unmixed black who took an active part in everything which would advance his race and shelter them from exploitation. In 1868 he started a newspaper, *The Missionary Record*, which soon became the most influential paper in the state. He even served as president of a small Methodist institution, Paul Quinn College in Waco, Texas. In 1880 Cain was appointed Bishop of the AME Church and served until his death in 1887.

Biographical Directory of the American Congress: 1774-1961 (Washington, D.C., 1961), p. 646.

SOUTH CAROLINA

John R. Lynch (1847-1939)

U. S. CONGRESSMAN
FROM MISSISSIPPI

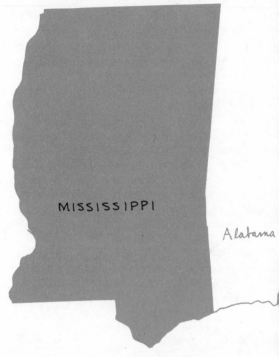

MISSISSIPPI

Alabama

John R. Lynch was one of the few Negro congressmen during the Reconstruction era to be elected three times to Congress from Mississippi as a Republican. John Lynch was elected to the Forty-third, Forty-fourth, and Forty-seventh Congress but served only two full terms. His last election to the Forty-seventh Congress in 1877, the end of the Reconstruction era, was contested and he was not allowed to take his seat. There is some belief that the state defrauded him of his rightful term. Lynch was aware of this and declared among other things that "the Republicans . . . and I am pleased to be able to say, thousands of honest Democrats as well, are anxious that this agitation will cease, upon such conditions as will secure to all citizens the equal protection of the laws, and a willing acquiescence in the lawfully expressed will of the majority."

Nevertheless Lynch remained active in public life. He was Chairman of the Mississippi Republican State Executive Committee (1881-1889), and towards the close of his political career he was appointed fourth auditor for the Treasury in the Navy. In 1898, he was appointed a paymaster in the regular army and served until his retirement in 1911.

Lynch was born a slave and was promised eventual freedom, but his father and owner died before he could be freed and he was sold to a Mississippian. Freed by the ending of the Civil War, Lynch, after educating himself,

came to the attention of politicians, one of whom appointed him a justice of the peace for Natchez County, Mississippi. In 1869, Lynch was elected a member of the Mississippi State House of Representatives, which led to his being elected to the Forty-third Congress.

John R. Lynch was the first black man to preside over a national convention of the Republican party. He served as a national party leader for most of the last decade of the nineteenth century. Following his retirement, Lynch occupied himself with the practice of law. He also wrote two rather influential books, The Facts of Reconstruction (1913) and Some Historical Errors of James Ford Rhodes.

The success of Lynch's self-education can be seen in this excerpt from a speech where he stresses the patriotism of the Negro immediately after the Civil War. "They were faithful and true to you there; they are no less so today. And yet they ask no special favors as a class; they ask no special protection as a race. They feel that they purchased their inheritance when, upon the battlefields of their country, they watered the tree of liberty with the precious blood that flowed from their loyal veins. They ask no favors, they desire and must have an equal chance in the race of life."

These words were to be echoed in the demands of Negro spokesmen from the time of John R. Lynch to the present.

William J. Simmons, Men of Mark (Cleveland, 1887), p. 1044; Richard Bardolph, The Negro Vanguard (New York, 1961), p. 88; Biographical Directory of the American Congress: 1774-1961 (Washington, D.C., 1961), p. 1232.

Jefferson Long (1836-1900)
U. S. CONGRESSMAN
FROM GEORGIA

When Jefferson Long took his seat in Congress in 1870, he became the first Negro to be elected to the United States House of Representatives. The day he was elected, white Georgians killed seven Negroes and chased Long to courthouse where he remained until friends sneaked him to an uncompleted sewer.

Throughout the state Negroes were intimidated, beaten, and abused by whites who could not stomach the idea of a Negro representing a district of that state in the U. S. Congress. Jefferson Long had been a leader of Negroes in Macon, Georgia where he had a thriving business as merchant tailor. When the white Congressman-elect was denied a seat in the House because of doubt about the honesty of his election, Long was persuaded to run for the vacancy. The merchant tailor won by only nine hundred votes, although it has been said that the votes for him would have been much larger had not many Negroes been terrorized into staying away from the polls.

Jefferson Long's first speech in Congress was devoted to ways and means of protecting Negroes who were qualified to vote, but who were unjustly prevented from voting by unreconstructed whites. The disheartening experience of Long's election made such an impression on him that he declined to stand for re-election, but he did retain an active interest in Republican politics. In 1880 he attended the Republican National Convention which met in Chicago and nominated James A. Garfield for President.

Upon the completion of his term in Congress, Long returned to his tailoring business in Macon, Georgia. His early training was typical of many other Negro Congressmen who followed him. He was largely self-educated, learning to read and write the best way he could. Born in Crawford County, Georgia, Long worked at a variety of odd jobs and occupations until he decided to open a tailoring business in Macon. This prospered and left him time and money for politics. Years after his leaving Congress, Republican politicians, Negro and white, would seek him out for advice which he dispensed freely.

Jefferson Long's term in Congress was very short, but he was the second Negro to ever enter that body in other than a menial capacity.

Richard Bardolph, *The Negro Vanguard* (New York, 1961), p. 88; *Biographical Directory of the American Congress: 1774-1961*, p. 1232.

Hiram Revels (1822-1901)

U.S. SENATOR FROM MISSISSIPPI

Just nine years after the Confederates fired on For
Sumter, Hiram Revels sat in the Senate seat of Jefferson
Davis. Revels had the distinction of being the first of the
only two Negroes ever to sit in this, the "world's most
exclusive club." Completing the term commenced by
Jefferson Davis, the ex-president of the Confederate States
of America, Hiram Revels represented the state of Mississippi from February 25, 1870 to March 3, 1871.

Senator Revels had been a state senator in Mississippi
and prior to this he had been an alderman. However, the
basis of his activity in politics lay in his career as a
minister of the gospel. In Natchez, Mississippi, he had
preached to a large congregation and was known as one
of the most able and popular ministers in the Delta.

Hiram Revels was born in Fayetteville, North Carolina in 1822. Negroes, slave or free, were forbidden to
learn to read and write at this time, and as soon as Revels
was old enough he left the state for Ohio where he studied
at a Quaker seminary. Later he was graduated from Knox
College, Galesburg, Illinois.

Like many of his contemporaries, Revels decided to
make a career in the ministry and entered the Methodist
Episcopal Church. He served congregations in Indiana,
Kentucky, Maryland, and Kansas. When the Civil War
started, he was preaching in Maryland but left the pulpit
to recruit soldiers for the first colored regiment organized
in the state.

During 1863-64, he taught school in St. Louis, Missouri,
and then worked with the U. S. Provost Marshal in handling the affairs of freedmen. In the chaos of Emancipation, Hiram Revels followed the Union Army, organizing
churches, attempting to start schools, and lecturing to the
freedmen. He finally settled at Natchez, Mississippi where
he started his second public career.

Hiram Revels became president of Alcorn University
(now Alcorn A & M College) near Lorman, Mississippi.
The same energy he displayed in political life was now
applied to the development of the college. In 1876 Revels
became editor of the *Southwestern Christian Advocate*. He
also served as an African Methodist Episcopal Minister
in the state of Indiana. The former senator maintained
a deep interest in education and religion up to the time of
his death on January 16, 1901.

William J. Simmons, *Men of Mark* (Cleveland, 1887), pp. 948-950.

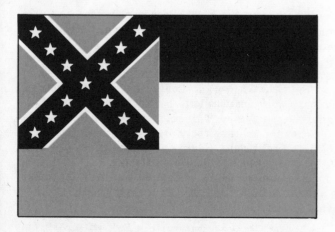

James T. Rapier (1839-1884)

CONGRESSMAN FROM ALABAMA

"I accept the civil and political equality of all men and [a]gree not to attempt to deprive any person or persons on [ac]count of race, color or previous condition, of any political [or] civil rights." Repeating this pledge with other delegates [to] the Alabama Constitutional Convention in 1867 was [J]ames T. Rapier, then twenty-seven years old. The dele[g]ates were meeting to help Alabama re-enter the Union.

Wise beyond his years and looking like an older man in [h]is long frock coat and with side whiskers, James T. [R]apier had been sent to the convention by his neighbors, [b]oth white and Negro, even though he had lived in the [st]ate only two years after the Civil War. He was destined [to] represent them in the United States House of Repre[se]ntatives from 1873 to 1875.

James T. Rapier had returned to his native Alabama [ri]ding a horse and carrying in his saddle bags literature [ur]ging Negroes to unite themselves into labor unions [w]here their scattered strength could be brought together [an]d used in their own interests. It was James T. Rapier [w]ho called the first conclave of laboring men in Alabama. [It] was he who drew up the first Republican party plat[fo]rm in the state of Alabama. Far-sightedly, his platform [ca]lled for a free press, free speech, and a public school [sy]stem. He even started his own newspaper, *The Sentinel*, [to] spread his views.

As a Congressman, Rapier was in the vanguard of [th]ose calling for strong enforcement of the civil rights [le]gislation passed during the years following the Civil [W]ar. He felt that only by stringent application of this [le]gislation could the average freedman be safe and learn [to] participate in public affairs.

Before the Civil War, Rapier's father and master sent [hi]m to Canada to be educated. He was tutored privately [an]d then sent to Montreal College and the University of [Gl]asgow, Glasgow, Scotland. Following his return to [Al]abama he became a planter and entered public life, [be]coming a notary public, tax assessor, and unsuccessful [ca]ndidate for office of secretary of state in Alabama.

After his term of office in the U. S. Congress ended, [Ra]pier was appointed collector of internal revenue in [Al]abama, a post he held until his death in 1884.

[Eu]gene Feldman, "James T. Rapier: 1839-1884," *Negro History Bulletin*, [V.] XX. #2 (1956), pp. 62-66.

Ebenezer D. Bassett (1833-1908)

FIRST NEGRO DIPLOMAT

Although the relations between the United States and Haiti were relatively stable but tense, Haiti and San Domingo were having serious difficulties. Haiti had long followed a policy of opposing foreign domination of San Domingo. At this time, the United States was considering annexing it. Haitian awareness of this created strong anti-American feelings among the Haitians. In addition to these problems, the Haitians were faced with serious internal difficulties. Bassett was expected to carry out United States policy and to keep his country informed of developments on the island.

Bassett's dispatches to Hamilton Fish, then Secretary of State, and others indicated a firm grasp of political developments in his host country. Appraisals of Bassett's work unanimously agree that he did the best job possible in the rather tense atmosphere of the early 1870's. As a maneuver in diplomacy, his appointment could hardly have been wiser, for the Haitians accepted Bassett with a confidence his predecessors never enjoyed.

Additional evidence of Bassett's success as a diplomat may be seen in the fact that after he completed his assignment in 1877, he was appointed a general consul *from* Haiti to the United States, a post he held for ten years.

In 1888, Bassett returned to Haiti to live as a private citizen. While there, he collected materials which were subsequently published in a *Handbook of Haiti*, printed in French, English, and Spanish.

In recognition of this work he was named a member of the American Geographical Society and the Connecticut Historical Society.

Born of a mulatto father and an Indian mother in Litchfield, Connecticut, Bassett studied at Wesley Academy, Wilbraham, Massachusetts; Connecticut Normal School; and, for a brief period, at Yale University. At the time of his appointment as minister-resident, Bassett was principal of the Institute for Colored Youth in Philadelphia, Pennsylvania.

Ebenezer D. Bassett was the first Negro to officially represent the United States abroad. Appointed by President Ulysses S. Grant as minister-resident to Haiti, Ebenezer D. Bassett set a high standard of achievement. "... With honor to himself and satisfaction to his country, he filled the position from 1869 to 1877, which was as long as the combined terms of his white predecessors."

James A. Padgett. "Diplomats to Haiti and their Diplomacy," *Journal Negro History*, XXV (July, 1940), pp. 265-330.

James Lewis (1832-1897?)

PORT of NEW ORLEANS tax COLLECTOR

Of the various figures who achieved prominence in Louisiana during the Reconstruction, James Lewis is one of the least known and appreciated. At various times, James Lewis was surveyor-general for New Orleans, colonel of the Second Regiment, State Militia, collector of the New Orleans Port, naval officer, and superintendent of the U. S. Bonded Warehouse in New Orleans. He was also administrator of police for New Orleans, and administrator of public improvements for New Orleans.

Lewis was born in Wilkinson County, Mississippi. His early life was spent on the Mississippi River where he, like Pinchback, worked his way up to steward and, at the time of the outbreak of the Civil War, was serving as steward aboard a Confederate ship, *The DeSoto*. On hearing of the Emancipation Proclamation, Lewis jumped ship and made his way to New Orleans. At this time he was 31 years old and eager to fight. New Orleans had just fallen into the hands of the Union, and Lewis persuaded the commanding officer to allow him to raise regiments of colored volunteers. He succeeded in raising two companies, serving for a short time in the First Louisiana Volunteer Native Guards as captain of Company K.

In 1864, Lewis resigned his commission and joined the Freedmen's Bureau as a traveling agent, setting up schools for the ex-slaves. He found this work more dangerous than soldiering. On one occasion, as agent of the Freedmen's Bureau, he was mobbed in northern Louisiana, but was saved in the nick of time. After this work, he was appointed to the post of United States inspector of customs, making him the first Negro in Louisiana to hold Federal appointive office.

In 1870, he was appointed colonel of the Second Regiment, State Militia, and in the same year was elected administrator of police for two years at the then considerable salary of $6,000 per year.

Becoming very active in Republican politics, Lewis in 1872 was nominated by the Louisiana State Convention for Congressman-at-large and served as chairman of the Louisiana delegation to the National Republican convention.

Shortly afterwards he was elected administrator of public improvement for New Orleans, a post then regarded as one of the most important in the city government. He was the only Republican in local government, but an appraisal of his handling of the city's improvement department may be found in a report of the City Council for 1873. After listing the great economies effected by Lewis in his department, the report states: "Colonel Lewis has devoted himself to his duties with great energy and industry, taking constant care that every dollar expended should benefit the city."

William J. Simmons, *Men of Mark* (Cleveland, 1887), pp. 954-958.

Henry Highland Garnet (1815-1882

ABOLITIONIST, MINISTER TO LIBERIA

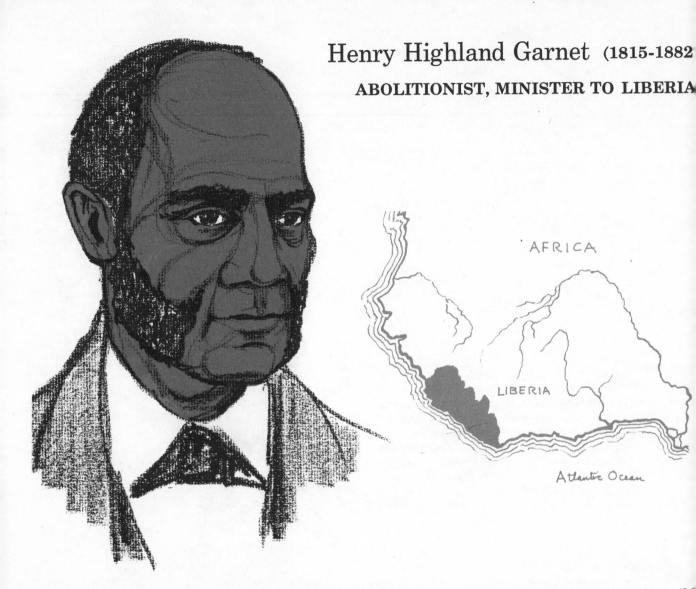

AFRICA

LIBERIA

Atlantic Ocean

"Brethren, arise, arise! Strike for your lives and liberties. Now is the day and the hour. Let every slave in the land do this and the days of slavery are numbered. You can not be more oppressed than you have been—you can not suffer greater cruelties than you have already. Rather die free men than to live and be slaves. Remember you are four million." This was the appeal of Henry Highland Garnet.

This was the year 1843. The occasion was a convention of free men of color gathered in Buffalo, New York. Over seventy delegates were present, among them Frederick Douglass, William Wells Brown, Charles Ray and Martin Delany.

For years Garnet had held the belief that slavery would not be ended by peaceful means, and, remembering Denmark Vesey and Nat Turner, he was an advocate of slave revolt. The convention was asked to adopt his remarks as a statement of sentiment of the delegates. Garnet's speech disturbed a number of abolitionists who did not favor violence. The vote was close, and Garnet's resolution lost by a single vote. While his speech attracted national attention, the vigor of his remarks to the slaves made Garnet increasingly ineffective as an anti-slavery worker, for the abolitionists had not yet moved to urge violence against slaveholders.

Henry's grandfather was a Congolese brought to thi country in chains. His father was a slave and had escape to Delaware where Henry was born. As a boy he at tended the African Free School in New York and the il fated New Canaan, Connecticut school for Negro yout which was destroyed. From there he went to Oneid Institute and later turned to the Presbyterian ministr In 1842 he was licensed and the following year he bega his ministry at Troy Liberty Street Presbyterian Churc He was highly successful as a minister. "His brigh unclouded eyes, large well-shaped head, commandin presence, great courage, strong will and fiery personality made him stand out in any gathering.

He was one of the most influential Negroes of his era until he made his controversial Buffalo speech. From th point on, his public influence waned. However, he becam very active in politics after the Civil War. He becam Recorder of Deeds for a time, and in 1881 was appointe Minister to Liberia. While serving as Minister in Liber he became ill and died in Monrovia.

"Garnet," *Dictionary of American Biography*, VII (1931), pp. 154-15 J. W. Schulte Nordholt, *The People That Walk in Darkness* (New Yo 1960), pp. 101-102. (Paperback.) William M. Brewer. "Henry Highla Garnet," *Journal of Negro History*, XII (January, 1928), pp. 36-52.

John H. Smythe (1844-1908)

U.S. MINISTER TO LIBERIA

John H. Smythe was one of the earliest and ablest ministers to Liberia during the years immediately following the Reconstruction period of American history. A measure of his ability may be seen in the fact that he not only represented the United States government there but also the governments of Belgium, Germany, Sweden and Norway. His reports on Liberia were perhaps the most competent of his era. All accounts of his life emphasize his ability and skill.

John H. Smythe was the first colored newsboy in Philadelphia, and the first Negro artist to become a member of the Philadelphia Academy of Fine Arts. He studied at a Quaker Institute for Colored Youth, headed by Ebenezer Bassett, himself destined to be the first Negro minister to Haiti. After a short period of teaching, John H. Smythe entered Howard University Law School in 1869 when John Mercer Langston was dean and, while attending this very recently established school, worked as a clerk in the Freedmen's Bureau. Later he was an internal revenue agent and an employee of the Freedmen's Bank.

In every position held by him, he served with obvious skill and soon came to the attention of highly placed politicians who felt him a perfect choice to represent the United States government in Liberia. As a result, in 1878 President Rutherford B. Hayes appointed Smythe minister to Liberia, and President Chester A. Arthur again appointed him in 1882.

Following his second tour of duty, John H. Smythe practiced law in Washington, where his fashionable home was a meeting place for all races.

Richard Bardolph, *The Negro Vanguard* (New York, 1961), p. 97; William J. Simmons, *Men of Mark* (Cleveland, 1887), pp. 872-878.

James Monroe Trotter (1844-1912)
RECORDER OF DEEDS

During the Reconstruction era, one of the government posts most prized by Negroes was the federal office of Recorder of Deeds, ranking only after ministerial posts to Haiti and Liberia. Frederick Douglass's first government post was in this office. The man who succeeded him was James Monroe Trotter, a writer and former assistant superintendent in the Post Office Department, Boston, Massachusetts.

Born in Gulfport, Mississippi, James Trotter grew up i Ohio where he attended school and studied music. Brigh apt and alert, he enlisted in the famous Fifty-fourt Massachusetts Regiment and in short order was pro moted from sergeant to lieutenant. For his service i Boston politics, he was appointed assistant superintend ent of the registered letter department in the Boston Pos Office. He left this position in 1883 due to the creepin color line which was being drawn in the office and als because he was disgruntled with the way the Republica party had handled its victory at Appomattox.

During this time he continued his interest in music an wrote a history of music which elicited favorable com ment from the critics.

However, his nomination for Recorder of Deeds a Washington provoked a storm which signaled the lacl of concern over the role of the Negro in the federa government. His nomination was held up for a time, or the grounds that he was not a resident of Washington Angrily, the Negro press and fair-minded journalist were quick to point out that this and many other office were filled with non-residents of the district. After mucl debate and procrastination, James M. Trotter wa: finally confirmed on March 4, 1887.

William J. Simmons, *Men of Mark* (Cleveland, 1887), pp. 656-661.

54

Jonathan J. Wright (1840-1885)
SOUTH CAROLINA JURIST

Sketch from 1863 cartoon commentary on racial injustice in South Carolina

From 1870 to 1877 Jonathan J. Wright was associate justice of the State Supreme Court of South Carolina. No other Negro rose to such a high judicial post during the whole of the Reconstruction era.

Wright was elected to fill out the few months left from the term of Solomon L. Hoge who had resigned to run for Congress. In the latter part of 1870, Wright was re-elected for a full six-year term. As an associate justice in the turbulent politics of South Carolina, Wright's decisions show evidence of considerable ability. Of the 425 cases heard by the State Supreme Court during his tenure, eighty-seven of the opinions handed down were written by him.

Born in Pennsylvania in 1840 Wright was the first Negro to be admitted to the bar in that state. In 1865, the American Missionary Society sent him to Beaufort, South Carolina to help organize schools for the freed men. From 1866 to 1868, he was a legal advisor employed by the Freedmen's Bureau to serve the legal needs of the ex-slaves.

In the roiling aftermath of slavery there was an acute demand for trained Negroes, particularly in politics. Realizing this, Jonathan J. Wright resigned his post with the Freedmen's Bureau and entered politics. He attended the South Carolina constitutional convention in 1868 and later was elected state senator from Beaufort, South Carolina. In the legislature, he was regarded as very "clear-headed, quick as a flash and could out-talk any man on the floor." Despite the corruption and vicious-ness of state politics at that time, there was no proof of any dishonesty in his action, either in the legislature or on the bench.

As the restoration of white supremacy continued apace, Jonathan J. Wright resigned from the court in 1877, thus symbolizing the high water mark of Negroes in the courts until the twentieth century.

R. H. Woody, "Jonathan J. Wright, Associate Justice of the Supreme Court of South Carolina, 1870-1877," *Journal of Negro History*, XVIII (April, 1933), pp. 114-131; *Dictionary of American Biography*, vol. XX (1936), p. 236.

George W. Williams (1849-1891)
SOLDIER, DIPLOMAT, HISTORIAN

Into his brief forty-two years, George Washington Williams crammed several lifetimes. At the age of fourteen he was serving in the Sixth Massachusetts Regiment of the Union Army. Because of his youth he was discharged but he promptly re-enlisted and became a sergeant-major on the staff of General N. P. Jackson. Serving in Texas, Williams was wounded, discharged again and then joined the Mexican Army. After less than a year in the Mexican Army, Williams resigned and joined the U. S. Cavalry and took part in the Comanche campaign where he served with conspicuous bravery. During each term of service Williams was noted for his courage and bravery. Because he was passed over as a candidate for the officer corps of the regular Army, Williams resigned from the Army altogether. He was only twenty years old and still saw his future before him.

Upon leaving the Army, George W. Williams enrolled in the Newton Theological Institution (now Seminary) where, in 1874, he became the first Negro to graduate. After a few years as a pastor of the 12th Street Church, Boston, Williams left Massachusetts for Washington, D.C. where he started a newspaper, *The Commoner*. John Mercer Langston and Frederick Douglass, among others, contributed articles to it, but, due to inadequate circulation, *The Commoner* failed.

Undaunted by this failure, Williams then went to Cincinnati, Ohio and was named minister of the Union Baptist Church which he served for two years. He continued his newspaper interests, having articles appear in the Cincinnati *Commercial* and the *South Western Review*. He even started reading law in the office of Alphonso Taft, a forebear of the present-day Tafts. In 1879 Williams was admitted to the Ohio bar and also elected to the Ohio state legislature for a term of two years.

While in Ohio, Williams developed a deep interest in Negro history. From 1876 to 1883 Williams diligently carried on his investigations of the Negro's past and finally published his two-volume *History of the Negro Race in America from 1619 to 1880*. The work created great excitement in scholarly circles and was generally regarded as the best book on Negro history published during the nineteenth century. Five years later Williams published his *History of Negro Troops in the War of Rebellion*.

In 1883 George Williams visited the Congo and wrote an article very critical of the Belgians' stewardship there. He served with distinction as United States Minister-Resident to Haiti in 1885-1886. Williams died in 1891 while living in Blackpool, England.

John Hope Franklin, "George Washington Williams, Historian," *Journal of Negro History*, XXXI (January, 1946), pp. 60-90; "George Williams," *Dictionary of American Biography*, XX (1936), p. 264.

Pinckney Benton Stewart Pinchback
(1837-1920)

LT. GOVERNOR OF LOUISIANA

Proud and imperious almost to a fault, Pinckney Stewart Pinchback rose from a canal-boat cabin boy to the lieutenant governorship of the state of Louisiana. Like Robert Smalls before him, Pinchback's early life was molded through his meeting all types of men during many years on the lakes and canals which were the main highways of commerce in the 1840's. Pinchback was born a slave on a Mississippi plantation, but, along with his mother, was given his freedom and moved to Ohio. At the age of twelve, he found himself alone and soon obtained work as a cabin boy first on the Ohio, and later on the Missouri and Mississippi rivers. His natural skills and aptitudes carried him to the rank of steward at which time he was bluntly told that only his race prevented him from rising any higher.

In 1861 a few weeks after the Confederates fired on Fort Sumter, Pinchback gave up the river-boat life and went to Louisiana where he enlisted in the Union Army. He even led volunteer efforts to recruit Negroes in Louisiana for the Union Army and by October, 1862, the Louisiana Native Guards, with Pinchback as captain, were mustered into service.

After this happy beginning, Pinchback ran into trouble, not with the Southerners, but with the Union troops who were openly hostile to him and his men. The Louisiana Native Guard was mistreated, despite all that Pinchback tried to do to avoid it. In disgust, Pinchback resigned his command. Still hoping to lead Negro troops, Pinchback again raised another regiment but was told by Union officials that, legally, no Negro could rise above the rank of non-commissioned officer. With his own desire to help the Union cause continuously frustrated, he gave up his military interests.

In 1865, he went to Mobile, Montgomery, and Selma, Alabama, denouncing the treatment of the newly freed Negroes. Two years later, Pinchback organized the Fourth Ward Republican Club of Northern Louisiana which elected him to the State Republican Caucus.

Pinchback as Captain, Second Louisiana Volunteers

57

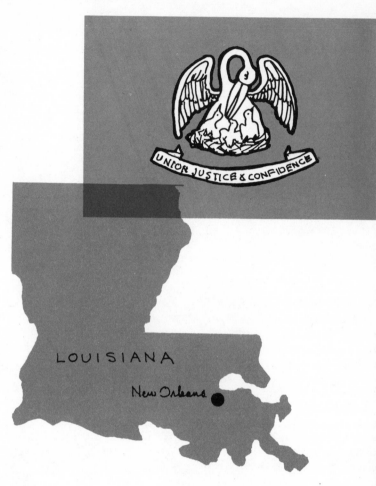

LOUISIANA

New Orleans

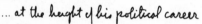

... at the height of his political career

Pinchback was later a delegate to the State Constitutional Convention. His major achievement was the successful introduction of the Thirteenth Amendment to the State's Constitution, guaranteeing civil rights to all people of the state.

From this point onward, Pinchback's political career moved rapidly; in short order he became a state senator, a delegate to the Republican National Convention in Chicago in 1868, school director to the School Board of New Orleans, and president *pro tem* of the State Senate. At a time when the state government of Louisiana was in chaos, Pinchback was elected acting governor for forty-two days, succeeding Governor Warmouth who had been impeached. According to Simmons, "the brief period he occupied the gubernatorial chair was the stormiest ever witnessed in the history of any state in the Union; but the governor was equal to the emergency and displayed administrative capacity of a high order."

However, the greatest drama in the life of Pinchback occurred when, in a hotly contested race, he was elected

to the United States Senate. Many other southern states in 1873 had disputed elections and the presentation of credentials to the clerk of the Senate was often a rather tense affair. In the case of Pinchback, the clerk had been instructed not to accept Pinchback's credentials until the Senate judicial committee had an opportunity to review them. An Alabama Senator-elect with the same problem had to wait only three days. After a three-year delay the Senate rejected Pinchback's credentials, thus denying him a seat in this conclave of gentlemen.

Pinchback was voted $16,666 of the Senate's contingency fund to cover the salary he would have earned up to the time he was finally denied his seat. In one of the rare flukes of politics, Pinchback was also denied a seat in the House of Representatives to which he had also been elected.

"Pinchback," *Dictionary of American Biography*, XVI (1934), p. 611; John Hope Franklin, *Reconstruction After the Civil War* (Chicago, 1961), p. 134; William J. Simmons, *Men of Mark* (Cleveland, 1887), pp. 759-781.

IV SCIENCE and INDUSTRY
And They Studied Man and Nature

Black Americans have made significant contributions to science despite the general absence of at least two basic conditions for scientific work: freedom from full-time pressures for personal survival, and a stimulating cultural environment. Slavery, segregation and cultural isolation have been the lot of most blacks in the United States. Nevertheless, scattered throughout the early history of Afro-Americans are individuals who made contributions of a scientific nature for the benefit of all.

One of the first American black men of medicine was the slave Santomee of New York who was trained in Holland and practiced medicine among the Dutch and English in New York. Another was Oneissimus who developed an effective antidote for the dreaded smallpox in 1721. Benjamin Banneker is well known as a surveyor who helped to lay out the nation's capital. He also made the first clock constructed in this country. His work in astronomy attracted the attention of learned men on both sides of the Atlantic. Through the use of mathematics, he was able to plot the cycles of the 17-year locust and thus help farmers to anticipate them.

James Derham is generally regarded as the first trained black physician. Derham secured a basic general education while growing up in Pennsylvania. He had the peculiar fortune to be owned by several individuals who were physicians. During the 1780's, he became one of the most prominent physicians in New Orleans, Norbert Rillieux, a native of New Orleans, revolutionized the early sugar industry by developing techniques for the more efficient use of steam in the reduction of cane liquids to sugar granules. He was educated in France, taught at the French Ecole Centrale, published papers on the steam engine, and spent a decade with the Champollions deciphering hieroglyphics. James McCune Smith, a graduate of the University of Glasgow, Scotland, was a native of New York. He came from a family which, on its maternal side, had been free of slavery for several generations. From the University of Glasgow, he received the A.B. degree in 1834, the A.M. degree in 1836, and the M.D. degree in 1837. Smith wrote scientific papers attacking the idea of racial inferiority. Some of his scientific papers bore such titles as "Comparative Anatomy of Races" and "The Influence of Climate on Longevity, with Special Reference to Insurance." Martin Delany was trained at the Canaan Academy and the Oneida Institute, both of New York State. This training was followed by an M.D. degree from Harvard in 1852. Delany was the author of a number of publications, the last being *Principia of Ethnology: The Origin of Races and Color, with an Archaeological Compendium of Ethiopian and Egyptian Civilization* (1879).

During the Reconstruction period, Edward Bouchet earned the Ph.D. degree from Yale University in 1876 for work on "Measuring Refractive Indices." In the last quarter of the 19th century, however, the scientific interest of blacks seems to have been directed more toward applied science or invention than pure science. This was also true of American science generally. This was the era of Elijah McCoy, Granville T. Woods and Jan E. Matzeliger. In the same era, Lewis H. Latimer made important applications of the principles of electricity. He took the work of Thomas A. Edison, and invented and patented the first incandescent electric light bulb with a carbon filament. As an employee of the Edison Company, he supervised the installation of electric lights in Philadelphia, New York City, Canada and England. Latimer wrote the first textbook on the Edison electric system, and even earlier did the drawings which accompanied the patent application for the telephone of Alexander Graham Bell. Granville T. Woods, the inventor of the "third rail," also worked for the Edison Company and received an annual salary of $10,000.

Other blacks with a scientific turn of mind were producing such things as rotary engines (A. J. Beard, 1892), pianolas (J. H. Dickinson, 1899), railway switches (W. H. Jackson, 1897), printing presses (W. A. Lavalette, 1878), electric railways (W. B. Purvis, 1894), refrigerators (J. Standard, 1891) and corn husking machines (Washington Wade, 1883). Granville T. Woods and Elijah McCoy made invention a profession. Few blacks were able to capitalize on their work because of the general hostility and difficulties which black entrepreneurs faced at every turn.

During the post-Reconstruction period, a sizeable number of blacks began to study the biological sciences with the establishment of Howard University's School of Medicine in 1876, and the founding of Meharry Medical School in Nashville in 1876. Black hospitals were founded in a number of cities, among them the Provident Hospital of Chicago (1891) and St. Louis (1894). By 1900 approximately 2,000 blacks were licensed to practice medicine in the United States. A few blacks were also fortunate enough to be able to pursue pure research. One of the most diligent researchers was Dr. Charles Turner of St. Louis, Missouri who wrote at least 47 learned papers in the field of biology. Dr. Daniel Hale Williams became known far beyond the halls of science and medicine by performing the first successful open heart operation in history. Prior to his time, the human heart had been regarded as off-limits for surgery. Removing this taboo was a necessary first step for the eventual transplanting of the entire heart.

Only with the coming of the present century did conditions for scientific endeavor among blacks improve to the point that gifted individuals were able to follow their interest in natural phenomena. The following are but a few of the Afro-Americans whose scientific work has been held in high esteem: Harold E. Finley (cytology and physiology of protozoa), Lloyd Hall (cereal chemistry and protein hydrolysates), Samuel M. Nabrit (embryology), David H. Blackwell and Joseph A. Pierce (statistics and the study of probability), Wade Ellis (abstract algebra and electromagnetic theory) and Ernest E. Just (egg fertilization and cellular phenomena).

Warren E. Henry (cyrogenics, thermodynamics and semi-conductors), Julius H. Taylor (electrical properties of semi-conductors and high pressure physics), Hubert M. Thaxton (theoretical physics and information theory) all did first-rate work in pure science. The list of outstanding black scientists could be extended to include such men as J. Ernest Wilkins, Jr., who earned a Ph.D. in mathematics from the University of Chicago at the age of nineteen, or Dr. Robert P. Barnes of Howard University whose students, according to one authority, at one point were publishing more articles in the *Journal of the American Chemical Society* than all of the chemistry professors in all of the black colleges combined, or Dr. Lloyd E. Ferguson who authored a chemistry text used in many colleges throughout the nation, or Dr. Cecil McBay, professor of chemistry at Morehouse college, who is famed for turning out students who subsequently earned the M.D. or Ph.D. degrees.

It is perhaps in the field of general medicine that a combination of inventiveness, scientific research and community service may be seen most clearly. Dr. Louis T. Wright, pioneer in the use of the antibiotic aureomycin on human beings, was a vigorous opponent of discrimination in the medical profession. Dr. William A. Hinton, a long-time member of the Harvard medical school faculty, originated what is known as the "Hinton Test" for syphilis. Dr. Peter Marshall Murray, a gynecologist, became the first black member of the House of Delegates of the American Medical Association. Julian Lewis, armed with an M.D. and a Ph.D., for a time was on the faculty of the University of Chicago and later was a professional pathologist with client-hospitals in the Chicago area.

The caliber of men now in medicine may be seen in the examples listed here. Dr. Nathaniel O. Calloway is a widely recognized expert in the area of internal medicine, the author of many scientific papers, a community leader and a hospital administrator. W. Montague Cobb, an outstanding anatomist at Howard University, has been a vice-president of the American Academy of Science and president of the American Association of Physical Anthropologists as well as president of the National Medical Association. In the latter organization of black physicians, Dr. Cobb has also been the editor of its *Journal* and historian of the profession. Asa G. Yancey is director of surgery at the Hughes Spalding Pavilion of the Grady Memorial Hospital in Atlanta, Georgia. Dr. Leonidas H. Berry holds a professorship of gastroenterology at Chicago's Cook County Hospital. Dr. J. Alfred Cannon is an eminent social psychiatrist in California. Dr. Middleton H. Lambright, Jr. of Cleveland has served as President of the Cleveland Academy of Medicine. Dr. Theodore K. Lawless of Chicago is one of the world's great dermatologists. He is also known for his philanthropy and civic consciousness. Dr. Percy Julian of Oak Park, Illinois, is primarily a research chemist whose work in sterols has done much to improve the medical treatment of arthritis and glaucoma. Shrewd management of his discoveries made him a millionaire.

The example of scientific and material success set by Dr. Julian is being emulated by other blacks. One of the most recent scientists to turn pure science to practical success is Meredith Gourdine, president of Gourdine Industries. Dr. Gourdine's specialty is electro-gasdynamics. He organized a company which conducts research and produces equipment in this field. His Gourdine Mark I generator received the Industrial Research Award as one of the 100 most significant new inventions of recent times. Black scientists are also finding employment for their talents in pure and applied science laboratories throughout the nation. Among those in this area of scientific endeavor are Timothy Wilson, project manager, Bio-Chemical Division, Applied Science, State College, Pennsylvania; Arthur Clark, Abbott Laboratories, University of Chicago; Dr. Emanuel B. Thompson, senior research pharmacologist, Baxter Laboratories, Morton Grove, Illinois; Spencer Robinson, head, Advanced Space Engineering Division, Douglas Aircraft Company; Dr. Joseph Logan, director, Research Laboratory, Aerospace Corporation; Raymond Wilkin, senior scientist, Rohm and Haas Chemical Co., Bristol, Pennsylvania; and Carl Fraction, microbiologist, Toni Corporation, St. Paul, Minnesota.

Black colleges are slowly beginning to evolve to the point where they can stimulate and train students for careers in the field of science. Fisk and Howard universities have helped to produce a good percentage of the black physicists in the country. Morehouse College and Lincoln University (Pa.), along with Fisk, have furnished solid background training for advanced work by blacks in chemistry and biology. Academic and social support for the production of black scientists is still limited by the effects of previously unfavorable social conditions and situations. This may be seen in the fact that between 1920 and 1962, 84,038 Ph.D.'s were awarded in the natural sciences. Of this number, only 250 were received by blacks. Consequently those individuals who study men and nature as their vocation usually are exceptional Afro-Americans whose careers represent a triumph over adverse circumstances.

Harry A. Ploski and Roscoe C. Brown, Jr. (eds.), *The Negro Almanac* (New York, 1967), pp. 643-649; Herman R. Branson, "The Negro Scientist," in *The Negro in Science* (Julius H. Taylor, ed.) (Baltimore, 1955), pp. 1-9; Benjamin Brawley, *A Short History of the American Negro* (New York, 1931), pp. 226-229; W. Montague Cobb, "A New Dawn in Medicine," *Ebony* (September, 1963), pp. 166-171.

Elijah McCoy (1843-1929)

"THE REAL McCOY"

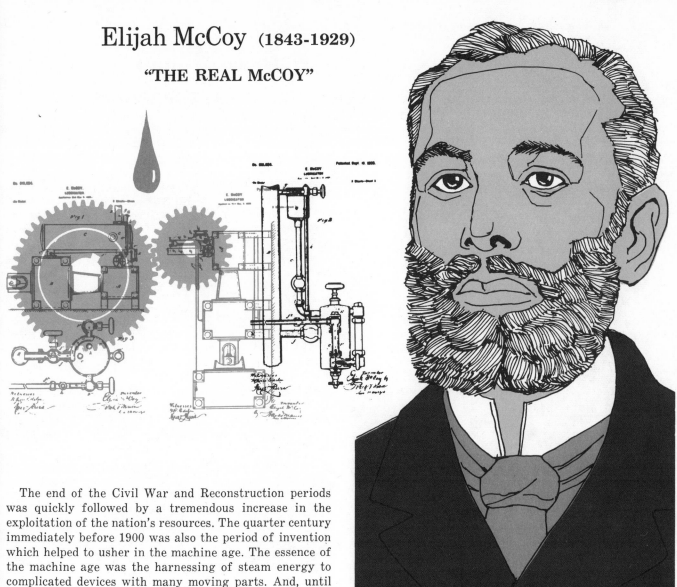

The end of the Civil War and Reconstruction periods was quickly followed by a tremendous increase in the exploitation of the nation's resources. The quarter century immediately before 1900 was also the period of invention which helped to usher in the machine age. The essence of the machine age was the harnessing of steam energy to complicated devices with many moving parts. And, until the inventions of Elijah McCoy were added to the complicated machines, even the most efficient of operations had to be halted until the machines were oiled to reduce the wear and tear of friction.

Elijah McCoy was a black inventor who was awarded over fifty-seven patents, mostly for various kinds of steam cylinder lubricators. His basic invention, the "drip cup," has been described as a "key device in perfecting the overall lubrication system used in large industry today." With this invention, it was no longer necessary to stop or shut down large machinery in order to apply the needed lubrication. McCoy received his first patent on July 12, 1872, and it was quickly adopted by the major industries using heavy equipment. So popular did his lubrication system become that persons inspecting new equipment generally inquired if it contained the "real McCoy." It is perhaps an indication of the widespread use of his inventions in that the phrase, "the real McCoy," is now a part of our language.

Elijah McCoy was born in Canada in 1843. His parents had been slaves who fled from their master in the state of Kentucky. As a youth, Elijah was fascinated with machines and tools. He enjoyed watching and working on them. He came to the United States after the Civil War and settled near Ypsilanti, Michigan, where he worked in a machine shop. In 1870, McCoy turned his attention to the problem of oiling machinery which was in motion. For two years he worked on the problem. In the spring of 1873, McCoy developed the small, oil-filled container with a stop cock to regulate the flow of oil to the innards of moving equipment.

Elijah McCoy subsequently invented twenty-three lubricators for different kinds of equipment as well as an ironing table, lawn sprinkler, steam dome, and dope cup. He eventually set up the Elijah McCoy Manufacturing Company in Detroit, Michigan to develop and sell his inventions. He worked with such intensity that he often patented two or three new devices each year. The continuous hum of the many industrial plants so characteristic of America is, in significant measure, due to the inventions of a self-taught mechanic, the son of fugitive slaves who fled America to lead the lives of free people.

Erwin A. Salk, *A Layman's Guide to Negro History* (Chicago, 1966), p. 79; Richard Bardolph, *The Negro Vanguard* (New York: Vintage edition, 1961), pp. 123, 124; Merle Eppse, *The Negro-Too, in American History* (New York, 1939), pp. 265-266.

N. Rillieux | Evaporating Pan.

No. 4.879   Patented Dec 10 1846

Norbert Rillieux (1806-1894)

SLAVE, SCIENTIST

As a freedman, Norbert Rillieux did not want to leave New Orleans. He was born there a slave and, after studying and teaching in France, returned to Louisiana to become the most famous engineer in the state. When he was assigned to reorganize a sugar refining plant, a fine house, complete with servants, was set aside for his exclusive use. He was one of the most important men in the state, yet he could not take part in its affairs unless he was invited. Rillieux accepted this until he was required to carry a pass. In 1854 he decided to leave Louisiana forever.

Norbert Rillieux was an important man wherever sugar was manufactured. Until 1846 the transformation of sugar cane juice into sugar was accomplished by a primitive method called the "Jamaica Train," a slow, costly process.

Before Rillieux, two other scientists, Howard and DeGrand, had developed vacuum pans and condensing coils which imperfectly utilized heat in evaporating the liquid portion of the sugar cane juice. ". . . it remained for Rillieux, by a stroke of genius, to enclose the condensing coils in a vacuum chamber and to employ the vapor from this first condensing chamber for evaporating the juice in a second chamber under higher vacuum."

The process developed by Rillieux greatly reduced the production cost and provided a superior quality of sugar. Sugar manufacturers immediately hailed the process as a revolution in the manufacturing of sugar. In the years that followed, the Rillieux process was adopted in Cuba and Mexico. Other industries having the problem of liquid reduction adopted the process.

Norbert's intelligence was recognized at an early age by his father who was master of the plantation on which his mother was a slave. He was sent to Paris to be educated and, at the age of twenty-four, Norbert became an instructor at L'Ecole Centrale. He published several papers on the steam engine and steam economy.

When Rillieux left Louisiana in 1854 and returned to France, he tried to interest the Europeans in his sugar processing, but found them lukewarm and finally gave up trying. He secured a scholarship and worked with the Champollions deciphering hieroglyphics. For ten years he was engaged in this work. Eventually his special process was adopted in Europe, and with renewed interest he turned again to invention. This time he applied his process to the sugar beet and cut production costs in half.

George Meade, "A Negro Scientist of Slavery Days," *Negro History Bulletin* (April, 1957), pp. 159-164.

Jan Ernst Matzeliger (1852-1889)

INVENTOR AND BUSINESSMAN

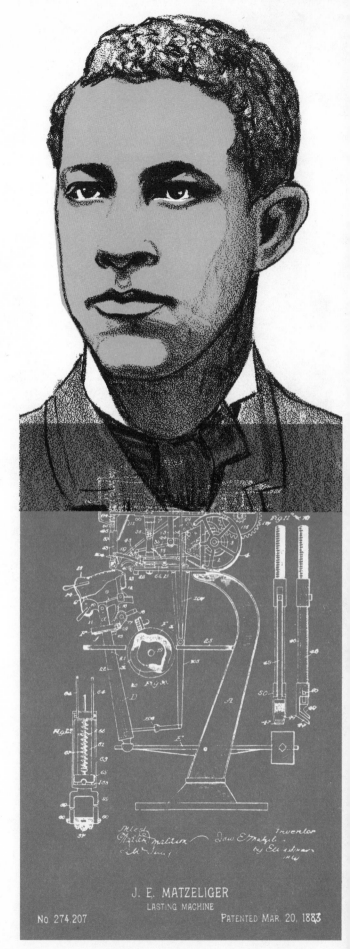

J. E. MATZELIGER
LASTING MACHINE

No 274,207   PATENTED MAR. 20, 1883

When young, slim, rather handsome Jan Ernst Matzeliger arrived in Lynn, Massachusetts in 1876, he could barely speak a word of English. No one knew him; he was poor and friendless, having been for two years a sailor. When he died thirteen years later, his name was known not only in Massachusetts, but wherever inventors gathered. During the years left to him, he laid the foundation of the shoe industry in the United States and made Lynn, Massachusetts the shoe capital of the world.

Before Matzeliger, hundreds of inventors had labored and thousands of dollars had been spent in an effort to make a complete shoe by machinery. Inventors such as Thompson, McKay and Copeland had developed crude shoe making machines but the final problem of shaping the upper leather over the last and attaching this leather to the bottom of the shoe stymied them. The "hand-lasters," as they were called, performed this crucial and final step. They were the aristocrats of the shoe industry and, in effect, had control of the shoe manufacturing industry. They were highly paid and temperamental, but no matter how fast the other portions of the shoe were completed, they could turn out only forty to fifty pairs each per day.

Matzeliger heard of the problem. Already extremely competent with mechanical things, such a challenge suited him perfectly. As he worked in shoe factories around Lynn and Boston, he heard it said many times that it was impossible to last shoes by machine; the job simply could not be done. In secret he started experimenting, first with a crude wooden machine, then with a model made out of scrap iron. For ten years he worked, steadily and patiently, with no encouragement. Indeed, when the news of his tinkering finally reached the public, there were jeers of derision. Matzeliger only smiled and continued working.

Meanwhile, after being denied membership in several churches, he finally joined a young adult group which made his days less lonely. Little did he hear of his Dutch father or Surinamese mother in his native Dutch Guiana. There is no record of his courting or marrying. Yet when he was working on his invention, acquaintances and friends would drop in to chat and perhaps smile condescendingly.

Finally in 1882, Matzeliger felt he had perfected his machine to solve the impossible problem. When he applied for a patent and sent his diagrams to Washington, patent reviewers could not even understand them. They were so complicated that a man was dispatched from Washington to Lynn, Massachusetts to see the model itself. On March 20, 1883, patent number 274,207 was granted to Jan E. Matzeliger. Six years later he died of tuberculosis.

Sidney Kaplan, "Jan Ernst Matzeliger and the Making of the Shoe," *Journal of Negro History*, XL (January, 1958), pp. 8-33.

Granville T. Woods (1856-1910)

PROLIFIC INVENTOR

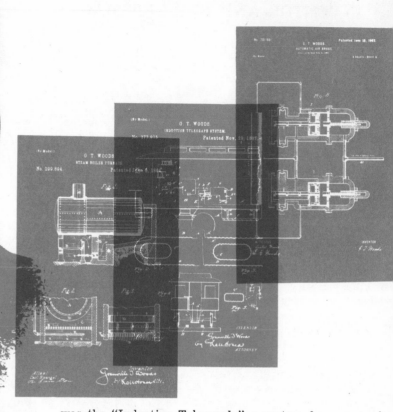

The Cincinnati, Ohio *Catholic Tribune* of January 14, 1886 carried an article which included this statement: "Granville T. Woods, the greatest colored inventor in the history of the race, and equal, if not superior, to any inventor in the country, is destined to revolutionize the mode of street car transit."

A little more than a year later, April 1, 1887 it said, "Mr. Woods, who is the greatest electrician in the world, still continues to add to his long list of electrical inventions."

Since the Woods' Railway Telegraph Company was located in Cincinnati at that time, the extravagance of these two statements may be partly attributed to civic pride, but they also truthfully reflect the inventive fertility of this mechanical genius. During his lifetime he earned over thirty-five patents, ranging from a steam boiler furnace (1884), and an incubator (1900) to the automatic air brake (1902). Many of his electrical inventions were sold to the American Bell Telephone Company and the General Electric Company; the Westinghouse Air Brake Company eventually obtained his air brake patent.

While he patented more than a dozen inventions for electric railways and many more for electrical control and distribution, his most noteworthy device in this area

was the "Induction Telegraph," a system for communicating to and from moving trains. Accidents and collisions were causing great concern both to the public and the railways at that time, and many electrical engineers were seeking improvement of the conventional telegraph as a solution. When Woods came out with his Synchronous Multiplex Railway Telegraph "for the purpose of averting accidents by keeping each train informed of the whereabouts of the one immediately ahead or following it; in communicating with stations from moving trains; and in promoting general social and commercial intercourse," he was contested by the Edison and Phelps Company which was working on a similar device. In the patent office's case of *Woods vs. Phelps*, Woods was twice declared the inventor.

G. T. Woods was born in Columbus, Ohio, April 23, 1856, where he attended school until he was ten and then worked in a machine shop. This basic mechanical knowledge was increased by jobs on a Missouri railroad in 1872, in a Springfield rolling mill in 1874, and mechanical engineering training at an Eastern college in 1876. In 1878 he obtained work as an engineer on board the *Ironsides*, a British steamer, and in 1880 actually handled a steam locomotive on the D & S Railroad. In spite of his background and engineering skill he was unable to advance in these jobs. He then started his own company to market his telegraph and other inventions.

Benjamin Brawley. *A Short History of the American Negro* (New York, 1931), pp. 227-228; Henry E. Baker. "The Negro in the Field of Invention," *Journal of Negro History*, II (January, 1917), p. 32.

Garrett A. Morgan (1875-1963)

INVENTOR FOR SAFETY

The time: July 25, 1916; the place: five miles out and 228 feet below Lake Erie and the Cleveland Waterworks. An explosion in Tunnel Number Five had trapped over two dozen men. No one knew for sure whether there were any survivors. And there was only one way to tell—have someone descend into the tunnel. With great quantities of smoke, natural gases, dust and debris, it was simply impossible for anyone to go into Number Five and live. At two A.M. when all seemed hopeless, someone recalled that one Garrett Morgan had been demonstrating a gas inhalator in an effort to interest manufacturers.

Immediately, a call went out for Morgan who wasted no time in reaching the scene of the disaster. Grim-lipped men and sobbing women moved aside as Garrett and his brother Frank arrived. Quickly donning their inhalators, the two brothers, assisted by two volunteers, entered the tunnel. Down, down, down, 100 feet, 200 feet into the darkness they descended. Soon Garrett Morgan stumbled into the body of a man. Quickly gathering up this body and locating other men, Garrett's small party returned to the tunnel's elevator which whisked them to the surface. Again and again, Garrett Morgan led rescuers into Tunnel Number Five to save over a score of the workmen.

Morgan's heroic act thrust him before the public. Many manufacturers and fire departments showed keen interest in his breathing device. Morgan was requested to demonstrate his inhalator in many cities and towns. In the Deep South it was necessary for Morgan to employ a white man to show off his invention. Orders began to pour into Cleveland as many municipalities purchased the Morgan inhalator. However, the orders soon stopped when the racial identity of the inventor became known.

Garrett Morgan was not discouraged. He returned to his workshop and in 1923 created a device which makes possible the orderly movement of the millions of automobiles in today's cities and towns—the automatic stop-sign. Rights to the stop sign were sold to General Electric for the sum of $40,000, a nice sum for a man who had come to Cleveland, Ohio a penniless native of Tennessee. Awarded a solid gold medal by the city of Cleveland for his heroic rescue, Garrett lived in that city until his death in 1963.

"Morgan," *Crisis* (February, 1914), p. 165; documents supplied by the inventor.

Martin R. Delany (1812-1885)

ETHNOLOGIST

"I thank God for making me a man simply; but Delany always thanks Him for making him a black man." Thus spoke Frederick Douglass of his old friend, Martin R. Delany, spokesman, physician, explorer and scientist.

Martin R. Delany was indeed proud of the Gullah and Mandingo blood which flowed in his veins. He was one of the leaders in the great debate following the passage of the Fugitive Slave Act in 1850. His pride of race was so great that he became a spokesman for those who felt that America was too inhospitable for persons of African descent. After serving as a prime mover in several conventions of free Negroes to discuss the possibility of emigrating to Africa, in 1859 Delany led the first and only exploratory party of American-born Negroes to Africa. In the region of the Niger River, Delany's party carried out scientific studies and made agreements with several African chiefs for the treatment of prospective emigrés from America.

Trained in the natural sciences, Martin Delany attended the International Statistical Conference meeting in London in 1860 and read a scientific paper before the Royal Geographic Society. When Lord Brougham commented favorably on Delany's presence at the Conference, several southern delegates withdrew from it.

Even before the Fugitive Slave Law was passed, Delany had already made a reputation as a writer and speaker on abolition and emigration. He helped Frederick Douglass to edit *The North Star* from 1847 to 1849. He received his medical and scientific training at Harvard and practiced medicine in Chicago and in Canada. When not practicing medicine, he often travelled about the country, speaking on abolition. Once in Ohio he was almost fatally beaten by a mob but continued to speak for the cause of freedom.

Delany was a free-born native of Charleston, West Virginia but spent his youth in Pennsylvania where he was taken to be educated. It was there that he became interested in seeking solutions to the plight of the Negro in America. For a short time he published his views in his own newspaper called *The Mystery*. After gaining journalistic experience with Douglass, Delany published two major books, *The Condition, Elevation, Emigration and Destiny of the Colored People of the United States Politically Considered* (1852), and *Principia of Ethnology: The Origin of Races and Color* (1879).

His devotion to the cause of freedom led him to seek audience with President Lincoln in 1865 to propose an army of Negroes, commanded by Negroes. Although he was not successful in persuading the President to do this, he was commissioned a major in the U. S. Colored troops, the first of his race to be so honored. He also served with the 109th Regiment.

After the war he worked with the Freedmen's Bureau for three years. Delany later became a customs inspector in Charleston, South Carolina and then a trial justice in the same city. Delany died on January 24, 1885.

Louis Mehlinger, "The Attitude of the Free Negro Toward African Colonization," *Journal of Negro History*, I (July, 1916), pp. 276-301; *Dictionary of American Biography*, V (1930), pp. 219-220.

Matthew A. Henson (1867-1955)

POLAR EXPLORER

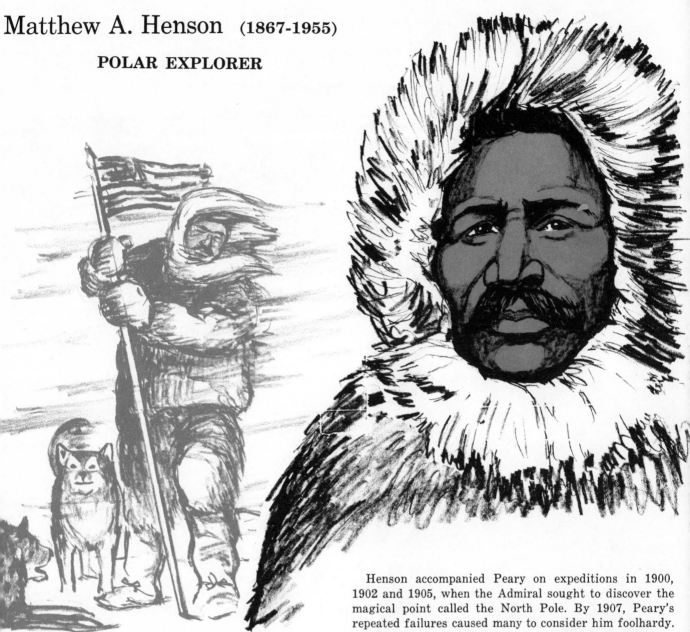

When Admiral Robert E. Peary, the renowned scientist and explorer, was surveying canal sites in Nicaragua in 1887, Matthew A. Henson was his trusty, versatile and resourceful companion. Four years later in June, 1891 when Peary set out on his expedition to Inglefield Gulf, Greenland, where he hoped to reach the North Pole by traveling the uncharted area to the north, he engaged Henson to accompany him.

On this first trip Henson was a valuable aid to Peary. He established a friendly relationship with the Eskimos, who believed him to be somehow related to them because of his brown skin. Arctic explorers at this time depended almost solely on their legs and dog sleds. Peary's expedition was greatly aided by Henson's expert handling of the Eskimos, dogs and equipment. On the first trip Matthew went as far as Cape York, Greenland with the Admiral who pushed on to discover Independence Bay.

Henson accompanied Peary on expeditions in 1900, 1902 and 1905, when the Admiral sought to discover the magical point called the North Pole. By 1907, Peary's repeated failures caused many to consider him foolhardy. In 1908, Peary and Henson set out for what they instinctively knew would be their last venture to the top of the world. Through their long association a brotherly bond existed between them, for Henson had given Peary the sincere moral support he sorely needed. Peary, Henson and four other explorers left Cape Sheridan, Greenland in February, 1908. The going was extremely hard. Snow-blindness, frostbite and sheer physical exhaustion felled all but Henson and Peary. April 4, 1908 found them accompanied by four Eskimos only sixty miles from their goal. On April 6, Peary called a halt and painfully took a reading with his sextant. Carefully calculating to avoid any possibility of error, Peary determined the precise point of the Pole on April 7 and asked Henson to place the American flag on the spot.

Matthew A. Henson has been recognized as the indispensable man who was responsible for getting Peary to the Pole.

Matthew A. Henson, *A Negro Explorer at the North Pole* (New York, 1912); Bradley Robinson, *Dark Companion* (New York, 1947).

George Washington Carver (1864-1943)

If an honest history of the Deep South is ever written, Dr. George Washington Carver will stand out as one of the truly great men of his time. Almost single-handedly, Dr. Carver revolutionized southern agriculture. He brought the findings of the laboratory to the land. He was a scientist, teacher, administrator and humanitarian.

From his small laboratory on the campus of Tuskegee Institute flowed hundreds of discoveries and products. From the once-neglected peanut. Dr. Carver extracted meal, instant and dry coffee, bleach, tan remover, wood filler, metal polish, paper, ink, shaving cream, rubbing oil, linoleum, synthetic rubber, and plastics. From the soybean he obtained flour, breakfast food, and milk. His mind laid bare over one hundred different products within the sweet potato. During World War II, he found over 500 different shades of dye to replace aniline dyes formerly imported from Germany; his work on dehydration attracted the attention of the United States government.

Dr. Carver was among the first advocates of the use of legumes to replace soil minerals depleted by cotton-growing. From *calcareous tripoli* and *siliceous tripoli* he made a universal scouring powder. Out of the Alabama clays he obtained a talcum powder. He discovered an exceptionally large deposit of *bentonite* extending from Montgomery to Mobile, Alabama. (*Bentonite* makes possible the re-use of newspaper pulp.)

Dr. Carver always had a practical bent to his mind but it took the boll weevil to focus his wizardry on the peanut and sweet potato. In 1914 the boll weevil, marching like some dreaded scourge from Mexico eastward, threatened to dethrone "king cotton" on which the South depended. Dr. Carver felt that the answer to this threat lay in the South finding some sources of income other than cotton. As news of his startling discoveries in the ordinary peanut and common sweet potato circulated around the country,

"SAVIOR OF SOUTHERN AGRICULTURE"

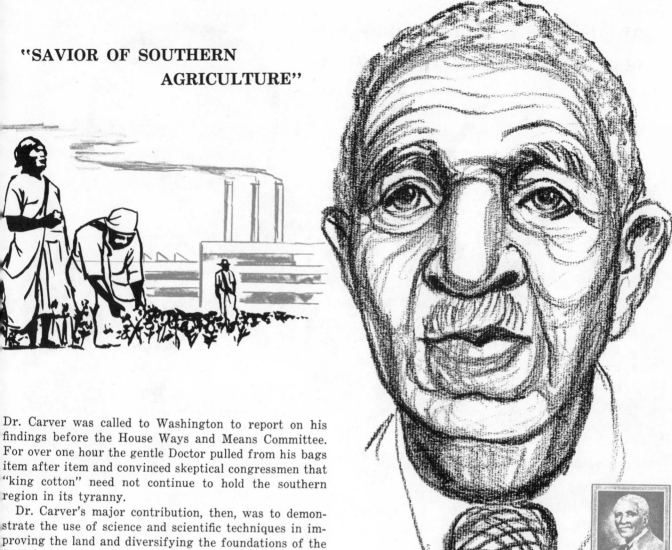

Dr. Carver was called to Washington to report on his findings before the House Ways and Means Committee. For over one hour the gentle Doctor pulled from his bags item after item and convinced skeptical congressmen that "king cotton" need not continue to hold the southern region in its tyranny.

Dr. Carver's major contribution, then, was to demonstrate the use of science and scientific techniques in improving the land and diversifying the foundations of the South's economy. The peanut and the sweet potato have become major items in the South's economy.

The "wizard of Tuskegee" was soon known throughout the world. Scientists, inventors, promoters, governmental officials all made their way to him. Thomas A. Edison, himself the inventor of the electric light and phonograph, wanted to employ Dr. Carver. Henry Ford set up a special laboratory for him. Men from Australia, Africa, Russia and India consulted him. In 1916 he was named a Fellow of the Royal Society, London; he received the Spingarn Medal in 1923.

Dr. Carver's achievements in science have perhaps obscured the fact that he was also a competent painter. Indeed, during the early part of his life he studied art at Iowa's Simpson College. His paintings were sufficiently competent to merit recognition and display in the Columbian Exposition held in Chicago in 1893. His "Yucca, Angustifolia and Cactus" was awarded an honorable mention. One of his most charming works in still life was a cluster of peaches which is housed in the Carver Museum at Tuskegee.

Humble and devout before God and nature, Dr. Carver was eager to see others benefit from his work and the study of science. In 1938 he donated $30,000 of his life's saving to the establishment of the George Washington Carver Foundation and, shortly before his death, willed the remainder of his estate to the Foundation whose purpose is to discover uses for agricultural wastes and to develop food products from common agricultural products with the aim of creating new markets for them.

Dr. Carver was born in Diamond Grove, Missouri in 1864. At the age of thirteen he was on his own. Enduring great hardships, he worked his way through Simpson and Iowa State Colleges. Booker T. Washington called him to Tuskegee Institute in 1896. Shortly afterwards an experimental farm was set up there under Dr. Carver, and the work began of re-educating farmers throughout the Tuskegee region.

The gentle, amiable and self-effacing Dr. George Washington Carver was first and foremost a research scientist whose work had immediate application. It is highly doubtful if any other individual has done as much for southern agriculture as Dr. Carver, who died in 1943 and was buried next to Booker T. Washington.

Rackham Holt, *George Washington Carver* (New York, 1943); *Negro Yearbook*, 1947, Tuskegee (1947), pp. 37-39, p. 415.

Daniel Hale Williams (1856-1931)

FIRST SUCCESSFUL HEART SURGEON

SEWED UP HIS HEART!

Provident Hospital - 1893

Dr. Daniel Hale Williams was raised from an unsung master of medicine to a position of national renown as one of America's greatest surgeons, by a husky, young street fighter named James Cornish. In a brawl, Cornish suffered a knife wound in an artery a fraction of an inch from the heart. Heart wounds, or even wounds in the thoracic cavity, prior to the date of this incident in 1893, were treated with sedatives and prayer, and the patient invariably died.

"Dr. Dan", as he was often called, decided to do something no other doctor had ever done: to open Cornish's chest and operate on the heart. X-rays, sulfa drugs, blood transfusion—now absolute necessities—were unknown medical tools at the time. Calling six of his colleagues on the staff of the struggling Provident Hospital in Chicago, Dr. Dan operated. The patient lived. The doctor had performed the impossible operation . . . "Sewed up his heart," headlined a Chicago paper.

From the age of twelve, Daniel was on his own, working as an apprentice shoemaker, a roustabout on a lake steamer, and barber, but with a constant eye on a medical career. From his birthplace in Pennsylvania, he drifted to Janesville, Illinois where he met a white physician who encouraged him to enter medicine. With the aid of friends, he finished Chicago Medical College in 1883 and opened his office on Chicago's South Side. His extraordinary skill earned him a post at his alma mater as a surgeon and demonstrator in anatomy.

At this time no hospital in Chicago allowed Negro doctors to use their facilities. In 1891, against great odds and almost single-handed, Dan Williams created Provident Hospital for the use of all physicians without regard to color, thus hastening the end to operations performed on couches and kitchen tables in the crowded tenements of Chicago's South Side. Dr. Dan's skill as a surgeon spread and physicians from far and near came to Provident to see the wizard of the scalpel perform.

In 1894 Dr. Williams was called to Washington to head Freedmen's Hospital, a collection of six old pre-Civil War buildings, with medical facilities equally as primitive. Dr. Dan organized Freedmen's into departments, collected a staff of twenty volunteer specialists, and created the beginning of the first nursing school for Negroes.

Desiring to resume his profession, and tiring of the pressure of administrative duties, Dr. Williams resigned from Freedmen's in 1898 and returned to Chicago where he became the first Negro to hold a post at St. Luke Hospital and Northwestern University Hospital. He also resumed his association with Provident Hospital. When he died in 1931, he bequeathed part of his estate for the advancement of Negro physicians and part to the NAACP, his major life interests.

Helen Buckler, *Dr. Dan; Pioneer American Surgeon* (Boston, 1954).

Ernest E. Just (1883-1941)
BIOLOGIST

Howard University College of Medicine

One of the most embarrassing moments in the life of Dr. Ernest E. Just occurred on the night of January 2, 1915. Accustomed to the laboratory and the passionless laws of science, the young Ernest E. Just did not want to endure the speeches and plaudits which accompany the awarding the Spingarn Medal, given by the NAACP to the individual who has done most during the year to advance the progress of the Negro. Young Mr. Just had even written to the NAACP explaining that he was upset over being the recipient of the award for 1914. Despite his modesty and embarrassment, this accolade could not be denied him.

Dr. Just was given the award not for making speeches about the condition of the Negro in the United States or leading demonstrations of protest; rather, he was being recognized for his work as a pure scientist who was making pioneer investigations into the mysteries of egg fertilization and the study of the cell. His work was earning him the title, "Scientist's Scientist," for he was a meticulously brilliant investigator of biological phenomena relating to the structure of the cell.

A measure of his contribution to biological knowledge may be seen in the words of the late Dr. Charles Drew, himself an outstanding researcher in blood plasma preservation. Dr. Drew described Dr. Just as a "biologist of unusual skill and the greatest of our original thinkers in the field." He was seen as producing "new concepts of cell life and metabolism which will make for him a place for all time."

Dr. Just wrote two major books and over sixty scientific papers in his field. He was for many years Howard University's outstanding professor in the biological sciences and received many awards and grants for his research. Scientists from all over America and Europe sought him out and studied his work. He loved Howard but from time to time he went abroad to study and confer with other scientists, researchers and investigators.

Ernest E. Just was a native of South Carolina and he worked his way from Charleston to Meriden, New Hampshire to enter Dartmouth College on a scholarship. His first two years at Dartmouth were lonely and discouraging but when his routine studies in biology introduced him to the intricacies of cellular reproduction, his entire mind caught fire and he graduated from Dartmouth magna cum laude and Phi Beta Kappa.

Mary White Ovington, *Portraits in Color* (New York, 1927); *Negro Yearbook, 1947*, Tuskegee (1947), pp. 35-36.

Ulysses Grant Dailey
(1885-1961)

SURGEON

Named for the victor in the war between the North and South, Ulysses Grant Dailey was one of the most distinguished surgeons in America. Whenever a roster of outstanding medical men is compiled, the name of Dr. Dailey ranks high on the list.

A native of Donaldsonville, Louisiana, Dr. Dailey rose to international prominence within his profession. A graduate of Northwestern University Medical School in 1906, Dr. Dailey's name was always associated with outstanding work in the fields of anatomy and surgery. Upon graduating from Northwestern he was appointed a Demonstrator in Anatomy at his alma mater. Following this he spent four years (1908-1912) as surgical assistant to the renowned Dr. Daniel Hale Williams, the founder of Provident Hospital, Chicago.

Not content with experience as an ambulance surgeon for the city of Chicago and his work with Dr. Williams, Dr. Dailey studied abroad in London, Paris and Vienna. In 1926 he set up his own hospital and sanitarium. Over the years, his brilliant mind and nimble fingers brought him increasing fame. He became a member of many medical societies, national and international. For thirty-eight years he was associate editor of the *Journal* of the National Medical Association. In 1948-49 he served as editor-in-chief of this publication. News of his competence spread as far afield as Pakistan and he was made corresponding editor of *The Medius* at Karachi.

In 1953, Dr. Dailey circled the world under the sponsorship of the International College of Surgeons of which he was a Founder Fellow. In 1951 and 1953, the U. S. State Department sent him as a health advisor to Pakistan and to India, Ceylon and Africa. He was named Honorary Consul to Haiti in 1954.

In the midst of all his travel and organizational work, Dr. Dailey for over two decades was Chief Attending Surgeon, Provident Hospital, located in the heart of Chicago's teeming South Side. He also found time to write numerous technical articles in different areas of his field. His death in 1961 ended an exceptional career of unstinting service to his fellowman.

Who's Who in Colored America, 1950, p. 132; Lucille A. Chambers, *America's Tenth Man* (New York, 1957), p. 82; *American Men of Science*, 3rd Edition (Farmingdale, New York, 1961), p. 157.

Charles Drew
(1904-1950)

PIONEER IN BLOOD PLASMA RESEARCH

One night in North Carolina a tired man fell asleep at the wheel, wrecked his car and was badly injured. For a time he lay bleeding and in a little while he died without ever regaining consciousness. The man had been a star athlete, scholar, scientist and surgeon who had already made his mark in his profession. The dead man was Dr. Charles Drew, head of Freedmen's Hospital, Washington, D.C.

Dr. Drew was not yet fifty years old, but already his contribution to medicine had saved hundreds of thousands of lives during World War II. Dr. Drew was a pioneer in blood plasma preservation. Before his time there was no efficient way to store large quantities of blood plasma for use during emergencies or for use in wartime where thousands of lives depended on the availability of blood for blood transfusions. After Dr. Drew this was no longer a problem, for he discovered ways and means of preserving blood plasma in what are commonly known as blood banks.

A native of Washington, D. C., Dr. Drew had been a letter man in track, a Mossman trophy winner in general scholarship, and a Spingarn Medalist for his contributions to human welfare. Dr. Drew's entire life was spent in the pursuit of excellence whether it was on the track cinders, in the operating room, or in the research laboratory. As an Amherst undergraduate, he was captain of the track team and an outstanding halfback on the football team. He received the Mossman trophy for having brought the most honor to the school over a four-year period. At McGill University in Canada, he won first prize in physiological anatomy and set track records which stood for several years.

Beginning his research into the properties of blood plasma at Columbia University, Dr. Drew became an authority on the subject and was asked by the British to set up a plasma program for them. He later did the same thing for the United States in 1942 and won the Spingarn Medal in recognition of his contributions to Negro progress. At the time of his death in 1950, Dr. Drew was chief surgeon and chief of staff at Freedmen's Hospital.

Current Biography, 1950; Negro Yearbook, 1947 (Tuskegee, 1947); Who's Who in Colored America, 1950, pp. 163-164.

Percy Julian (1899-   )

CHEMIST

The citation on one of Dr. Percy Julian's many honorary degrees sums up his career by saying in part: "Education's investment in him has been returned manyfold in the magnificence of his service to mankind." His greatest single scientific contribution helped millions suffering from the excruciating pain of arthritis.

Dr. Percy Julian is, perhaps, the most famous living Negro scientist. Just as George Washington Carver demonstrated what could be done with the ordinary peanut, Dr. Julian took the soybean, which was until his time just another bean, and extracted from it an ingredient to relieve inflammatory arthritis.

Until the late thirties, Europe had a monopoly on the production of sterols, the basis of Dr. Julian's research. These sterols were extracted from the bile of animals at a cost of several hundreds of dollars a gram. Substituting sterols from the oil of the soybean, Dr. Julian reduced the cost of sterols to less than twenty cents a gram, thus making cortisone, a sterol derivative, available to the needy at a reasonable cost.

Today (1969) Dr. Julian is a millionaire and is president of two companies bearing his name. His route to fame was not easy and, like others who have achieved it, had to toil and sacrifice. The son of a railway clerk, he worked his way through DePauw University at Greencastle, Indiana. For a time he lived in an attic of the fraternity house where he worked as a waiter. Applying himself to his studies, he graduated with Phi Beta Kappa honors and was valedictorian of his class. His mother was so impressed with his achievements as a student at DePauw that she moved the entire Julian family from Montgomery, Alabama to Greencastle so that the other children might have the same advantages of good schooling. Two of Dr. Julian's brothers are physicians and his three sisters have earned their master's degrees.

Graduating from DePauw in 1920, Percy Julian spent several years teaching at Fisk and Howard universities and West Virginia State College. He attended Harvard and then took his doctorate at the University of Vienna. For several years he taught at DePauw and later became director of research and manager of fine chemicals at the Glidden Company and formed his own company which was devoted mainly to the production of sterols. When he totaled up Julian Laboratories' earnings for the first year he found a net profit of $71.70. The next year however he counted a profit of $97,000. In 1961 his company merged with the huge Smith, Kline and French Pharmaceutical Company in an arrangement which paid Dr. Julian several millions of dollars.

Living at this time (1969) in the exclusive residential section of Oak Park, Illinois, a prosperous suburb of Chicago which first rejected him as a resident, he and his family have become full members of the community.

Richard Bardolph, *The Negro Vanguard* (New York, 1961), pp. 428-? *Ebony*, XIII (January, 1958), pp. 51-56.

Julian Laboratories, Franklin Park, Ill., founded 1953

Theodore K. Lawless (1892-   )
DERMATOLOGIST-PHILANTHROPIST

In 1963, as they had been doing for many years, people lined the sidewalk running past an old mansion in the heart of Chicago's black metropolis. Slowly they moved forward, up the steps and into the waiting-room of a doctor. The doctor heard their complaints in accents representing every social strata and section in America. Often the accent was French, German or Italian. Sometimes the patients spoke in halting English, for many were not Americans at all, but citizens of another country who were there solely because of Dr. Theodore K. Lawless, the man who saw and listened to them all.

Known wherever dermatologists gather, Dr. Lawless is one of the world's leading skin specialists. His career stretches back over a period of forty years. Born in Thibodeaux, Louisiana in 1892, Dr. Lawless achieved eminence in his chosen field by hard work, superb training and outstanding intellect. He was educated at Talledega College in Alabama, the University of Kansas, Columbia, and Harvard. He received the M.D. degree from Northwestern University in Evanston, Illinois. He has done special work in Vienna, Freiburg, and Paris and has made signal contributions in the scientific treatment of syphilis and leprosy. From 1924 to 1941 Dr. Lawless taught at the Northwestern University School of Medicine. For many years he has been Senior Attending Physician at Provident Hospital, seven blocks from his office.

Although Dr. Lawless is a millionaire, he works as hard as ever and sees an average of one hundred patients daily. He once declared that "I am happiest when I work and I work as much as I can." The distinguished dermatologist is as prodigal with his earnings as he is with his skill. As an example of his liberality, Dillard University New Orleans, Louisiana has a $700,000 apartment building which was secured through his efforts in 1956. A chapel on the Dillard campus bears his name. Several other colleges attended by Negroes have benefited from his largess. His philanthropy, however, is not restricted to his race. In the state of Israel at the Beilinson Hospital Center stands a $500,000 dermatology clinic, erected mainly through the efforts of Dr. Lawless. The clinic bears his name.

On May 16, 1963, civic leaders, the mayor of Chicago and the governor of the state of Illinois attended a testimonial dinner in his honor. As early as 1929 he won the Harmon Award for outstanding achievement in medicine; in 1954 the NAACP gave him the Spingarn Medal. Dr. Lawless has served on numerous boards and committees in the areas of education and health. Neither his great wealth, his international reputation, nor his many honors keep him from treating the rich and the poor with the same care and devotion he showed when he was unknown and obscure.

Who's Who in Colored America, 1950, p. 332; Chicago Sun-Times (June 2, 1963), p. 54.

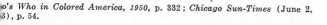
Lawless Chapel, Dillard University, N.O., Louisiana

V BUSINESS PIONEERS

In 1788 a French traveler in America, J. P. Brissot de Warville, wrote that "if . . . Negroes here are limited to the small retail trade, let us not attribute it to their lack of ability, but rather to the prejudices of the whites who put obstacles in their way." De Warville understood those obstacles to be: extreme difficulty in securing credit, general exclusion of Negroes from positions whereby they could gain business experience, and the absence of educational opportunities. Abram Harris in 1935 and Andrew F. Brimmer in 1966, both eminent black economists, came to the same conclusions nearly two hundred years later.

In 1769, an ex-slave bearing the name of Emmanuel operated a rather successful ale house in Rhode Island and accumulated an estate valued at $2,500. After the American Revolution, James Forten of Philadelphia managed to develop a sail loft enterprise worth $100,000 at his death in 1842. Richard Allen, the founder of the African Methodist Episcopal church, was engaged in the real estate business and left $25,000 to his survivors. Occasionally slaves were permitted to earn extra money by trading. One of the most successful was Lunsford Lane of North Carolina who had sales outlets for his special smoking tobacco mix in Raleigh, North Carolina. Lane earned several thousands of dollars, and spent over $4,000 to secure freedom for himself and his family.

In the state of Georgia, Solomon Humphries had a grocery business worth at least $20,000. A Negro named John Jones operated hotels worth $40,000 in Charleston, South Carolina. The free blacks of antebellum New Orleans, some 10,000 strong, jointly owned possessions valued at $15,000,-000 in 1860. Up in Lancaster, Pennsylvania, William Whipper and Stephen Smith were partners in a lumber business which grossed over $100,000 annually. Smith also was the owner of nearly a hundred brick houses in different parts of the state. Henry Boyd, a Kentucky professional cabinetmaker, was worth $26,000 in 1859. James Garrett in Detroit and John Jones in Chicago were merchant tailors, each grossing $1,000 weekly during the same period. William Leidesdorff in California had amassed property worth $1,500,000 at the time of his death in 1848.

After the Emancipation Proclamation was issued in 1863, ex-slaves in the South were the possessors of property valued at $25,000,000. Afro-Americans in other parts of the nation were estimated to have property worth a total of $50,000,000. Most of this was in the form of homes, land and livestock. Negro businesses were still rather scarce.

From about 1875 onward, Negroes attempted to emulate white entrepreneurs through inventions and joint financial speculation. Nearly a thousand patents were issued to black inventors. In 1897, Andrew Beard received $50,000 for inventing the "Jenny Coupler," an automatic device which securely hooks railroad cars without endangering the lives of workmen. Elijah McCoy was a profession inventor who received more than fifty patents for lubri cating devices. He set up the Elijah McCoy Manufacturin Company in Detroit, Michigan. Trained as a mechanic engineer, Granville T. Woods sold many of his invention through his own company. In 1893, E. R. Robinson receive patent number 505,370 which acknowledged him as th inventor of the electric railway trolley. J. H. and S. Dickinson received patents for inventing the player pia in 1899. Ironically, Jan E. Matzeliger who invented th shoe lasting machine and revolutionized the shoe indust did not profit at all from his handiwork.

During the last quarter of the nineteenth century, N groes attempted to develop their economic resources entering small scale service and trade enterprises. In 190 more than 20,000 service and retail establishments exist in the black community. In 1888, the first bank organiz entirely by Negroes opened its doors in Washington, D. and bore the title "Capital Savings Bank." In that sa year, the "Savings Bank of the Grand Fountain of t United Order of True Believers" was founded in Ric mond, Virginia. Banks, of course, were more complex erations than the burial aid societies, mortuary establis ments, restaurants and the like which were typical of t possibilities confronting black business men. In the 1800 Wiley Jones of Pine Bluff, Arkansas, accumulated $200,0 as the owner of a street car line. Thomy Lafen of New C leans made a half million dollars from real estate inve ments. In Tennessee, Robert R. Church, father of Ma Church Terrell, amassed hundreds of thousands of doll from his speculation in Memphis lands. In Harlem, N York, Philip A. Payton, Jr. organized the Afro-Americ Realty Co. which had assets of $500,000 and 200 employe

By 1900, scores of Negroes organized and operated b ial aid societies, newspapers, shirt factories, carpet f tories, drygoods stores, small cotton mills, and many oth types of enterprises. Some set up co-operative business The most notable of them were the Bay Shore Hotel co pany of Hampton, Virginia, the Southern Stove Holle Ware and Foundry Company in Chattanooga, Tenness and the South View Cemetery Association of Jacksonvi Florida. Between 1900 and the beginning of World Wa the number of retail establishments rose from 10,000 25,000. The number of banks increased from four in 1 to fifty-one by 1915.

Black-owned banks generally were based on the finan custody of funds from fraternal and lodge groups. For ample, the Independent Order of St. Luke organized the Luke Bank and Trust Company of Richmond, Virgi This particular order, by 1924, possessed the build which housed its bank, an insurance company and its ne paper, the *St. Luke Herald*. Not only did Negroes organ banks, but they also assisted in the development of legi

Having Been Faithful With a Few Talents

n protecting depositors. One such individual was Pearl
. Chavers, the founder and first president of the Doug-
s National Bank of Chicago. In 1924, two years after
tablishing the National Bank, Mr. Chavers drafted a
l (H.R. 8977) which has been described as "the earliest
l introduced into the Congress . . . providing for pro-
tion of bank deposits by requiring banks to purchase
rety bonds in an amount equal to their deposits."

Banking and finance continue to be among the more
table achievements of the black communities of Amer-
a, particularly when the general lack of capital is taken
to consideration. The leading Negro-owned banks in
nerica include the Citizens Trust Company of Atlanta,
orgia; the Industrial Bank of Washington, D.C.; the
echanics and Farmers Bank of Durham, North Carolina;
e Tri-State Bank of Memphis, Tennessee; the Citizens
d Southern Bank of Philadelphia, Pennsylvania; the
eedom National Bank of New York City; the Independ-
ce Bank, and Seaway National Bank of Chicago. In
gro America there are also a considerable number of
vings and loan associations. Some of the more outstand-
g associations are the Mutual Savings and Loan Asso-
tion of Atlanta, Georgia; the Broadway Savings and
an Association of Los Angeles; the Mutual Savings and
an Association of New York City. This last named asso-
tion is the largest black-owned establishment of its
nd in America. In 1969, the Carver Federal Savings and
an Association had assets in excess of $30,000,000. In
icago there is the Service Federal Savings and Loan
mpany and the Illinois Federal Savings and Loan Com-
ny. Chicago also boasts of its Sivert Mortgage Company.
few Negroes have moved into top positions in predom-
antly white banks: Norman A. Simon is president of the
niversity National Bank in Chicago's Hyde Park area.

Closely associated with banks and savings and loan as-
ciations are the Negro-owned and operated insurance
mpanies. Today there are nearly three score of these
mpanies in America. Among them are the Atlanta Life
surance Company; the Golden Gate Mutual Life Insur-
ce Company of Los Angeles; the Great Lakes Mutual
fe Insurance Company of Detroit, Michigan; the Rich-
ond Beneficial Insurance of Virginia; the Supreme Life
surance Company of America in Chicago, Illinois; and
e North Carolina Mutual Life Insurance Company of
urham, North Carolina. The nation's largest of these
egro-owned and operated insurance companies is the
orth Carolina Mutual Life Insurance Company with as-
ts in 1968 approaching $95,000,000.

In the field of journalism a few Negro publishers have
et with financial as well as journalistic success. Among
e newspapers which were sound economic investments
e the New York *Age*, the Baltimore *Afro-American*,
the Atlanta *Daily World*, the Los Angeles *Sentinel*, the
Norfolk *Journal and Guide*, and the Chicago *Defender*.
Since the publication of the *Anglo-African* in the late
1850's, Negroes have attempted to enter the popular periodical and magazine field. In our time have been published
monthlies such as *Color, Our World,* and *Ebony*. The latter publication, *Ebony*, is the financial mainstay of the
Johnson Publishing Company which also produces *Jet,
Tan,* and *Negro Digest*, a serious periodical. Founded by
John H. Johnson in 1945, the Johnson Publishing Company in 1968 grossed more than $7,000,000 annually and
provided employment for more than 200 individuals.

In the South, Negro businessmen today are engaging
in a wide variety of successful business enterprises. They
own and operate a bus company in Winston-Salem, North
Carolina; highly successful poultry companies in West
Virginia; lumber companies in North Carolina; fishing
fleets off the coast of South Carolina; an aerospace-elec-
tronics firm in Philadelphia, and scores of other types of
businesses. Arthur G. Gaston of Birmingham, Alabama
is perhaps the most successful of southern entrepreneurs.
He owns a complex of businesses that include the B.T.W.
Business College, the B.T.W. Insurance Company and the
Citizens Savings and Loan Association of Birmingham.
His holdings have been valued at more than $12,000,000.

Beginning with the creation of the Small Business Administration in the mid-fifties and continuing with the
Equal Employment Opportunity Act of 1964, the federal
government has recognized and assumed some of the responsibility for the reduction of poverty and the stimula-
tion of Negro business enterprise. The private sector of
the general American economy to some extent has assumed
new and positive responsibilities toward the economic
condition existing in urban communities which are increasingly becoming the home of Afro-Americans leaving
the rural and semi-rural areas of the South. Negroes themselves have initiated such programs as the Opportunities
Industrialization Center in Philadelphia, Pennsylvania;
the Rochester Business Opportunities Corporation in
Rochester, New York; Operation Breadbasket in Chicago;
and similar ventures in other major cities of the nation.

The business enterprises listed above are exceptions to
the relative scarcity of large-scale business organizations
owned and operated by Afro-Americans. The men and
women who founded and developed them were a shrewd
and hardy breed, competing against the odds of a restrictive society and environment.

James Tobin, "Improving the Economic Status of the Negro," *Daedalus:
The Negro American* (Fall, 1965), pp. 889-896; Harry Ploski and Roscoe C.
Brown, Jr. (eds.), *The Negro Almanac* (New York, 1966), pp. 433-441;
Abram Harris, *The Negro Capitalist* (1936); Joseph A. Pierce, *Negro Busi-
ness and Business Education* (New York, 1947).

John B. Russwurm (1799-1851)

FIRST EDITOR-PUBLISHER

FREEDOM'S JOURNAL.

"RIGHTEOUSNESS EXALTETH A NATION."

CORNISH & RUSSWURM,
Editors & Proprietors

NEW-YORK, FRIDAY, MARCH 30, 1827

[VOL. I. No. 3.

The first Negro newspaper published in the United States was *Freedom's Journal*, and John B. Russwurm was its editor. Russwurm, along with Samuel E. Cornish, began publishing *Freedom's Journal* on March 16, 1827. By this time, the liberalism of the American Revolution had faded. Serious proposals were advanced by some of the leading men of the country to send all free men of color to Africa. A few states had enacted laws prohibiting them from migrating across their boundaries. Free blacks had to compete with immigrant whites for the least desirable available menial jobs. The liberal Quaker newspapers opposing slavery had all but ceased publication by the mid-1820's.

In the very first issue of *Freedom's Journal*, Russwurm and Cornish declared their objectives: immediate emancipation of slaves, full civil and political equality for free Negroes, unceasing opposition to racist publicity, and truthful information about Africa. Sensing their declining position in the nation, a few Negroes publicly lamented the lack of any organ to express their views on public matters affecting them. The immediate cause of the establishment of *Freedom's Journal* was the appearance of a rabidly anti-black publication in New York city which ridiculed free Negroes and defended slavery. A number of prominent New York Negroes met at the home of Bustin Crummell, father of Alexander Crummell, and subscribed funds for the establishment of *Freedom's Journal*. John B. Russwurm, who had just graduated from Bowdoin College in Maine a year before, was made editor. Samuel E. Cornish assumed responsibility for the business side

of the venture. Men such as James Forten, Richard Allen and David Walker served as correspondents.

Freedom's Journal was published at #5 Varick Street, Manhattan. It consisted of four tabloid size pages totalling sixteen columns. About a fourth of these columns were devoted to domestic and foreign news. The others contained reports on the condition of the African Free School of New York City, the achievements of prominent Negroes, marriage and death notices, and the like. Except for the lack of pictures and advertisements, *Freedom's Journal* is strongly reminiscent of the average Negro newspaper today. *Freedom's Journal* appeared each Friday until financial difficulties terminated it in February of 1829. Both the absence of extra cash for purchasing newspapers and the scarcity of literate Negroes contributed to its demise. At the time of his editorship of the newspaper, Russwurm was the second of two Negroes who had ever completed college in America. (Edward A. Jones of Charleston, South Carolina was the first: Amherst, Class of 1826).

John B. Russwurm was a native of Jamaica. His father was his owner and his mother was a slave. He was named John Brown, but his master's widow insisted that he take the family surname. In addition, she sent him to Canada and quietly financed his preparatory education and then his college years at Bowdoin. Russwurm had been interested in the work of Paul Cuffe, the colonizationist, and shortly after the collapse of *Freedom's Journal*, he emigrated to Liberia. Here he was first superintendent of schools and later governor of the Maryland province before it was united with Liberia proper. Historians are generally agreed that Russwurm was a good editor, an excellent school superintendent and an able governor.

I. Garland Penn, *The Afro-American Press and Its Editors* (Springfield, Mass. 1891), pp. 25-31; Lerone Bennett, "Founders of the Negro Press," *Ebony* (July, 1964), pp. 96-100.

William Whipper (1805-1885)

NON-VIOLENT BUSINESS ACTIVIST

An abolitionist, businessman and banker, William Whipper was one of the most significant, but perhaps least recognized Negroes of the nineteenth century. At a time when most Negroes could own no property, Whipper was a partner in the leading lumber company of Lancaster, Pennsylvania. When most black abolitionists were pessimistic about the future of the black man in America, Whipper was optimistic.

William Whipper was the son of a Lancaster County, Pennsylvania white businessman and his Negro domestic servant. He learned early some of the principles of sound financial investment and management. Upon the death of his father, Whipper inherited a small retail lumber yard. He took Stephen Smith, another black, as his partner and together they built up a resoundingly successful whole-sale enterprise with outlets in Morristown and Columbia, Pennsylvania.

By the 1850's, the firm of Whipper and Smith had twenty-seven of the "finest merchantman cars on the railroad from Philadelphia to Baltimore," and had bought $8,000 worth of stock in the Columbia Bank. During the time when private individuals could build bridges and charge for their public use, Whipper and Smith invested $9,000 in the Columbia Bridge. In 1859, the lumber yards of Whipper and Smith contained over 2,250,000 feet of lumber, and their warehouses contained thousands of bushels of grain. In 1871, William Whipper became cashier of the Philadelphia Freedmen's Bank. Stephen Smith, Whipper's partner, was regarded as one of the wealthiest blacks in America, at one time owning fifty-eight brick houses in the city of Philadelphia and fifty-three others in Columbia and Lancaster County.

But, while William Whipper was deeply involved in the abolition movement, giving much of his time to the cause, Smith devoted himself completely to business. Whipper gave much time and considerable sums of money to the Negro Convention Movement of the 1830's, the first national effort by blacks to plead their cause in America. In contrast to David Walker's appeal for direct revolution by slaves, Whipper advocated moral suasion and non-violence. In this respect he was the forerunner of Thoreau, Ghandi and Dr. Martin Luther King. In 1833, he became active in the American Moral Reform Society, a black originated group with several thousand members dedicated to pricking the moral conscience of America. He financed and edited its journal, the *National Reformer* (1833-1839).

Whipper spent at least $1,000 annually assisting fugitive slaves to escape to Canada from Lancaster. During the Civil War, Whipper likewise spent $1,000 annually helping to "put down the rebellion." In 1870, he told William Still, "I would prefer today to be penniless in the street rather than to have withheld a single hour's labor or a dollar from the cause of liberty, justice and humanity."

Vernon Loggins, *The Negro Author: His Development in America to 1900* (Port Washington, New York, 1964), edition, p. 79; William Wells Brown, *The Rising Son, or the Antecedents and Advancement of the Colored Race* (Boston, 1874), pp. 494-495; William Still, *Underground Railroad* (Records, Philadelphia, 1883), pp. 773-774.

William Leidesdorff (1810-1848)

MANEUVERING MILLIONAIRE

In the downtown section of cosmopolitan, multi-racial San Francisco, there is a short street named Leidesdorff, which few know is named after a crafty, multi-racial individual, William Alexander Leidesdorff. Leidesdorff was a ship captain, trader, Mexican citizen, American diplomat, merchant, city treasurer of San Francisco, owner of several city blocks in what is now downtown San Francisco and owner of 35,000 acres of land near Sutter's Mill, the birthplace of the California gold rush.

Born at St. Croix in the Danish Virgin Islands, Leidesdorff was the son of a Danish planter and an African mother, Anna Marie Sparks. As a young man, he was sent to New Orleans to work in the office of his two brothers in the cotton business. Both brothers died and Leidesdorff came into considerable wealth. He left New Orleans for California in 1841 because, legend has it, of an unhappy love affair, and landed in California, captain of a 160-ton schooner, the *Julia Ann*.

At this time California was in the middle of a three-way power struggle between Mexico, who owned it, and the United States and Great Britain, who coveted it. Leidesdorff threaded his way through this political maze by first securing from Mexico, in 1843, a land grant of two 300-foot lots on the corner of Clay and Kearney streets. Upon these lots he built a store and a home where he entertained American social and political big-wigs. Soon afterwards, he was appointed American Consul in California. With the Mexican land grants in mind, he became a naturalized Mexican citizen in 1844, and promptly acquired from the Mexican government 35,000 acres of ranch land on the bank of the American River. This strategy was rewarded when, in 1845, he was appointed American sub-consul at Yerba Buena. In 1846 the last Mexican mayor of San Francisco gave him the corner of what is now Leidesdorff and California streets. Upon this Mexican-given property he built a warehouse which he leased to the U. S. Government.

The power struggle for California came to a head in July, 1846. Leidesdorff was given a proclamation of the take-over of the city by Captain Montgomery of the U. S. Marines. This proclamation had to be translated into Spanish for the benefit of the Mexican citizens who could not understand English. The Marines landed and raised their flag on a pole just vacated by the Mexican flag which had been given to Leidesdorff for safe keeping. Two months later Leidesdorff held a ball at his home for the "conquerors." A week later he was named treasurer by the city council of which he was a member.

Before his fabulous career ended he bought a steamship from the Russian-American Fur Company, and also staged the first formal horse race in California history. On May 18, 1848, he died at the age of thirty-eight, leaving an estate of $1,500,000.

Ebony Magazine (November, 1958), Johnson Publishing Co.

John Jones (1816-1879)

BUSINESSMAN CRUSADER

Though born of free parents in Greene County, North Carolina, on November 3, 1816, John Jones did not obtain his liberty until January, 1838. In the intervening twenty-two years he acquired both a knowledge of slavery and the means for fighting it. His mother, a free mulatto, fearing that his father, a German, would sell John into slavery, apprenticed the boy to a local tailor. Through a series of moves and job transfers, John found himself in Tennessee, a virtual slave, at twenty-one. He filed a petition for his freedom which was finally granted him in the Judicial Court at Somerville, Tennessee.

After working in Memphis for about three years and saving $100, he moved to Alton, Illinois, where he married Mary Richardson, the daughter of a Memphis blacksmith. In Alton the newlyweds were made aware of the Illinois "Black Laws" which required all blacks and mulattoes to carry freedom papers and to hold a bond. To protect themselves, both John and Mary obtained their papers from the Clerk of Madison County in 1844.

Still searching for complete freedom, Jones moved to Chicago in 1845, where he established the first Negro tailor shop in that city. Here his early apprenticeship served him well.

He built an excellent business catering to the aristocracy of the Gold Coast. By the time he was twenty-five, he had constructed a four-story office building at 119 South Dearborn Street. His business prospered, and he was soon considered one of the city's more substantial citizens.

A fighter as well as a businessman, Jones refused to accept the dictates of the "Black Laws," as they were called. He took to the streets with a petition to have them stricken from the books. He approached friends and strangers alike, asking them to sign in support of his fight for full civil rights. His efforts were finally rewarded in 1865, when the notorious "Black Laws" were repealed. Jones built up a large following during his business career and crusading. He was encouraged to enter politics where he made a remarkable showing. He became the first Negro on the Board of County Commissioners when he was elected for a short term in 1871, and was reelected in 1872 for three years. He later became a powerful man in Chicago politics and used his influence to wipe out the practice of segregation in Chicago public schools. He was the first Negro appointed to the Chicago Board of Education.

Although Jones spent much of his time in politics and business, before the Civil War he set up his palatial home

as a station of the Underground Railroad. Many a night, fugitive slaves, in fear and trembling, knocked at his door and were received with open arms and aided toward their destination.

Jones was so admired among Chicagoans that, when he celebrated his thirtieth year as a resident in 1875, most of the leading social and business personalities of both races were present. It was reported at that time that he had amassed an estate worth $100,000 before the destructive Chicago Fire of 1871; when he died on May 21, 1879 he left an estate of $60,000.

Edward T. Clayton, "Four Chicago Pioneers," *Negro Digest*, Vol. 8 (September 1950), p. 91; Bessie L. Pierce, "A History of Chicago," Vol. 3 (New York, 1957), p. 48; I. C. Harris, *The Colored Man's Business Directory of Chicago* (Chicago, I. C. Harris, 1885-1886).

Isaac Myers (1835-1891)

BUSINESSMAN, LABOR ORGANIZER

A businessman and labor organizer, Isaac Myers was one of the outstanding personalities of the Reconstruction period. He founded a shipyard and was the spark plug of the first important movement to organize black workers in America. His shipyard at one point employed over three hundred Negroes. During his lifetime, Isaac Myers had the same relation to black labor as A. Phillip Randolph in modern times.

Isaac Myers was born of free parents in Baltimore, Maryland. He was privately tutored by one Rev. John Foster until he reached his sixteenth birthday, then he became an apprentice ship caulker. In the days when the hulls of ships were constructed of wood, the occupation of caulker was very important, having the responsibility of applying pitch and gum to openings and crevices between the planks and beams of the hull to prevent leakage. Myers learned this trade so well that within four years he was a supervisor in one of the largest shipyards in the bustling harbor of Baltimore.

Blacks had been engaged as caulkers and mechanics on ships for decades. In the late 1830's, Frederick Douglass had worked at the caulker's trade. After the Civil War, however, a movement developed to remove blacks from the shipbuilding industry. This movement was especially vigorous around Baltimore. Isaac Myers took steps to deflate this effort by raising ten thousand dollars from among the Negroes of Maryland and setting up a black-owned and controlled shipyard. He raised the necessary beginning

capital, recruited workmen, and set up an all-black uni[on] called the Baltimore Caulker Trade Society to which on[ly] highly competent workmen were eligible for membershi[p].

Isaac Myers and the men he supervised had an ou[t] standing reputation for excellence of workmanship. Th[is] reputation stood the new shipyard in good stead, for se[v] eral white ship owners switched their business to Meyer[s'] firm. Even the United States government awarded t[he] new yard several ship caulking and building contrac[ts] and within five years Myers was able to liquidate t[he] $40,000 mortgage on his company.

The white labor movement was in its formative stag[e] at this time and Myers desired to organize the masses [of] black workers throughout the country. In 1869 an all-whi[te] group called the National Labor Union, composed of [a] number of local federations, was organized. Myers a[t] tended their convention as an observer and pleaded t[he] cause of unity among all laborers. He was requested [to] investigate the prospects of setting up a national netwo[rk] composed of scattered black unions of Philadelphia, Ne[w] York, Baltimore, and Richmond, Virginia.

In December, 1869, Isaac Myers spearheaded the o[r] ganization of a black National Labor Union. His reput[a] tion was such that he had little trouble persuading 1[30] delegates to gather in Washington, D.C. for its init[ial] meeting. The black National Labor Union lasted for ab[out] three years, succumbing to the opportunism of certa[in] black politicians, but Myers continued to be active in h[is] own local, preaching the doctrine of collective action f[or] better working conditions and more pay for black labore[rs]. He was prominent in Republican politics until his death [in] 1891.

Charles H. Wesley, *Negro Labor in the United States, 1850-1925* (New Yo[rk] 1927), p. 159; John R. Commons et al. (eds.), *Documentary History of Am[er] ican Industrial Society*, IX (New York, 1958 edition), pp. 139-140; Sterl[ing] D. Spero and Abram Harris, *The Black Worker: The Negro and the La[bor] Movement* (New York, 1939), p. 29.

John Merrick (1859-1921)

INSURANCE PIONEER

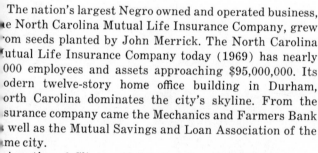

The first office building of the company on Parrish St. (1906)

The nation's largest Negro owned and operated business, the North Carolina Mutual Life Insurance Company, grew from seeds planted by John Merrick. The North Carolina Mutual Life Insurance Company today (1969) has nearly 000 employees and assets approaching $95,000,000. Its modern twelve-story home office building in Durham, North Carolina dominates the city's skyline. From the insurance company came the Mechanics and Farmers Bank as well as the Mutual Savings and Loan Association of the same city.

A native of Clinton, North Carolina, John Merrick was born in 1859. There is no record of his ever having attended school. He began his adult life as a brick layer. Later he was a barber, building and operating five barber shops in Raleigh, North Carolina. Merrick's shops were profitable, catering to a prosperous clientele. In 1899, John Merrick joined six other Negroes in organizing an insurance company out of the faltering remains of a mutual aid society known as the Royal Knights of David. The new company set up shop in a spare room with four chairs in the office of one of its founders, Dr. A. M. Moore of Durham, North Carolina.

John Merrick was elected president, a position he held until 1919. The first year of operation for the company was so discouraging that five of the seven founders withdrew from the company, leaving only Merrick and Moore. These two men hired a rather quiet, but persuasive and aggressive young man bearing the name C. C. Spaulding as the company's salesman, bookkeeper, advertising man and janitor. Spaulding had to depend upon cash received from the sale of policies for his travel expenses. The three men had also to face the ridicule of Negroes who doubted that black men could operate an insurance company. Spaulding, in particular, had to endure the amused smiles of prospective customers who had never heard of a Negro insurance company or salesman.

Backed by Merrick and Moore, Spaulding eventually sold his first policy for sixty-five cents. This "bonanza," however, was soon wiped out by the death of the policy holder to whose estate a forty dollar claim was due. John Merrick and A. M. Moore, together, contributed $39.71 toward paying off the claim. The remaining twenty-nine cents was paid by Spaulding, an expenditure which left him flat broke. The claim was paid and the receipt of payment was used in many subsequent sales talks to convince doubters that the company did indeed, honor its obligations. This episode helped the struggling company to realize about $800 in premiums within a year.

As the insurance company began to earn substantial profits, Merrick skillfully reinvested them. The Mechanics and Farmers Bank grew out of the insurance company, and John Merrick was named its first president in 1907. Under the leadership of John Merrick and others associated with the insurance company, Lincoln Hospital of Durham, North Carolina was organized with Merrick as first president of the board of directors. When John Merrick died in 1921, the North Carolina Mutual Life Insurance Company was well on its way to the position it holds today in the financial world of black America.

The Whetstone, Second Quarter (1966), pp. 1, 23; Richard Bardolph, *The Negro Vanguard* (New York, Vintage edition, 1961), pp. 261, 326-264.

Madame C. J. Walker
(1869-1919)

COSMETICS MANUFACTURER

While America has produced hundreds of millionaires, few ex-washerwomen are numbered among their ranks. One of the first American women of any race or rank to become a millionaire through her own efforts was Sarah Breedlove Walker.

Orphaned in her native Louisiana at six, married to one C. J. Walker at fourteen and widowed at twenty, Madame C. J. Walker invented a new method of straightening hair. Before her time, Negro women who wanted to de-kink their hair had to place it on a flat surface and press it with a flat iron. In 1905 Madame Walker invented her hair softener and a special straightening comb. For millions of women at that time these inventions were a godsend. Overnight she found herself in business, with assistants, agents, schools and, eventually a manufacturing company. Before her death in 1919, Madame Walker could count over 2,000 agents selling an ever-expanding line of Walker products and demonstrating the "Walker System" of treating hair.

A former laundress, Madame Walker proved hersel[f] competent businesswoman. She organized her agents i[n] clubs, trained operatives for her system, allocated fr[an]chises and provided the cosmetics and equipment [re]quired. Her payroll was over $200,000 annually. S[he] donated large sums to charity and to educational insti[tu]tions. She even founded an academy for girls in W[est] Africa and bequeathed $100,000 to it.

Madame Walker constantly made headlines, both w[ith] her business and her social activities. In New York [at] Irvington-on-the-Hudson, she built Villa Lewaro, [a] $250,000 mansion. She furnished it with a gold-pla[ted] piano, a $60,000 pipe organ, Hepplewhite furnitu[re] Persian rugs and many huge oil paintings. A "who's wh[o]" of Negro America entered her doors. Through it [all] Madame Walker remained a pleasant, kindly pers[on] genuinely interested in those less fortunate than hers[elf].

Madame Walker's ingenuity and ability laid the foun[da]tion of the cosmetics industry among Negroes and spur[red] the interest in personal beautification among colo[red] women.

Dictionary of American Biography, XIX, 1936; Roi Ottley. *New W[orld] A-Coming*, New York, 1943, pp. 172-173.

Maggie L. Walker
(1867-1934)

BANKER, ORGANIZER

"If the state of Virginia had done no more in fifty years with the funds spent on the education of Negroes than to educate Mrs. Walker, the state would have been amply repaid for its outlay and effort." Thus spoke the governor of Virginia in 1924 when the city of Richmond was paying tribute to the foresight and genius of Maggie L. Walker.

Mrs. Walker was being honored at the time for her contribution to Richmond's economic and civic progress. Her contributions could be seen in the huge structure which housed the St. Luke Bank and Trust Company, the national headquarters of the Independent Order of St. Luke, and an insurance concern, all of which she headed. Newspaper readers could follow the course of her progress in the *St. Luke Herald,* another of her enterprises.

She was the prime mover in the establishment of a home for delinquent Negro girls in Richmond, having organized 1400 women into a council which paid the first $5,000 to purchase the land for the institution. Richmond could also boast of a community center in 1924, mainly because Mrs. Walker spurred an inter-racial group of women to build one.

When Maggie Walker became secretary for the Order of St. Luke in 1889, she accepted a salary of $8.00 a month and continued to teach school for her living. The Order had 3,408 members but no funds of any consequence, no property of value, and virtually no staff. Yet dues-paying members expected coverage for sickness and a decent burial. By 1924 Mrs. Walker had built the Order's membership to over 100,000, increased its headquarters staff to fifty-five full-time employees working in a $100,000 building constructed with funds advanced by the Order. Throughout Virginia and the surrounding states, 145 field workers provided excellent service to the members of the Order of St. Luke.

Maggie Walker, who grew up in dire poverty, was a native of Virginia. She managed to finish high school and became a teacher. Her contemporaries described her as having enough energy for a dozen women. She remained charming and pleasant throughout the hustle and bustle of her business and civic life.

Benjamin Brawley, *Negro Builders and Heroes* (Chapel Hill, North Carolina 1937), pp. 267-272.

Jesse Binga (1865-1950)

BANKER—FINANCIER

Binga before and after the collapse of his financial empire

Cleverly purchasing property on the southern fringe of the black ghetto, Binga's own little real estate business prospered to the extent that he could count over 300 units of real estate and collect rent from nearly 1200 apartments. Following the southern exodus, Binga opened a new real estate office on the southwest corner of Chicago's 36th Place and State Street. He opened the Binga State Bank in 1908 in the same building. The then busy 35th and State Street intersection was his real goal and over the years he was able to buy most of the land in that block. The block, naturally, was called the "Binga Block."

Binga became known as the financial wizard of the South Side. He was a power in the Negro community and had earned the respect of a number of white financiers and bankers. He moved into a white neighborhood over the protests of its residents, determined to enjoy his right to live where he was able.

The Binga financial and real estate empire prospered during the booming twenties. At the height of his success Binga could count deposits of nearly one and a half million dollars. But as the signs of the coming depression caused more and more people to seek loans from his bank, the empire began to totter. Jesse Binga found it hard to say no to impecunious depositors and businessmen. He soon found himself in dire financial difficulties. Unable to meet his many pressing obligations, Binga desperately tried to save his businesses and, in the opinion of some, overstepped the bounds of legality.

The Binga State Bank had to close its doors in May of 1932. In 1933 Jesse Binga went to prison but later received a presidential pardon. Ever the optimist, Binga was nevertheless unsuccessful in his efforts to regain the high status he had enjoyed during the balmy twenties.

Jesse Binga was born the day after General Robert E. Lee surrendered his sword to General Ulysses S. Grant at Appomattox. A native of Detroit, Michigan, Binga received only a high school education and, after a variety of menial jobs, decided that one day he would go into business for himself and become his own boss. He had no idea of ever owning two banks and numerous parcels of real estate.

Coming to Chicago during the World's Fair of 1895, Binga became a huckster selling wares to Negroes in Chicago's burgeoning South Side. Through his peddling he came to know thousands of people, their needs, desires and aspirations. As his own small business grew, he met and married Eudora Johnson, the niece of a wealthy sportsman, known as "Mushmouth" Johnson, who had strong political connections and a private fortune of nearly a quarter of a million dollars. After Johnson's death, Binga's wife inherited his estate which was to be the nucleus of the Binga enterprises.

Inez V. Cantey, "Jesse Binga; the Story of a Life," *Crisis*, XXXIV (December, 1927); Abram L. Harris. *The Negro as Capitalist* (Philadelphia, 1936).

Anthony Overton (1864-1946)

BANKER, MANUFACTURER

Ex-slave, judge, manufacturer, newspaper publisher, and business executive, Anthony Overton was one of the outstanding businessmen of his generation. In a career covering almost sixty years, Anthony Overton left an indelible mark on the history of Negro business. In recognition of his achievements in the business world, Overton was awarded the Harmon Award in 1927 and the Spingarn Medal in 1929 as the individual who contributed most to the progress of the Negro in the preceding year.

A native of Monroe, Louisiana, Overton's career began in Kansas in 1888 when he received the A. B. degree in law from the University of Kansas Law School and was admitted to the bar. In a short time, he was appointed to the municipal bench in Topeka. The call of the business world was stronger than that of the law and, after a period in Oklahoma as a merchant, Overton returned to Kansas and founded the Overton-Hygienic Products Company, manufacturing and selling baking powder, flavor extracts and toiletries.

In 1911 Overton moved his business operations to Chicago, and within nine years Overton-Hygienic Products Company was in the million-dollar class. In 1922 Overton ventured into the field of banking and assisted Pearl W. Chavers in his successful efforts to set up the Douglass National Bank, which was housed in the Overton Building at 36th and State Street. The Douglass National Bank operated for ten years, and, when it closed its doors in 1932, its depositors received thirty-eight cents on the dollar, the highest amount paid by any bank involuntarily closing its doors at that time. Anthony Overton next launched the Victory Mutual Life Insurance Company, which for a time was operated by his son, Anthony Overton III. Following the success of the Victory Mutual Life Insurance Company, Overton turned to journalism and became the publisher of the *Chicago Bee*, a weekly news-paper which quickly gained a large readership on Chicago's South Side.

Anthony Overton was an energetic and frugal man who did not display the customary signs of success; instead he believed in returning profits to the enterprise that created them. He had little truck with abstraction, but felt that one should "make each day count for more than the previous day." His own career was a perfect illustration of this motto.

Richard Bardolph, *The Negro Vanguard* (New York, 1961), pp. 256, 261; Abram Harris, *The Negro as Capitalist* (Philadelphia, 1936).

Robert S. Abbott (1870-1940)
THE LONELY WARRIOR

Chicago Defender
WORLD'S GREATEST WEEKLY

DEFENDER PLATFORM May 5, 1905

"American race prejudice must be destroyed"
The opening up of all trade Unions to black
Representation in the President's Cabinet
Engineers, firemen and conductors on all rail
roads, and all jobs in government
Representation in all
Government schools ope
preference to foreigners
Motormen and conductors on surface and
motorbus lines throughout America
Federal legislation to abolish lynching
Full enfranchisement of all

CHICAGO
Daily Defender

The road to real success is usually a long and hard one. Without moral support and encouragement it can also be heart-breakingly lonely. Behind the *Chicago Defender*, the only Negro daily newspaper in Chicago, with its magnificent offices at 2400 South Michigan Avenue, stands a man who trod this lonely road, Robert Sengstacke Abbott.

Without bitterness, he recalled his long battle to establish his newspaper: "My friends made fun of me . . . they thought it was foolish of me to anticipate success in a field in which so many men before me had failed . . . but I went on fighting the opposition of my adversaries and the indifference of my friends; I emerged victorious but battle-scarred."

Abbott's dream of setting up a newspaper started in his youth. A native of St. Simon Island, Georgia, Robert was enrolled at Beach Institute in Savannah and later entered Claflin University in Orangeburg, South Carolina. It was at Virginia's Hampton Institute where, on the advice of his stepfather, John J. J. Sengstacke, he learned the printing trade that was to be his career some twelve years later. In the interim, Abbott migrated to Chicago in 1896, where he attended Kent Law School and supported himself by working in a Loop printing house. Obtaining his law degree in 1899, he wandered about the Midwest for several years before he became convinced that he could do a better job of defending his people in public print than he could in a courtroom.

He returned to Chicago and his work as itinerant job printer and set foot on the lonely road. Combining a small amount of capital with borrowed money, and equipping his landlady's dining room with a folding card-table and kitchen chair as his office, he started the *Chicago Defender* on May 5, 1905. Three hundred copies of the 4-page, handbill-size sheets were printed on his employer's press. Abbott himself sold them for two cents a copy, going from door to door, visiting every South Side barber shop, poolroom, drugstore and church.

For fifteen years the lonely warrior contended for social justice and political and economic equity. The strong editorial policy of the *Defender* pushed the newspaper's national circulation to more than a quarter million copies. The *Defender* became a thriving institution.

John H. Sengstacke, nephew of Robert S. Abbott, inherited the *Defender* upon the death of his uncle. Sengstacke, a graduate of Hampton Institute, brought to the newspaper a new perspective on the specialized type of journalism it represented, and built steadily on the foundation he inherited.

Sengstacke was not satisfied with the prospects of the weekly paper and made plans for daily publication. On February 6, 1956 the first copy of the *Daily Defender* made its appearance, and, although skeptics said it could not be done, it has prospered and grown. Abbott would be proud of the *Defender* today and even prouder of the modern plant which houses it.

Roi Ottley, *The Lonely Warrior; the Life and Times of Robert S. Abbott* (Chicago, 1955).

Robert L. Vann (1887-1940)

PITTSBURGH COURIER FOUNDER

Robert L. Vann, as a boy, lived so far "on the other side of the tracks" that he was ten years old before he saw his first train. His parents were tenant farmers trying to eke out a living in the backwoods of North Carolina. He had no idea that one day his name would appear from coast to coast each week in a nationally distributed newspaper or that he would be the owner and publisher of that newspaper, the *Pittsburgh Courier*.

The *Pittsburgh Courier*, like Robert L. Vann himself, sprang from a rather modest beginning. A worker in a Pittsburgh pickle factory had started a two-page sheet as a vehicle for printing his occasional verse. Vann, by this time a struggling young lawyer, saw how eagerly Negroes read the nondescript sheet and decided to convert it into a newspaper. Gathering associates and capital, Vann published the first edition of the *Pittsburgh Courier* on March 10, 1910. At first he thought he had erred in launching a newspaper, for as a struggling young lawyer just out of the University of Pittsburgh Law School, he had precious little time to spend on profitless ventures.

The *Pittsburgh Courier* caught on and Negroes came to swear by it. Staunchly Republican in those days, the newspaper spoke for the Negro community in Pittsburgh and was brutally candid in reporting the news. Over the years the *Pittsburgh Courier* grew. Hundreds of people soon found employment at the *Courier* plant. Across the country, hundreds of vendors sold the sprightly publication, and many reporters were hired in various states. A number of well known Negro authors wrote for it, and in many homes, it was the only paper read with interest. In 1940 the *Courier* was the most widely-read Negro newspaper in America, with branches in the leading metropolitan cities.

While the paper grew, Robert L. Vann's legal career also developed. In 1917 he was made city solicitor for Pittsburgh and remained in this post for four years. In 1924, he was alternate delegate-at-large from Pennsylvania to the National Republican Convention. He also served as a Republican publicity director of the campaign which saw Calvin Coolidge enter the White House. In 1935, Robert L. Vann was appointed to a committee to revise the constitution of the State of Pennsylvania. Switching from the Republican to the Democratic party at the end of the depression, he was appointed Assistant United States Attorney General by Franklin D. Roosevelt.

Robert L. Vann died in 1940, at the beginning of World War II. However, his newspaper lives on as a tribute to his energy and enterprise.

Richard Bardolph, *The Negro Vanguard* (New York, 1961, Paperback), pp. 192-196.

Frank L. Gillespie (1867-1925)

FOUNDER OF THE
SUPREME LIFE INSURANCE COMPANY

of Illinois. Then he joined a future congressman, Oscar DePriest, in the real estate business in 1914. When this did not prove to be very rewarding, Gillespie found a job with a small white-owned company, the Royal Life Insurance company in 1916. In less than eight months he was named superintendent of the company which prospered handsomely under the management of Gillespie who now felt that he had found his true vocation.

Word of his abilities spread throughout the white Chicago business world, and in 1917 a group of white business men invited him to help organize and manage a new insurance company named the Public Life Insurance Company. Gillespie remained with this company for two years but yearned for an opportunity to set up a Negro-owned insurance company which would serve the black community of Chicago.

In 1919, with the support of a few optimistic black businessmen, Gillespie set about raising the sum of $100,000 the amount of capitalization required by Illinois law. The new company, which called itself the Liberty Life Insurance Company, issued 10,000 shares of stock. In less than sixteen months, $300,000 had been raised. In June 1921 the company began writing policies. By December of the same year, they had a total of $254,000 of insurance in force. At the time of Gillespie's death, on May 1, 1925 the Liberty Life Insurance company had over $5,000,000 of insurance on its books.

Over the succeeding years, the Liberty Life Insurance company expanded, absorbing a number of smaller companies. The present name of the company, Supreme Life Insurance Company of America, was adopted in 1961 when its assets stood at $31,000,000 and the amount of insurance in force amounted to $200,000,000. Other outstanding legal and business notables such as Truman K. Gibson and Earl B. Dickerson contributed mightily to the enterprise that was guided through its first critical years by Frank L. Gillespie.

Frank L. Gillespie founded the black owned and operated institution known as the Supreme Life Insurance Company of America, an institution often referred to as the largest Afro-American business in the North. He was born in Osceola, Arkansas on November 8, 1876, but grew up in Memphis, Tennessee and St. Louis, Missouri. After completing three years of high school work at Sumner High School of St. Louis, Gillespie went to Boston and entered the Boston Conservatory of Music. His intention was to develop his unusual talent as a violinist, and he completed his secondary education while attending the conservatory. Then he entered Harvard Law school with the hopes of pursuing a legal career. Family reverses completely halted his education and he had to leave Harvard.

Adrift in the world and faced with the need to earn a living, young Gillespie headed for Chicago. There by chance, he met a prominent white businessman, Edward Stutte, who hired him as a private secretary. This employment turned Gillespie's interest toward the world of business and finance. After a few years of comfortable employment, Gillespie suddenly found himself again without a job due to the death of Edward Stutte.

Following a series of nondescript jobs, Gillespie became the first Negro hired by the Automatic Telephone Company

Liberty Life Insurance Company of Illinois, *Book of Achievement* (Chicago, n.d.), pp. 3-6; Gillespie Memorial Committee, *In Memoriam* (Chicago, n.d.) pp. 1-4; Richard Bardolph, *The Negro Vanguard* (New York, Vintage Edition, 1961), pp. 261, 264-65.

C. C. Spaulding (1874-1952)

BUILDER OF THE NORTH CAROLINA MUTUAL LIFE INSURANCE COMPANY

John Merrick and A. M. Moore were the men who actually founded the huge North Carolina Mutual Life Insurance Company when, in 1898, they converted a burial aid association into a mutual life insurance company. But Charles Clinton Spaulding built the company into what it is today, an enterprise with more than $3 million worth of insurance in force.

The company was so small when Spaulding joined Merrick and Moore that it was almost left bankrupt by a forty-dollar claim. Spaulding, a quiet, earnest young man, was the company's only employee and served as bookkeeper, salesman, advertising director and custodian. For many years Spaulding travelled the highways and byways of North Carolina, developing business for his struggling company and patient partners.

A pioneer in saturation advertising, Spaulding made sure that barbershops, lodges, stores, and offices had their share of matchbooks, fans, calendars, pens, and paper weights. The Negro press carried advertisements of North Carolina Mutual in almost every edition. School teachers were enlisted as agents for the company, thus creating an image of confidence and respectability. Under Spaulding the company grew from ten to twenty and, finally hundreds of agents scouring the east coast to bring a measure of security to thousands of Negroes.

In 1923 C. C. Spaulding was made president of North Carolina Mutual and remained in this office until the day of his death. The habits of hard work, dependability, and thrift which Spaulding had shown in his youth were infused into the growing company. Spaulding became a national figure and his advice and counsel were sought by hundreds of citizens, public and private. Spaulding gave unstintingly of his time and energy to numerous causes.

Born in comparative poverty and one of fourteen children, Spaulding rose to national prominence. Schools, parks, and playgrounds are named after him. His story is another of the authentic success stories of our history.

The Whetstone "In Memoriam," 3rd Quarter, 1952; Richard Bardolph, *The Negro Vanguard*, New York, 1961 (Paperback), pp. 260-264.

1963 home office in Durham, N.C.

Claude A. Barnett (1889-1967)

FOUNDER OF THE ASSOCIATED NEGRO PRESS

brutalities visited upon blacks in different parts of the country were accused of having an anti-American bias. In setting up the Associated Negro Press, Barnett formed a national news-gathering body of competent reporters to present a national picture of black America each week. For years, the Associated Negro Press was the only black organization devoted mainly to collecting and disseminating news from the four corners of the world. In its prime years, this brainchild of Claude A. Barnett, had member newspapers in the U.S., Caribbean and Africa.

Claude A. Barnett was born in Sanford, Florida on September 16, 1889. He was educated in Mattoon, Oak Park and Chicago, Illinois and was a graduate of Tuskegee Institute (Alabama) in 1906. After a number of odd jobs, Barnett attempted to make a living selling photoprints of outstanding Negroes before organizing the ANP.

The interests of Claude A. Barnett were reflected in his membership on the Board of Directors of the Liberia Company, the Supreme Life Insurance Company, Provident Hospital (Chicago) and the Phelps-Stokes Fund. He successfully fought for the assignment of black reporters to the fighting fronts in World War II. From 1944 to 1952, he was Special Assistant to the Secretary of Agriculture. As his news service expanded, he developed a deep interest in things African. Barnett was a member of the Board of Directors of the Booker Washington Institute in Kakata, Liberia (1944-1945). In 1951, he was inducted into the Chevalier Order of Honor of Merit in Haiti; in 1952, he was named a Commander in the Order of Star of Liberia. He and his wife, the famed singer and actress Etta Moten, made many trips abroad. They turned their home in Chicago into a miniature repository of African life and culture. This pioneer in black journalism died in Chicago on August 2, 1967.

From the days when John B. Russwurm edited *Freedom's Journal* (1827), the central aim of the black press has been to "tell it like it is." However, few newspapers had the funds to send correspondents beyond the limits of the localities where the papers were published. When Claude Albert Barnett founded the Associated Negro Press in Chicago, Illinois in 1919, the smallest black newspaper was given a newsline to the world.

The Associated Negro Press (ANP) followed the format of the Associated Press and the Scripps-Howard News Service. Barnett and his correspondents in different parts of the country, gathered news of interest to blacks and made it available to client newspapers at rates determined by the size of their circulation. This innovation in the handling of Afro-American news was immediately reflected in the columns of subscribing newspapers. Negro newspapers reporting events such as the race riots of St. Louis (1917) and Chicago (1919), as well as the routine

Who Was Who in America, IV, 1961-1968 (Chicago, Illinois, 1969; Richard A. Bardolph, *The Negro Vanguard* (New York, Vintage Edition, 1961), pp. 192, 194, 195; *Jet* (August 17, 1967).

A. G. Gaston (1892-   )

MILLIONAIRE, FREE ENTERPRISER

Growing with Birmingham!

HOME OFFICES OF...
B.T.W. BUSINESS COLLEGE · VULCAN REALTY & INVESTMENT CO.
B.T.W. INSURANCE CO. · CITIZENS FEDERAL SAVINGS & LOAN ASSN.
A.G. GASTON, President

The eminence of Arthur G. Gaston does not rest on the fact of his wealth alone, even though he is one of the few Negro millionaires in the U. S. today. Credit is due him for the way he made his money rather than its amount. Gaston is a self-made millionaire in an age when individual enterprise is a rarity. He made his millions in business ventures—slowly and legitimately. He has invested and re-invested in business projects which directly help meet the needs of his race.

His philosophy, both business and personal, that "success is founded on seeing and satisfying the needs of people" has proven to be a rewarding one in his business and an enriching one in his life. Today he is president and owner of seven different companies and corporations in Birmingham, Alabama, including an insurance company, a chain of fourteen funeral homes, a business college, a realty and investment corporation, a string of motels, a housing development, a large farm, a savings and loan association, and a cemetery. His business interests alone have assets totaling more than $20 million.

But there was a time when Arthur G. Gaston worked for about $3 a day. Like most Negroes of that day, Gaston's parents were poor when he was born in Demopolis, Alabama in 1892. His father died while Arthur was a boy and when his mother had to work in Birmingham as a domestic, he stayed with his grandmother. Here there was a yard with a swing which was a favorite playing place for the children in the neighborhood. Gaston's business acumen manifested itself at this early age when he started charging admission to the yard, of buttons and pins.

After he finished eighth grade (Tuggles Institute, Birmingham) and a stint in the Army, he settled in Westfield, Alabama and went to work for the Tennessee Coal Iron and Steel Company for $3.10 a day. To supplement this meager income he sold peanuts and loaned money to his less thrifty co-workers at the rate of 25 cents on the dollar. In 1921 he saw the need for a burial society and,

with his father-in-law as partner and $35, he started the Booker T. Washington Burial Society which grew into the incorporated insurance company. The need for Negro housing led to the founding of the Citizens Federal Savings and Loan Association in 1923. In order to get the typists and clerks necessary for these businesses, he started the Booker T. Washington Business College, which today is fully accredited and supplying graduates for positions in business and government throughout the country.

His awareness of the needs of people, particularly the needs of his own people, spurred the organization of the 11,000 member Smith and Gaston Kiddie Club in 1945 and the sponsoring of the Gaston Statewide Spelling Bee for Negro students. This is no mere indulgence in the philanthropic tradition of millionaires or the tax-write-off operation of a shrewd businessman. It is an action motivated by a belief in his people. He says, "If I ever had a conviction that the Negro wasn't capable, I would sell out. But I'm convinced, and I want to convince others."

Ebony Magazine (Jan., 1963).

93

John H. Johnson (1918-   )

PUBLISHER WITHOUT A PEER

at DuSable High and soon became editor of the schoo
newspaper and later president of the student body. He
continued his education at Northwestern University and
the University of Chicago while employed in the public
relations department of the Supreme Life Insurance Com
pany, where he was later to become chairman of the board

Encouraged by Harry H. Pace and Earl B. Dickerson
president of the insurance company, Johnson launched
Negro Digest in 1942 with five hundred dollars borrowed
using his mother's furniture as collateral. The 5,000 copies
of the first printing sold out within a week. By the end
of 1943, Negro Digest had a monthly circulation of 50,000
copies. Ebony magazine was started in November 1945
with a first printing of 25,000 copies. As of August 1968
Ebony had a guaranteed circulation slightly in excess of
1,000,000 copies monthly. In November 1951, John H
Johnson began the publication of Jet, a pocket-size weekly
news round-up. By 1968 this publication had a circulation
of 450,000 copies weekly. Tan, a woman's magazine, appeared a year earlier than Jet and in 1968 had a circulation approaching a quarter-million copies per month.

In 1963 John H. Johnson entered the field of hardcover
books with the publication of Before the Mayflower, by
Lerone Bennett, Jr., the senior editor of Ebony. Mr.
Bennett has since published several other works under
the Johnson Publishing Company sponsorship. The late
Freda DeKnight popularized features such as "Date with
a Dish" and the Ebony Fashion Shows, the latter being
continued under the direction of Mrs. Eunice Johnson,
wife of the publisher.

John H. Johnson is laden with honors. In 1951 he became
the first black to be recognized by the U.S. Junior Chamber
of Commerce as one of the ten outstanding young men of
the year. In 1957 he was among the members of the press
team which accompanied Vice-President Nixon on a tour
of nine African countries. In 1961 the late President John
F. Kennedy named him special ambassador to the Independence Ceremonies of the Ivory Coast. In December
1963, President Lyndon B. Johnson appointed him to a
similar post and mission to Kenya. In 1966 John H.
Johnson was named winner of the Horatio Alger Award
and the John B. Russwurm Award.

John H. Johnson has been the most successful black
publisher since Samuel E. Cornish and John B. Russwurm
started Freedom's Journal, the first Negro newspaper, in
1827. His publications—Ebony, Jet, Tan, and Negro Digest
—have a combined circulation of nearly two million. Several
hundred employees collect data, write and edit articles, and
distribute hundreds of thousands of Johnson Publishing
Company magazines each month. John H. Johnson, the
company's founder, president, and publisher, is known
throughout America.

A native of Arkansas City, Arkansas, Johnson was
brought to Chicago in 1937 by his mother. Her occasional
jobs as a domestic were insufficient to keep them off the
public assistance rolls. Johnson plunged into his schoolwork

Who's Who in Colored America, 1950, pp. 305-306; Chicago Defender (January 6, 1962), p. A-15; Chicago Sun-Times (May 19, 1963), p. 60.

Paul R. Williams (1896-   )

ARCHITECT OF FAME AND FORTUNE

Paul Revere Williams is generally acknowledged to be one of the leading architects in America. A native of Los Angeles, Paul Williams was attending the Polytechnic High School when he first expressed a desire to become an architect. His teachers thought they were being kind when they advised him to aspire to something else, as "Negroes had no future in architecture." Determined to pursue his dream, he continued to prepare himself for his career. He studied at the Beaux Arts Institute of Design, the Los Angeles School of Art and Design, and earned a degree from the University of Southern California. In 1915, Williams was certified as an architect.

Upon completing his work at the University of Southern California, Williams made a systematic canvass of all practicing architects in Los Angeles, but was only able to find a job with a landscape architect at seven dollars a week. It was this experience, however, that provided the background for one of the hallmarks of his buildings: the perfect blending of structure and surroundings. He finally managed to find work as an architect with Reginald D. Johnson, an excellent designer of private residences. This contact landed him a job as chief designer with John C. Austin, an architect specializing in commercial buildings.

In 1923, Paul Williams opened his own office. His teachers were only partly correct in warning him of the difficulties facing an Afro-American whose specialty was architecture. Many white builders hesitated before entrusting expensive plans to an independent black. Often builders who came to Williams' office did not know that he was not white, and sometimes, upon learning of his racial background, they would attempt to withdraw their offers. In order to keep this to a minimum, Williams would use all sorts of devices to keep the interest of potential clients on their projects and away from himself. He taught himself to draw upside down so that they could see his designs take form before their very eyes. He learned to produce full preliminary plans in twenty-four hours, rather than the usual week or so. Thus, the client would have less time to speculate upon his ancestry. Such speed also became known to other builders who then sought out Williams for the one commodity he had for sale . . . efficient, competence as an architect.

Among the more notable structures designed by Williams are the Music Corporation of America Building in New York; the Federal Customs and Office Building in Los Angeles; Franz Hall and the Botany Building on the University of California campus at Los Angeles; the W. J. Sloan and Haggerty buildings in Beverly Hills, California; several of the public school buildings of Los Angeles city and county; and a score of private homes, ranging as high as $100,000 in cost.

Paul R. Williams has been a vice-president and director of the Broadway Federal Savings and Loan Association (Los Angeles), president of the Los Angeles Art Commission, a member of the President's Committee on Housing, a member of the California Redevelopment Commission and the California Housing Commission. In 1963, Paul R. Williams received the Spingarn Medal, the highest award of the N.A.A.C.P., for his contributions to the quality of American life.

Who's Who in America (1964-65), p. 2174; Richard Bardolph, *The Negro Vanguard* (New York; Vintage Edition, 1961), pp. 258-259.

VI RELIGION

A Balm in Gilead

When Negroes were first brought to America no effort was made to convert them to Christianity, as the slave owners felt that a baptized Christian could not be held in bondage. But around 1700 the general attitude of whites changed. The new view was that holding a Christian in slavery was not incompatible with the tenets of Christianity. From this point forward, slaveowners encouraged the adoption and promotion of religion among slaves with the hope that they would be easier to control, particularly if they learned patience and humility. There was also the notion that perhaps the slaves did have souls to save.

Negroes, slave and free, were allowed to attend white churches in the North and South, provided they were kept separated from the congregation. In the Deep South slaves were allowed to start plantation churches of their own. Quite often it had to be with the specific consent of the whites or under their general supervision. While the basic content of the ministers' sermons was taken from the Bible, little effort was made to control their ideas and utterances as long as they were confined to a discussion of the Hereafter.

In the time of the American Revolution, Negro churches existed. Usually they were quite small and their ministers totally untrained. There are historical accounts of Baptist churches being organized in Aiken, South Carolina in the 1780's. George Liele, baptized in 1775, preached in Georgia while the Revolution was in progress. Thomas Paul and M. C. Clayton organized churches in the North during the early nineteenth century.

The Negro church as an institution did not develop until Richard Allen united a scattered group of Methodist churches to organize the African Methodist Episcopal Church in 1816. Shortly after this, Allen's associate Absalom Jones, organized the first Episcopal Church among Negroes, and James Varick laid the foundation of the African Methodist Episcopal Zion Church. John Chavis, at a somewhat later period, developed into a prime mover in bringing the Presbyterian Church to the attention of Negroes. Daniel Coker and Lott Cary were pioneer Negro missionaries to Africa.

For the most part these ministers were without formal training in religion and theology. They were natural leaders and, with due allowance for their being "called" to the ministry, the Negro church at that time was the one relatively open path to leadership. John Chavis, for example, illustrates the possibilities confronting a talented Negro during the early nineteenth century. Born in Charleston South Carolina, Chavis was a brilliant unmixed black who was sent to Princeton University by kindly whites. In 1805 Chavis returned to his native Charleston a Presbyterian minister who preached to both Negro and white congregations within the state. He even organized a preparatory school for white pupils. Among his "prep" students were a future U.S. senator, a governor lawyers, doctors, and ministers. The Nat Turner insurrection in 1831 made it impossible for him to continue his ministry and his school.

These pioneer ministers were most active in the agitation for freedom in this world, although they couched their words in the accents of angels. Most of them were self-supporting as their congregations were too poor to support them. They worked with the various abolitionist societies, took part in the underground railroad movement, and were active workers in the so-called Convention movement. In general, they were the spokesmen for the free Negroes in the North.

During the 1840's and thereafter, Negro leadership continued to emanate from the pulpit. Men such as Alexander Crummell, Henry Highland Garnet, Daniel Payne, Henry McNeal Turner, J. W. C. Pennington, and Benjamin Tucker Tanner came to the forefront of religious endeavor and race protest. The turn of the century found ministers still the major spokesmen and leaders despite the rise of worldly men such as Booker T. Washington, William Monroe Trotter, T. Thomas Fortune, and W. E. B. DuBois, or Kelly Miller and Eugene Kinckle Jones.

While the influence of ministers declined in the twentieth century, many of them continued to remain national figures within and without the church. Among them are William Holmes Borders, Mark Miles Fisher, Howard Thurman, J. H. Jackson, Adam Clayton Powell, Jr., James H. Robinson, and Benjamin E. Mays. It is perhaps interesting to note that the more prominent ministers are known in more than one field, as in the cases of Adam Clayton Powell, Jr., who was also a U. S. Congressman, and James H. Robinson, head of Operation Crossroads Africa.

As the 1960's drew to a close, black ministers continued to be rather prominent in the fight for a better America. In the SCLC, the late Dr. Martin Luther King, Jr. was succeeded by the Rev. Ralph D. Abernathy, ably assisted by Hosea Williams and Andrew Young. The Rev. Jesse Jackson, the national director of Operation Breadbasket, continued to remain visible as a probable prototype of the black minister of the future whose concerns are with the well-being of the body as well as the soul. The Rev. Albert Cleage captured public attention with his conception of the black Christ, one which, he argued, was more relevant to the experience of Christians whose skins are black. Amidst debate over the "death" of God in white religious communities, Negro churches continued to be sources of leadership in the black communities as the decade ended.

Carter G. Woodson, *The History of the Negro Church* (Washington, D.C. 1921), passim; *Ebony*, March 1969, pp. 170-178.

Martin de Porres (1579-1639)

A SAINTED LIFE

Priestly prejudice was not the only handicap surmounted by Brother Martin. He was the illegitimate offspring of Don Juan de Porres of Burgos, a Spanish nobleman, and Ana Velasquez, a young, freed Negro slave. Eight years after Martin's birth on December 9, 1759 in Lima, Peru, his roving father returned and provided for his apprenticeship as a barber-surgeon.

At the age of eleven he took a job as servant in the Dominican priory and performed his chores with such devotion that he was called "the saint of the broom." He was later promoted to the job of the convent's almoner and became so efficient at begging that he was soon collecting an average of $2,000 a week from the rich. This was dispensed as food, clothing and medical care to the sick and the poor. Placed in charge of the Dominicans' infirmary, he became known for his spectacular cures of the sick and his tireless comforting of the afflicted. In recognition of his fame and devotion, his superiors dropped the color bar to his becoming a friar. Martin, at the age of twenty-four, was vested in the full habit and took solemn vows as a Dominican brother.

His admission to brotherhood only increased his humility and desire to help others. He established an orphanage and foundling hospital and even extended his love to animals. He filled the convent with ailing stray cats and dogs which he nursed back to health. He set up a shelter in the garden for the convent mice and supplied them with scraps of food. In self-imposed austerity, he never ate meat, but fasted completely from Holy Thursday until Easter noon. Inspired by St. Dominic, he lashed himself three times nightly with a whip armed with iron hooks on the ends.

Brother Martin was venerated almost from the day of his death. In 1657 Fray Salvedor started the beatification investigation; he was beatified by Pope Gregory XVI in 1837. In 1926 Pope Pius XI opened the investigation required for sainthood after devotion to Brother Martin had spread world-wide from Peru.

Although miraculous cures—including raising the dead—had been attributed to Martin, these were not sufficiently authenticated for his canonization. The first of the two required "certified miracles" reported was the case of a girl in Paraguay who, in 1948, recovered from an "incurable" intestinal ailment. The second was reported in 1959 from Canary Islands where a boy "instantly recovered" from a gangrene-infested foot after prayers to the saint-to-be.

The official Vatican account of his sanctity notes: ". . . he made it clear that every race and nationality has the same dignity, the same equality, because we are all sons of one heavenly Father and redeemed by Christ the Lord."

In May of 1962, the late Pope John XXIII, in a ceremony at St. Peter's Basilica in Rome, made Martin de Porres the Catholic church's first mulatto saint. In doing this, he amended a centuries-old order of the Dominican's Convent in Lima, Peru, which stipulated that "those who are begotten on the side of either one of their parents of Indian or African blood . . . may not be received to the holy habit or profession of our order."

"Mulatto Saint," *Time* (May 11, 1962), p. 87; *Ebony* (July, 1962), pp. 21-26.

Thomas Paul (1773-1831)

PIONEER BAPTIST ORGANIZER

"His understanding was vigorous [sic], his personal appearance interesting, and his elocution was grateful [sic]." He could spellbind thousands for hours, and when he left them, if they did not have an organized church, they organized one. This was the summation of the life of Thomas Paul, a Baptist minister who began the movement of independent Baptist churches in the United States.

Although there are records of small Baptist congregations among Negroes being organized as early as 1776 in Virginia, the movement toward separate denominations did not really get under way until the first decade of the nineteenth century. Thomas Paul was one of the leaders in this development. Until that time free Negroes had worshipped alongside whites; however, the conservative reaction following the American Revolution and the increased migration of free Negroes to the North made attendance at white churches an uneasy affair.

Shortly after his ordination as a minister in 1805, Thomas Paul organized a congregation of free Negroes in a church on Joy Street in Boston. Word of his oratorical ability and organizing skill spread among free Negroes in Boston and Philadelphia, and Paul became an early Billy Graham, taking the word of God to all who wanted to listen. By 1808, he was so famous that he was invited to speak to white churches in New York where Negroes were growing restless with their position as members of Baptist congregations. When Thomas Paul finished a series of sermons there, whites and Negroes agreed that it was possible for separate Negro congregations to be organized. The First Baptist Church thereupon granted letters of honorable "Dismission" to sixteen of its members, who, under the leadership of Thomas Paul, organized a Baptist congregation which became known as the Abyssinian Baptist Church of New York City.

Brilliant, energetic and tireless, Paul did not end his labors with the organization of churches in the United States. With the aid of the Massachusetts Baptist Society, he spent six months in Haiti teaching and preaching to the Haitians.

Because he could not speak French, Paul was not as successful as he had been in the United States. On his return from Haiti he continued his labors in the North until his death in 1831.

Some church-goers of the early 1800's

Carter G. Woodson, *The History of the Negro Church* (Washington, 1922), pp. 76-77.

Augustus Tolton (1834-1897)

FIRST NEGRO PRIEST IN AMERICA

On Easter Sunday in the year 1886, a black man offered Holy Mass on the High Altar at St. Peter's Basilica in Rome, Italy. As a rule only the Pope himself offers Mass over the tomb of St. Peter in this holy of holies of the Christian world. But this was no regular occasion. Instead, it was the Church's way of honoring the first full-blooded American Negro ever to be ordained for the priesthood. Augustus Tolton, the priest, was from Quincy, Illinois and the road to Rome had not been easy.

The pomp and circumstance of St. Peter's was a stark contrast to the austere life which lay behind and before the twenty-seven year old priest who has been described as having the "vivid and striking likeness of a solid man, true as steel, without a shadow of pretension." Augustus Tolton was born in Ralls County, Missouri but had grown up in Quincy, Illinois where his mother had taken him after escaping from slavery. Before Augustus reached his teens, he was put to work in a tobacco factory where for twelve years he worked from sunrise to sunset.

Being a devout Catholic, Martha Tolton, his mother, saw that he attended mass and confession. His intelligence and piety quickly brought Augustus to the attention of the priests and bishops at St. Boniface's parish. They encouraged him in his studies and, when he was sure of his true vocation, helped to secure his admission to the College of Propaganda (De Propaganda Fide) at Rome in 1880. Brilliantly mastering the language and theological requirements, Augustus Tolton was ordained a priest on Holy Saturday, April 24, 1886.

Returning to Quincy, Illinois in the summer of 1886, the Reverend Father Augustus Tolton was made pastor of St. Joseph's Catholic Church for Negroes. St. Joseph's was an extremely small church and Father Tolton had time to tour the country. The newspapers made much of the fact that he was the first Negro priest in America, but he was more interested in service than in publicity. In 1889, a wealthy individual donated $10,000 for the establishment of St. Monica's Church for Negro Catholics in Chicago in the 2200 block of South Indiana Avenue. The doors of St. Monica opened in 1890, and for seven years Father Tolton went about his clerical duties, giving himself to his parishioners without reservation. The long years of work in his early youth, intense study, and later service took their toll and the good Father Tolton died on July 10, 1897.

William J. Simmons, *Men of Mark* (Cleveland, 1887), p. 444; Albert S. Foley, *God's Men of Color: The Colored Catholic Priests of the United States, 1854-1954;* pp. 32-41.

Richard Allen (1760-1831)

FOUNDER of AFRICAN METHODIST EPISCOPAL CHURCH

The African Methodist Episcopal Church has the distinction of being the oldest and largest institution among Negroes. It was founded in Philadelphia in 1787 by Richard Allen, an extraordinary organizer and minister. In the reaction which followed the end of the Revolutionary War, Negroes were discouraged from worshipping at churches with white congregations. One Sunday in November 1787, Richard Allen and several of his friends rebelled against the increasing restrictions of segregation that were imposed upon their right to worship in St. George's, one of Philadelphia's leading Methodist churches. Richard Allen led an exodus of Negroes from the church and set about organizing a new denomination—the African Methodist Episcopal Church.

In less than two years, Richard Allen and his group had constructed a new church called "Bethel" and Philadelphia's Negroes joined it. In 1816, Richard Allen was a prime mover in calling together sixteen independent Negro Methodist congregations from different states and organizing them into one group. Richard Allen was elected as the first bishop of this new denomination and thus began a career of preaching and organizing which ended only with his death in 1831.

Richard Allen seemed to have a natural gift for organization. During the Revolutionary War, he was a slave who made enough money as a wood cutter and wagoner to buy his and his brother's freedom in 1783. Converted to Christianity while yet a slave, Allen used the first years of his freedom to preach the gospel to Negroes in and around Pennsylvania. He was present at the organizing conference of the general Methodist Church in 1784. On April 12, 1787, Richard Allen and several other Negroes formed the Free African Society whose purpose was the improvement of the social and economic conditions of the free Negroes. Using this society as his foundation, Allen was able to bring together enough people to launch the African Methodist Episcopal Church which has endured to this day.

During the period between 1815 and 1830, Richard Allen was the commonly recognized leader of free blacks in the North. His Bethel Church in Philadelphia was the scene of the first general mass meeting by blacks in 1817 to protest the deportation policies of the newly formed American Colonization Society. The Negro Convention movement was launched in 1830 at Bethel with Richard Allen dominating the proceedings. This movement was the first interstate political movement of blacks in North America and had as its objectives the abolition of slavery in the South and racial discrimination in the North.

Charles H Wesley, *Richard Allen; Apostle of Freedom* (Washington, 1935) ; Rt. Rev. James A. Handy, *Scraps of African Methodist Episcopal History* (A.M.E. Book Concern, Philadelphia, 1902).

Some church-goers of the late 1700's

Daniel Alexander Payne (1811-1893)

A GIANT OF THE A. M. E. CHURCH

If Richard Allen founded the African Methodist Episcopal Church, then Daniel Payne educated it, for it was he who insisted that the A. M. E. ministry have some standards of education. Long before he rose to eminence, Payne dreamed of a college where the "peace of God and the light of learning would shine." A native of Charleston, South Carolina, Daniel Payne secured the semblance of an education. When he was eighteen years old, he opened a school for free Negroes in Charleston. His student body consisted of three children and three adult slaves, each of whom paid fifty cents a month tuition. Payne could not buy books from bookstores as education of Negroes was discouraged in the state; he had to secure them by stealth and cunning. After the publication of Walker's *Appeal* in 1829 and Nat Turner's revolt two years later, the state of South Carolina became alarmed and, in 1835, made it illegal for any person to operate a school for the education of Negroes.

Disappointed but not discouraged, Daniel Payne went to New York and soon made the acquaintance of Alexander Crummell and others interested in the abolition of slavery. With their help he continued his own education at a Lutheran Seminary in Gettysburg, Pennsylvania. He preached for a while in Troy, New York and then opened another school in Pennsylvania.

However, it was not until 1844, two years after he united with the African Methodist Episcopal Church in Philadelphia, that Daniel Payne really found an opportunity to combine his love of learning with religion. In that year, he was appointed chairman of a committee on education by the General A. M. E. Conference to study the best type of training a minister should have for the denomination. His studies made him familiar with the A. M. E. Church throughout the country. In 1852, he was elected a bishop.

Nine years later he was chosen to become the first Negro president of Wilberforce University in Ohio. From 1852 to 1876, Bishop Payne presided over the destiny of Wilberforce and saw many of his charges develop into the capable ministers he thought the church should have. The oldest institution of higher learning founded by Negro Americans, Wilberforce University stands today as a testimony to the pioneering spirit of the African Methodist Episcopal Church.

William J. Simmons, *Men of Mark* (Cleveland, 1887), pp. 1078-1085; Saunders Redding, *The Lonesome Road* (New York, 1958), pp. 26-29; 32-38; Rt. Rev. James A. Handy, *Scraps of African Methodist Episcopal History* (A.M.E. Book Concern, Philadelphia, 1902).

Building of Wilberforce U. burned April 14, 1865

James Augustine Healy
(1830-1900)
FIRST NEGRO CATHOLIC BISHOP

James A. Healy received the best possible training for his post of Bishop. For over a decade he was assistant to Bishop John Fitzpatrick of Boston. Bishop Fitzpatrick appointed him chancellor and "deputized him to handle most of the routine business of the diocese—the Bishop's account books, his official correspondence with other Bishops, with the sixty-one priests of the diocese, with the many seminarians in American and foreign seminaries and with the religious orders of men and women working in the diocese."

Healy had been pastor of St. James Church on Boston's southeast end, amidst the teeming Irish where he performed his office during the various epidemics of typhoid, pneumonia and tuberculosis. The Boston Irish were at first reluctant to accept him but eventually overcame their reservations and "came to recognize him as a true priest all the way to his sacred finger clasp."

A native of Macon, Georgia, James Augustine Healy was sent north to be educated. He attended the Franklin Park Quaker School in Burlington, New York and Holy Cross College, Worcester, Massachusetts. In 1849 he graduated from Holy Cross with highest honors in the first class to complete the course. Friends of his wealthy father enabled him to go abroad to continue his education.

Catholics of Massachusetts, Maine and New Hampshire came to revere Bishop Healy whose career was terminated by his death in 1900.

Albert S. Foley, *God's Men of Color: The Colored Catholic Priests of the United States, 1854-1954*, pp. 32-41.

James Augustine Healy, the mulatto son of a Georgia planter and his household servant, was the first Catholic Bishop of African descent in the United States. For twenty-five years, Bishop Healy presided over the diocese of Maine and New Hampshire. Under him, sixty-eight mission stations, eighteen parochial schools, and fifty church buildings were erected. The number of Catholic communicants more than doubled. The Church recognized Bishop Healy's work by making him Assistant to the Papal Throne, a rank just below that of Cardinal.

Henry Mc Neal Turner
(1833-1915)
MINISTER EXTRAORDINAIRE

The extraordinary talents of Henry McNeal Turner enabled him to become a bishop, politician, orator, philosopher, and one of the most influential American Negroes of his day. The roots of these talents were not ordinary either. His maternal grandfather, David Greer, was the son of an African King who, after being brought to this country as a slave, was freed through a rarely observed British law forbidding the enslavement of royal blood. His paternal grandmother was German; however little is known of her, but his maternal grandmother was well known in his home town as "not so notable for female modesty . . . but physical resources; an athlete which men dreaded meeting in combat."

Henry Turner was born February 1, 1833 in South Carolina, the oldest child of Howard and Sarah Turner. Though born free, he suffered the hardships common to all Negroes of that time; these were aggravated by the absence of his father. As a boy, he worked in the cotton fields and apprenticed as a blacksmith. He had an intense desire for education—which was forbidden by state law. However, with the help of some defiant white benefactors, he had learned half of the old Webster's spelling book by the time he was thirteen. When he was fifteen, he got a menial job in the office of some white lawyers who recognized his intellect and taught him to read. He not only finished the spelling book but studied the lawyers' books on history, theology and law.

He joined the Methodist Episcopal Church South in 1848 at the age of fifteen, and was licensed to preach five years later, in 1853. In 1858, he joined the A.M.E. Church. He was ordained deacon in 1860 and elder in 1862. He became the twelfth Bishop of the A.M.E. Church in 1880 at the general Conference in St. Louis. In 1863 he was appointed by President Lincoln as the first colored chaplain to the colored troops. Ten days after he mustered out in 1865, he was re-commissioned in the regular army by President Johnson and detailed to work with the Freedmen's Bureau in Georgia. In 1867 he was delegated by the National Republican Executive Committee in Washington to organize the Negro in Georgia, and served as a member of that state's constitutional convention. In 1868 he was elected to the Legislature and re-elected in 1870. President Grant made him postmaster of Macon, Georgia in 1869 at a salary of $4,000, and later, customs inspector and government detective.

He was awarded the title of Doctor of Literature by University of Pennsylvania in 1872 and the title of Doctor of Divinity by Wilberforce in 1873. As a politician he wrote a document defining the status of the Republican and Democratic parties which circulated more than four million copies. As a church man, he compiled a hymn book and wrote a catechism for the A. M. E. Church. He also authored the *Methodist Polity* which defined the duties of the church officers. He was a forceful and eloquent orator, and many of his speeches and lectures were printed or noted by *Harpers Weekly* and other magazines.

Rt. Rev. James A. Handy, *Scraps of African Methodist Episcopal History* (A.M.E. Book Concern, Philadelphia, 1902); William J. Simmons, *Men of Mark* (Cleveland, George M. Rewell Co., 1887), pp. 805-819.

John Jasper (1812-1901)

OUTSTANDING SLAVERY-EMANCIPATION PREACHER

The last of his mother's twenty-four children, John Jasper spent his life at the center of crowds and controversy. Inspired to preach while a slave, John Jasper attracted wide attention as a Baptist minister during the 1880's with his flaming oratory, dramatic sermons, and original views. Theologians, scholars, and laymen debated Jasper's ideas of the universe.

A spell-binder in the days of free-wheeling oratory, John Jasper preached to throngs of entranced listeners. His most famous sermon was "The Sun Do Move." In it he argued that the earth is the center of the solar system and that the sun and other heavenly bodies revolve around it. Although Galileo, in the seventeenth century, had proved this view to be false, millions of people in Jasper's time still believed that the earth stood still at the center of things. Many other ministers felt the same way but few could outdo Jasper in using the Bible to "prove" this particular view of the universe.

Combining the force of a Daniel Webster with the dramatics of a Billy Sunday, for over sixty years John Jasper preached to white and Negro congregations in Virginia, Washington, Maryland, and New Jersey. Newspapers announced his sermons, and his appearances were usually major events. In London, Paris, and Berlin, scholars took note of his views and sayings even when they disagreed with them.

A native of Virginia, John Jasper was born during the War of 1812 and lived until the Spanish-American War was over. He was freed after Appomattox and started his career as a literal-minded believer in the Bible. Even his scientifically-inclined critics admitted his sincerity. Jasper's concrete descriptions of hell persuaded many people to join the church. A. S. Thomas, a minister who knew him well, said that "it did seem to me sometimes that Rev. Jasper came into the world with a Bible in his heart, head and tongue."

Benjamin Brawley, *Negro Builders and Heroes* (New York), pp. 80-87.
William J. Simmons, *Men of Mark* (Cleveland, 1887), pp. 1064-1076.

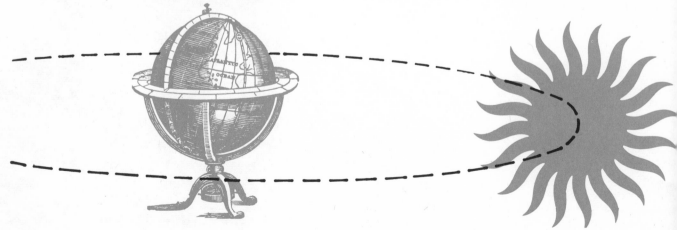

Adam Clayton Powell, Sr.
(1865-1953)

BUILDER OF AMERICA'S LARGEST NEGRO CONGREGATION

The world's largest Negro congregation is the Abyssinian Baptist Church of New York. Established by Thomas Paul and eighteen other Negroes in 1808, this church has over 15,000 members and is a major force in the total life of the Negroes of New York City. A community in itself, the Abyssinian Baptist Church is the elongated shadow of one man—Adam Clayton Powell, Sr:

Born in a one-room log cabin set on five acres of hard scrabble dirt in the backwoods of Virginia, Adam Clayton Powell, Sr. built the Abyssinian Church to the point where it could care for thousands of the needy, furnish recreation for hundreds of the young, and serve as the seat of power for a United States Congressman.

Powell started life in a hurry. As a seven-year old, on his first day at a rural school, he learned his alphabet, and on the second, could recite it backwards. His family, composed of sixteen brothers and sisters, could not afford to send him to school regularly. Between school sessions, Powell worked in the mines of West Virginia. Finally finishing high school, Powell decided to enter the ministry.

In 1888 he entered Wayland Academy, now Virginia Union University, and worked his way through the institution as a janitor and waiter. After graduating from Wayland Academy, he continued his education at Yale University School of Divinity. While at Yale he served as pastor of the Immanuel Baptist Church in the small Negro community in New Haven.

In 1908 Powell became pastor of the Abyssinian Baptist Church which was then located opposite the present site of the *Herald Tribune*. At this time the church had a membership of 1600 and an indebtedness of $146,354. In 1921 the church was moved to its present location and housed in a $350,000 Gothic structure of New York bluestone.

In addition to building the church, Powell was a vigorous crusader against vice and prostitution. When the Depression of 1929 reached Harlem, Powell opened soup kitchens which served thousands of meals. With his son, Powell was in the forefront of the Harlem push for job equality and for a fair share of the city's services.

After twenty-nine years, Adam Clayton Powell, Sr. retired in 1937. The Abyssinian Baptist Church had 14,000 members and $400,000 in assets. Before he died in 1953, Adam Clayton Powell, Sr., had the satisfaction of seeing his church continue its growth and service in the hands of his son and heir, Adam Clayton Powell, Jr.

Ben Albert Richardson, *Great American Negroes* (New York, 1945), pp. 185-196; *Who's Who in Colored America, 1950*, pp. 422-423.

Howard Thurman (1900-   )

THEOLOGIAN-AUTHOR

For two years, Howard Thurman was a pastor in Oberlin, Ohio. In 1928, he returned to Morehouse College and remained for three years as Professor of Systematic Theology. In 1935, he received the Doctor of Divinity degree from Wesleyan College (Connecticut). In that same year, he toured Canada, lecturing on many college campuses there. A bit later, he travelled to India and delivered lectures. From 1934 to 1944, Thurman served as Dean of the Chapel at Howard University, Washington, D.C. Upon leaving Howard, Dr. Thurman went to San Francisco as minister of the inter-racial, interfaith Church for the Fellowship of All Peoples. For a decade, he made this church one of the major assets of the city.

In 1953, Howard Thurman was persuaded to join the faculty of Boston University as Professor of Spiritual Discipline and Resources in the School of Theology. He was also named director of religious counselors and preacher at the university. Dr. Thurman continued to lecture widely, speaking at such institutions as Harvard, Radcliffe, and many predominantly black institutions of higher learning.

Howard Thurman has been a prolific author. Among his works are *The Greatest of These* (1945), *Deep River* (1946), *Meditations for Apostles of Sensitiveness* (1947), *The Negro Spiritual Speaks of Life and Death* (1947), *Jesus and the Disinherited* (1948), *Deep is the Hunger* (1951), *Meditations of the Heart* (1953), *The Creative Encounter* (1954), *Apostles of Sensitiveness* (1956), *Footprints of a Dream* (1959), *The Inward Journey* (1961), *Mysticism and the Experience of Love* (1961), *Disciplines of the Spirit* (1963), and *The Luminous Darkness* (1965).

Dr. Howard Thurman retired as Dean of the Chapel at Boston University in 1965. He is still active, however, in the fields of religion and social justice.

Founded in 1839 as a Methodist school of theology, prestigious Boston University installed a new Dean of the Chapel in March 1953. The new dean was Howard Thurman, born and bred a Baptist—and black. The road Howard Thurman took to the Chapel began in Daytona Beach, Florida in 1900. It wound through Georgia, Washington, D.C., Pennsylvania, New York and California, with brief detours through Canada and India. Howard Thurman had a national reputation as a sensitive theologian and eloquent preacher whose themes were the brotherhood of man and the reality of God. Beginning in 1945, Thurman expressed his thoughts on man and God in nearly a dozen books. He gained fame as an outstanding orator and preacher on both the east and west coasts of America.

Born on November 18, 1900, Howard Thurman was reared by an ex-slave grandmother. He managed to attend high school only through the kindness of a relative who took him in and furnished him one meal a day. By 1923, he had worked his way through Morehouse College in Atlanta, Georgia. From Morehouse, Thurman entered the Colgate Rochester Divinity School in New York, and his career was on its way.

Elizabeth Yates, *Howard Thurman: Portrait of a Practical Dreamer* (New York, 1965), pp. 166-194, 241-242; *Who's Who in America* (1964-65), p. 20.

VII LEADERS and SPOKESMEN
Voices for the Multitude

In his progress down the winding road from slavery toward freedom, the Afro-American has relied on leaders and spokesmen to carry the beacon of hope. Negro leaders have been the means of communicating to the nation the wishes of the inarticulate masses. Their tactics have ranged from the petitions of free Negroes during the infancy of the Republic to the moral exhortation of Frederick Douglass; from the example and opportunism of Booker T. Washington to the rage and daring of Marcus A. Garvey; from the blunt anger of W. E. B. DuBois to the cool calculation of Charles H. Houston and Walter White; and from the blazing zeal of Mary McLeod Bethune to the consuming pacificism of Martin Luther King, Jr.

Organized Negro leadership dates from the time of the American Revolution. During this early period of American history, small groups of free Negroes banded together to point out the inconsistency and immorality of holding black men in bondage while fighting for political freedom from the Old World. The most active and vocal opposition to slavery, apart from the Quakers of New England, was to be found among the free Negroes of Massachusetts and Pennsylvania.

In 1780 Paul Cuffe led his people in a protest against taxation of Negro tax payers without representation. In 1788 Prince Hall petitioned the Massachusetts Legislature to end the practice of permitting free Negroes to be sold into slavery. Under the leadership of the redoubtable Absalom Jones, the free Negroes of Pennsylvania petitioned Congress for repeal of the fugitive slave act of 1793. In the city of Philadelphia, James Forten in 1813 headed opposition to plans to have all free Negroes registered with the city. At the suggestion of Hezekiah Grice, James Forten and other leaders in Philadelphia held the first of a famous series of conventions which served as forums of debate over issues facing Negroes in the North and South.

While white abolitionists such as William Lloyd Garrison, Wendell Phillips, Arthur Tappan, James Birney, Elijah P. Lovejoy, John Brown, and others were gaining public notice for their activities, several Negro leaders achieved fame as "conductors" on the underground railroad. Foremost among them were William Still, David Ruggles and Harriet Tubman. Journalists of the caliber of Samuel Cornish, John Russwurm and Charles Bennett Ray, and orators such as Sojourner Truth, Henry Highland Garnet and Theodore S. Wright publicized the views and opinions of the masses. To this list may be added the names of William Cooper Nell, Charles L. Remond, William Wells Brown and J. W. C. Pennington. Soaring above all of these was the golden voice of the leonine Frederick Douglass.

Following the Civil War, a new group of leaders came to the fore. Robert Smalls, Hiram Revels, Blanche K. Bruce, John R. Lynch, John Mercer Langston, Robert B. Elliott, P. B. S. Pinchback and James T. Rapier are only a few of the extremely able men who were nationally prominent during the early years of freedom. Many less well known Negroes achieved prominence in southern state and local governments. Samuel J. Lee was speaker of the South Carolina House of Representatives in 1872. A. K. Davis was lieutenant governor of Mississippi in 1873. Jonathan C. Gibbs was successively secretary of state and state superintendent of public instruction in Florida during the period of 1868-1872.

At the end of the Reconstruction era in the late 1870's the political power and influence of Negro leaders declined. While many of the older leaders such as Douglass, Langston and Lynch continued to define the issues and propose solutions to the economic and political handicaps foisted on the group, men such as Isaiah T. Montgomery, Benjamin "Pap" Singleton and Henry Adams led tens of thousands of freedmen northward to Missouri, Kansas, Indiana and other states to escape the oppressive economic and political conditions in the Deep South. By 1895 Booker T. Washington was the most famous Negro in America; however, with Ida B. Wells writing and lecturing against the evils of lynching, and DuBois protesting the philosophy of accommodation to the status quo, the ground was being prepared for the birth of organizations directly devoted to the cause of racial advancement.

Excluded from the mainstream of politics, many leaders found outlets for their ambitions in organized religion. William Heard, once a minister to Liberia in the 1890's, was soon to find himself a bishop in the African Methodist Episcopal church. His influence lasted for decades. Reverdy Ransom was famous as an A. M. E. bishop and as a major figure in politics and social reform. He even ran for Congress in 1916. The masses looked to such men for leadership during the long struggle for first-class citizenship.

The Afro-American League organized in 1890 by the journalist, T. Thomas Fortune; the National Association for the Advancement of Colored People organized in 1909 with DuBois as its first Negro member; the Urban League organized in 1910 under George W. Haynes and Eugene Kinckle Jones; and the formation of other race relations groups marked the professionalization of the fight for freedom. Down to the middle of this century, the NAACP bore the brunt of the fight. Among its more illustrious leaders were DuBois, James Weldon Johnson and Walter White. Today this oldest of protest organizations carries on under the leadership of Roy Wilkins.

The new urgency in the civil rights movement has given rise to groups such as the Congress of Racial Equality (CORE) founded in 1942, the Southern Christian Leadership Conference (SCLC) organized by the famed Rev. Martin Luther King, Jr. in 1957 and the Student Non-Violent Coordinating Committee (SNCC) which dates from 1960. These groups and their leaders have different emphases and tactics but their objectives are in the historic tradition of Negro leadership: the achievement of a condition of freedom which would render the question of color irrelevant in American life.

Richard Bardolph, *The Negro Vanguard* (New York, 1961), p. 88; *Biographical Directory of the American Congress: 1774-1961* (Washington, D.C., 1961).

Benjamin "Pap" Singleton
(1809-1892)

WALK AND NEVER TIRE

All Colored People THAT WANT TO GO TO KANSAS, On September 5th, 1877, Can do so for $5.00

"Pap" Singleton was only partly right in his statement to the Congressmen. Other causes for the migration were economic exploitation, denial of political recognition, and the dreaded activity of the Ku Klux Klan. The Negroes buoyant dreams of early Reconstruction had changed to nightmare of repression in many parts of the Deep South. "Pap" was the Pied Piper urging them away.

A native of Tennessee, "Pap" Singleton had escaped from slavery. For a time he lived in Canada. After the Emancipation Proclamation, he returned to the South. He had been a carpenter and cabinet-maker during slavery and now supported himself through these trades. A tall, thin tawny man who could barely read, Singleton was a most persuasive talker and a compulsive promoter.

In his travels, Singleton discovered thinly populated areas in Kansas, the now-tranquil land of John Brown. While Negro intellectuals were debating the merits of emigration to Africa and South America, Singleton marched through the South advertising and preaching a haven of ease and dignity just over in Kansas. The newspapers picked up his stories and he himself produced pictures and clippings showing Negroes living where the living was easy.

In 1873 "Pap" led some three hundred Negroes to Cherokee County, Kansas to found "Singleton's Colony." Henry Adams in Louisiana and Isaiah T. Montgomery in Mississippi also headed northbound migrations from their respective states. On foot, by boat, rail and horseback, they swarmed into Kansas and Missouri and went as far north as Indiana and Illinois. Over 5,000 Negroes left South Caroina in one week; in twenty months, Kansas was inundated with over 19,000 "Exodusters" as they were called. Although these Negroes did not find an Eldorado and had to be assisted by northern philanthropy, few returned to the South.

The great exodus halted in 1881; "Pap" Singleton died in Tennessee, the state where he was born.

"I started it all; I was the cause of it all," said Benjamin "Pap" Singleton to a congressional committee investigating the causes of the great "Exodus of 1879" when tens of thousands of Negroes simply packed up and moved northward from Tennessee, Texas, South Carolina, Mississippi, and Louisiana. In this great movement of Negroes were some sixty to eighty thousand men and women seeking some better place, some more tolerable clime away from the South.

Roy Garvin, "Benjamin "Pap" Singleton and His Followers," *Journal Negro History*, XXXIII (January, 1937), pp. 50-92; John G. Van Deusen, "The Exodus of 1879," *Journal of Negro History*, XXI (April, 1936), pp. 111-129.

Ida B. Wells (1862-1931)

ANTI-LYNCH CRUSADER

One cold night in March, 1892, a mob of cursing, shout-
ng white men broke into the jail at Memphis, Tennessee,
ustled three black prisoners out into an open field and
ddled them with bullets. The blacks were lynched for the
rimes of being "uppity" and "too successful" in the small
rocery business. Ida B. Wells, writing under the pen name
[ola," published a detailed expose on the mob and its dirty
ork in her newspaper, *Free Speech*. The very night that
er newspaper appeared with the expose, a mob invaded her
ffices and destroyed the printing equipment and all the
opies of *Free Speech* that it could find. A determined
earch for Miss Wells was made, but her friends had spir-
ed the outspoken editor away from danger.

After her press was destroyed, Miss Wells made her way
New York and joined the staff of the *New York Age*,
lited by T. Thomas Fortune. With the encouragement of
uch men as Frederick Douglass and William Monroe
rotter, Miss Wells publicized the facts of lynching. In
895, she wrote "Red Record," the first serious statistical
reatment of the tragedy of lynching. She appealed to
resident William McKinley for support in the fight
gainst lynch law. She said that "nowhere in the civilized
orld, save in the United States, do men go out in bands of
fty to 5,000, to hunt down, shoot, hang or burn to death,
single individual, unarmed and absolutely powerless."

A native of Mississippi, Ida B. Wells was orphaned at
ourteen, but managed to attend Rust College and Fisk
niversity. After a few courses at Fisk, she went to work
s a school teacher. The young Miss Wells began writing
bout the inferior facilities of black schools around
lemphis, and, as a result, lost her teaching position.
reed of dependence on the whims of others for her liveli-
ood, she devoted all of her time to journalism and the
xposure of crime and injustice.

In 1895, Miss Wells married a Chicago newspaper-
an, Ferdinand L. Barnett. Together they continued their
ght against injustice. Mrs. Ida B. Wells Barnett organ-
ed many civic and self-help clubs in Chicago. She was one
f the six blacks who signed the initial call for the great
ational conference out of which grew the N.A.A.C.P. in
909. In 1915, she became chairman of the Chicago Equal
ights League.

Ida B. Wells in her time was perhaps the most famous
black female journalist in the country. She was a correspondent for the *Detroit Plain-dealer*, the *Christian Index*,
the *People's Choice* and had written for the *New York
Age*, the *Indianapolis World*, the *Gate City Press* (Mo.),
the *Little Rock Sun*, the *Memphis Watchman*, the *Chattanooga Justice* and the *Fisk Herald*. She was a columnist
for *Our Women and Children*, edited by the author of
Men of Mark, William J. Simmons. She was also a part-
owner of the *Memphis Free Speech* and the *Head Light*.
Twice Miss Wells had been secretary of the Afro-American
Press Association.

Writing of her in 1891, T. Thomas Fortune, the outstanding black editor of the period, said, "She has become
famous as one of the few of our women who handle a goose
quill, with diamond point, as easily as any man in the
newspaper work."

I. Garland Penn, *The Afro-American Press and Its Editors* (Springfield.
Mass., 1891), pp. 407-410; Harry A. Ploski and Roscoe C. Brown, Jr. (eds.),
The Negro Almanac (New York, 1967), pp. 755-756.

William Monroe Trotter
(1872-1934)

PIONEER IN PROTEST TECHNIQUES

But, Trotter was far from being a rowdy. He was born of affluent parents on April 17, 1872 in Boston. His childhood was unusually favored. He attended high school in Boston, went on to Harvard University where he was elected to Phi Beta Kappa, graduated *magna cum laude* in 1895, and received his M.A. in 1896. In 1901, in spite of a promising career in real estate, he started the *Boston Guardian* with George Forbes, another member of the Boston elite. The *Boston Guardian* was started in the same building and on the same floor from which William Lloyd Garrison had published the *Liberator* seventy-one years earlier.

With the same intensity that Garrison fought slavery, Trotter struggled against racial discrimination. The pages of the *Boston Guardian* carried the outline of what are now commonly accepted demands of blacks: an immediate end to racial discrimination, prompt admission of blacks to the franchise, freedom of association, positive enforcement of the Fourteenth Amendment's equal protection provision, and massive support for public education. Trotter was a charter member of the first militant post-Reconstruction group, the Niagara Movement which was spearheaded by W. E. B. Du Bois. When the NAACP was organized in 1909 by whites, Trotter refused to become a member on the grounds that he felt that it was too moderate.

Trotter's counsel was sought by scores of leaders and activists, and, on at least five occasions, he led black delegations to call on the president of the United States. When he complained to Woodrow Wilson about segregation in the federal service, the latter was so angered that Trotter was forbidden to return to the White House. However, he did consult with successors to Wilson. During World War I, Trotter protested against discrimination in the training of black soldiers. He organized picket lines to protest the showing of the anti-Negro film, *Birth of a Nation*, and defended the rights of the Scottsboro boys in the *Guardian*.

William Monroe Trotter died on April 17, 1934, the day of his birth. Like David Walker, the author of the *Appeal to the Slaves*, he died under circumstances still shrouded in mystery.

August Meier, *Negro Thought in America, 1855-1915* (Ann Arbor, Michigan, 1963), pp. 174-176, 182-184; Richard Bardolph, *The Negro Vanguard* (New York; Vintage Edition, 1961), pp. 194-195; John Hope Franklin, *From Slavery to Freedom* (New York; Alfred A. Knopf, 1956 edition), pp. 438-448.

The modern protest techniques of confrontation, mass mobilization and direct action were most effectively used in the black resistance movements of the early 1900's by a little-known, handsome, well-to-do Negro graduate of Harvard: William Monroe Trotter. One of the prime targets of these techniques was Booker T. Washington who, in the eyes of many, was the brightest star in black America. Trotter, like his friend W. E. Du Bois, refused to accept Booker T.'s submissive strategy of accommodation to the racial status quo, championing instead "full equality in all things governmental, political, civil and judicial."

This ideological difference came to a head on July 30, 1903, at the Zion A.M.E. church in Boston where Booker T. Washington was speaking. Stationed in the audience, Trotter's supporters heckled Washington throughout his speech. At one point, Trotter himself, stood and asked, ". . . would it not be a calamity at this juncture to make you our leader?" As the audience became more polarized and unruly, someone tossed red pepper. The crowd panicked, and the police were called. Trotter, with several of his supporters, was arrested. He served thirty days in jail for rioting.

Colonel Charles Young
(1864-1922)

FIRST NEGRO OF DISTINCTION AT WEST POINT

Colonel Charles Young was the first Negro graduate of West Point to achieve distinction in the military. Henry [.] Flipper was the first Negro to finish that institution in [8]77 but was separated from the service in 1881.

Colonel Charles Young entered West Point in 1884; he [co]mpleted his studies there in 1889. The young lieutenant [th]en began a career of active service that was to take him [to] Mexico, Haiti, Liberia, and to Cuba where he rode with ["T]eddy" Roosevelt and his Rough Riders in the famous [ch]arge up San Juan Hill in Cuba.

Colonel Young was not only a good soldier but also a [ge]ntleman and a scholar. He was proficient in several lan[gu]ages, including Latin, Greek, German, French, Spanish, [an]d Italian. The colonel owned a magnificent library with [vo]lumes in these languages. He was a writer of pageants [an]d poetry; he played the piano and violin and composed [m]usic for both instruments. While teaching military [sc]ience and tactics at Wilberforce University in Ohio, his [ho]me was a gathering place for such men as Paul Laurence [D]unbar and W. E. B. DuBois.

However, his career was that of a soldier and it was in [th]is connection that he achieved his greatest fame. Soldiers [ar]e trained to fight. With the outbreak of World War I, [Co]lonel Young expected to be given an active assignment [ov]erseas. The Negro press clamored for him to be given a [co]mmand. Military doctors examined the colonel only to [an]nounce that his health was too poor at that time for [ac]tive duty.

Angered by this, Colonel Young mounted his favorite [ho]rse at Chillicothe and rode the five hundred miles back [to] Washington, D.C. as proof of his fitness for service. [In]stead of being retired for "reasons of health," he was [as]signed to train Negro troops at Fort Grant, Illinois. [La]ter he was sent to Liberia as military attache in Mon[ro]via. Shortly after his arrival in Africa, the colonel died [at] Lagos, Nigeria in 1922. He was returned to America [to] be buried in the Valhalla of heroes—Arlington National [Ce]metery.

[We]sley Brown, "Eleven Men of West Point," *Negro History Bulletin*, XIX [(A]pril, 1956), pp. 147-157; Bernie Young Mitchell Wells, "A Versatile Rela[tiv]e of Mine: Colonel Charles Young," in Herman Dreer, *American Litera[tur]e by Negro Authors* (New York, 1950), pp. 179-184.

Benjamin O. Davis, Sr.
(1877-   )

FIRST NEGRO GENERAL
IN THE U. S. ARMY

For ten years he remained a colonel until the pressur[e] of World War II forced his promotion to brigadier ge[n]eral. During the long years since joining the regular arm[y] Davis had served in the Philippines, had been milita[ry] attache at Monrovia, Liberia. Stateside, he had been [an] instructor in the Ohio National Guard, professor of mi[li]tary science and tactics at Wilberforce in Ohio and lat[er] at Tuskegee Institute. He was also an instructor and co[m]mander of the 369th Infantry, New York National Gua[rd].

After 1940, Brigadier General Benjamin O. Davis, S[r.] served as a special advisor and co-ordinator in the Eur[o]pean theater of operations. He rendered extremely val[u]able service in the desegregation of the military establis[h]ment. From 1945 to 1947 he was assistant to the inspe[c]tor-general of the army. In 1947 General Davis w[as] appointed special assistant to the secretary of the arm[y].

After fifty years of outstanding service to his countr[y] Brigadier General Benjamin O. Davis, Sr. retired in 194[8]. He could count among his military decorations medals f[or] service in the Philippines, the Spanish-American War, a[nd] along the Mexican Border; he could point to service meda[ls] of two world wars, including the Bronze Star, the Fren[ch] Croix de Guerre with Palm, and the Distinguished Servi[ce] Medal. And, even more than the decorations, he could ta[ke] pride in a son following in his military footsteps and de[s]tined to surpass the achievements of the father.

Although Negroes have served in the United States Armed Forces since the War of Independence, it was not until 1940 that any had earned the rank of general. In that year Colonel Benjamin Oliver Davis, Sr. was named a brigadier general in the regular army.

His career began in 1898. Because of his skill and ability, he was promoted to the rank of first lieutenant in the Ninth United States Volunteers shortly after he was graduated from Howard University. Mustered out of the volunteers in 1899, he re-enlisted in the regular army that same year. By 1901 he had moved up to the rank of second lieutenant in the cavalry.

Step by step he mounted the military ladder. In 1905 he was a first lieutenant; in 1915, a captain; in 1917, a major (temporary); in 1918-20, a lieutenant colonel; and in 1930, a full colonel.

Who's Who in Colored America, 1950, p. 139; Lee Nichols, *Breakthrough the Color Front* (New York, 1954), pp. 28-41.

Benjamin O. Davis, Jr.
(1912-   )

LEADER ALOFT

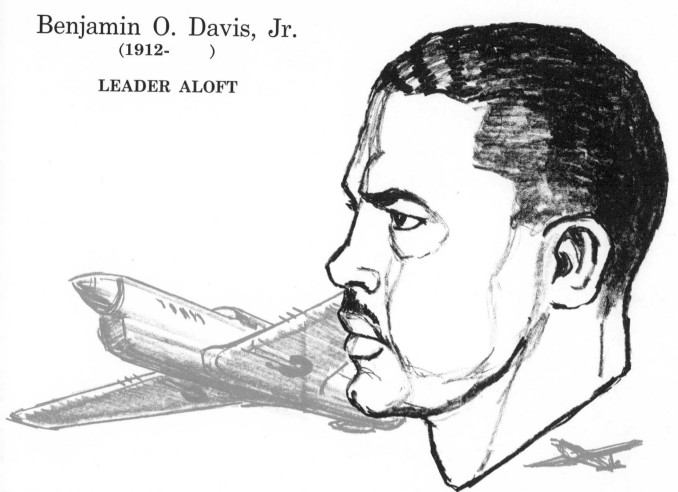

In 1944, Brigadier General Benjamin O. Davis, Sr. pinned the Distinguished Flying Cross to the chest of one Colonel B. O. Davis, Jr., who had led the 332nd Pursuit Squadron, a Negro group, on a successful bombing raid against a German installation located deep in occupied France. This was more than a ceremony of decoration, it was a father saying to his only son, "Well done."

For B. O. Davis, Jr., this was also a particularly sweet moment—a moment of realization and culmination, the realization of who and what he was, and the culmination of his father's, as well as his own struggles to prove the worth of the Negro as a "fighting man."

There was a time when B. O. Davis, Jr., did not know what to make of himself—when he was first appointed to West Point he was not particularly elated. He was well aware of the fact that it took his father over thirty years to attain the rank of colonel. Young Davis's indifference was so great that he failed his first West Point examination. But after 1932 when he finally entered West Point, his indifference was replaced by a purposefulness born of the awareness that he had to succeed, because failure would be interpreted by many as a failure of his race.

Born in 1912 and traveling about the country with his soldier-father, young Davis was well prepared for a career in the military. He also possessed the necessary physical and mental equipment; he was 6'2" tall and had a sharp mind. In school, his main academic interest was mathematics and he was president of his class. His grades at the University of Chicago and Northwestern were above average.

This same mental and physical equipment stood him in good stead at a time when he was the only Negro student at West Point. During his first year and intermittently thereafter, he was subjected to the silent treatment. He overcame this hostility and became the first Negro to be graduated from West Point in forty-seven years. But he was under this same type of pressure at Tuskegee Air Base where he took his flying training, and, later, when he led the 99th Fighter Squadron, 332nd Fighter Group in the European theater during World War II. Here Davis earned the Distinguished Flying Cross and Silver Star for personal bravery, and his group won a Presidential Unit Citation.

When B. O. Davis, Jr., was assigned to the top position at Godman Field, Kentucky in 1945, he became the first Negro to command an air base. Davis later served as commander of the Thirteenth Air Force at Clark Air Force Base in the Philippines. He has commanded bases in Korea, Formosa, and Germany. From 1961 to 1965, General Davis was director of manpower and organization for the U.S. Air Force, and from 1965 to 1967 he was chief of staff of the United Nations command in Korea.

In addition to the Distinguished Flying Cross and the Silver Star, General Davis has received the Decorated Legion of Merit, the Air Medal with Clusters, the Croix de Guerre with Palm (France), and the Star of Africa.

Who's Who in Colored America, 1950, p. 139; Lee Nichols, *Breakthrough on the Color Front* (New York, 1950), pp. 47-50; *Who's Who in America, 1968-1969,* p. 553; *Ebony* (August, 1968), pp. 56-60.

John Hope (1864-1936)
BUILDER OF MEN

The Atlanta University System is the hub of academia for Negro America. From the portals of the colleges within the system—Morehouse, Spelman, Clark, Morris Brown and Gammon Theological Seminary—come many of the leaders and spokesmen of the black race. John Hope was the man most responsible for changing the separate schools into a unified system of education for thousand of young men and women. A reserved, genteel, but energetic man, John Hope's impact on the Atlanta University System was so great that, years after his death, men still spoke of him as though he were yet alive.

The different colleges in the Atlanta University System were started in the aftermath of the Civil War; Morehouse and Spelman existed through the efforts of northern philanthrophy and the American Baptist Association. Clark and Morris Brown Colleges were created by the labors of the African Methodist Episcopal Church. Before the advent of John Hope these colleges got along as though their nearness to one another was merely coincidental. After Hope, the foundation existed for a system of cooperation and mutual assistance which preserved their administrative independence but unified their academic programs so that students could benefit from what each college was able to do best.

John Hope came to Morehouse College (then Atlanta Baptist Institute) as an instructor in classics in 1897, a year after W. E. B. Du Bois went to Atlanta University. Georgia was not new to Hope, for he was a native of Augusta where Morehouse College was begun in 1867. Soon he became an indispensable aid to Rev. George Sale, a Canadian minister who was the president of the institution. While Du Bois was turning out his volumes on the status of the Negro and feuding with Booker T. Washington, Hope was preaching the need for Negroes trained in the liberal arts.

In 1906 Hope became the first Negro President of Morehouse College and soon began to envision a cooperative center of education in Atlanta. In 1929 his dream came true when Morehouse, Spelman, and Atlanta University agreed to affiliate and to work in concert for their mutual benefit. John Hope was elected President of Atanta University and, hence, head of the System.

During these years, he found time to travel in behalf of the YMCA and to serve on numerous boards, committees and commissions. Today every college within the area has benefited from John Hope's faith, foresight and vision.

Ridgely Torrence, *The Story of John Hope* (New York, 1948).

Atlanta Baptist Seminary

Marcus A. Garvey (1887-1940)
LOOK AWAY TO AFRICA

To some people he was a charlatan, a naive dreamer; to others a messiah. To himself, Marcus A. Garvey was the Negro's best hope of finding dignity and honor, not in America, but in his original home of Africa.

Coming to America from Jamaica in 1916, Marcus Garvey found dissatisfaction, discontent, and frustration among millions of Negroes pushed northward by oppressive conditions in the South during World War I. Within two months, Garvey had recruited 1500 followers for his Universal Negro Improvement Association (U.N.I.A.). Five years later he claimed upwards of one million members.

A short, stocky, dark man possessing a shrewd sense of crowd psychology, Garvey preached economic independence and the return of Negroes to Africa as the solution to being a "Negro" in the western world. In 1921 he called an international convention which attracted thousands of Negroes to New York City from twenty-five countries, and laid the foundation for a steamship company, The Black Star Line, and the Negro Factory Corporation as devices for business and industry among Negroes.

For five years Garvey led many of the discontented masses in New York, Chicago, Cleveland, Detroit and other cities. He praised everything black and was suspicious of everything white. He formed the Universal Black Cross Nurses, the Universal African Motor Corps, and the Black Flying Eagles. His newspaper, *The Negro World,* carried his views and information about the U.N.I.A. to all corners of the country.

While millions in the masses followed him without hesitation, Negro intellectuals were skeptical of him and his promises. In 1925 Garvey was imprisoned for using the United States mails to defraud in connection with the sale of stock in his Black Star Line, and his dream began to fade. After serving two years in prison, he was deported from America and died in London in 1940, a lonely and penniless man.

Marcus A. Garvey captured the interest of the ordinary Negro as no other leader before or since, but his dream was based on a fatal flaw: his failure to understand that the overwhelming mass of Negroes considered America their rightful home and had no real desire to leave it. His weakness lay in thinking that the Negro, after helping to build America, would abandon it. His greatness lies in his daring to dream of a better future for Negroes somewhere on earth.

Edmund Cronon, *The Story of Marcus Garvey and the Universal Negro Improvement Association* (Madison, Wisconsin, 1955); E. U. Essien-Udom, *Black Nationalism: A Search for an Identity in America* (Chicago, 1962), pp. 36-39.

AFRICA

Oscar DePriest (1871-1951)

FIRST NEGRO CONGRESSMAN
IN THE 20TH CENTURY

During the Reconstruction era when the Negro population numbered between five and six million, some twenty-two Negroes represented them in the U.S. Congress. From 1901 to 1929, despite a doubling of the number of black Americans, not a single Negro sat in the nation's highest legislative tribunal.

When Oscar DePriest took his seat on April 15, 1930, in the U.S. House of Representatives, he was the only Negro there. He was elected as a Republican to the Seventy-first, Seventy-second and Seventy-third Congresses.

Oscar DePriest was shaped in the crucible of Chicago politics. His first public office was that of County Commissioner which he held from 1904 to 1908. In 1915 he became the first Negro member of the Chicago City Council. He also served as a member of the Illinois Commerce Commission and was a delegate to several Republican National Conventions. He was a member of the board of directors of the famed Binga State Bank.

After his election to Congress, he was constantly in demand as a speaker. He had no grandiose plans to lead 12,000,000 Negroes. He did realize that he was not only a representative of voters from Illinois' Twenty-first Congressional District, but also a symbol of the Negro in politics. He urged his many audiences to study political organization to learn their rights under the federal constitution, and to see campaign activity as a public duty.

Oscar DePriest was a native of Florence, Alabama but spent his youth in Salina, Kansas. He went to Chicago, Illinois in 1889. DePriest's early interest in politics can be traced back to his father, Alexander DePriest, who knew and admired James T. Rapier, the Alabama representative in Congress during the days of Reconstruction. The elder DePriest learned people and politics while a drayman; Oscar DePriest learned them through his successful career as a real estate entrepreneur. Through his long life he maintained a keen interest in politics and in the progress of the Negro. His success in business and politics did not change him; he insisted to his dying day in 1951 that "I am of the common herd."

Harold F. Gosnell, *Negro Politicians* (Chicago, 1935), pp. 163-195; *Who in Colored America, 1950*, p. 151.

Arthur Mitchell (1883-   )

U. S. CONGRESSMAN FROM ILLINOIS

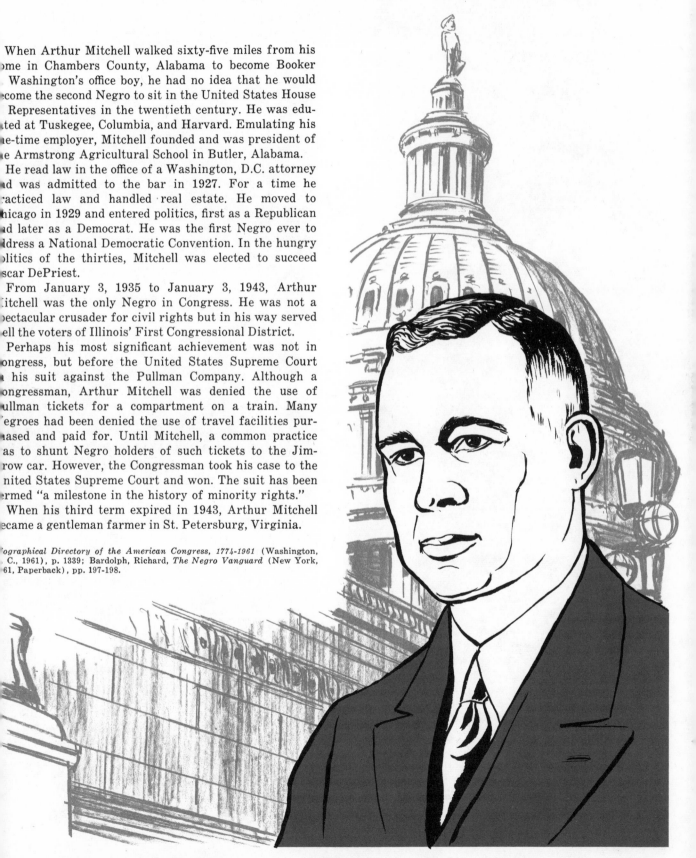

When Arthur Mitchell walked sixty-five miles from his [h]ome in Chambers County, Alabama to become Booker [T.] Washington's office boy, he had no idea that he would [be]come the second Negro to sit in the United States House [of] Representatives in the twentieth century. He was edu[ca]ted at Tuskegee, Columbia, and Harvard. Emulating his [on]e-time employer, Mitchell founded and was president of [th]e Armstrong Agricultural School in Butler, Alabama.

He read law in the office of a Washington, D.C. attorney [an]d was admitted to the bar in 1927. For a time he [pr]acticed law and handled real estate. He moved to [C]hicago in 1929 and entered politics, first as a Republican [an]d later as a Democrat. He was the first Negro ever to [ad]dress a National Democratic Convention. In the hungry [p]olitics of the thirties, Mitchell was elected to succeed [O]scar DePriest.

From January 3, 1935 to January 3, 1943, Arthur [M]itchell was the only Negro in Congress. He was not a [s]pectacular crusader for civil rights but in his way served [w]ell the voters of Illinois' First Congressional District.

Perhaps his most significant achievement was not in [C]ongress, but before the United States Supreme Court [in] his suit against the Pullman Company. Although a [c]ongressman, Arthur Mitchell was denied the use of [P]ullman tickets for a compartment on a train. Many [N]egroes had been denied the use of travel facilities pur[ch]ased and paid for. Until Mitchell, a common practice [w]as to shunt Negro holders of such tickets to the Jim-[C]row car. However, the Congressman took his case to the [U]nited States Supreme Court and won. The suit has been [te]rmed "a milestone in the history of minority rights."

When his third term expired in 1943, Arthur Mitchell [b]ecame a gentleman farmer in St. Petersburg, Virginia.

[Bi]ographical Directory of the American Congress, 1774-1961 (Washington, [D.]C., 1961), p. 1339; Bardolph, Richard, *The Negro Vanguard* (New York, [19]61, Paperback), pp. 197-198.

J. Finley Wilson (1881-1952)

RENOWNED FRATERNAL LEADER

J. Finley Wilson once described himself as a form[er] "bellboy, newsboy, bootblack, porter, hotel waiter, co[w] boy, miner, newspaper reporter, newspaper editor a[nd] publisher, and president of the Negro Newspaper Asso[ci] ation." However, for twenty years, he was known [to] millions as the Grand Exalted Ruler of the Improv[ed] Benevolent and Protective Order of Elks of the Wo[rld] (IBPOE).

The IBPOE was started in 1897 when Arthur J. Rig[gs] in Cincinnati, Ohio and B. F. Howard in Covington, K[en] tucky organized Elk lodges in their respective states. T[he] social and fraternal organization showed a moderate ra[te] of growth and by 1921 claimed a membership of 36,3[00]. With the election of J. Finley Wilson as Exalted Gra[nd] Ruler, the IBPOE took on new life. During his first ye[ar] in office he travelled over 50,000 miles and the Elk me[m] bership rose to 51,491. Wilson could count eighty-f[ive] new lodges when he made his first annual report.

Under Wilson's leadership, the Elks' scholarship p[ro] gram was launched in 1925 and the famed Elks Oratori[cal] Contest in 1927. The Elks initiated the first systema[tic] health survey among Negroes. During the war years [the] organization assisted in drives for Allied War Relief fun[ds,] contributed books to servicemen in its Victory Bo[ok] Campaign, initiated campaigns for buying defense bon[ds] and stamps, and sold over $2,000,000 worth in New Yo[rk] City alone.

J. Finley Wilson was forever on the move, promoti[ng] the causes and programs of his beloved order. Each ye[ar] some city would see the small, dynamic, and somewh[at] flamboyant Exalted Grand Ruler leading a long and col[or] ful parade of fellow lodgemen. Few men in public life he [did] not know. He came to exercise great influence in Repu[b] lican party platform drafting and patronage politi[cs.] When Wilson died in 1952 the IBPOE had net assets [of] $450,000, including $181,390 in cash, and could lo[ok] back on scores of young people who had benefited fr[om] its scholarship and oratorical contests.

A native of Tennessee, Wilson left home at the age [of] thirteen. He wandered west and worked with Buffalo B[ill] in Arizona and Colorado, where he joined the IBPO[E.] At Salt Lake City, Utah, he edited a newspaper called [the] *Plaindealer*. In the East he was a reporter for the *Bal[ti] more Times*, edited the *Washington Eagle*, and worked [on] the *New York Age* with T. Thomas Fortune.

The entire course of Wilson's life is summed up in [his] favorite saying: "Forward!"

Charles H. Wesley. *History of the Improved Benevolent and Protective Or[der] of Elks of the World: 1898-1954*, Washington, D. C., 1955. *Who's Who [in] Colored America*, 1950, p. 565.

Mary Church Terrell (1863-1954)

CHAMPION OF WOMEN'S RIGHTS

Mary Church Terrell was born in 1863, the year of the Emancipation Proclamation. Her entire life was devoted to the fight for equality. A writer, lecturer, organizer, and demonstrator, Mrs. Terrell was active in the successful campaign to secure women the right to vote. She was instrumental in the campaign to desegregate the restaurants in the nation's capital.

Her achievements were numerous. In 1895 she was appointed to the District of Columbia school board; in 1896 she became one of the charter members of the National Association of Colored Women. In 1909 she joined the NAACP, then less than a year old. In 1913-14 she helped to organize the Delta Sigma Theta sorority, and twenty-six years later wrote its famous creed, setting up a code of conduct for Negro women. She was also active in politics, campaigning and speaking out against discrimination and segregation. In World War I, she worked with the War Camp Community Service, an organization which, among other things, aided in the demobilization of Negro servicemen.

Mary Church Terrell was a United States delegate to several international conferences. In London she met the famous writer, H. G. Wells, and other luminaries. At the International Council of Women in Berlin, she delivered her address in three languages—English, French, and German—to the amazement of the assembled delegates. Her theme was the same: equal rights for women and the Negro, wherever they may be found.

A strikingly handsome woman, Mary Church was born to wealth and ease. She was a "rare combination of the high intellectual in close understanding with the mass." A native of Memphis, Tennessee, she was the daughter of Robert Church, an ex-slave of extremely high business skill who amassed a fortune in real estate before the turn of the century. Unwilling to have his daughter face discrimination in Tennessee, Robert Church sent Mary to Ohio where she attended private and public schools, and later, Oberlin College from which she was graduated in 1884 with a major in the classics.

By her own choice, Mary Church Terrell made her home in Washington in the 1890's, at that time a heavily segregated city. Except for public transportation, Washington remained segregated until 1953. In that year, at the age of eighty-nine, Mrs. Terrell won the biggest and toughest battle of her life-long struggle against racial intolerance. She headed a committee of distinguished citizens to demand enforcement of a seventy-five-year-old law banning discrimination of "respectable persons" from restaurants. With several other Negroes, she went to a number of restaurants and was refused service. A suit was filed and the resulting test case went to the United States Supreme Court which held that the old law was still valid. Shortly thereafter, the walls of segregation began to crumble in hotels, theaters and other places hitherto off-limits to Negroes.

Mary Church Terrell died in Annapolis, Maryland in 1954, a few months after hearing the United States Supreme Court declare that segregation itself was unconstitutional.

Mary Church Terrell, *A Colored Woman in a White World* (Washington, 1940).

Mary McLeod Bethune (1875-1955)
COTTON PICKER, EDUCATOR, WHITE HOUSE ADVISOR

Bethune-Cookman College

Mary McLeod Bethune ranks high among the great women of America. Her life story is one of an ennobling rise from a field hand picking cotton to the position of confidante and friend of Franklin D. and Eleanor Roosevelt. The last of seventeen children born to South Carolina sharecroppers, Mary Bethune lifted herself from the cotton fields to the White House as an advisor to the President of the United States. Almost single-handedly she built Bethune-Cookman College.

Mary McLeod Bethune rose by no golden stair or silver spoon, but by sheer courage, faith and perseverance. She was the only one of the McLeods born this side of slavery. She had a burning desire for an education and used the three-month school term between planting and harvesting to good advantage, so that when a seamstress in Colorado offered to pay the cost of educating one Negro girl at Scotia Seminary in Concord, North Carolina, Mary was selected. Graduating from this institution in 1893, Mary McLeod journeyed to Chicago where she enrolled in Moody Bible Institute with the idea of becoming a missionary to Africa. Instead, she returned to the Deep South to teach at Haines Institute in Augusta, Georgia.

It was in Georgia that she reached the real turning point in her life. She heard of railroads being constructed on the east coast of Florida. Mary Bethune immediately thought of the hundreds of Negro railroad laborers' children clustered in many squalid section settlements, destined to grow up without any sort of education. With only $1.50, nerve, and determination, she set out to build a school for them.

In her own words, she summed up her effort to build the school: "I rang doorbells . . . , I wrote articles for whoever would print them, distributed leaflets, rode interminable miles of dusty roads on my old bicycle, invaded churches, clubs, lodges, chambers of commerce." Slowly the school rose from old crates, boxes and odd rooms of old houses near the Daytona Beach city dump. The student body grew from an enrollment of five little girls to a co-ed institution numbering its pupils in the hundreds. By 1923 when Bethune College merged with Cookman Institute, it had an enrollment of 600 students and 32 teachers; its property was worth well over half a million dollars. Today, Bethune-Cookman graduates number in the thousands.

By 1935 Mary McLeod Bethune was nationally known. That year she received the NAACP's Spingarn Medal as a symbol of distinguished achievement. The following year Franklin D. Roosevelt appointed her director of Negro Affairs Division of the National Youth Administration. She became a familiar figure at the White House as Roosevelt came to demand her wisdom and insight.

Edward R. Embree, *13 Against the Odds* (New York, 1946), pp. 9-24.

A. Philip Randolph (1889-   )
IN UNION—STRENGTH

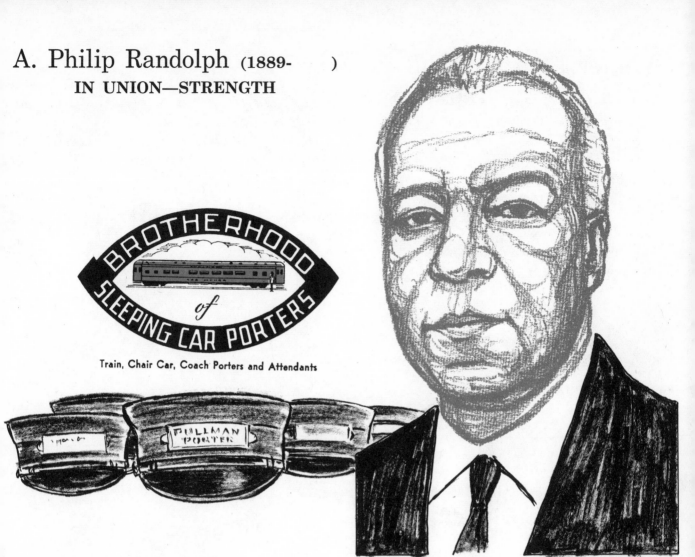

Train, Chair Car, Coach Porters and Attendants

A. Philip Randolph is the elder statesman of Negro [lab]or leaders. For almost forty years he has been in the [th]ick of the fight for improved working conditions and [hi]gher wages for all laborers. He has been particularly [vi]gorous in his opposition to racial discrimination within [th]e labor movement.

In 1925 Randolph organized the Brotherhood of Sleep[in]g Car Porters, the strongest labor group among Negroes. [W]ith the Pullman car porters as a foundation, A. Philip [Ra]ndolph rose to the topmost hierarchy of the labor [mo]vement to become the only Negro vice-president of the [AF]L-CIO. He is the founder and organizer of the Negro [Am]erican Labor Council. During World War II he was [th]e prime mover in the celebrated "March on Washing[to]n" movement which prodded the United States govern[me]nt into banning discrimination in the industries having [go]vernment contracts. He was one of the most effective [lo]bbyists for the establishment of a permanent Fair Em[pl]oyment Practices Committee.

[T]he basic character of the man may be seen in the bitter [str]uggle to organize porters and maids working on trains [du]ring the late twenties and early thirties. Railroad man[ag]ement fought Randolph and his union every step of the [wa]y. Nonetheless, Randolph never compromised his prin[cip]les or the goals of the Brotherhood. The union survived [ev]ery onslaught of management and became a potent [for]ce in American labor generally.

A native of Crescent City, Florida, A. Philip Randolph had no specific desire to develop into a spokesman for labor and the Negro. He fancied himself a writer and, with Chandler Owens, edited *Messenger*, a rather outspoken magazine of comment and opinion. He also wrote for *Opportunity* magazine, the journal of the Urban League.

In addition to his writing, Randolph gained wide acclaim with his oratory. His speeches have reflected the influence of frequent readings of Shakespeare and other literary masters. Because of his vocal opposition to World War I, he was imprisoned. Upon his release, however, he promptly threw himself into the fight for the underdog. While the president of the Brotherhood of Sleeping Car Porters, Randolph frequently shook the house of labor with his thunderous demands that blacks be allowed a full share of the fruits of their work in the American economy. In 1960 he formed the American Negro Labor Council in which nearly a hundred black labor leaders pledged themselves to work for the reduction of prejudice and discrimination within the union movement. Randolph dominated the steering committee of the Council until his retirement in 1966. At the age of seventy-four, A. Philip Randolph was one of the organizers and leaders of the famous 1963 March on Washington.

Edwin Embree, *13 Against the Odds* (New York, 1946), pp. 211-230.
Brailsford R. Brazeal, *The Brotherhood of Sleeping Car Porters* (New York, 1946).

Walter Francis White (1896-1955)
A GUIDE TO THE PROMISED LAND

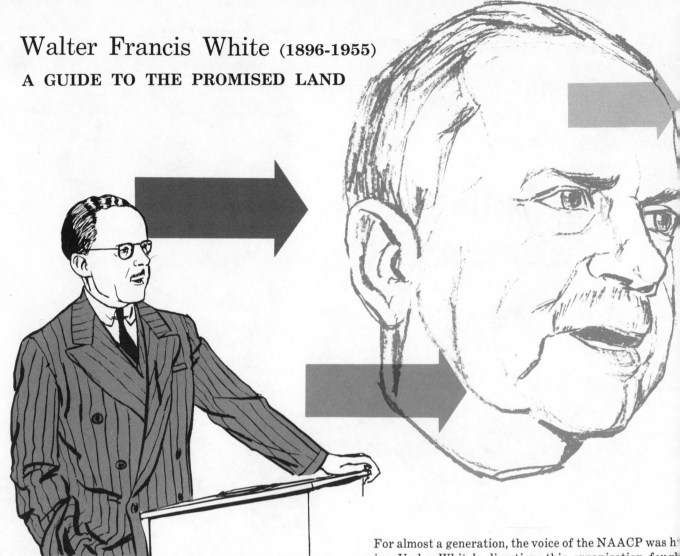

Completely out of breath, the blue-eyed, pink-skinned Negro with reddish hair flopped down in his seat. The conductor was passing through the train collecting tickets from passengers coming aboard at the little depot in Arkansas. As he neared the slender blue-eyed man still gasping for breath, he said "Mister, you're leaving town just as the fun is about to start. They're after a yaller nigger down here passing as white."

The "yaller nigger" referred to was Walter Francis White, special investigator of lynchings for the National Association for the Advancement of Colored People. This was Walter White, destined to become the leader of the Negro's oldest and largest civil rights organization. This was Walter White beginning a long fight against lynching, discrimination, and segregation.

Walter White, a native of Atlanta, Georgia could have slipped across the "color line" and vanished into white anonymity. Instead, he chose to remain identified with America's most oppressed minority. His abilities doubtless would have earned him security, ease, and respect beyond the color curtain. But he, like his father before him, was a fighter and a strong believer in simple justice.

For almost a generation, the voice of the NAACP was h[is] voice. Under White's direction, this organization fough[t] forcefully for equality in voting rights, turned the eyes [of] America to the real evil and horror of lynching, and move[d] against segregation and discrimination in travel and ed[u]cation. During the era of Walter White, NAACP criti[cs] felt that the NAACP was moving too fast on too ma[ny] fronts, that White wielded too much power over the o[r]ganization for his and the organization's own good. B[ut] he felt that America had much too far to go for his organ[i]zation to move slowly.

Perhaps he had a special interest in moving the organ[i]zation rapidly. Perhaps he could not forget that his fathe[r] whom he revered, died from neglect in a Georgia hospit[al] while the doctors argued over whether or not he was Negr[o]. Perhaps he could never forget the night a rampaging m[ob] of racists tried to burn down his father's home in Atlant[a] Georgia while he and his father waited inside with draw[n] guns. In any event, Walter White moved himself and t[he] NAACP as though the world was aflame. The tutelage [of] men such as Charles Houston, James Weldon Johnso[n] and W. E. B. Du Bois was too strong for him to ignore.

Walter White was also an urbane man, equally at hom[e] at the White House or a Harlem tenement. The fight f[or] freedom was one that consumed his every waking hou[r.] In matters racial, his theme was always "Now is the time[."]

Edwin R. Embree, *13 Against the Odds* (New York, 1946), pp. 71-95; *Wh*[o] *Who in Colored America*, 7th Edition (1950), p. 550.

122

Whitney M. Young, Jr. (1921-1972)

LEADER OF THE NATIONAL URBAN LEAGUE

Only a dedicated man could turn down a $75,000-a-year vice-presidency with a major corporation to work for Negro progress at less than half that salary. But Whitney M. Young, Jr., executive director of the National Urban League, in doing just that, was following the example of his father, who, in 1920, gave up his $300-a-month job with the Ford Motor Company to teach at a struggling school for blacks at $68 a month. The inherent dedication of Whitney Young, Jr. is commonly credited with revitalizing the Urban League, organized in 1910 to assist the Negroes moving into northern cities to find jobs and housing.

The Urban League, a year younger than the N.A.A.C.P., began by assisting Negro immigrants, studying the economic conditions of the ghetto, training social workers, and breaking down job barriers. When Young succeeded Lester Granger as head of the League in 1961, it was operating with an annual budget of $250,000 and a national staff of 4. By 1968, the budget had grown to $3,500,000 and the national staff to more than 200. The programs of its ninety branches include a Special Skills Bank for professionals, anti-poverty workshops, tutorial centers, veterans adjustment guidance clinics, and an on-the-job training program which in 1967 resulted in the employment of over 8,000 Negroes.

The path leading Whitney Young to the front ranks of black leadership stretches back to Lincoln Ridge, Kentucky where he was born in 1921. His primary education began with a white tutor and ended at Lincoln Institute where his father had become president. Graduating at 14 with an A average, he entered segregated Kentucky State College and again earned high grades.

Enlisting in the army during World War II, he was sent to the Massachusetts Institute of Technology for electrical engineering but, despite this training, ended up an enlisted man in a Negro road-construction company commanded by whites. Here he first realized his talents as a mediator between white and black men, and resolved to make race relations his life's work.

After the war, Young earned a master's degree in social work at the University of Minnesota with a thesis on the Urban League of St. Paul. This led to employment with League groups in St. Paul and Omaha, Nebraska and in 1954, to the position of Dean of the Atlanta University Graduate School of Social Work. Following further study at Harvard University, he was selected executive director of the League, whose prestige he lent to the March on Washington (1963), the Selma March (1965) and the Meredith Mississippi March (1966). Young has served on no less than nine presidential panels and became a founding member in 1967 of the ambitious Urban Coalition, a group devoted to solving the economic problems of the inner city.

Continuing his dedication to race relations and the League through his book *To be Equal*, Whitney Young has warned, "We will either help Negroes to become constructive, productive citizens . . . or they will become destructive dependents."

Ebony (November, 1965), **XXI**, pp. 164-170; *Time* (August 11, 1967), pp. 12-15; *Newsweek* (May 15, 1967), pp. 28-29; *Who's Who in America* (1964-65), p. 2230.

Charles H. Houston
William H. Hastie
James B. Parsons

LAWYERS AND JUDGES

In a nation of law, the American Negro, for the most part, has been an "outcast, asylumed 'neath these skies." Yet he has maintained faith in the ideals of democracy and has relied upon the law as one of the avenues to a fuller role in the democratic experiment. Where existing law has been directed toward his repression and degradation, the Negro has tried to bring about new laws more in keeping with the fulfillment of the American dream.

Ever since Macon B. Allen was admitted to the bar in the state of Maine in 1854, Negro lawyers have played an important role in the fight for equality. Of the twenty-two Negroes who sat in the U.S. Congress during the Reconstruction era, six were lawyers. Among the most brilliant of them was Robert B. Elliott who had one of the finest law libraries in the South. John Mercer Langston was an ex-dean of the Howard University Law School when he took his seat in the U.S. House of Representatives in 1889. Jonathan J. Wright was an associate justice of the State Supreme Court of South Carolina from 1870 to 1877.

However, not until the twentieth century did the Negro lawyer come into his own. The best brains and talents of the legal profession were directed toward securing of the constitutional rights of Negroes. For decades the Negro's top legal talent was focused on Howard University in Washington, D.C. From Howard, either as students or teachers, have emerged some of the giants in the history of Negro lawyers: William Hart, James Cobb, Herman E. Moore, William Hastie and Charles H. Houston, to name only a few. Other lawyers such as Spottswood Robinson; Raymond and Sadie T. Alexander of Philadelphia; A. T. Walden of Atlanta; Robert Ming of Chicago; Henry J. Richardson, Jr. of Indianapolis, Indiana; Perry Howard of Washington, D.C.; Arthur Shores of Birmingham, Alabama; and scores of other brilliant lawyers have served the Negro and the nation with valor and distinction.

A closer view of some of the lawyers in the history of civil rights litigation will perhaps give some indication of the quality of the men before the bar and on the bench.

Charles Hamilton Houston (1895-1950) has been credited with laying the legal strategy for the justly famous case of *Brown v. Board of Education* in which the U. S. Supreme Court in 1954 declared segregation itself to be unconstitutional. Working with the NAACP he "set the pattern for *fundamental* attacks on barriers to equal justice, in place of the former practice of meeting emergencies and opportunities as they arose." His was the strategic thinking behind the brilliant series of cases on restrictive covenants, discrimination in education and in labor as well as in interstate travel.

HOUSTON

In the course of his work at Howard University from 1924 until his death in 1950, Charles H. Houston raised the Howard Law School to unrivalled superiority in the area of civil rights law. Houston's own formal training was obtained at the Harvard University Law School from which he was graduated in 1922. Earlier he had graduated from Amherst with a brilliant record.

Charles Houston attracted many able men to the Howard Law School. Outstanding among them are William Hastie and Thurgood Marshall. When William Hastie was appointed U. S. District Judge for the Virgin Islands in 1937, he became the first Negro ever appointed to the federal bench. He had been a law partner of Houston, and followed him to Howard in 1930. Hastie, too, could claim Amherst and Harvard as his alma maters.

In 1939, William Hastie became Dean of the Howard Law School. A year later he took a leave of absence to serve as civilian aide to the secretary of war (now defense). All policy questions regarding Negro servicemen were to be referred to him. While Hastie was in this post only two years, he made heroic efforts to accelerate the integration of the armed forces. In 1944 he was appointed Governor of the Virgin Islands. Since 1949, he has been

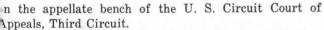

HASTIE

PARSONS

n the appellate bench of the U. S. Circuit Court of Appeals, Third Circuit.

Since the early days of Hastie and his successor in the Virgin Islands, Herman E. Moore, many outstanding lawyers have become judges in different states. Most famous among the new generation of Negro judges is James Benson Parsons, who was appointed to the U. S. District Court for the Northern District of Illinois in 1961, just twelve years after he was admitted to the bar. An example of lawyers giving effective service in their states is the instance of attorney Henry J. Richardson, Jr., of Indiana. A stalwart fighter against the Indiana Ku Klux Klan, Richardson won a seat in the Indiana state legislature in 1932. His first act in the legislature in 1933 was to successfully introduce legislation outlawing the Klan and prohibiting the wearing of masks by marchers. As chief counsel of Indiana's NAACP, Richardson won the first case at the federal level on housing desegregation in 1953.

The field of law has not been the exclusive preserve of men. A number of brilliant women have made outstanding reputations as lawyers and jurists. With her famous husband, Sadie T. Alexander became a veteran of many legal battles in Philadelphia. Edith Sampson, formerly a practicing attorney and United Nations delegate, later became a judge with the Cook County Municipal Court. Constance Baker Motley was associate counsel of the NAACP Legal Defense Fund. In 1964 she was elected to the New York State Senate. Jewel Stratford Lafontant of Chicago was the first Negro woman United States assistant district attorney. Juanita Stout of Pennsylvania became a judge in the city of Philadelphia. After a distinguished career as an attorney, Marjorie Lawson went to work with the Juvenile Court in Washington, D.C.

Negro lawyers and judges, men who argue and decide, are thus an extremely important group. They have been makers not only of black history but also of American history. Neither their profession nor their successes have come easy. Theirs has been the task of weaving the final patterns of equal justice for all citizens into the incomplete fabric of American law.

Saunders Redding, *The Lonesome Road* (New York, 1958), pp. 319-320; Langston Hughes, *Fight for Freedom: The Story of the NAACP* (New York, 1962), Berkley Medallion Edition, p. 69; Richard Bardolph, *The Negro Vanguard* (New York, 1962), Vintage Edition, pp. 254-255.

Thurgood Marshall (1908-   )

"MR. CIVIL RIGHTS"

On October 2, 1967, Thurgood Marshall began his duties as an associate justice of the Supreme Court of the United States. He thus became the first Negro ever to sit on the highest court in the nation. From August 24, 1965 to his nomination to the nation's highest court, Justice Marshall was solicitor general of the United States, the first black man to be the government's lawyer. Before assuming his duties as solicitor general, he had served for a number of years as a member of the U.S. Second Circuit Court of Appeals. While chief attorney for the NAACP, Marshall made his reputation as perhaps the greatest constitutional lawyer of this century and certainly the most widely known legal mind in America. From 1936 until his appointment to the federal bench in 1961, "Mr. Civil Rights" exerted "an influence as a mover and shaker of American society that few of his white contemporaries in the profession could match."

Thurgood Marshall laid the basis of legal cases firmly establishing the right of Negroes to serve on juries and to vote in Democratic primaries in the South, to travel from state to state free of jim crow, to be free of restrictive covenants denying them the equal right to the use and purchase of property, and to receive a public school education without discrimination or segregation.

As the NAACP's lawyer, he won not only thirty-two out of thirty-five cases taken by him before the United States Supreme Court but also the respect of his opponents by his careful, precise, and objective arguments. Warm and friendly, a man's man among intimates, he was the most feared antagonist of the best legal brains the South could buy. As his reputation grew, Marshall received lucrative offers from some of the nation's leading law firms to pay him several times more than the NAACP, but he felt it his duty to remain in the thick of the battle to make America what it ought to be. He once said, "My commitments have always been to justice for all people, regardless of race, creed, or color."

The son of a dining room steward and a school-teacher mother, Marshall was born on July 2, 1908 in Baltimore, Maryland and finished his public school education in that city. Hard work and a sense of humor carried him through Lincoln University, where he waited tables and hopped bells, and through Howard University Law School, which he helped to make the legal arsenal for all civil rights suits in recent decades.

After finishing Howard with honors in 1933, Marshall returned to his native Baltimore, where he made a modest living. It was here that he "learned what rights were." His clients were poor, usually victims of dispossession, eviction, police brutality and the like. He handled many cases knowing full well there would be no fee. Soon he was known in Maryland as the "little man's lawyer." His life since has been dedicated to the defense of the "little man," because "the United States Constitution was designed for the least as well as the greatest Americans."

Saunders Redding, *The Lonesome Road*, pp. 314-329; *Jet* (October 2, 1967); *Negro History Bulletin* (October 1967), pp. 4-5; *Newsweek* (October 16, 1967); *New York Times* (June 18, 1967), p. 6E.

Ralph J. Bunche (1904-   )

DIPLOMAT, U. N. MEDIATOR

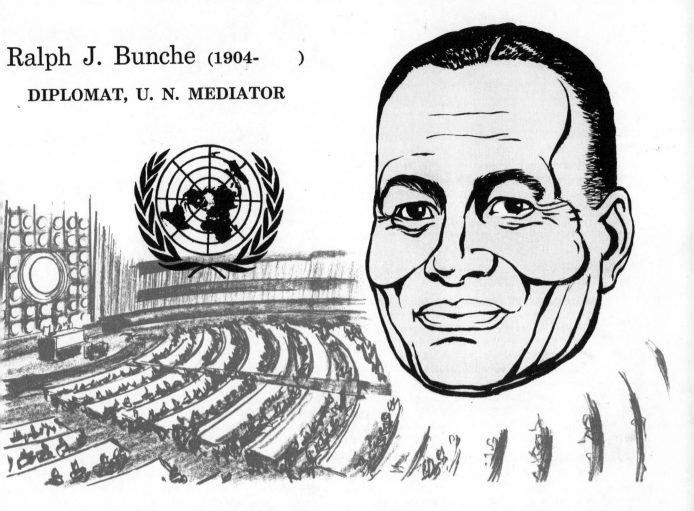

Dr. Ralph Johnson Bunche's forty-odd honorary degrees and one Nobel Prize are eloquent testimony to the contributions he has made to America and to world peace. High school class valedictorian at Los Angeles's Jefferson High School; magna cum laude graduate of the University of California; winner of the Tappan Prize at Harvard University for the best doctoral dissertation in the social sciences in 1934; post-doctoral study at Northwestern University, the London School of Economics and the University of Capetown, Johannesburg, South Africa: such is the academic background of one of America's most honored Negroes.

After a career at Howard University which paralleled his academic advancement, Dr. Bunche was named chairman of Howard's political science department in 1937, and a year later he joined the Swedish economist, Gunnar Myrdal, to begin the comprehensive study of the American Negro, published in 1945 as *An American Dilemma*.

By 1942 Dr. Bunche was at work in the Office of Strategic Services as a research analyst of material relating to Africa. By 1946 he had advanced to the position of associate chief of the State Department's Dependent Areas section. Already a foreign affairs adviser of growing reputation, Dr. Bunche left the State Department for the Trusteeship Division of the United Nations. In quick succession, he was head of the United Nations Trusteeship Department and personal representative of the United Nations secretary-general in the extremely dangerous Arab-Israeli

dispute. Following the assassination of the United Nations Palestine mediator in 1947, Dr. Bunche was named acting mediator and achieved a historic settlement of the Palestine question.

In 1949, Dr. Bunche was awarded the Spingarn medal. In 1950 he received the Nobel Prize for Peace. Other honors and offers came to him, including a professorship at Harvard University, the presidency of the City College of New York and the post of assistant secretary of state. However, Dr. Bunche has remained with the United Nations and is now its under secretary-general. He went to the Congo in 1960 as the United Nations special representative during the height of the turmoil there.

The achievements of Dr. Bunche are based on a extraordinary personal ability and hard work. His father was a poor Detroit barber; his mother, an amateur musician. Both parents died before Bunche reached his teens and he found himself living in California with his grandmother and several aunts. When he won an athletic scholarship to the University of California, he paid his other expenses by working as a campus janitor. Friends and neighbors raised money for his living expenses for one year after he won a tuition scholarship to Harvard. From this point onward, Ralph Johnson Bunche depended on nothing but his brains to carry him the rest of the way.

Current Biography, 1948, pp. 77-79; *Who's Who in Colored America,* 1950, pp. 74-75; *Who's Who,* 1962-63, p. 427.

Martin Luther King, Jr. (1929-1968)

THE NON-VIOLENT CRUSADER

Ten years before his death, Martin Luther King, Jr., was described by Dr. Benjamin E. Mays of Morehouse College in the following words: "You are mature beyond your years, wiser at twenty-nine than most men at sixty, more courageous in a righteous struggle than most men can ever be, living a faith that most men preach about and never experience . . . . Your name has become a symbol of courage and hope for oppressed people everywhere." Dr. Martin Luther King's public career began in 1955 in Montgomery, Alabama where he led the working blacks' fight against segregation on the public buses. It ended on April 4, 1968 in Memphis, Tennessee where he had joined the fight to secure better wages and working conditions for the garbage collectors. Between these two places the world was his platform; between these years universal brotherhood was his message.

Martin Luther King's broad public career and the black "revolt" began about the same time. On December 1, 1955, Rosa Parks, a Montgomery seamstress, refused to yield her bus seat to a white male as required by the laws and customs of Alabama as they existed on that date. Rosa Parks was hauled away to jail, and the long-standing grievances and systematic humiliation of Montgomery's blacks were shown in unbearable relief. Within five days after the arrest of Mrs. Parks, the blacks organized the Montgomery Improvement Association (MIA) and elected the Reverend Martin Luther King, Jr., president.

Under the leadership of Martin Luther King and the MIA, the Negroes simply refused to ride the buses. The boycott was almost 100 percent effective. A car pool of 300 vehicles transported Negroes to and from their jobs. Neither protests by whites nor threats, nor petty harrassment hurt the new-found pride of Montgomery's black citizens, who stayed off the buses for 381 days.

Rev. King and some seventy of his followers were arrested and convicted for "illegally boycotting" the buses. The convictions were appealed and eventually overturned, and on December 20, 1956 the city of Montgomery officially declared an end to racial segregation on the city buses. When the buses resumed their rounds, Dr. King was among the first to ride them.

While eschewing violence, King himself was the target of violence a number of times. His home was bombed and shotgunned; he was slugged and stabbed and stoned. He went to jail more than thirty times. Through it all, Dr King continued to say, "Let no man drag you so low as to hate." King's non-violent social philosophy was a mixture of old-fashioned Christianity, the social gospel of Walter Rauschenbusch, and the "Satyagraha" or love-force of Gandhi's views.

Dr. King's deep Christian faith in God and man served him well as he led the Southern Christian Leadership Conference (SCLC) in forays against racism in the North as well as the South. He was one of the first to sense the connection between the nation's conduct in foreign affairs and the quality of its domestic life. In season and out he sought the truth about racism and attempted to arouse the nation's conscience over the gap between its preachments and practices. In his classic "Letter from Birmingham Jail," Dr. King explained the considerations that drove him ever onward: ". . . when you have seen vicious mobs lynch your mothers and fathers . . . down your sisters and brothers; when you have seen hate-filled policemen curse, kick, brutalize, and even kill your black brothers and sisters . . . when you are forever fighting a degenerating sense of 'nobodyness'—then you will understand why we find it difficult to wait." He pursued the dream described in his famous speech before the hundreds of thousands who marched on Washington on August 28, 1963: "When we let freedom ring, when we let it ring from every village and every hamlet, from every state and every city, we will be able to speed up that day when all of God's children, black men and white men, Jews and Gentiles, Protestants and Catholics, will be able to join hands and sing in the words of that old Negro spiritual, 'Free at last! Free at last! Thank God Almighty, we are free at last.'"

Born Michael Lewis King, Dr. King adopted the name of the great Protestant Reformer, Martin Luther. A native of Atlanta, King attended the local Booker T. Washington High School, entered Morehouse College, and under the influence of its famed president emeritus, Dr. Benjamin E. Mays, entered the ministry in 1947. Martin Luther King graduated from Morehouse in 1948

nd in 1951 received the B.D. degree from Crozer Theo-
ogical Seminary, where he was an outstanding student.
While there, he received the Pearl Plafkner Prize for ex-
ellence in scholarship and was elected president of the stu-
ent body. In 1955 he earned the Doctor of Philosophy
egree from Boston University.

Two years before finishing Boston University, Dr. King
married attractive Coretta Scott, a native of Marion,
Alabama. They were the parents of four children at the
ime of the assassination. From his first pastorate at the
Dexter Avenue Baptist Church in Montgomery, Martin
Luther King moved to Atlanta where he continued to head
he SCLC and to assist his father, the Rev. M. L. King,
Sr., in the management of the Ebenezer Baptist Church.
Dr. King in life gave everything to the SCLC and its
goals. When awarded the Nobel Peace Prize in 1964, he
kept the medallion and presented the $54,000 to SCLC.
His earnings from lectures and writings generally went
o the organizations supporting the civil rights movement.
Following his death, his estate was appraised at less than
5,000. Honors and awards cascaded upon him; college
presidencies and professorships were his for the asking.
Dr. King casually accepted the honors and just as casually
urned down offers that would take him away from SCLC.

When James Earl Ray, the convicted assassin of Dr.
Martin Luther King, Jr., pulled the trigger of his rifle
hat fateful evening in Memphis, he set off an explosion
hat rocked the world. Scores of cities erupted in flames
and violence as thousands of people gave vent to rage
oo strong for silence. Americans, black and white, suddenly saw Dr. King as the real keeper of the dream of what
he nation could become. Two months before his death,
Dr. King said to his congregation at Ebenezer Baptist
Church the words that perhaps most appropriately
summed up his life. Referring to his funeral, he said,
'I'd like somebody to mention that day Martin Luther
King, Jr., tried to give his life serving others . . . . And
I want you to say that I tried to love and serve humanity."

L. D. Reddick, *Crusader Without Violence* (New York, 1959); Lerone Bennett, *What Manner of Man* (Chicago, 1968); *Jet* (April 18, 1968), entire
issue; *Newsweek* (March 24, 1969), pp. 29-32; *Ebony* (April 1969), pp. 80-88.

Edward W. Brooke (1919-   )

NEW-BREED POLITICIAN

Saltonstall. As chairman of the Boston Finance Commission from April 1961 to September 1962, attorney Edward Brooke's accomplishments as a public servant in uprooting corruption, graft, and conflict of interest by public officials won wide acclaim. His investigations resulted in the dismissal of the Boston City Auctioneer who was illegally disposing of public land.

Brooke has attained an impressive list of honors in military and civilian life. He received the Distinguished Service Award of the American Veterans of World War II and is a former National Judge Advocate of that organization. Former President Eisenhower appointed him chairman of the Massachusetts Advisory Committee, U. S. Civil Rights Commission, and he was reappointed by President Kennedy. President Kennedy thought highly of Brooke and once said, "You know, you'd make a good Democrat, Ed."

Senator Brooke was born in Washington, D.C. on October 26, 1919. After completing public school he went to Howard University, where he received his B.S. degree in 1940. After World War II, he entered the Boston University Law School, where he received the L.L.B. degree (1948) and the Master of Laws degree (1949).

During World War II, he served five years with the 366th Infantry and was awarded the Bronze Star and Combat Infantryman's Badge, attaining the rank of captain. As a result of his knowledge of Latin and French, he was put through a crash course in Italian and assigned as an intelligence officer, working with a group of partisans in Italy.

Knowing Italian was also very helpful when it came to courting Remigia, a pretty Italian girl whom he eventually married in 1947. Winning the hand of Remigia was one of Captain Brooke's more difficult achievements. For after meeting her parents and proposing, he was at first refused. But he was determined, and from Boston University, where he was a law student, came a steady stream of letters to Remigia until she finally said "yes." They now have two teen-age daughters, Edwina and Remi who help Brooke keep in touch with the thinking of young people. Edward Brooke, however, is in tune with people of all ages, and is sensitive to their anxieties, aspirations, and their needs. He is aware of the problems which beset the black man and other minorities, and has attacked them on every count. However, he has championed most forcefully solutions to the problems which assail all Americans.

The Honorable Edward W. Brooke has the distinction of being the first member of his race to occupy a seat in the United States Senate since March 3, 1881, when Hiram Revels and Blanche K. Bruce of Mississippi were in the Senate. Prior to his election to the Senate in 1966, Brooke had the honor of serving as the first popularly elected Negro attorney general of any state. His election to this office in 1962 was "a stunning and dramatic victory," as he was the only Republican to win statewide office.

In his first attempt to win statewide office in 1960, Brooke was the unsuccessful Republican nominee for secretary of state, but polled 1,095,054 votes, more than any Republican except Governor Volpe and Senator

Official biographical sketch (1964); *Time* (February 17, 1967) pp. 20-23.

Malcolm X (1925-1965)

MARTYRED MILITANT

Just as Frederick Douglass emerged from the depths of slavery, so Malcolm X rose from the heart of the black ghetto. Born nearly a hundred years apart, these two men ascended from the underside of black America during periods of extreme social unrest. Frederick Douglass thundered against slavery; Malcolm X lashed out against racial segregation and oppression. Each resisted to the end the forces which attempted to deny them their sense of self. Each tried to articulate the outrage of their black brothers.

Malcolm X was born on May 19, 1925 in Omaha, Nebraska. His father Earl Little, an undiluted black from Georgia, was murdered by whites in 1931. Louise Little, the mother of Malcolm X, was a mulatto native of the island of Grenada. She moved to Detroit, Michigan shortly after her husband's death. Without the support of his parents, Malcolm began an almost predictable pattern of delinquency and crime, but showed better than average talents before dropping out of school at the age of fifteen.

By his sixteenth birthday, Malcolm had moved east, first to Boston to live with relatives, and later to New York. In Harlem, he drifted into the underworld of "numbers," bootlegging, dope, commercial sex and confidence games. By this time he was variously known as "Detroit Red," "Big Red," and simply "Red" because of his height and reddish hair. Before his twenty-first birthday he had been convicted and sentenced to prison for burglary.

It was in the state prison at Charlestown, Massachusetts that he learned of the Black Muslim movement and the teachings of Elijah Muhammad. In prison from 1946 to 1952, Malcolm re-entered society a dedicated follower of Elijah Muhammad. In 1953 Malcolm Little, now known as Malcolm X, became assistant minister of the Muslim's Detroit mosque. Elijah, pleased with his work, transferred him to Philadelphia and later assigned him to Mosque number 7 in Harlem. By the end of 1956, the New York mosque was one of the most successful in the movement. By the early 1960's, Malcolm X overshadowed his nominal superior, Elijah Muhammad.

In 1963, Malcolm X was suspended as minister of the New York mosque and attempted to organize a group of his own, the Organization of Afro-American Unity. He travelled the length and breadth of the nation with a message of black manhood and independence, and made two voyages to the Middle East and Africa. The effect of these journeys was to increase his optimism regarding brotherhood between blacks and whites the world over.

He had made many enemies, black and white, before and after his break with Elijah Muhammad, and feared for his life. On February 21, 1965, what he feared came true. He was assassinated in the Audubon Ballroom in New York City. His death was headlined around the world. Most commentators on the life of Malcolm X agreed that his greatest contribution was "telling it like it is" in a style and manner that made America listen to the voice of an outraged *man*.

Malcolm X, "I'm Talking to You White Man," *Saturday Evening Post* (September 12, 1964), pp. 30-52; *"The Autobiography of Malcolm X"* (New York: Grove Press, Inc. 1965); George Breitman (ed.), *Malcolm X Speaks* (New York Grove Press, Inc. 1965).

Robert C. Weaver (1907-   )

FIRST NEGRO CABINET MEMBER

the Housing Authority. During World War II, Weaver held a succession of posts connected with the mobilization of black manpower.

After the war, Robert C. Weaver served as executive secretary of the Mayor's Commission on Race Relations in Chicago, taught at Northwestern University, and also at Columbia and New York universities. From 1949 to 1955, he directed the Opportunity Fellowships Program of the John Hay Whitney Foundation. In 1955, Weaver returned to public life, becoming Deputy Commissioner of Housing for New York State. In 1960, he was named vice-chairman of the New York City Housing and Redevelopment Board. In 1961, President John F. Kennedy named him administrator of the Federal Housing and Home Finance Agency. When the various sub-divisions of the government's housing bureaus were brought together in the Department of Housing and Urban Development in 1966, Robert C. Weaver was appointed secretary of the department.

Robert Weaver is a native of Washington, D.C. He was educated in the public schools of the District and then went to Harvard University where he earned the B.S. degree *cum laude* in 1929 and the M.S. degree in 1931. He taught economics briefly at A & T College (now University), at Greensboro, North Carolina and then returned to Harvard to earn the Ph.D. in economics in 1934. He married Ella V. Haith in July, 1935.

Dr. Weaver managed to blend the worlds of government and academia rather smoothly. He served on numerous college and foundation boards, including the Visiting Committee of the Harvard MIT Joint Center for Urban Studies and the Advisory Council of the Woodrow Wilson School of Public and International Affairs. He is the author of four books: *Negro Labor: A National Problem* (1946); *The Negro Ghetto* (1948); *The Urban Complex* (1964); and *Dilemmas of Urban America* (1965). He has also written more than sixty articles for various periodicals and journals. Recently Dr. Weaver was made president of the Bernard Baruch School of Business Administration, New York City.

On January 18, 1966, Robert Clifton Weaver was sworn in as the secretary of the newly created Department of Housing and Urban Development. Only one man was his superior: that man was the president of the United States. Robert C. Weaver thus became the first black man ever to hold a cabinet position in the United States Government.

Robert C. Weaver brought to this post thirty-three years of experience as a specialist in public affairs. He first entered the federal service in 1933 as an associate adviser on Negro Affairs, Department of the Interior. The next year, Weaver became special advisor to Harold L. Ickes, the Secretary of the Interior. From 1934 to 1938 Weaver was special assistant to Nathan Straus, administrator of

Harry A. Ploski, and Roscoe C. Brown, Jr. (eds.), *The Negro Almanac* (New York, 1967), pp. 45-47; Richard Bardolph, *The Negro Vanguard* (New York, 1959), pp. 361-363.

VIII EDUCATION

They Carried The Lamp

The African-American has long possessed a deep faith in the power of education to bring about a change in his status and in the conditions affecting his personal life. He has believed that education is the key to many of the shackles that bind him. In the days of slavery this was also believed by his master, who made it a crime for him to learn to read and write.

Like the history of all education in America, the history of the education of black Americans can be traced to the church. Under the impetus of the Quakers in Philadelphia, schools were provided for Africans as early as 1774. In the North the hunger for education was manifested in schools such as the African Free School, which was opened in New York by the Manumission Society in 1787. In 1798 a school was set up in Boston, Massachusetts in the home of Primus Hall, a prominent Negro.

General public support for the education of free blacks commenced with the state of New Jersey in 1777. From this time forward, there was some tax support for the maintenance of African-American schools in the North. Small schools were set up in Virginia at the beginning of the nineteenth century. New York set aside money for the operation of the Free African Schools in 1824. By 1830, Connecticut, Rhode Island, and other northern states supported a few schools for Negroes. In the South, schools were operating in some cities of Virginia, North and South Carolina, Kentucky, Georgia, Florida, and Tennessee.

In 1829 Daniel Payne, an educator and a minister of the African Methodist Episcopal church, opened a school in his native Charleston, South Carolina with three free-born children and three adult slaves. Payne had to purchase his books secretly from peddlers as no bookstores would sell them to him. After the Nat Turner uprising, a wave of repression hit the South. In 1835 Daniel Payne was forced to close his little school, which by this time had sixty students.

John Chavis, another native of Charleston, had been teaching whites by day and blacks at night. He too had to close his school. In Canterbury, Connecticut during the same general period, Prudence Crandall operated a girls' school for whites. When she admitted a few girls from prosperous black families who came from other states, her school was stoned and she was taken to court for violating a state law forbidding non-residents to study in Connecticut schools.

The search for education went underground. Many whites risked fines and possible imprisonment by secretly teaching eager blacks. Many aggressive slaves such as Frederick Douglass often exchanged their services or meager valuables for tidbits of learning. By 1838 thirteen private schools were open in Philadelphia. In 1840 the wealthy colored people of New Orleans founded the Ecole des Orphelins Indigents and several other educational and charitable institutions. The Methodist Episcopal Church purchased 120 acres of land in Green County, Ohio and established the basis for Wilberforce University in 1847.

The big drive for education came following the Civil War. Military service experience during the war had helped to educate tens of thousands of the more than 180,000 black soldiers engaged in the conflict. After the war, the Freedmen's Bureau and many missionary societies made education their major objective. During its short life-span (1865-1872), the Freedmen's Bureau "established altogether 4,239 schools and these had 9,307 teachers and 247,333 students."

The major religious denominations were most instrumental in laying the foundation of higher education among the freedmen. The American Baptist Home Missionary Society, the Freedmen's Aid Society of the Methodist Church, the conferences of the African Methodist Episcopal Church, and similar groups brought education to more than a million southern blacks between 1865-1875. Negroes raised large sums, particularly for elementary education.

Prior to the Civil War there were only two Negro institutions of higher learning: Wilberforce and Lincoln Universities. During the first decade of the Reconstruction era (1865-1876) ten colleges and universities were founded in the Southern states. In the next decade nearly all of the ex-Confederate states set up various agricultural and manual arts or agricultural and industrial ("A & M" and "A & I") colleges which today dot the South. By 1900 there were nearly one hundred institutions bearing those titles. The most celebrated of these was Tuskegee Institute, established in 1881 by Booker T. Washington.

Since that time many changes have come about, first with blacks attending white colleges in the north and later with a law for school desegregation. Black educators and administrators hold key positions in all areas of education. Most of the Northern institutions of higher learning have one or more black faculty members, with some as heads of departments.

In the late 1960's, the demand for black study programs in the colleges and universities of the nation was one of major confrontation. Lower standards of education in the elementary and high schools, in addition to the cry for black study programs, was a dominant concern of the black communities. The answer to these needs and demands is a problem which remains to be resolved today.

Leon Litwack. *North of Slavery*, (Chicago, 1961); Willard Range. *The Rise and Progress of Negro Colleges in Georgia: 1865-1949*, (Athens, Georgia, 1951); Ridgely Torrence, *The Story of John Hope*, (New York, 1948), pp. 312-367; Gunnar Myrdal, *An American Dilemma* (vol. II), (New York, 1944), pp. 887-903.

William Scarborough
(1852-1926)

LECTURER, SCHOLAR, LINGUIST

Wilberforce University, near Xenia, Ohio (early 1900's)

A lecturer, linguist and college president, William Saunders Scarborough was a member of that unusual band of ex-slaves who achieved eminence in freedom. Like many of his contemporaries, Scarborough early showed a desire to learn and secured his basic education by stealthy reading, with the help of sympathetic white playmates and adults. Although he became a minister at an early age, he did not devote himself solely to the pulpit but concentrated on the Greek classics. Extremely proficient with languages, he was elected to the American Philological Association in 1882, the American Spelling Reform Association in 1883, the Modern Language Association and the American Social Science Association in 1884 and 1885 respectively.

Scarborough was born on February 16, 1852 in Macon, Georgia and began school at the age of six. At the age of ten he could read and write, and during the Civil War was able to forge passes for his fellow slaves and to read the war news to men at the shoemaker's shop where he worked part-time. At the age of twelve, he began the study of music; at fifteen he entered the Lewis High School and completed the course in two years. He then attended Atlanta University and later Oberlin College,

earning the B. A. degree from the latter institution in 1875, and the M.A. degree in 1878. He managed to get to Africa and attended Liberia College, completing his studies there in 1882 with the LL.D. degree.

Even before receiving his M. A. degree, Scarborough had taught Latin, Greek and mathematics at his former high school. In 1881 he authored a Greek textbook which was published by A. B. Barnes Company, New York and received high critical acclaim in academic circles. In 1886 Scarborough wrote *"The Birds" of Aristophanes: A Theory of Interpretation*, a scholarly analysis. With an early grounding in Greek and Latin, Scarborough became an able student of Slavonic languages, Sanskrit and even Hebrew. He read papers before a number of scholarly societies, including the American Philological Association.

After a short period as president of a small denominational college in Columbia, South Carolina, Scarborough joined the faculty of Wilberforce University in Ohio and in 1908 became president of the institution. He rendered outstanding service as an administrator during this time, and finally retired at the age of sixty-eight in 1920.

William J. Simmons, *Men of Mark* (Cleveland, 1887), pp. 410-418; *Dictionary of American Biography*, XVI (1935).

William J. Simmons
(1849-1890)

BIOGRAPHER, EDUCATOR, CLERGYMAN

William J. Simmons ranks with William Cooper Nell and William Wells Brown as a chronicler of the lives of black men during the nineteenth century. Greatly influential in his own era, Simmons continues to contribute to the history of the black man through his monumental work, *Men of Mark: Eminent, Rising, Progressive* (Cleveland: George M. Rewel, 1887). This work is a storehouse of biographical data on historical Negro leaders. It contains over 1,000 pages and 106 engraved portraits. In 1891, I. Garland Penn, the author of *The Afro-American Press and Its Editors*, described *Men of Mark* as a "book of priceless value to all who desire to know and learn of the chief scribes and orators of the Negro race."

William J. Simmons was well known before the appearance of his master work. In 1882, he was chairman of the Executive Committee of the Convention of the Colored Men of Kentucky. He addressed the Kentucky state legislature in a memorable speech listing the grievances of over a quarter million black citizens of that state whose rights were being violated. Over 2,000 copies of this address were printed and distributed to the public. Simmons edited a number of newspapers and periodicals, chief among them being the *American Baptist* and *Our Women and Children*. The latter journal was the first Negro publication devoted exclusively to the concerns of mothers and children. In 1887 he was president of the Colored Press Association, an organization of editors interested in developing a unified policy for fighting racial discrimination and segregation.

Simmons was prominent in the ministry and education. He pastored churches in Florida and Kentucky, and at one time was Secretary of the Southern District of the American Baptist Home Mission Society. He organized the American National Baptist Convention in St. Louis, Missouri in 1886. As an educator, he was president of the Normal and Theological Institution of Kentucky and later of the State University of Kentucky at Louisville.

William J. Simmons was a native of Charleston, South Carolina. His mother was a slave; his father unknown. Carried from bondage via the underground railroad, Simmons spent his adolescence in Philadelphia and in Bordenton, New Jersey where he was apprenticed to a dentist. He aspired to become a physician but found his way blocked because of his race. In 1864, at the age of fourteen, young Simmons volunteered for the 41st U.S. Colored Troops and participated in skirmishes around Petersburg, Hatches Run and Appomattox, Virginia.

Following his discharge from the army in 1865, Simmons began his study of religion and theology. After attending Madison and Rochester Universities in New York for short periods, he enrolled at Howard University from which he was graduated in 1873. Simmons made his mark in history in less than two decades before his premature death in 1890.

I. Garland Penn, *The Afro-American Press and Its Editors* (Springfield, 1891), pp. 120-122; Henry McNeal Turner, "Introduction," *Men of Mark* (Cleveland, Ohio 1887) pp. 1-63.

Booker T. Washington (1856-1915)

When the Board of Commissioners of Tuskegee Normal Institute asked General Samuel C. Armstrong of Hampton Institute for a principal to head their institution, they wanted a white man. Instead, Booker T. Washington was selected, and he searched the map in vain for the location of Tuskegee. When he arrived at Tuskegee in June of 1881, the institute consisted of a rickety church and a small shanty, plus thirty-one students from the nearby farms.

Two men were responsible for the creation of the institute: Lewis Adams, a successful Negro farmer and W. F. Foster, a local white politician who was trying to win votes among the Negroes of Macon County, Alabama. Foster had obtained an annual appropriation of $2,000 and a few acres of land for the school.

On July 4, 1881, Booker T. Washington opened the doors of the school. Physical survival was the main problem confronting the principal and his young charges. Food had to be grown and buildings erected, for the two dilapidated structures were totally insufficient. With a directness typical of him, Washington led the way in felling trees, clearing the land, digging wells for water and constructing buildings to house the new school.

A natural politician, Washington cultivated the good will of whites and Negroes in Macon County. He explained that Tuskegee was to be an industrial training school, not a liberal arts college. All of the students were to work to pay their way, and to run the school. His gospel of self-help appealed to many people. The student body in-

creased, and permanent buildings replaced temporar shelters and shanties. By 1900 over forty buildings dotte the clearing that was Tuskegee, erected mainly by studer labor and paid for by northern philanthropy.

Booker Washington spoke to numerous audiences i the North and seemed to offer a solution to the naggin problems of the freedmen. His industrial school was turn ing out graduates who were successful farmers, carpenter and bricklayers; these were sober, hard-working citizen who "minded their own business." His name was know throughout the South.

In 1895 Booker T. Washington was invited to speak a the Atlanta Exposition. This was the first such invitatio extended to a Negro leader in the deep South. Muc speculation developed over what he was going to say Washington himself realized that this was a special occa sion and took great pains in composing his speech.

Birthplace replica at Rocky Mount, Va.

THE LENGTHENED SHADOW

On September 18, Booker T. Washington, on the same platform with Georgia's governor and other dignitaries, rose to make his speech. James Creel, a noted correspondent for the New York *World*, described Washington as he appeared that day: "There was a remarkable figure; tall, bony, straight as a Sioux chief, high forehead, straight nose, heavy jaws, and strong, determined mouth, with big white teeth, piercing eyes and a commanding manner...."

In his speech Washington apologized for the "errors" his race had made in beginning "at the top instead of at the bottom" in seeking seats in state legislatures rather than developing skills in industry and real estate, in pursuing politics rather than cultivating truck gardens. He urged the southern Negro to "cast down your bucket where you are" in agriculture, mechanics, commerce, domestic service and the like. He said that "the wisest among my race understand that the agitation of questions of social equality is the extremest folly," and he felt that "in all things that are social we can be as separate as the fingers, yet one as the hand in all things essential for mutual progress."

The white audience went wild; the governor shook his hand publicly. The nation's press heralded his speech as the greatest utterance of an American Negro. Overnight Washington was a national figure with more speaking engagements than he could possibly handle. Philanthropists pressed money upon his Institute.

At this time Tuskegee had eight hundred students, a staff of fifty-five, $200,000 worth of buildings and one-hundred sixty-five graduates taking the Tuskegee idea throughout the South. After the speech, enrollment increased: Dorothy Hall, Douglas Hall, Institute Chapel, and other buildings rose on the wings of northern cash.

Washington himself helped to institutionalize northern philanthropy. In 1907 he helped set up the Anna T. Jeanes Foundation for Negro rural schools; in 1910 he was host to the formative meetings of the General Education Board fund; in 1911 he cooperated in the establishment of the Phelps-Stokes Fund and the Carnegie Foundation. Two years later he participated in the development of the Rosenwald Fund idea.

By 1915 Tuskegee had over sixty buildings and an endowment of nearly three million dollars. Both the school and the man were internationally famous. Washington never slackened the tempo of his work. He suffered a fatal heart attack on November 14, 1915.

Debate over his racial adjustment philosophy continues to this day; however, there was never any question of his role and place in the building of Tuskegee Institute.

Booker T. Washington, *Up From Slavery* (New York, Bantam Pathfinder Edition, 1963); Samuel R. Spencer, Jr., *Booker T. Washington and the Negro's Place in American Life* (Boston, 1955).

First U.S. stamp to honor a Negro, issued April, 1940

...at the time he founded Tuskegee

William Edward Burghardt Du Bois (1868-1963)

WITH FLAME AND SWORD

If any scholar deserved to become a legend in his own time it was William Burghardt Du Bois. Throughout his life he hacked at the enslaving chains of racism and prejudice with the sword of scientific truth, and thrust the flame of his intellect into the dark caves of degrading myth and stereotype. The sheer brilliance of his scholarship and the passionate vigor of his pen accounted for more than twenty books and over one hundred scholarly articles, not to mention the dozens of chapters in volumes edited by him and the many newspaper columns under his name.

Born February 23, 1868 in Great Barrington, Massachusetts, Du Bois was the son of a wandering, mixed-blood father and a mother who had to take in washing and boarders to support the family. Finishing prep school with honors and a scholarship, he received his B.A. from Fisk University in 1888, graduated *cum laude* from Harvard in 1890, and earned his Ph.D. there six years later. As a graduate student at the University of Berlin between 1892 and 1894, he gained broadening experience through extensive travel in Europe. However, it was not until 1927 that he made the first of several trips to Russia which influenced him to join the Communist Party much later in his life.

No single title does credit to the prodigious talents of Du Bois. He has been labeled educator, author, historian, sociologist, philosopher, poet, leader, radical, apostle of peace, and prophet. He earned each label and deserves others which might describe how he has inspired black youth all over the world.

Du Bois was a pioneer social scientist. He authored one of the standard books on the Reconstruction Era and conducted the first studies of the Negro in Philadelphia and Atlanta. He organized the Atlanta University Studies of the Negro Problems, editing papers on business, common school, college, art, church, crime, health, and family life. His economic study, published in 1901, revealed facts about the Negro in Georgia which were pertinent to investigations conducted by the Civil Rights Commission sixty years later.

The first major work which earned for him the title of historian was *The Suppression of the African Slave Trade to the United States of America, 1638-1870* which contained 335 pages with voluminous footnotes and bibliography. Du Bois was twenty-four years of age when he worked on this subject, and, ironically, was a professor of Greek and Latin when it was published two years later in 1895.

Perhaps his greatest fame came, not from his scholarly work, but from his debate at the turn of the century with Booker T. Washington over the type of education needed by the Negro in America. Washington, of course, stressed vocational education whereas Du Bois insisted on training in the liberal arts and the humanities. After the death of Booker T. Washington, W. E. B. Du Bois became the one generally recognized spokesman for the Negro.

The Ordeal of Mansart (Volume one of The Black Flame) (1957)

Darkwater: Voices from within the Veil

The World and Africa (1947)

John Brown (1909)

The Negro (1915)

Dark Princess (1928)

The Souls of Black Folk

Black Folk, Then and Now (1939)

In Battle for Peace: The Story of My 83rd Birthday (1952)

Worlds of Color (Volume three of The Black Flame) (1961)

The Quest of the Silver Fleece (1911)

Mansart Builds a School (Volume two of The Black Flame) (1959)

The Gift of Black Folk: Negroes in the Making of America (1924)

Dusk of Dawn: An Essay toward an Autobiography of a Race Concept (1940)

Color and Democracy: Colonies and Peace (1945)

He was a prolific promoter of the written word. Among the various publications founded and edited by him are: *The Moon* (Tenn., 1906); *The Horizons* (Washington, D.C., 1907-1910); *Crisis*, the official organ of the NAACP 1910-1934); *Phylon*, an Atlanta University quarterly 1940-1944); *The Brownies' Book*, a magazine for children (1920-1921).

As an organizer and leader Du Bois was both tireless and fearless. In 1905 he launched the Niagara Movement, advocating the immediate ending of racial discrimination and segregation, and in 1909 was one of the founders of the NAACP which grew out of this movement. In 1919 he initiated the Pan-African Conferences in Paris with the hope of focusing world opinion on the conditions of black men everywhere. On behalf of the NAACP at the United Nations he tried to get a firm anti-colonial commitment from the United States in 1945, and in 1947 presented a protest against American jim crow. In 1949 he helped to organize the Cultural and Scientific Conference for World Peace in New York, and later attended their meetings in Paris and Moscow.

His leadership of the Peace Information Center resulted in his being indicted, along with four other Americans, for being an "unregistered foreign agent." This was during the McCarthy era of the 1950's, and suspected subversives were being hunted without restraint. Du Bois, then 83 years old, said, "It is a curious thing that I am called upon to defend myself against charges for openly advocating the one thing all people want—peace." In spite of intimidation, liberals rallied to his support and petitions of two million signatures were collected. Before Du Bois could take the stand in his own defense in November 1951, the case was dismissed. But the Cold War against Communism continued and, because of Du Bois' radical views and activities, the press and the public accomplished what the courts could not. Many halls were closed to his speeches and newspapers denied him their pages. Even some leading Negro organizations avoided the now controversial figure. It was a bitter experience and Du Bois bent beneath it. But he did not break. The civil rights confrontations of the young students in the South sustained his hope. They were fulfilling some of his prophecies.

The prophetic historical insights of Du Bois are perhaps the most impressive evidence of his intellect. Long before the Negro Revolution of the late sixties he championed "economic democracy" and the channeling of "black power"—physical, political, economic, and spiritual —through a unified Negro society. He said, "We must smash segregation *with* segregation." Though he was near white himself, his keen awareness of the beauty of Negritude, both culturally and physically, pre-dated by many years the "black is beautiful" concept of the mid-century

militants. His "black pride" was manifested by his stated belief that black people had a special mission to humanity: through racial integrity ("soul power") to humanize the civilized world.

Du Bois died at 11:40 P.M., August 27, 1963, the day before the great demonstration in Washington, D.C. Though ninety-five years old and a rather lonely citizen of Ghana, at the time of his death he was hard at work on a mammoth compendium of African culture entitled *Encyclopedia Africana*.

Frances L. S. Broderick. *Du Bois: Negro Leader in a Time of Crisis* (Stanford, 1959); Elbert L. Tatum. *The Changed Political Thought of the Negro, 1915-1940* (Chicago, 1942). *Freedomways: W.E.B. Du Bois Memorial Issue*, Vol. 5, No. 7 (Winter 1965).

Arthur Schomberg (1874-1938)

BIBLIOPHILE-ANTIQUARIAN

The study of black history in the United States has been greatly facilitated by the existence of the Arthur Schomberg Collection of the Harlem (135th street) Branch of the New York Public Library. Scholars from all parts of the nation gather at the collection which contains more than 45,000 books, periodicals and pamphlets, 4,000 manuscripts, 200 scrapbooks, over 1,000 microfilm reels of Afro-American newspapers, and 140 pieces of African art. At the Schomberg, a reader may see copies of the 1792-93 almanacs of Benjamin Banneker, *Clotel*, the first novel published by a black American, early editions of the poems of Phillis Wheatley, the addresses and broadsides of free men of color in their conventions of protest, and may find many other items in the aging building located diagonally across the street from the famed Harlem YMCA building.

The Schomberg Collection is an extended rebuttal by Arthur Schomberg to one of his teachers who claimed that the black man had no significant history. Born in San Juan, Puerto Rico, Arthur Schomberg attended the elementary schools of San Juan, St. Thomas College, Danish West Indies and was graduated from the Institute de Instruccion, San Juan. He left the island for the States in April, 1891 hoping to become a lawyer. Young Schomberg headed for New York where he read law for five years, but found work with Afro-American study groups more rewarding than law. He was founder and secretary of the Negro Society for History Research (1911), and president of the American Negro Society (1922-26). For a time he worked as a clerk for the New York Bankers Trust Company. At his own expense, he often took extended vacations to Europe, North Africa and South America in search of books, pamphlets, manuscripts and etchings.

In 1926, the Carnegie Corporation paid Arthur Schomberg the sum of $10,000 for his collection. Schomberg then gave up his job at the bank and became the curator of the Negro collection at Fisk University in Nashville, Tennessee. In 1932, however, he was invited to become the curator of the 135th Street Branch of the New York Public Library. He had the unique pleasure of maintaining a collection which he had put together over the years while being paid to do so by the city of New York. This collection was called the Schomberg Collection after his death in 1938.

Ebony (October, 1967), pp. 55-60; Harry Ploski and Roscoe C. Brown, *The Negro Almanac* (New York, 1966), p. 156.

Alain L. Locke (1886-1954)

RHODES SCHOLAR, PHILOSOPHER

The Rhodes Scholarship is to the world of academic preparation what the Nobel Prize is to the world of international achievement. Both awards represent the highest pinnacle. In addition to intellectual ability, the Rhodes Scholarships are given on the basis of moral character and the potentialities of the applicant for significant achievement in later life. Alain LeRoy Locke was the first Negro recipient of this most prestigious graduate scholarship since it was created by Cecil Rhodes in 1899, and he more than satisfied its criteria on all three counts.

(To date, only three Negroes have been selected for the Rhodes Scholarship since: John E. Wideman of Pittsburgh, Pennsylvania and Joseph S. Sanders of Los Angeles, California in 1962; and William McCurine of Chicago, Illinois in 1969.)

A native of Philadelphia, Alain Locke went to Oxford as a Rhodes Scholar in 1907. After three years he left Oxford for the University of Berlin. Upon his return to America from Germany in 1912, Locke joined the faculty of Howard University that same year, and became a full professor of philosophy in 1917, a year before he received his Ph.D. from Harvard University.

In the area of philosophy, Locke's writings have been regarded as "original contributions in a highly controversial field." His philosophical works include *The Problem of Classification in the Theory of Value* and *Values and Imperatives in American Philosophy: Today and Tomorrow.*

Dr. Locke's intellectual influence spread far beyond his academic specialty. In 1925 he edited a collection of significant literature by young Negro authors in an epochal volume called *The New Negro*. During the Negro Renaissance (sometimes called the "Harlem Renaissance") Locke became the leading intellectual spokesman for the remarkable upsurge of creativity among Negroes in literature, art and drama.

In 1933 he published *The Negro in America;* in 1936, *The Negro and His Music*. The next year he wrote *Negro Art: Past and Present* and in 1941 published *The Negro in Art*. For a number of years he wrote annual reviews of the developments in literature by black authors. He encouraged many promising young writers and artists.

Many awards and honors came to Dr. Locke. He was the first Negro to be elected president of the National Council of Adult Education. He was an exchange professor to Haiti in 1943, and a visiting professor at several universities, including Fisk and the University of Wisconsin.

So busy was Dr. Locke in encouraging others, his own masterwork *The Negro in American Culture* was completed by Margaret Just Butcher after his death. Alain Locke lived up to every expectation of the donor of the Rhodes Scholarships.

Who's Who in Colored America, 1950, pp. 342-343; *Negro Yearbook, 1947,* pp. 411-412; Margaret Just Butcher, *The Negro In American Culture.*

Carter G. Woodson (1875-1950)

FATHER OF NEGRO HISTORY

William Cooper Nell, William Still, William Wells Brown, George Washington Williams and W. E. B. DuBois wrote books on various aspects of the history of the Negro. Despite their pioneering efforts, however, systematic treatment of Negro history was not begun until 1915 when Carter G. Woodson, an ex-coal miner and school teacher, organized the Association for the Study of Negro Life and History. Over the years the still-thriving Association has published many important volumes in this field. Today most educational institutions are conscious of the Negro's past. Many of them are developing study programs to fill this neglected gap in the education of most Americans.

Woodson himself set the pace for research in this area. Among his books are *The Education of the Negro Prior to 1861, A Century of Negro Migration, The Negro in Our History, Negro Makers of History, The Story of The Negro Retold, The Mind of the Negro as Reflected in Letters Written During the Crisis of 1800-1861, Negro Orators and Their Orations* and *The History of the Negro Church.*

In the year 1916, Dr. Woodson started the *Journal of Negro History,* a scholarly repository of research which is used by students throughout the world. He initiated the observance of Negro History Week in 1926. Eleven years later the Association began the publication of *The Negro History Bulletin,* a more popular vehicle for disseminating the findings of scholars and researchers.

Carter G. Woodson was born in Canton, Virginia in 1875. Having little opportunity or money to attend school, he was twenty-two years old when he completed high school. During this period Woodson supported himself by working as a coal miner. He continued his education at Berea College in Kentucky and at the University of Chicago. He terminated his formal studies with a Doctor of Philosophy degree from Harvard in 1912. Three years later he organized the Association for the Study of Negro Life and History. Dr. Woodson firmly believed that "the achievements of the Negro properly set forth will crown him as a factor in early human progress and a maker of modern civilization." His life and work are eloquent testimony to that belief.

Who's Who in Colored America, 1950; p. 572; John Hope Franklin, "The Place of Carter G. Woodson in American Historiography," *The Negro History Bulletin* (May, 1950), pp. 174-176.

Charles S. Johnson (1893-1956)

EDUCATOR, SOCIAL SCIENTIST

Jubilee Hall, Fisk University, Nashville, Tenn.

While the field of sociology has attracted hundreds of black scholars, none of them has ever achieved the eminence of Charles Spurgeon Johnson. In volume after volume of social research, Charles S. Johnson revealed to the world the status and strivings of the Negro on the farms and in the cities. Any serious study of the Negro in America must include his work.

The very titles of his books give some indication of his interests: *The Negro in Chicago* (1922); *The Negro in American Civilization* (1930); *Negro Housing* (1932); *Economic Status of the Negro* (1933); *Shadow of the Plantation* (1934); *Collapse of Cotton Tenancy* (1934); *Growing Up in the Black Belt* (1941) and *Into the Mainstream* (1947).

In 1946 Charles Johnson was named president of Fisk University in Nashville, Tennessee. He was the first Negro to head this institution since it was founded in 1865. Before and after his elevation from his directorship of the able social science department at Fisk University, Johnson helped this institution to remain a leader in the scientific study of race relations in America.

Dr. Johnson's training in social science research may be traced back to his student days at the University of Chicago when he witnessed the Chicago race riot of 1919. The Chicago Urban League selected him to head an investigation of the social forces causing the riot. For six years (1923-29) he was associate executive director of the Chicago Commission on Human Relations. In 1928 he was appointed to the faculty of Fisk University and remained with this institution the balance of his life.

His knowledge and experience were sought at several White House conferences on youth. He was a consultant to, and a member of, many commissions, including those devoted to educational problems in Japan, and with the United Nations.

A native of Bristol, Virginia, Dr. Johnson received his formal education at Virginia Union University and the University of Chicago from which he received the Ph.B. in 1928. As a youth shining shoes in Bristol, he developed the detachment, the curiosity, and the concern about people which characterized all of his scientific work. His death in 1956 created a void in the study of race relations in America.

Who's Who in Colored America, 1950, pp. 302-320; Edward Embree, *Thirteen Against the Odds* (New York, 1956).

Mordecai Johnson (1890-   )

ORATOR, EDUCATOR

For over thirty years, Mordecai Johnson was one of the most renowned university presidents in America. As president of Howard University in Washington, D.C. he became a near-legendary figure in his own lifetime. Under Dr. Johnson, Howard University, founded in 1867 in an abandoned dance-hall and beer saloon, changed from a cluster of second-rate departments to nationally-approved units of distinction. The University's School of Law is preeminent in the area of civil rights.

When Mordecai Johnson came to the University at the age of thirty-six, many people questioned his ability. When he retired thirty years later, he was acknowledged as *the* great president of the school. The faculty had tripled; salaries had doubled. Congressional appropriations which support the school, had increased to $6,000,000 annually. Freedmen's Hospital was turning out half of the Negro physicians in the country. The University's physical plant was valued at $34,000,000.

Before assuming the presidency of Howard Universit in 1926 Mordecai Johnson had been a successful Baptis minister in Charleston, West Virginia. Prior to this h had taught economics and history at his alma mater Morehouse College (class of 1911). He had also served a student secretary with the national office of the Youn Men's Christian Association.

Born in Columbus, Tennessee, Mordecai Johnson wa an only child. His father, a minister and laborer, was rather stern man who worked at a mill six days a week twelve hours a day for forty years. His mother cushione the sternness of the father and encouraged him in hi education.

Johnson's oratorical ability won for him acclaim eve while in high school and was quite evident at Morehous and Harvard where, in 1922, he attracted national atten tion with a commencement speech entitled "The Faith o the American Negro." Mordecai Johnson earned his A. B degree from Morehouse in 1911, the Master of Sacre Theology degree from Harvard in 1923, and the Doctor o Divinity degree from Gammon Theological Seminary i 1928.

Dr. Johnson was active in numerous religious and governmental bodies, including a presidential commission for the study and review of conditions in Haiti and the Virgin Islands. He was a member of the Advisory Council of the National Youth Administration and a member of the National Advisory Council on Education. In addition to many honorary degrees, Dr. Johnson is one of the few Negroes who have won the Spingarn Medal (1929) as having done the most to contribute to the progress of the Negro during the previous year.

Who's Who in Colored America, 1950, p. 307; Richard Bardolph, *The Negro Vanguard* (New York, 1961, Paperback), pp. 168-169.

Benjamin E. Mays (1895-   ) PREACHER, EDUCATOR, LEADER

A distinguished looking black eulogist at the funeral of
. Martin Luther King in 1968 said, in reference to
ng's all-too-brief life, "It isn't how long, but how well."
e speaker was Dr. Benjamin E. Mays, King's dear
end, former teacher and himself an example of his own
rds. In 1967, Dr. Mays had retired from the presidency
Morehouse College in Atlanta, Georgia, after twenty-
en years of outstanding service. During this time, the
lege came to be dubbed the "black Oxford of the South."
. Mays had placed the college on a sounder financial
ting, collected a faculty nearly half of whom held the
.D. degree, expanded the school's physical plant, and
ced on campus "as much scientific equipment per stu-
t as any college in the country."

But Dr. Mays is known far beyond the Morehouse
mpus. In a career beginning in the 1920's, he has been a
cticing minister, a professor of higher mathematics and
glish, an Urban League official (Tampa, Florida, 1926-
28), national student secretary of the YMCA (1928-
0), director of the first scientific study of the status
black churches in America (1930-1932), vice president
the Federal Council of Churches (1944-1946) and a
mber of numerous national boards and panels. He has
o represented educational and religious groups in differ-
parts of the world.

3orn on August 1, 1895, Dr. Mays is a native of Ep-
rth, South Carolina and grew up as the last of seven
ldren of ex-slaves and semi-literate farmers. His bril-
nce was recognized early and he grew accustomed to the
udits of the public as he won a local reputation for skills
mathematics and oratory. Stunned by the assertion that
cks were intellectually inferior to whites, he was deter-
ned to destroy this myth. After completing the ele-
ntary and high school in the state, Mays first entered
rginia Union University. After a year, however, he was
e to enter Bates College (Maine) where he settled

for himself the question of inferiority by winning a Phi
Beta Kappa key and graduating in 1920. He later entered
the University of Chicago to earn a M.A. degree in 1925; a
decade later he was awarded the Ph.D. degree by the same
university. In 1934, Dr. Mays joined Howard University
as Dean of its school of religion, and in 1940 he was named
the president of Morehouse College. One of his first acts as
president was to appoint students to all major committees
involving campus-wide responsibility, a step that most colleges have only recently begun to consider.

Dr. Mays is the author or co-author of five books, including *The Negro's Church* (1933) and *The Negro's God as
Reflected in His Literature* (1938). He has contributed to
more than 14 other books, and has had over 70 articles
published in magazines and journals. Twenty-three institutions of higher learning have awarded him honorary
degrees in recognition of his achievements and contributions. For years, through his column, "My View," in Negro
newspapers, he has projected his pride of race and his faith
in America.

Morehouse College Bulletin: Commencement Issue (July 1965), p. 38; *Who's
Who in America* (1964-65), p. 1313; Lerone Bennet, Jr., "Men of Morehouse,"
Ebony (May 1961), pp. 25-32.

jamin E. Mays Hall Dormitory and Dining Room

John Hope Franklin (1915-

HISTORIAN, EDUCATOR

John Hope Franklin, chairman of the sixty-man history department of the University of Chicago is acknowledged to be one of the most scholarly historians in the world today. Requests for his services as a lecturer, consultant, and writer are overwhelming. Although Dr. Franklin's duties at the university are demanding, his commitments as a lecturer, consultant, writer, and member of national and international institutions and societies are equally so.

Among his civic and public services in the past has been his membership on the United States National Commission for UNESCO and the Board of Directors of the American Council on Human Rights. In 1962 President Kennedy appointed him to a three-year term on the Board of Foreign Scholarships. He serves as a member of the Fisk University Board of Trustees, the Board of Directors of the American Council of Learned Societies, and the Board of Directors of the Salzburg Seminar in America.

John Hope Franklin was born in Rentiesville, Oklahoma on January 2, 1915. When he was ten, the family moved to Tulsa, where his father practiced law. Franklin received the degree of Bachelor of Arts (magna cum laude) from Fisk University in 1935. Pursuing graduate studies in history, he went to Harvard University where he earned his A.M. and Ph.D. degrees in 1936 and 1941 respectively.

Although he received the Edward Austin and the Jul Rosenwald Fellowships to help foster his Harvard e cation, he earned his keep by waiting table and typi Ph.D. dissertations. Franklin continued his education w grants from the Social Science Research Council and Guggenheim Memorial Foundation. He was a Foundat Member of the Fisk University Chapter of the Society Phi Beta Kappa, and is a charter member of the Howa University Chapter of Phi Alpha Theta, honor society history.

Professor Franklin has taught at Fisk University, Augustine's College, North Carolina College at Durha and Howard University. In 1956 he became chairman the Department of History at Brooklyn College. He serv as visiting professor in several American universiti including Harvard, Cornell, Berkeley and the Universit of Wisconsin, California, and Hawaii. Abroad he h served twice as Professor at the Salzburg Seminar American Studies in Austria and also as visiting lectu at the Seminar in American Studies at Cambridge Univ sity in England. In 1962-63 he was Pitt Professor of Am ican History and Institutions at Cambridge Universi His educational activities have taken him to the Univ sities of Calcutta, Madras, Bombay, Australia, and Nigeria to study higher education in that country for t Department of State.

His first book, *The Free Negro in North Carolina, 179 1860*, was published in 1943. In 1947, *The Civil War Dia of James T. Ayers* and *From Slavery to Freedom* we published and, in 1956, *The Militant South*. These we followed by *A Fool's Errand* and *Reconstruction After t Civil War* (1961); *Army Life in a Black Regiment* (1962 and his *Emancipation Proclamation* (1963). For twen years he has been working on a biography of George Williams, the first serious Negro historian, and conten "Eventually I'll find time to finish it."

Dr. Franklin is chairman of the Fulbright Board a helps to select scholars. "International education is my b outside interest," he says, and believes that it transcen prejudice and is the best path to peace.

Time (January 11, 1963), p. 65; *The Negro Handbook* (Chicago, John Publishing Co., 1966), p. 401; Additional data supplied by John H Franklin.

IX LITERATURE
Tellers of Troubled Tales

The growth of an important body of literature in Negro America is very recent. In centuries past, however, individual Negroes made notable contributions to the literature of their respective adopted cultures. Jacques E. J. Capitein in Holland, Juan Latino in Spain, Alexander Pushkin in Russia and Alexandre Dumas, *pere* in France were men of color whose writing skill brought them to public notice.

While Jupiter Hammon and Phillis Wheatley wrote poems of some merit in the eighteenth century, the birth of a real literary tradition dates from around 1853, when William Wells Brown wrote *Clotel, or The President's Daughter,* a story of the hardships of a mulatto family. This novel went through several editions. Brown's book was published during the period when the slave narrative was in vogue.

In the eighteen nineties, a number of Negro authors wrote novels and poems which attracted small audiences. For the most part these were works of protest and propaganda. Frances Ellen Harper wrote *Iola, or Shadows Uplifted,* in 1892. In 1896 McHenry Jones published *Heart of Gold.* In 1900 Pauline Hopkins tried to portray the life of free Negroes in the North and South in her *Contending Forces.* Beginning in 1896, Sutton E. Griggs wrote, published, and distributed a number of novels devoted to themes of miscegenation, black leadership and southern politics. His novels such as *Imperium in Imperio, Unfettered* and *The Hindered Hand* received a rather wide distribution among literate Negroes.

These early writers were neophytes in letters. Charles Waddell Chesnutt was perhaps the first Negro writer to give serious consideration to the artistic requirements of the short story and the novel. National magazines were publishing his short stories as early as 1887. In subsequent years he published several novels, all of which were artistically superior to those of his contemporaries. He was the first Negro writer to rise above the double standard of literary criticism then applied to black authors. Charles Waddell Chesnutt's work was judged alongside the best general American fiction.

Between 1903 and 1923 only W. E. B. DuBois and James Weldon Johnson commanded a national audience. In 1903 DuBois published his influential collection of essays *The Souls of Black Folk.* In 1912 James Weldon Johnson produced his *Autobiography of an Ex-Coloured Man,* and saw the publication of *Fifty Years and Other Poems* five years later. In the year 1922 Claude McKay burst into print with his *Harlem Shadows.* Countee Cullen carried Negro poetry to a peak which was probably unsurpassed during this period. James Weldon Johnson brought a classical elegance to black poetry in his *God's Trombones* which continues to move readers. Between the publication of Cullen and Johnson's work during this period, poetry lovers were introduced to Langston Hughes, perhaps the most prolific and durable of all the writers of the "Negro Renaissance." *The Weary Blues,* a precursor of several collections of Hughes' poems, came off the press in 1925.

A casual reading of the lists of books written by Negroes during this period might suggest that poetry was the only medium of literary expression open to Negroes. A closer view, however, reveals important writers of prose. Jean Toomer's *Cane,* Walter White's *The Fire in the Flint,* Wallace Thurman's *The Blacker the Berry,* Eric Walrond's *Tropic Death* and Rudolph Fisher's *The Walls of Jericho* were published between 1923 and 1929. Alain Locke, the intellectual guide and interpreter of the era, attempted to explain the background and significance of the Negro Renaissance in his famous preface to *The New Negro,* an anthology of prose and poetry by black authors.

Langston Hughes opened the decade of the thirties with an excellent first novel entitled *Not Without Laughter.* George Schuyler wrote *Black No More* and the prolific Arna Bontemps penned *God Sends Sunday* in 1931. Jessie Redmond Fauset, perhaps the leading woman author of the "Negro Renaissance" wrote *The Chinaberry Tree* in the same year. George W. Lee, George Henderson, Waters Turpin and William Attaway were among the newer writers in this period. Zora Neal Hurston, a prolific but strangely neglected author, published *Jonah's Gourd Vine* in 1934. Hurston wrote *Their Eyes Were Watching God* (1937), *Moses, Man of the Mountain* (1939), and *Seraph on the Suwannee* (1948). By this time poetry-lovers were acquainted with the work of Melvin B. Tolson, Owen Dodson, Sterling Brown and Gwendolyn Brooks.

The publication in 1940 of Richard Wright's *Native Son* is often considered the beginning of the present stage of the evolution of the Negro's literary tradition. He was perhaps the first Negro writer of fiction to have reached hundreds of thousands of readers of all races both in America and abroad. Willard Motley with *Knock on Any Door,* Chester Himes with *If He Hollers Let Him Go,* and Ann Petry with *The Street* preceded Ralph Ellison who received the National Book Award in 1952 for *Invisible Man.* A year later James Baldwin exploded on the literary scene with *Go Tell It on the Mountain.*

In the 1960's the number of black novelists increased enormously. Among the more notable authors were John O. Killen, William Melvin Kelly, Margaret Walker Alexander, John A. Williams, and Robert Dean Pharr. In poetry, the virtuoso voice of Gwendolyn Brooks (*In the Mecca,* 1968) continued to be heard. Several newer poets made their appearance, perhaps the most impressive being Don L. Lee. Eldridge Cleaver was generally acclaimed the most forceful and penetrating new essayist. His *Soul on Ice* mirrored the rage, anguish—and artistry—of black men of letters during the closing years of a strident decade.

Hugh M. Gloster, *Negro Voices in American Fiction* (Chapel Hill, 1948); Herman Dreer, *American Literature by Negro Authors* (New York, 1950).

Phillis Wheatley (1753-1784)

A DUSKY SAPPHO

Mrs. Wheatley had a lot of time on her hands and im mediately began to teach the new slave girl. She nam her Phillis and became very fond of her. Within a fe months, little Phillis could speak and write English though she had been reared in Boston all of her life. Aft seven or eight years, Phillis was reading the classic roma tic poets, such as Horace and Virgil. She eventually re Alexander Pope who had died ten years before she w born in Senegal. His verses so impressed her that s mastered his poetic style and unconsciously used it in mo of her own poems.

When thirteen years old, Phillis Wheatley wrote " the University of Cambridge in New England." When s translated a poem from the Latin of Ovid, her admirers Boston were so astounded that they had the poem pu lished. In 1768 she wrote "To the King's Most Excelle Majesty" and a year later "On the Death of Rev. I Sewall." These were followed by other occasional poem

By 1773 Phillis Wheatley had turned out enough poer to have a collection of them published in London und the title *Poems on Various Subjects*. In 1772 she compos "A Farewell to America: To Mrs. S. W." who freed her the same year and helped her secure passage to Englar On both sides of the Atlantic, her poems won widespre admiration. The abolitionists pointed to her skill as pro that the Negro should be freed. A former Lord Mayor London presented her with a copy of the great Jo Milton's *Paradise Lost*.

After she returned to America, she sent a letter and poem to George Washington in 1775 who replied and i vited her to visit him. After the death of her former ma ters, Phillis Wheatley married a handsome Negro, Jo Peters, and bore him several children, the last of whi caused her death in childbirth in 1784.

Vernon Loggins, *The Negro Author* (New York, 1931), pp. 17-29; I *tionary of American Biography*, vol. XX (1936), pp. 36-37.

One day in 1761 John Wheatley wandered up and down the stalls and auction blocks of the Boston, Massachusetts slave market. He wanted to buy a female slave as a companion for his wife. Already he had looked over several possibilities but was not pleased. Then his eye fell upon a dark little girl with delicate features and an inborn sense of dignity. After having the slave-dealer place her on the auction block, he decided that the eight-year-old slave was just what Mrs. Wheatley wanted even though the child was a little frail. With the same casualness he showed in buying a bolt of cloth for his prospering tailoring business, John Wheatley made his purchase. He then led the little girl home to his wife.

Alexander Pushkin (1799-1837)

RUSSIA'S GREATEST POET

Russia's greatest poet, Alexander Sergeyevich Pushkin, was the grandson of Abram Hannibal, the transplanted African who achieved greatness in the armies of the Czars. Pushkin's poetry is still widely loved and read in Russia and, despite the passing years, holds front rank in the land of Tolstoy and Dostoevski.

Pushkin's physical appearance does not fit the common ideas of how a poet should look. He had a short muscular frame, a head of thick, dark, curly hair, a flat nose, thick lips and a swarthy complexion. Only his intensely brilliant eyes suggested the poet within.

For his early education Pushkin was sent to Tsarkoe Selo near St. Petersburg in 1811. He left this school in 1818 and joined the Russian foreign ministry as a clerk. His early poems "Ode to Freedom" and "Noel" were thought to be critical of the government of Czar Alexander I, and he was sent to the south of Russia to Ekaterinoslav. Here, he wrote "Ruslan and Ludmila," epic of six parts, containing 3,000 lines.

After two years in Ekaterinoslav, Pushkin was then transferred to the small village of Kishinev in the Caucasus. Here he began his "Eugene Onegin" under the influence of Lord Byron's work and after three years in Kishnev, he was shifted to Odessa, where he wrote the "Bakchisarai Fountain." In 1824, he was discharged from the government's service and returned to his mother's native village of Mikhailvskoe.

Poetry became his life. In 1825 Pushkin finished "Boris Godunov," and in 1832, "Eugene Onegin." Both later became operas of the same title. Already behind him were his *The Captive of the Caucasus,* a novel and "Ode to Napoleon," plus "The Gypsies." In his "The Bronze Horseman," Pushkin expressed his concern with the rights of the individual as opposed to those of the state. His novel *The Captain's Daughter* was to influence greatly subsequent novels in Russian literature.

Alexander Pushkin was far from the brooding poet. He had a fiery temperament; his considerable charm saw him through many love affairs and dashing escapades. He married a beautiful but frivolous woman, Nathalie Goncharova, whose cousin engaged him in a fatal duel over her. Stilled by death at the age of thirty-eight, Pushkin still speaks to the world through his impassioned poetry.

Samuel H. Cross and Ernest J. Simmons, *Alexander Pushkin, 1799-1837: His Life and Literary Heritage* (New York, 1937).

149

Alexandre Dumas
(1802-1870)

TIME DOES NOT DIM

Dumas' famous "Three Musketeer[s]"

Sooner or later every boy and girl learns of *The Three Musketeers* and *The Count of Monte Cristo*, romantic sagas of an earlier day. Few of them get to know of their author, Alexandre Dumas, who also wrote over two hundred volumes of plays and historical romances under that name.

Alexandre Dumas was born Alexandre Davy de la Pailleterie, and was a blue-eyed, olive-complexioned, curly-haired mulatto. His Haitian-born father, General Thomas Alexandre Dumas, was the natural son of Antoine Alexandre Davy, Marquis de la Pailleterie, and Marie Cessette Dumas, a black woman of Haiti. When Thomas became estranged from his father, the Marquis, and joined the French army at the age of twenty-two, he renounced the noble name Davy and from then on used his mother's name, Dumas, as did his son Alexandre.

The young Dumas was born at Villers-Cotterets in comparative poverty and obtained a smattering of education from a local priest. As an unknown and unproduced playwright, he made his way to Paris in 1827. While supporting himself as a clerk, he and a friend, Adolphe de Leuven, began writing vaudeville sketches and plays. Dumas first won recognition as a playwright with *Henri III et Sa Cour* (1829), a play which has been described as the first great triumph of Romantic drama.

With the Duke of Orleans as his patron, Dumas began turning out one play after another. In fifteen years, he wrote more than forty of them. *Antony*, *Richard Darlington*, and *Mademoiselle de Belle-Isle* were among his more prominent efforts.

In 1839 Dumas began writing historical novels with t[he] intention of reviewing the history of France in them. [In] 1844 appeared the world-famous *Three Musketeers* (eig[ht] volumes); in 1845 *Twenty Years After* (ten volumes[).] Readers in England as well as in France followed the a[d]ventures of the musketeers—Porthos, Aramis, and Atho[s.]

Keeping several works in progress at the same tim[e,] Dumas completed *The Count of Monte Cristo* (twel[ve] volumes) in 1844 and *La Reine Margot* in 1845. Oth[er] historical romances and plays flowed from his pen, a[nd] all of Paris turned to his writings. A corps of assistan[ts] worked on outlines which Dumas then used and tran[s]formed into literature peculiarly his own.

Dumas even started a newspaper, *Le Mousquetaire;* f[or] four years he wrote most of the copy that appeared in [it] each day. In addition, he travelled in Italy and Russi[a.] Thousands of francs poured in, and he spent them on [a] prodigious scale. Dumas constructed his own theatre f[or] the performance of his plays and maintained a splend[id] residence. He was a most regal host.

Paris became accustomed to Dumas' "great height, h[is] strong and squarely-built figure, his perpetually smili[ng] face, his large head crowned with curly grey locks, . [. .] his deep chest and his firm step." He reminded them of [a] "good tempered Hercules."

A great favorite with the ladies, Dumas had one natur[al] son, Alexandre Dumas, *fils*, who became a distinguishe[d] author in his own right.

Beatrice Flemming and Marion Pryde, *Distinguished Negroes Abro[ad]* (Washington, 1946), pp. 81-82.

Charles Waddell Chesnutt
(1858-1932)

FICTION'S
"PIONEER OF THE COLOR LINE"

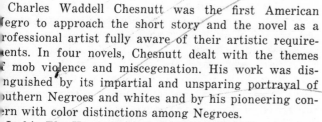

Charles Waddell Chesnutt was the first American Negro to approach the short story and the novel as a professional artist fully aware of their artistic requirements. In four novels, Chesnutt dealt with the themes of mob violence and miscegenation. His work was distinguished by its impartial and unsparing portrayal of Southern Negroes and whites and by his pioneering concern with color distinctions among Negroes.

In his *The House Behind the Cedars* (1900), Chesnutt handles the problems involved in racial "passing." In *The Marrow of Tradition* (1901), he wrote of the blurring of the color "lines" and the problems of the culturally superior Negro in the South. Chesnutt's last novel, *The Colonel's Dream* (1905) was a candid treatment of the South in which a Confederate Colonel's ideas of social reform are thwarted by the bigotry of a small North Carolina town.

Although born in Cleveland, Ohio in 1858, Chesnutt was carried by his family to North Carolina when he was quite young. Fair enough to pass for white, he was a bookkeeper in a white saloon when he was fourteen years old. He attended the local public schools for Negroes near Fayetteville, North Carolina but spent a good deal of time in the libraries of prominent whites, reading everything on which he could lay his hands. Chesnutt was made the principal of the State Normal (high) School for Negroes at Fayetteville when he was only twenty-two. Chesnutt spent some time studying stenography, not knowing that later this would be the major source of his income. Leaving Carolina in 1883, Chesnutt headed for New York where he worked as a stenographer for Dow Jones, a commercial reporting firm, and from there he went to Cleveland, Ohio where he spent the remainder of his life.

In Cleveland, Chesnutt became a commercial and legal stenographer. His fiction began appearing in the Cleveland newspapers and the famous *Puck* magazine. By reading law, in 1887 Chesnutt passed the Ohio bar examination with the highest scores recorded for that period. However, he never practiced law, for his legal stenography business was more lucrative.

From 1905 until his death in 1932 Chesnutt wrote no fiction but contributed many essays and articles to various newspapers and magazines. In 1927 he was awarded the Spingarn Medal for contribution to literature.

Helen M. Chesnut, *Charles Waddell Chesnutt: Pioneer of the Color Line;* Herman Dreer, *American Literature by Negro Authors* (New York, 1950), pp. 229-230.

Paul Laurence Dunbar
(1872-1906)

THE PEOPLE'S POET

Be proud my Race, in mind and soul;
Thy name is writ on Glory's scroll
In Characters of fire.
High 'mid the clouds of Fame's bright sky
Thy banners' blazoned folds now fly,
And truth shall lift them higher.

Dunbar was equally capable of
Little brown baby wif' spa'klin eyes,
Who's pappy's darlin' an' who's pappy's child?
Who is it all de day never once tires
Fu' to be cross, er once loses dat smile?

It was for his poems in dialect that Paul Lauren
Dunbar became famous, although he longed to be re
ognized for his work in conventional English. In the diale
poems of *Majors and Minors* (1895) and *Lyrics of Lou*
Life (1896) Dunbar captured the humor and gentlene
of the lives of Negroes in the rural South. He was primari
a gentle poet who did not try to shock his predominant
white reading audience. Nevertheless Dunbar's deep
feelings would often show up in disquieting poems su
as "We Wear the Mask."

Dunbar's poetic genius was evident in his high scho
days when he was class poet at Dayton, Ohio's Centr
High School. Dunbar, the only Negro in his class, w
the editor of the school paper and edited the yearbo
for his graduating class. Several of his early poems we
published by the Wright brothers of later aviation fam
when they experimented with printing newspapers
their homemade press.

Upon finishing high school, the best job Dunbar cou
find was that of an elevator operator at a local hot
William Dean Howells, then the reigning critic in Ame
can letters, discovered Dunbar in 1893. From this point
Dunbar's career as a poet took a turn for the better.
became one of Dayton's better known native sons. His fir
two volumes sold out rather rapidly and in 1896 the be
poems in them were published in *Lyrics of Lowly Life.*

Dunbar also tried his hand at fiction. He wrote thr
collections of short stories and four novels, including
passably good novel entitled *The Uncalled.* Paul Lauren
Dunbar turned out the bulk of his work in just ten year
It is suspected that the strain of such heavy productic
undermined his health and weakened him for a fatal sie;
of pneumonia in 1906.

Shortly after his first collection of poems *Oak and Ivy*
had been published, Paul Laurence Dunbar was invited
to address the West End Club of Toledo, Ohio. Dunbar
walked into the club's meeting room just as one Dr.
Chapman finished reading a paper denouncing the Negro
and doubting his basic intelligence. When the good doctor
had finished, Dunbar was called upon to recite. He said,
"I shall give you one poem which I had not intended
reciting when I first came in." In measured and stately
tones, the twenty-one year old poet gave his "Ode to
Ethiopia," putting extra stress on the lines

Brawley Benjamin, *Paul Laurence Dunbar, Poet of His People* (Chapel H
1936); Virginia Cunningham, *Paul Laurence Dunbar and His Song* (N
York, 1947); Robert A. Bone, *The Negro Novel in America* (1958), pp. 38–

Claude Mc Kay
(1890-1948)

"HOME TO HARLEM"

If we must die, let it not be like hogs
Hunted and penned in an inglorious spot,
While round us bark the mad and hungry dogs,
Making their mock at our accursed lot.
If we must die, O let us nobly die, . . .

Thus commented Claude McKay on the race riots of 1919. Claude McKay was perhaps the most blunt and outspoken of the "Harlem Renaissance" poets and novelists as can be seen in the above lines from his famous protest poem "If We Must Die." In his prose McKay celebrated the joyful and the primitive in preference to the sedate and sanctimonious. Some critics felt that he placed the lusty, easy-going virtues of an island paradise above the stern, cheerless inclinations of an industrial civilization, even if he did declare that:

"I love this cultured hell that tests my youth . . ."

A native of Jamaica, McKay came to America to attend Tuskegee Institute in 1912. After a few months he left for the University of Kansas where he remained for two years. Then, with the help of a timely inheritance, McKay cut short his formal education and headed for New York to pursue his interests among kindred souls in Bohemian circles. Supporting body and soul with a variety of odd jobs, McKay continued his writing which had started in Jamaica with the publication of his first book of verse *Songs of Jamaica* (1911).

In 1919 McKay was living abroad; in 1920 he published his second collection of verse, *Spring in New Hampshire*. Back in America by 1922, McKay saw the publication of *Harlem Shadows*, still another collection of verse. *Harlem Shadows* made his reputation as a writer of poetry. Six years were to pass before he produced another major work. In 1928 McKay wrote *Home to Harlem*, the first of three thematically related novels. This was followed by *Banjo* (1929) which was set in Paris and then in 1933, he produced *Banana Bottom* with Jamaica as the setting.

Claude McKay lived in many parts of the world, including Paris, Morocco, Marseilles and Russia. He was well-versed in the intellectual discourse of his time. He enjoyed living among the masses and felt that despite his artistic achievements, he was always a part of them.

In his later years when he no longer wrote, he joined the Catholic Youth Organization in Chicago. McKay retained his concern for the young and the free until his death in 1948.

James Weldon Johnson, *Black Manhattan* (New York, 1930), pp. 264-266; Herman Dreer, *American Literature by Negro Authors* (New York, 1950), pp. 36-37.

Countee Cullen
(1903-1946)

WHAT IS AFRICA TO ME?

What is Africa to me:
Copper sun or scarlet sea,
Jungle star or jungle track,
Strong bronzed men or regal black
Women from whose loins I sprang
When the birds of Eden sang?

To most readers of poetry by Negroes, these lines identify Countee Cullen, one of the leading poets of the "Negro Renaissance" of the twenties. Precocious, enormously talented, Countee Cullen was a nationally acclaimed poet at the age of twenty-one with the publication of his first book of poems, *Color,* which won the Harmon Award for high achievement in literature in 1925. Sure of his ability in poetry and despite the predominance of Negro themes in his work, Cullen wanted to be known simply as a poet rather than as a Negro poet.

In addition to *Color,* Cullen published other collections of poems under the titles of *The Ballad of the Brown Girl* (1927), *Copper Sun* (1927) and *The Black Christ and Other Poems* (1929). He also edited an anthology of poems called *Caroling Dusk* (1929). In 1932 he saw the publication of his only novel, *One Way to Heaven.*

Countee Cullen was born in New York City and reared by a Methodist minister who gave him the name Cullen. While a high school student, Cullen's poetic skill was recognized and encouraged. After completing his high school education, Cullen entered the undergraduate division of New York University. Here he distinguished himself by winning the Witter Bynner poetry prize for undergraduates in American colleges. More than a dozen campus literary journals published his work. After earning a Phi Beta Kappa key from New York University, Cullen entered Harvard and received the master of arts degree in 1926.

While Cullen wrote in the classical idiom, he was able to adapt his style to the protest motif which was present in the "Negro Renaissance," particularly in his long poem on lynching, *"The Black Christ."* An example of the classical style applied to a racial theme might be noted in the concluding lines of "Black Majesty," a poem about the Haitian revolutionists, Henri Christophe, Dessalines, and Toussaint L'Ouverture:

"Lo, I am dark, but comely," Sheba sings.
"And we were black," three shades reply, "but kings."

Countee Cullen. *The Black Christ and Other Poems* (New York, Harper and Brothers, 1929).

154

James Weldon Johnson
(1871-1938)

A GENTLEMAN OF LETTERS

James Weldon Johnson has been called "the only true artist among the early Negro novelists." Not only as a novelist but also as a poet, NAACP official and diplomat, Johnson left a lasting impression on the cultural and social life of the Negro in America. His famous poem "Lift Every Voice and Sing" (1900), when set to music by his talented brother, John Rosamond Johnson, became a sort of Negro national anthem during the early forties. His strikingly dramatic poem "God's Trombones" (1927) may still be heard recited from the stages of many high schools and colleges in the South. In one of Johnson's collections of verse, *St. Peter Relates an Incident* (1917) his poem "O Black and Unknown Bards" is still accepted as the best poetic explanation of the origins of the spirituals. His *Autobiography of an Ex-Colored Man* (1912) was one of the earliest accounts of a Negro exploring different levels of American society by "passing," and is still being reprinted in soft cover editions. This fictional "autobiography" was so real that Johnson felt the need to publish his own life's story in his now classic *Along This Way* (1933).

Aside from his creative work, Johnson edited the New York *Age* and ran an extremely popular column in it for ten years. He also published an anthology, *The Book of American Negro Poetry* (1922). He wrote articles for the *Nation* on the conduct of United States Marines in Haiti and helped to make the United States' occupation of that country a presidential campaign issue in 1921. His essays on the roots of the Negro's cultural contributions helped to explain the foundation of the Negro's achievements in literature and music, especially during the decade of the twenties. In *Negro Americans, What Now* (1934), he eloquently set forth his own philosophy and beliefs.

In 1916 James Weldon Johnson joined the NAACP and for many years was its executive secretary. Among his many achievements with this organization are: sparking the drive behind the Dyer Anti-Lynching Bill in 1921; leading the fight against the lily-white primary which made it illegal for Negroes to be denied participation in southern primary elections. Before he joined the NAACP, Johnson served as consul to Nicaragua and Venezuela.

James Weldon Johnson was a native of Florida with family roots stretching as far south as the Bahamas. He was educated at Atlanta and in New York. He was the first Negro to pass a written examination for the bar in Florida, and after practicing law and teaching school for a few years, he moved to New York where he joined his brother in writing successful musical comedies. His last major post was that of Professor of Creative Literature at Fisk University in Nashville, Tennessee.

Robert Bone, *The Negro Novel in America* (New Haven, 1958), pp. 45-49; James Weldon Johnson, *Along This Way* (New York, 1933); *Dictionary of American Biography*, XXII (1958) Supplement 2, pp. 345-346.

Richard Wright (1908-1960)

A SOUND OF THUNDER

The shattering sound of the clock in Richard Wright's *Native Son* was heard throughout America and echoed overseas. Wright's raw and powerful account of the life and death of "Bigger Thomas" in Chicago resounded in the conscience of America. Published in 1940, *Native Son* sold over 300,000 copies and was translated into six languages. It was a Book-of-the-Month Club choice. It was made into an equally powerful play starring Canada Lee. Overnight, Richard Wright was famous; his royalties exceeded his wildest dreams.

Prior to the publication of *Native Son*, Wright's volumes of short stories, *Uncle Tom's Children*, heralded the advent of a writer to be reckoned with. *Uncle Tom's Children* had won the author a Guggenheim fellowship and a $500 prize. His earlier work had appeared in the smaller magazines, *The Daily Worker* and the radical *New Masses*. During the Depression he had toiled on the Federal Writers Project in Chicago and New York.

Born in Natchez, Mississippi, Wright wandered to Memphis, Tennessee and in 1925 found himself in Chicago where, for years, he earned his living from a variety of odd jobs. Although he had been keenly interested in writing before he reached his teens, Richard Wright's formal education ended with high school. In Chicago he was able to meet other aspiring writers and studied the techniques of bending words to his will. His experiences in Mississippi and Chicago furnished the material for his fiction; the power and fervor of his earlier work came from his truthfulness, honesty and deep social concern.

In recognition of his literary talent Richard Wright received the Spingarn Medal in 1939. Over the next twenty years he was to write additional books: *The Outsider* (1953), *The Long Dream* (1958) and *Lawd, Today* (1963). *Black Boy* (1945) was his autobiography, *Black Power* (1954) was an account of his travels in Africa, and *The Color Curtain* (1956) was his report on the Bandung Conference of 1955.

A man deeply troubled by the crudities and dilemma of race, Wright became an expatriate and spent his last years in Paris. Wright's work was protest fiction which approached art. While other writers have approached the themes of race and personality with greater finesse and subtlety, few have surpassed Richard Wright in calling the world's attention to the consequences of exploitation of man by man on the basis of color. The significance of Richard Wright to black awareness was indicated by the revival of interest in the man and his career as the 1960's drew to a close. Constance Webb, in her book, portrayed the life and thoughts of Richard Wright as she understood them over a period of twenty years. Horace Cayton, an author and close friend of Wright, began a mammoth biographical study, and *Negro Digest* devoted an entire issue to Richard Wright. No serious discussion of Afro-American literature is complete that excludes him.

Edwin Embree, *Thirteen Against the Odds* (New York, 1946), pp. 25-46; Harold Isaacs, *The New World of American Negroes* (New York 1963), pp. 247-260; Constance Webb, *Richard Wright* (New York, 1968); *Negro Digest* Vol. 18, No. 2 (December 1968).

Langston Hughes (1902-1967)

A BARDIC VOICE

Langston Hughes was so prolific that he seemed to be three-fourths print and one-fourth person. In reality, however, the man and his works were one. In his writing, Hughes tried almost every conceivable form men have used to arrange their words and thoughts on paper. Poems, songs, novels, plays, biographies, histories and essays were the vehicles employed by him to communicate with his fellow men.

Known primarily as a poet, Hughes published many volumes of verse. Among them were *Weary Blues, Fine Clothes to the Jew, The Dream Keeper, Dear Lovely Death, Shakespeare in Harlem, Fields of Wonder, One Way Ticket* and *Ask Your Mama*. His novels were *Not Without Laughter* and *Tambourines to Glory*. For the theatre Langston Hughes wrote *Scottsboro Limited* and *Mulatto;* the later work was also staged as an opera, *The Barries*. In the field of biography Hughes books include *Famous American Negroes, Famous Negro Heroes* and *Famous Negro Music Makers*. He also wrote books for juveniles and lyrics for William Grant Still, Elmer Rice and Kurt Weill.

Langston Hughes was one of the most honored authors in America. He began by winning the Witter Bynner undergraduate prize for excellence in poetry for 1926. He was a Rosenwald and Guggenheim fellow, as well as a grantee of the American Academy of Arts and Letters. In 1959 he received the Anisfield-Wolfe award and in 1960 he won the Spingarn Medal for contributions to the progress of the Negro.

A native of Joplin, Missouri, Langston Hughes has lived in many parts of the world including Haiti, Mexico, France, Italy and Russia. No poet of the ivory tower, he worked as a busboy, clerk, cafe bouncer, and office boy with the *Journal of Negro History*. He was a part of the "Harlem Renaissance" and achieved a measure of fame during the twenties; however, he did not begin to depend on his writings for a living until 1930. Although his education ended with his undergraduate days at Columbia University, Langston Hughes lectured at leading schools and colleges in the country.

The theme of his work was the common man, more specifically the ordinary Negro and his pleasures, joys and sorrows. Of the hundreds of poems written by him perhaps the best-known and most durable is "The Negro Speaks of Rivers," part of which is reproduced below:

I have known rivers:
I've known rivers ancient as the world and older than
the flow of human blood in human veins.
My soul has grown deep like the rivers.

James M. Ethridge (ed), *Contemporary Authors* (Detroit, 1962), p. 143; *Who's Who in Colored America, 1950*, p. 278; Edwin R. Embree, *Thirteen Against the Odds* (New York, 1946), pp. 117-138. Donald C. Dickinson, *A Bio-bibliography of Langston Hughes, 1902-1967* (Hamden, Connecticut, 1967); James A. Emmanuel, *Langston Hughes* (New York, 1967).

Gwendolyn Brooks
(1917-   )

PULITZER PRIZE WINNER

Book reviewers heaped praise upon her first volume of poems, *A Street in Bronzeville* (1945), which won for her the Merit Award of *Mademoiselle* magazine as the outstanding woman of the year. Her second volume *Annie Allen* (1949), brought her the Pulitzer Prize for Poetry. Her other major writings include *Bronzeville Boys and Girls* (1956) and *The Bean Eaters* (1960). She also wrote a novel, *Maude Martha*.

Miss Brooks' career is studded with honors and awards. She has received two Guggenheim Fellowships with substantial stipends; the American Academy of Arts and Letters awarded her a prize of $1,000. She received the prestigious Eunice Tietjeans award from *Poetry* magazine, and for three consecutive years Miss Brooks won the Midwest Writers Conference Prize.

Miss Brooks was born in Topeka, Kansas, but has spent virtually all of her life in Chicago. Although she is amazingly erudite, her formal education ended at Wilson Junior College in Chicago. Married since 1936 to Henry Blakely, a Chicago businessman, Gwendolyn Brooks manages to rear two children and to write some of the finest poetry of our time.

An example of Miss Brooks' work is this description of changing neighborhoods. The title of the poem: "The Ghosts at the Quincy Club":

> *Where velvet voices lessened, stopped, and rose*
> *Rise raucous Howdys. And a curse comes pure.*
> *Yea it comes pure and challenges again*
> *All ghost airs, graces, all daughters-of-gentlemen*
> *Moth-soft, off-sweet. Demure.*
>
> *Where Tea and Father were (each clear*
> *And lemony) are dark folk, drinking beer.*

From *The Bean Eaters*, by Gwendolyn Brooks.

She tells you that she is a "simple housewife." She dresses rather plainly. Utterly without affectation, she is almost painfully shy and unassuming. She does not stand out in a crowd. Perhaps the most distinctive feature about her is her eyes: soft, gentle, quizzical. There is absolutely nothing about her appearance to suggest that she is one of America's leading poets. Her name is Gwendolyn Brooks and she is the only Negro ever to win the Pulitzer Prize.

In *Contemporary Authors* (vol. I, 1962, p. 36) under the name of this "simple housewife" is the following description: "Career: Writer, lecturer at Universities and Colleges." Under her deceptive exterior Miss Brooks leads an intense poetic and intellectual life. She studies the techniques of her craft as well as the people, sights and sounds of Chicago's crowded South Side and creates superb poetic renditions of urban Negro life. Her brilliant and succinct book reviews indicate a close acquaintance with a rather wide range of modern literature.

Arna Bontemps
(1902-   )

MANY-FACETED WRITER

Arna Wendell Bontemps is probably the most prolific black author other than Langston Hughes. In a career stretching over a period of three decades, Bontemps has written nearly a score of novels, poems and biographies, and has published many works in the fields of sociology and history. For years he was head librarian and publicity director at Fisk University in Nashville, Tennessee. Since 1966, he has been a member of the social science division at the Chicago Circle campus of the University of Illinois.

Arna Bontemps was born on October 13, 1902 in Alexandria, Louisiana. He attended the Pacific Union College of California from which he received the B.A. degree in 1923, earned the M.A. degree at the University of Chicago in 1943, and has been a teacher at every major level of education. As a poet, he received the Crisis Magazine Prize in 1926, and for two consecutive years (1926-1927) was awarded the Alexander Pushkin Prize. He has also been awarded a Rosenwald Fellowship, and, in 1949-1950, received a Guggenheim Fellowship for creative writing.

From the pen of Arna Bontemps has come *God Sends Sunday* (1931), *Popo and Fifina: Children of Haiti* (1932), *You Can't Pet a Possum* (1934), *Black Thunder* (1936), *Sad Faced Boy* (1937), *Drums at Dusk* (1939), *Golden Slippers: An Anthology of Negro Poetry for Young People* (1941), *The Fast Sooner Hound* (with Jack Conroy, 1942), *They Seek a City* (with Jack Conroy, 1945), *They Have Tomorrow* (1945), *Slappy Hooper, The Wonderful Sign Painter* (1946), *Song of the Negro* (1948), *The Poetry of the Negro: 1746-1949* (anthology, 1949), *George Washington Carver* (1950), *Chariot in the Sky* (with Jack Conroy, 1959), *Sam Patch, the High, Wide and Handsome Jumper* (1951), *The Story of George Washington Carver* (1954), *Lonesome Boy* (with Langston Hughes, 1955), *The Book of Negro Folklore* (1958), *Frederick Douglass: Slave, Fighter, Free Man* (1959), *100 Years of Negro Freedom* (1961), *American Negro Poetry* (Anthology, 1963), *Personals* (1964), and *Famous Negro Athletes* (1964).

Arna Bontemps is among the last of the survivors of the Black Renaissance movement of the twenties, a movement that starred such artistic blacks as Langston Hughes, James Weldon Johnson, Claude McKay, Jean Toomer, Countee Cullen, Jessie Redmond Fauset and others. Bontemps once stated that he witnessed the Black Renaissance from a grandstand seat: From the twenties onward, he found himself in the center of the field. Before his first fiction was published, he made a splash with his Pushkin Prize poems: "Golgotha is a Mountain" (1926) and "Nocturne at Bethesda" (1926).

In all of his works, poetical, fictional and non-fictional, Arna Bontemps has attempted to convey the richness and variety of the Negro's experience in the western hemisphere.

James M. Ethridge and Barbara Kopala (eds.), *Contemporary Authors* (Detroit, 1962), p. 99; John Hope Franklin, *From Slavery to Freedom* (New York, 1956), pp. 502, 505-506.

X THE THEATRE

The history of the Negro in the American theatre goes back to the first decades of the nineteenth century. As early as 1821, free blacks in New York City were presenting Shakespearean plays. The African Company, located at the "corner of Bleecker and Mercer streets," catered to a small community of black playgoers. James Hewlett, the leading member of this company, specialized in portraying the title roles of *Othello* and *Richard III*. With few exceptions, however, the development of the theatre among Negroes had to wait until the twentieth century.

The *Creole* (1891), The *Octoroon* (1895) and *Oriental America* (1896) are landmarks in the emergence of blacks in the theatre. Perhaps the most outstanding black theatrical personalities at the turn of the century were Bert Williams, Bob Cole, and Will Marion Cook. Bert Williams starred in *Abyssinia* and *Dahomey*. Cole was a noted producer, singer, dancer and librettist. Cook produced the music for such plays as *Shoofly Regiment* (1906) and *The Red Moon* (1908). Around 1909, the Lafayette Theatre in New York presented all-black melodramas, among them *The Servant in the House, On Trial* and *Within the Law*. In 1917, three one-act plays by Ridgeley Torrence—*The Rider of Dreams, Granny Maumee* and *Simon, the Cyrenian*—gave black actors a chance to show their talents in a rustic comedy, a tragedy and an historical drama.

In 1920, Charles Gilpin became a national star in Eugene O'Neill's *The Emperor Jones*. The same year Paul Robeson appeared in *All God's Chillun Got Wings*. The next year Noble Sissle and Eubie Blake produced *Shuffle Along*. Josephine Baker starred in *Chocolate Dandies* in 1925; Florence Mills opened spectacularly in *Blackbirds* in 1926. In 1927, the durable *Porgy* was presented. This decade ended with Richard B. Harrison achieving international stardom as "De Lawd" in *The Green Pastures*.

The Federal Theatre Project was started in 1937 as a federal effort to succor the performing arts. Almost 900 blacks were participants in this project. With the Lafayette Theatre of New York as a base, Negroes appeared in plays such as Frank Wilson's *Walk Together Children*, Rudolph Fisher's *Conjur' Man Dies* and William Du Bois' *Haiti*. An unusual version of *Macbeth*, transposed to the tropics, created some excitement. Cities outside of New York also felt the effects of the Federal Theatre Project. In Chicago, *Swing Mikado* was so successful that it was sold to the commercial theatre. In Los Angeles, Hall Johnson's *Run Little Chillun* ran for over a year. In Seattle, the Federal Theatre group presented *Lysistrata, Noah, In Abraham's Bosom* and *Stevedore*.

Following the termination of government support in 1939, there was a temporary falling off in the number of theatrical productions by or about blacks and Afro-American themes. Canada Lee portrayed "Bigger Thomas" in the 1941 stage version of Richard Wright's *Native Son*. Beginning in 1944, Hilda Simms carried *Anna Lucasta* from the basement of the 135th street branch of the New York Public Library to Broadway for a run of 956 performances. Other important plays followed. Lillian Smith's novel, *Strange Fruit*, was brought to the stage. Ethel Waters starred in Carson McCuller's *A Member of the Wedding* (1950). Sidney Poitier and Claudia McNeill brought to life Lorraine Hansberry's *A Raisin in the Sun* (1959). Ruby Dee and Ossie Davis, along with Godfrey Cambridge, lampooned the myths of the plantation era in *Purlie Victorious* (1961). Cambridge won an "Obie" for the 1960-1961 theatre season's most outstanding performance in *The Blacks*.

The 1960's saw a resurgence of interest in the theatre by blacks. Occupying a special place in the pages of contemporary theatrical history is Ellen Stewart, the founder and director of Cafe La Mama in New York City. La Mama was the launching pad for such off-Broadway avant-garde plays as *Hair*, by Ragni and Rado, *Viet Rock* by Megan Terry, *Futz* by Rochelle Owens and *America Hurrah* by Jean-Claude van Italie. James Baldwin produced two works for the stage, *The Amen Corner* and *Blues for Mr. Charlie*. LeRoi Jones created a sensation with *Dutchman* and *The Toilet*. William Branch wrote *A Wreath for Udomo* and Loften Mitchell, a veteran playwright, authored *A Land Beyond the River*. Ronald Milner attracted attention with *Who's Got His Own*. Ed Bullins, competent and prolific, became known as the creator of *In the Wine Time* and *The Electronic Nigger*. Bullins also edited "Black Theatre," one of the newer periodicals devoted exclusively to black drama and theatre. Douglas Turner Ward impressed black and white theatre goers with his *Day of Absence* and *Happy Ending*. In 1969 Lonnie Elder was mentioned as a Pulitzer Prize nominee for *Ceremonies in Dark Old Men*.

In New York City, the Negro Ensemble Company (NEC) was formed under the leadership of Douglas Turner Ward, Robert Macbeth and Robert Hooks, best known for his role on the T. V. program "N.Y.P.D." The NEC received a grant of $434,000 to produce plays and encourage playwrights of the black community. The New York Greenwich Mews Theatre produced *The Strong Breed* and *The Trial of Brother Jero*, both by the talented Nigerian, Wole Soyinka. In Philadelphia, Ed Bernard led in the establishment of the Afro-American Thespians. Moving back and forth on the east coast, The Spirit House Movers and Players of Newark, New Jersey performed several of the works of LeRoi Jones, its founder.

And the World's a Stage

In Chicago, Ted Ward founded the South Side Center of the Performing Arts. In the same city, Phil Cohran [ai]ded in the formation of the Artistic Heritage Ensemble which was concerned not only with drama, but also history, music and non-western languages. David Rambeau estab[l]ished Concept East/Theatre in Detroit Michigan. Down [i]n New Orleans, Tom Dent, along with Carmel Collins and [E]luard Burt, pioneered in the development of the Free [S]outhern Theatre.

On the west coast, blacks around San Francisco, Cali[f]ornia have formed the Aldridge Players/West. The early [s]tandouts among the Aldridge Players were fledging writers Elton Wolfe, Leonard McDonald and Leslie Perry. [I]n the spring of 1968, there were several important black theatre groups in the Los Angeles area. Ebony Showcase, [D]ouglass House Foundation, the Mafundi Institute and the Performing Arts Society of Los Angeles were perhaps the most active. The Mafundi Institute enjoyed the talents of the actor William Marshall and the composer-performer Oscar Brown, Jr. Working closely with the Douglass House Foundation was Harry Dolan whose work *Losers, Weepers* was aired coast-to-coast. The Performing Arts Society had as its central aim the development of black theatre in black communities.

In the sixties new names and faces also appeared in the ranks of black performers. Diana Sands appeared in plays as unlike as *The Owl and the Pussycat* and *St. Joan*. Earl Hyman had developed a reputation as one of the leading "Othellos". Gloria Foster appeared in *Yerma* by García Lorca, *Medea*, and *The Trojan Women*, in addition to plays that were directed toward black audiences. Clarence Williams was able to swing from *The Mod Squad* to *King John*. Ivan Dixon appeared in *Hogan's Heroes* on TV as well as in the film *Nothing But a Man* with the singer, Abby Lincoln. Other players of great competence were Cicely Tyson, Barbara Ann Teer, Thelma Oliver, Leon Bibb, Louis Gossett, Al Freeman and James Earl Jones. Jones, in particular, achieved an unusual measure of fame for his portrayal of Jack Johnson in *The Great White Hope*, winning the Tony award for best dramatic actor in 1969.

In the area of mass entertainment, a few blacks have become household names. Sidney Poitier has been described as a "superstar." Jim Brown left a dazzling career as a superstar of the gridiron for the klieg lights of Hollywood. He has appeared in films such as *The Split, Ice Station Zebra, Rio Conchos, The Riots, Dark of the Sun, The Dirty Dozen, 100 Rifles* and *Year of the Cricket*. Raymond St. Jacques, Rafer Johnson and Percy Rodrigues also had featured roles in movies. At the end of 1968 there were at least fourteen television programs which featured blacks. Bill Cosby broke the ice in *I Spy*. Ivan Dixon became a regular on *Hogan's Heroes*. Robert Hooks shared the spotlight with the stars in *N.Y.P.D.* Don Mitchell in *Ironside* and Greg Morris in *Mission Impossible* both had featured roles. Otis Young became the first black TV cowboy in *The Outcasts*. The versatile Diahann Carroll became the first black prime-time star of a television series in *Julia*, a situation comedy which ranked among the top ten programs of the 1968 season. Gail Foster was regularly seen in *Mannix* as was Nichelle Nichols in *Star Trek*. While these performers represented an increase in the number of programs which featured blacks, Afro-Americans constitute only a small percentage of the number of actors whose faces are seen in television. In 1967, for example, only 23.9% of the 3,000 actors in America were regularly employed. Of this percentage (817 jobs), blacks held slightly under fifty. Ossie Davis and Ruby Dee were perhaps the most consistently employed black professionals during this period.

Behind the cameras even fewer blacks were to be found. Robert Goodwin, a writer, had more than a dozen scripts produced for such shows as *Judd for the Defense, The Big Valley* and *Julia*. Jean Ferdinand, Harry Dolan and Gene Boland all have had at least one script developed into a TV production. The closing years of the sixties also saw the introduction of black newscasters. Mal Goode of ABC, and Bill Matney and Bob Teague of NBC represented another advance of blacks in the communications and broadcasting areas.

In all of the performing and informing arts, Afro-Americans debated their roles: could they write, act or report independent of their status as black men and women? The growth of black theatre groups on both coasts was generally accepted as the answer some groups were giving to this question. On the other hand, actors were still doing non-black classics. During the first part of 1969, for example, veteran actor Frank Silvera was appearing in the lead role of *King Lear*. Pearl Bailey and Cab Calloway starred in an all-black version of *Hello Dolly*, and Julian Mayfield and Raymond St. Jacques appeared in an all-black version of *The Informer* that bore the title *Uptight*. As the decade ended, more blacks were engaged in the performing arts than ever before, and they were asking more profound questions than ever about themselves and their relationship to the society in which they found themselves.

Black Theatre, #1, 1968, pp. 3-4; Margaret Just Butcher, *The Negro in American Culture*, (New York, 1956), p. 187-206; Edith Isaacs, *The Negro in the Theatre*, (New York, 1947), passim; *New York Times*, (February 2, 1969), Sec. 2, pp. 1, 9; *Newsweek*, (July 17, 1967), pp. 63-67; *Ebony*, (January, 1969), pp. 27-35; *Saturday Evening Post*, (November 30, 1968), pp. 42-44, 82, 84.

Ira Aldridge (1805-1867)

BLACK TRAGEDIAN

Such was the skill that made Ira Aldridge the toast of the European continent and the leading Shakespearean actor of his era. He played *Othello* in the major cities and capitals, including Berlin, Vienna, Dresden, Frankfort-am-Main, Krakow, Amsterdam and St. Petersburg, Russia. Until Aldridge appeared, white actors, wearing black-face make-up and black gloves, played the jealous Moor. In Aldridge, at last was found the perfect Othello. However, this great actor was not limited to playing Othello. He also played Macbeth, King Lear and the leading roles in plays which had no Negro or Moorish characters.

Honors and awards came to Ira Aldridge. Dukes, princes and kings honored him. From the King of Prussia, he received the First Medal of the Arts and Sciences. From the Emperor of Russia, he received the Cross of Leopold. He was named a member of many high-ranking societies. His success as an actor enabled him to maintain a fashionable home near London where he received the nobility and distinguished men of arts and letters. Among his dearest friends was Alexandre Dumas, the author of the *Count of Monte Cristo* and *The Three Musketeers*.

The place and precise date of his birth is uncertain. Some accounts say that Aldridge was born in Africa. Others give Belaire, Maryland as his birthplace. Various authorities list 1804 and 1805 as his birthdate. It is known that he was apprenticed as a carpenter in Maryland, and in association with immigrant Germans he picked up the German tongue. Aldridge's interest in the theatre was stimulated by Edmund Kean, himself a leading Shakespearean actor who encouraged and aided him to enter the theatre. Years later, Aldridge was to play Othello to Edmund Kean's Iago. For a long time, Aldridge performed on the continent and, briefly, in America. He was married twice, first to an Englishwoman who died shortly thereafter, and then to a Swedish baroness who was with the actor when he died in Lodz, Poland in 1867.

Mildred Stock, *Ira Aldridge, the Negro Tragedian* (New York, 1959) ; Walter Monfried, "The Great Ira Aldridge," *Negro Digest* (March, 1963), pp. 67-70.

The ornate theatre in St. Petersburg, Russia is crowded. The cream of Russian society is present. On the stage, the powerfully-built black man playing the title role of Othello, the Moor, comes to the fateful lines where he prepares to kill Desdemona :

"It is the cause, it is the cause, my soul.

Let me not name it to you, you chaste stars."

Up leaps a young man from his seat, crying in a terrified voice. "She is innocent, Othello, she is innocent." Not moving a muscle, Ira Aldridge finishes his speech. The young man is so carried away by the actor that he has forgotten the events on the stage were merely part of a play, and Aldridge and the white female pretending sleep were only actors. The next day while dining with a Prince, Aldridge learns that the excited spectator had died shortly after making his outcry. On another occasion, as Aldridge, again playing Othello, prepared to kill Desdemona, the young actress playing the part screamed in real fright. She, too, had forgotten she was in a play.

Charles Gilpin (1878-1930)

PIONEER DRAMATIC ACTOR

Gilpin as Emperor Jones

James Weldon Johnson once wrote that Charles Gilpin "by his work in *The Emperor Jones* . . . reached the highest point of achievement on the legitimate stage that had yet been attained by a Negro in America." In *The Negro in American Culture*, Margaret Just Butcher declared that "Gilpin was the first modern American Negro to establish himself as a serious actor of first quality." In writing of Charles Gilpin's portrayal of Brutus Jones, Edith Isaacs asserted that when "the play and the player met they became one."

Charles Gilpin astounded theatre-goers with his dramatic talents in a most demanding role which required him to carry O'Neil's play alone for six lengthy scenes. With Gilpin in the lead role, *The Emperor Jones* ran in New York for four years (1920-1924). In 1921 Gilpin won the coveted Spingarn Medal for his contribution to the theatre and to the progress of the Negro.

Success did not come to Charles Gilpin the easy way. When Eugene O'Neill decided to present *The Emperor Jones*, Gilpin had just finished playing the small role of Reverend William Custis in John Drinkwater's *Abraham Lincoln*. O'Neill quickly recognized him as just the man to play the island ruler in his daring drama.

Gilpin had been connected with vaudeville and the theatre since 1890 but was unable to make a steady living as an actor. Between occasional appearances in vaudeville houses and parts with touring troupes, he supported himself with employment as a printer, elevator operator, porter and as a trainer for prize-fighters. In 1911-1914 he toured with a group called the "Pan-American Octette." In 1914 he had a small role in *Old Man's Boy*. In 1916 he was organizer and manager of the Lafayette Theatre Company, one of the first Negro dramatic stock companies in New York. Behind him was experience with the Pekin Stock Company of Chicago and appearances with Bert Williams and George Walker in *Abyssinia* and with Gus Hall's *Smart Set*.

A small intense man, Charles Gilpin was a native of Virginia. After briefly attending St. Francis's Catholic School for colored children in Richmond, he took a job as a printer's devil on the *Richmond Planet*. Whenever an opportunity arose for him to perform, Gilpin forgot all else, for he lived for the stage. In 1926, two years after *The Emperor Jones* closed, Gilpin lost his voice and had to go back to running an elevator for a living. He died in 1930, and a year later was included among notable Americans in the *Dictionary of American Biography*.

Edith Isaac, *The Negro in the American Theatre* (New York, 1947), p. 63; James Weldon Johnson, *Black Manhattan* (New York, 1930), pp. 184-185; *Dictionary of American Biography*, vol. VII (1930), p. 314.

Bert Williams
(1878-1922)

A COMEDIAN'S COMEDIAN

The late W. C. Fields once described Bert Williams as "the funniest man I ever saw; the saddest man I ever knew." Booker T. Washington declared that "Bert Williams has done more for the race than I have. He has smiled his way into people's hearts. I have been obliged to fight." From about 1909 until his death in 1922, Bert Williams was perhaps the most famous Negro entertainer in America. He made thousands double with laughter in his portrayal of the lazy comical stage Negro speaking an outlandish dialect. His talent as a comedian made him one of the highest paid performers in America.

Many theatre-goers declared that Williams was successful because he was "himself" on the stage. He was seen as the funniest flower of the school of blackface comedians. A closer view of Bert Williams shows that his triumphs came from his talents as an actor rather than from his personal life. His stage characterizations were based on what he observed around him.

In physical appearance Williams was a six-foot tall handsome man with decidedly Caucasian features. For his portrayals he had to use the regular blackface make-up. His weird stage dialect and drawl were a marked contrast to his natural speech which was the king's English of his native Antigua in the British West Indies. The fun-loving, shiftless, ignorant buffoon role Williams played on the stage was a far cry from the quiet, rather melancholy man that was the real Egbert Austin Williams. Instead of blackface comedy, the serious stage was his real interest.

Bert Williams spent his early youth on the huge plantation of his grandfather, the Danish Consul in the Indies. Both of his parents were quadroons. Williams came to the U.S. while he was still a young boy, and upon completing his high school education in California, he decided to seek his fame on the stage. He first appeared in California dives and honky tonks with a line of patter and a banjo. In 1895, he teamed up with George Walker. By 1903, Williams and Walker were so successful that they took his hit "Dahomey" to England and repeated their earlier New York triumph. In 1909 George Walker died and the following year Williams joined the Ziegfeld Follies and remained with them as the star for nearly ten years. This was followed by his appearance in *Broadway Brevities* and *Under the Bamboo Tree*.

Mabel Rowland (ed), *Bert Williams, Son of Laughter* (New York, 1947).

The famous comedy team of Williams + Walker

164

Richard B. Harrison
(1864-1935)

THE ORIGINAL "DE LAWD"

"Gangway! Gangway for de Lawd . . . God . . . Jehovah!" announced the angel Gabriel one night in 1929. And "De Lawd" in the person of Richard B. Harrison came on the stage of the Mansfield Theatre in New York wearing a simple black suit. From this point on, Richard B. Harrison dominated and gave lasting form to Marc Connelley's *Green Pastures*. His performance as "De Lawd" during the season of 1929 was regarded as among the finest of the year.

One critic was moved to say this of *Green Pastures* and Richard B. Harrison: "Call it fable or allegory or what you will; his dramatization of an idea of primitive faith was so moving in its tender simplicity that it deserves a place among the classics of life and letters where all greatness is truly simple . . ." In 1930, Richard B. Harrison was awarded the Spingarn Medal as the person who contributed most to the progress of the Negro during the preceding year. Several colleges awarded honorary degrees to him. *Green Pastures* toured the North and South and ran for 557 performances

Green Pastures was Harrison's first and only legitimate stage role. He was over sixty-five years old when he agreed to play "De Lawd."

Before *Green Pastures*, he had toured the country reciting excerpts from Shakespeare, Kipling, Poe and Paul Laurence Dunbar. He treated Negro social and church groups to one-man versions of *Macbeth*, *Julius Caesar*, and *Damon and Pythias*.

Born in Canada, Richard B. Harrison went to Detroit as a boy and earned his keep as a handyman, waiter, porter and railway clerk. Whenever it was possible he would climb to the gallery of theatres to see stage productions. Noting his enthusiasm for the stage, friends assisted him in getting an opportunity to study drama in Detroit. After developing his repertoire of readings and recitations, he made his debut in Canada in 1891, then came to America where he worked with amateur groups. When he was called to the cast of *Green Pastures*, he was an instructor in drama at A. and T. College, Greensboro, North Carolina.

Richard B. Harrison appeared in *Green Pastures* a total of 1,656 times and at the time his heart gave way in 1935, was at the peak of his fame. His performance in the play has been the standard by which all subsequent revivals have been measured.

"Richard B. Harrison," *The National Cyclopedia*, Vol. XXVI, 1937, p. 364. *Who's Who in Colored America, 1928-29*, p. 166.

Frank Silvera (1914-   )

AN "EVERYMAN" OF THE THEATRE

Frank Silvera has become a sort of "everyman" of the acting profession. In a career stretching back over two decades, he has proved the Negro's ability to play a wide range of parts far beyond the racial stereotypes. He has portrayed Mexicans, Spaniards, Italians as well as white and black Americans. At various times Silvera has been active on the legitimate stage, screen, television and radio, giving convincing performances of any roles assigned to him.

Frank Alvin Silvera was born in Kingston, Jamaica 1914. He was brought to America while still a child an became a naturalized citizen in 1922. His education i cluded two years of law at Northeastern Universit Boston, Massachusetts. In 1934, however, the lure of th theatre proved irresistible. In that year he appeared in Pa Green's *Potter's Field* presented at the Plymouth Theatr Boston. The following year he performed in *Stevedor* From 1935 to 1938 Silvera appeared in plays such as *Th Trial of Dr. Beck, Macbeth* and *Emperor Jones,* all spo sored by the Federal Theatre Project. In 1939 Silver toured with the New England Repertory Theatre.

While serving in the Navy during World War II, Silver wrote and directed radio shows at the Great Lakes Nav Training Station. In 1945 he appeared in the Broadwa production of *Anna Lucasta.* Two years later this versati actor had a role in *John Loves Mary* which was sponsore by the Urban League.

In the hey-dey of radio, Frank Silvera performed o such shows as *Perry Mason, Up for Parole, Countersp* and *Two Billion Strong, The U.N. Story.* On television h appeared in *Captain Video, The Big Story* and *The U touchables.* In the movies, his most memorable roles wei in *Viva Zapata, Mutiny on the Bounty,* and *Hombre.*

Who's Who in Colored America, 1950, p. 469; Lucille Arcola Chamber America's Tenth Man (New York, 1956), p. 191.

166

Canada Lee (1907-1951)

"BIGGER THOMAS"

Canada Lee is best known for his sensitive portrayal of "Bigger Thomas," the bitterly frustrated central character the screen and stage version of Richard Wright's book, *ative Son.* Although he had never taken an acting lesson his life, Lee earned rave notices in this role. Richard atts, in the *New York Herald Tribune,* declared that anada Lee was ". . . a fine actor giving one of the season's 947) best performances."

Canada Lee explained his success thusly, "I've *known* uys like Bigger Thomas all my life."

Canada Lee, christened Leonard Lionel Cornelius Cane-ata after his West Indian grandfather, was born in Man-attan's San Juan Hill district and attended high school Harlem. Although he started studying violin at the age seven and was approaching concert status, when he was urteen he ran away from home to become a jockey. After ree or four years, his racing career was ended by excess eight. He drifted into boxing where he soon rose to ama-ur lightweight champion. In 1926 he turned pro, moved p to the welterweight division and, after winning more an seventeen of twenty-two bouts, became a leading ntender for the welterweight crown. It was during this eriod, 1926 to 1933, that Leonard Canegata became known s Canada Lee. But this budding career, too, was short-ved. A hard blow to the head blinded him in one eye and e had to quit the ring.

Perhaps it was this performing in front of a crowd that led him to the career where he really found his niche. After casually reading for, and winning, a role in the W.P.A. stage play, *Brother Mose,* he played in *Stevedore,* the Federal Theater production of *Macbeth, Othello,* and *Haiti,* and obtained a small part in *Mamba's Daughters.* About this time Orson Welles chose him for the Bigger Thomas role, and from here his star ascended. *Anna Lucasta, South Pacific, The Tempest,* a screen version of *Macbeth,* and William Saroyan's *Across the Board on Tomorrow Morning.* His career reached its zenith when, in addition to much radio work, he was given a leading role in the Tallulah Bankhead picture, *Life Boat.*

Canada Lee's life was cut short in 1951 by a fatal heart attack.

Edith Isaacs, *The Negro in the Theatre* (New York, 1947).

Ethel Waters
(1900-   )

THIRTY YEARS ON STAGE

...in the 1949 movie
"Pinky", with Jeanne Crain

Ethel Waters had an unusual voice—high, clear, plaintive—which, in her heyday, she projected seemingly without effort. When she was seventeen, her singing landed her a job at the Lincoln Theater in Baltimore where she made nine dollars a week. This was followed by years of singing in honky-tonk dives and night-clubs which led to her big break in 1923 when she substituted for Florence Mills at New York's Plantation Club and created a sensation with her unique rendition of "Dinah," "I'm Coming, Virginia," and other currently popular songs.

In 1927 she made her first stage appearance at Daly's West Sixty-Third Street Theater in a musical called *Africana*. After this she earned roles in *Blackbirds* (1930), *Rhapsody in Black* (1931-32), *As Thousands Cheer* (1933), and *At Home Abroad* (1935). She gained added stature in motion pictures such as *Cabin In The Sky*—where she sang her famous version of "Stormy Weather"—and *Pinky*.

Her place as a mature and sensitive actress was assured with her starring role in the Broadway play *The Member of the Wedding*, in 1950. When the play was made into a movie, millions were moved by the big-hearted warmth and strength of the house servant who was more than a servant. Ethel Waters' years on the stage have enriched all who have been privileged to see her perform.

Although there have been better singers and actresses than Ethel Waters, none typifies the rise from rags to riches more dramatically than she. She started life in Chester, Pa., in 1900 with two strikes against her. Her parents, Louisa Tar Anderson and John Wesley Waters were poverty-stricken, and she was born out of wedlock. There was seldom enough food for the family. There were many days when the only meals she had were supplied by the sisters of the convent school she attended as a child.

She was married at twelve years of age and went to work as a maid and laundress in a Philadelphia hotel for $4.75 a week. A few years later she could jokingly make the claim that she "went through" swanky Swarthmore College in two weeks!—as a charwoman. Some twenty-five years later she was making $2,000 a week as a versatile performing artist on stage and screen, and owned two apartment houses in Harlem. But the path from maid to movies was long and tortuous.

Ethel Waters, *His Eye Is On The Sparrow* (New York, 1951).

Katherine Dunham
(1910-   )

ITH ROOTS IN RHYTHM AND RACE

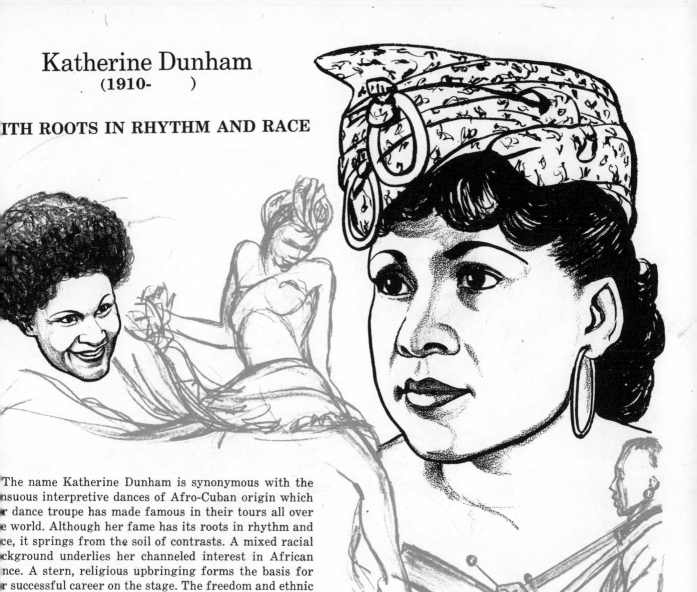

The name Katherine Dunham is synonymous with the
nsuous interpretive dances of Afro-Cuban origin which
r dance troupe has made famous in their tours all over
e world. Although her fame has its roots in rhythm and
ce, it springs from the soil of contrasts. A mixed racial
ckground underlies her channeled interest in African
nce. A stern, religious upbringing forms the basis for
r successful career on the stage. The freedom and ethnic
xuality of her dance belies an early parental vise which
gidly confined her conscious life.

Miss Dunham was born in Chicago, the daughter of
nny June Taylor, a fair-skinned divorcee of French
nadian ancestry, and Albert Dunham, a hard-working
ilor. After the death of her mother, her father remarried
d moved to Joliet, Illinois, where Katherine attended
hool. Here, at the age of eight she evidenced her first
terest in dancing. At nine, she staged her first production
en she organized a group of children to present a dance
vue for a church-raising project—which grossed thirty-
o dollars.

In high school she excelled in athletics and music, which
erged into her great interest in dancing. As a member
the Terpsichorean Club she laid the disciplined founda-
n for her future career with endless hours of running,
ping and arm-waving to the cadence of a gong and tom-
m. As a college student at the University of Chicago,
e financed her education by giving dance lessons which
cluded the cultures and religions of the peoples from
om the dances originated.

In 1936 she received special field training in a West
dies research project from Northwestern University.
ter that year she won a Julius Rosenwald Travel Fellow-
ip to the West Indies where for two years she studied

the life of Koromantees, a tribe of blacks brought over
from the Gold Coast of Africa during the colonial days.
When she returned to the University of Chicago she was
awarded her bachelor's degree in anthropology for her
thesis on life in the Caribbean.

In 1939 she was made a supervisor on the Writers
Project of the Works Progress Administration. Here she
was associated with writers Arna Bontemps and Richard
Wright. She went to New York in 1940 as a dance director.
Shortly afterward she appeared in *Cabin In The Sky* and
Stormy Weather. She was engaged as choreographer for
Pardon My Sarong and *Windy City*. In 1943 she was guest
artist for the San Francisco Symphony Orchestra, and in
1945 for the Los Angeles Symphony Orchestra. With her
own Tropical Revue she made several appearances at the
Hollywood Bowl. Tours with her troupe took her to almost
every country on the globe. She has written several books
and articles for many magazines, including *Esquire* and
Mademoiselle.

Katherine Dunham, *A Touch of Innocence* (New York, 1959).

169

Sidney Poitier (1927-)

OSCAR-WINNING DRAMATIC STAR

Once in New York, Sidney found the going rough.
worked as a dishwasher and odd-job man. Once he w
reduced to sleeping on Harlem rooftops under old new
papers. In 1945, he got up enough courage to audition f
membership in the American Negro Theatre (ANT), b
was rejected because of his thick West Indian acce
He learned the correct pronunciation of English by liste
ing to a radio for six months. He again auditioned f
the ANT and was accepted. One of his early classmat
was another West Indian, Harry Belafonte.

In 1946, he got bit parts in off-Broadway productio
of *You Can't Take it With You* and *Lysistrata*, and was
understudy in the major production of *Anna Lucasta*. H
first film role was in *No Way Out*. Then over the yea
Sidney Poitier appeared in one film after another: *R
Ball Express; Cry, the Beloved Country; Go, Man G
Blackboard Jungle; Good Bye, My Love; Edge of the Cit
Something of Value; Band of Angels; Mark of the Haw
The Defiant Ones; Lilies of the Field; To Sir, With Lov
In the Heat of the Night; Guess Who's Coming to Dinne
and For Love of Ivy*. For his performance in *Lilies of t
Field*, he became the first Negro actor to receive t
Academy Award as "best actor of the year." Sidney Poiti
had the male lead in two major plays, *A Man is Ten Fe
Tall* and *Raisin in the Sun*.

The success of Sidney Poitier is to some extent due
the increasing boldness of movie producers to cast Negro
in feature films. No one denies the tremendous talent
Poitier the actor, but some critics have complained th
many of his roles have been for characters too good or t
brilliant to be "real." Fully aware of this, Sidney Poiti
plans to remedy this with productions from his own co
pany. The presence of his name in the cast assures t
success of the film at the box office.

Lerone Bennett, "Hollywood's First Negro Movie Star," *Ebony* (May, 195
pp. 100-108; Charles L. Sander, "Sidney Poitier: The Man Behind
Superstar," *Ebony* (April, 1968), pp. 172-182.

Sidney Poitier is the first black actor to make it "really
big" in the movie industry. He succeeded with only one
major asset: consummate skill which enables him to move
with ease from comedy to tragedy. He has won the Academy Award, the highest accolade Hollywood gives in recognition of talent. He has over two dozen film credits to
his name. In 1968 he commanded three quarters of a million dollars per film and ranked among the top ten as a
box office draw.

Sidney Poitier was born of West Indian parents in
Miami, Florida on February 20, 1927. As a youth, however, he spent most of his childhood in his parents' native
Bahamas where he attended school for less than two years.
Hard pressed to support him and his seven brothers and
sister, his parents permitted him to return to Miami in his
early teens to live with relatives. In 1943, young Sidney
set out for New York, carrying only $1.50 in cash and
the clothes on his back.

XI MUSIC

Lift Every Voice and Sing

The story of Negro music goes back to Africa where song was a medium by which the past was recorded, the present rendered more tolerable, and the future made less insecure. Due to the bewildering number and variety of languages and dialects, the development of writing was greatly impeded in Africa. On the other hand, a tremendous oral tradition and literature took the place of the written word and acted as a reservoir for memories of the past. The custom and habit of singing and dancing as a means of historical, emotional, and intellectual expression survived the awesome "Middle Passage" across the Atlantic and laid the foundation for the development of Negro music in the New World.

Although Africans came to America from many different points and tribes on the West Coast of the African mainland and spoke a variety of languages, in the Deep South they found a means of communicating with one another via the English and French of their masters. To this new speech they joined the remembered African rhythms and passed them down through the generations. In the words of Mark Miles Fisher, "with concern for the music of their masters, Negroes employed rhythmical song to provide creature comforts, to accompany menial labor, to learn facts, to sell commodities and to share religion."

From their experiences as slaves, African-Americans developed the spirituals which "rank among the classical folk expressions because of their moving simplicity, of their characteristic originality, and universal appeal." In his famous essay "Of the Sorrow Songs," W. E. B. DuBois called the spirituals the "music of an unhappy people, of the children of disappointment; they tell of death and suffering and unvoiced longing toward a truer world, of misty wanderings and hidden ways."

The spirituals caught the interest of the nation during the abolitionist agitation but soon died away until the Fisk Jubilee Singers took them before the world in the 1870's. While the sacred and secular songs of the Negro slaves were taking form in the Deep South, free Negroes in the North were participating in the formal music of their day. Eugene V. McCarty, an excellent singer, pianist and composer of popular music, studied at the Conservoire Imperial in Paris in the 1840's. About the same time, Sarah Sedgewick Bowers sang operatic arias in Philadelphia and New York. Elizabeth Taylor Greenfield made a name for herself as a professional singer. She earned the title "The Black Swan" with a fine voice which carried her before Queen Victoria at Buckingham Palace in 1854. Mrs. Sampson Williams, a soprano, made a successful tour of Europe in 1880 using the professional name "Mme. Marie Selika." In the decade of the nineties Isseretta Jones made triumphal tours as "Black Patti."

A year after the Fisk Jubilee Singers began their astounding tour of the East and Europe in 1871, the Colored Opera Company, under John Esputa, presented such works as Eichberg's *The Doctor of Alcantra*. Negroes in Massachusetts formed the Boston Musical Union in 1875 and the next year Negroes in New York organized the Philharmonic Society of New York. The Samuel Coleridge-Taylor Musical Society of Washington, D.C., boasted over two hundred members in 1903 and was probably the largest Negro musical group of its era.

Scholars have traced the history of secular music among Negroes back to the sources of the spirituals. Both types of music are blends of West African and European rhythmic and harmonic forms. While the patterns of Negro secular music—the earthy blue tonality, the call-and-response, the field holler and the falsetto break—are very old, the emergence of individual musicians whose names are recorded may be dated from the turn of the century. Scott Joplin and his ragtime out of Missouri; Will Marion Cook and his syncopated musicals in New York; W. C. Handy and the blues out of Memphis and St. Louis; James Reese Europe with his promotion of the Handy music; and Ferdinand "Jelly Roll" Morton and his jazzband were important forerunners of today's secular music. Then followed Louis Armstrong with his trumpet in the thirties, Charlie Parker in the fifties, and Miles Davis with Thelonius Monk in the sixties. Indeed the list is much longer; the field of jazz is so vital that it possesses a literature of its own. Started by Negroes, jazz seems to be the characteristic musical idiom of the mid-twentieth century.

Throughout the long evolution of jazz, serious music has not been neglected. Harry T. Burleigh was arranging spirituals for the concert stage during the century's first two decades. J. Rosamond Johnson, Carl Diton, Nathaniel Dett, and John R. Work also made reputations as arrangers of Negro spirituals and as composers in their own right. Following them, William Dawson as a composer and Dean Dixon as a conductor gained national recognition. As concert artists, Roland Hayes, Paul Robeson, Marian Anderson and Etta Moten Barnett carried vocal music to new heights of technical finesse. Other artists including Lillian Evanti, Todd Duncan, Dorothy Maynor, Carol Brice, Gloria Davy, Mattiwilda Dobbs, Camilla Williams, Robert McFerrin, Leontyne Price, William Warfield, Lawrence Winters, and Grace Bumbry continued the fine tradition of superb singing in concerts, folk opera and grand opera.

W. E. B. DuBois, *The Souls of Black Folk* (Greenwich, Connecticut, 1963) Premier Americana edition, p. 183; Mark Miles Fisher, *Negro Slave Songs in the United States* (Ithaca, 1953), p. 1; Marshall Stearns, *The Story of Jazz,* New York, 1960 (Paperback), pp. 11-19, 183-200.

171

George P. Bridgetower
(1779-1860)

COMPOSER

"At home, on May 18. Although we have not spoken, I do not hesitate for all that, to speak of the bearer, Mr. Bridgetower, as a master of his instrument, a very skillful virtuoso worthy of recommendation. Besides concertos, he plays in quarters in a most praiseworthy manner and I wish very much that you would make him better known. He has already made the acquaintance of Lobkowitz, Fries and many other distinguished admirers. I believe that it would not be unwise to bring him some evening to Theresa Schonfeld's who I know has many friends . . ."

These words were written by the immortal Ludwig van Beethoven. He was singing the praises of George Polgreen Bridgetower, one of the outstanding violinists and composers of his day. Bridgetower was at the beginning of his career and Beethoven was taken by the skill and ability the Polish-born Bridgetower demonstrated in music.

At the age of ten, Bridgetower had taken Paris by storm with his first major violin concert. This was in 1789. The next year Bridgetower repeated his success in London at the Drury Lane Theater. So great was his skill and appeal that he was sponsored by the Prince of Wales.

His parents recognized his musical ability early and did their best to develop it. He studied under the finest available teachers, for who could ask for better instructors than Haydn, Barthelemon, or Giornovichi. As a matter of fact, the many friends of the young prodigy insisted that he meet Beethoven. The great composer was not disappointed and he himself quickly joined the ranks of Bridgetower admirers. Beethoven even appeared in concert with the Abyssinian Prince, as Bridgetower was called.

In addition to playing the music of others, Bridgetow composed works of his own, the best known being t "Henry" ballad which was dedicated to the Princess Roy in London. More than forty pianoforte suites flow from his pen.

George Bridgetower was the son of an African who ha emigrated to Poland where he met and married a lady Polish descent. His parents found little prejudice again them and lived the life of any other upper-class famil They were quick to take an interest in George and h brother, T. Bridgetower, who became a well known celli Often the two brothers appeared in concert together.

Not very much is known of Bridgetower's later li although he continued to perform in various countries. his death in 1860 at the age of 81, George Bridgetower w able to bequeath the sum of $5,000 to his sister-in-la

Beatrice Fleming and Marion Pryde, *Distingushed Negroes Abroad* (Wa ington, 1946), pp. 160-165.

Samuel Coleridge-Taylor (1875-1912)

ENGLISH COMPOSER

On November 16, 1903 a slim, somewhat short, mulatto from England stood before the 200-voice Samuel Coleridge-Taylor Society in Washington's Convention Hall and led in a performance of *Hiawatha*, a cantata of his own composition. A cross-section of Washington's society, cabinet members, congressmen and hundreds of music lovers turned out to hear the Society and to see the composer and conductor, Samuel Coleridge-Taylor. *Hiawatha* had already been presented in England with much success before an audience of thousands in London's famed Albert Hall.

After the Washington performance, the twenty-eight-year-old composer was presented with a baton made of cedar from Frederick Douglass's home, an autographed picture from Theodore Roosevelt and a loving cup from Washington Negroes inscribed with the words "Well for us, O brother, that you come so far to see us."

The son of an African father from Sierra Leone and a mother from England, Samuel Coleridge-Taylor was born in London in 1875. He began to study the violin at the age of six and showed an early aptitude for composition. In 1890 he entered the violin department of the Royal Academy of Music, and in his third year won a prize for composing. He graduated from this institution with honors in 1894.

The *Hiawatha* cantata was the work which catapulted him to fame. In *The Death of Hiawatha* and *Hiawatha's Wedding Feast*, Coleridge-Taylor elaborated the Hiawatha theme. Nevertheless the young composer made his most distinctive contribution to music in his symphonic works based on Negro melodies of Africa and America. For the piano he wrote *African Suite, African Dances* and *African Romances*, the latter with words by Paul Laurence Dunbar whom he met and performed with in England. Among his vocal works are *The Blind Girl of Castle-Cuille* and *The Atonement* which was presented in Washington in 1906 during his second and last trip to America. Coleridge-Taylor composed a suite for the piano based on *Othello* and an interesting choral work, *A Tale of Old Japan*.

Critical estimates of his work rank Coleridge-Taylor high on the lists of English composers. He made his living entirely from his work as a musician. He supported himself by public appearances and by teaching the violin at the Croyden Conservatory of Music. Music was his life. When he died in Croyden in 1912, he imagined that he was conducting his unfinished *Violin Concerto*.

W. C. Berwick Sayers, *Samuel Coleridge-Taylor: Musician* (New York, 1915); Maud Cuney-Hare, *Negro Musicians and Their Music* (Washington, 1936), pp. 244-247.

James Bland (1854-1911)

COMPOSER OF SOUTHERN SONGS

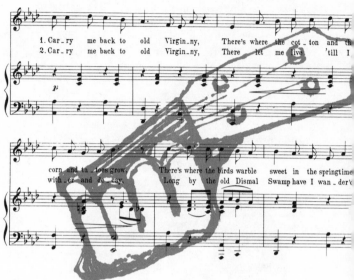

CARRY ME BACK TO OLD VIRGINNY

SONG AND CHORUS

Words and Music by
JAMES BLAND
Author of "In the morning by the bright light," &c.

Virginia, the proudest of the southern states, is perhaps the only state in the Union whose official song was written by a Negro. Whenever citizens of the Old Dominion rise to sing *Carry Me Back to Old Virginny*, they are also giving homage to James Bland, a Negro composer who was born free in Long Island, New York.

Other old-time favorites such as *Oh, Dem Golden Slippers*, *In The Evening By The Moonlight*, *Tapioca*, *Pretty Little Carolina Rose*, *Listen to the Silver Trumpets*, and scores upon scores of other songs flowed from the pen of this untrained composer.

Contrary to popular legend, James Bland was not a white-haired ex-slave writing songs of fealty and affection for his former masters. He was a self-made professional descending from a long line of free Negroes. Having the distinction of being the first Negro employed as an examiner in the United States Patent Office, his father, Allen Bland, was a graduate of Wilberforce and Oberlin Colleges and had a degree from the Howard University Law School. His mother was a native of Wilmington, Delaware.

James Bland fell in love with the banjo while in his teens. He began his career singing and playing for parties and weddings. At the age of fourteen Bland was hired to sing at a hotel in Washington, D.C. Thinking to discourage his son from a show business career, Allen Bland sent his son to Howard University. Once there, James promptly started organizing glee clubs and minstrel groups. Finishing his courses at nineteen, Bland soon took to the road as a regular professional. He appeared with such groups as Billy Kersand's Minstrels and Callenders' Original Georgia Minstrels.

In 1878 while working with George Primrose, James Bland published *Carry Me Back To Old Virginny*, which became an instant success. Popular singers rushed to add the song to their repertoire. Bland was in great demand for personal appearances. On the strength of his popularity in America, James Bland went to England in 1881 and found even greater professional and personal success. He gave a command performance for Queen Victoria. The leading vaudeville houses vied for his services. At one point James Bland was earning $1000 weekly. He was called the "Prince of Negro Performers."

Dispensing with blackface and burnt cork, Bland could be seen as he was: a rather handsome, debonair man with an engaging smile. He wore the finest products of English tailoring and lived on a lavish scale. After twenty years abroad, James Bland returned to America only to find that old-time minstrelsy was no longer the vogue. He died in 1911, two years after Bert Williams hit the big time as a comedian.

John J. Daly, *A Song in His Heart* (Philadelphia, 1951); Langston Hughes, *Famous Negro Music Makers* (New York, 1955), pp. 29-34; David Ewen (ed.), *Popular American Composers* (New York, 1962), pp. 30-31.

Blind Lemon Jefferson
(1897-1929?)

BEST OF THE EARLY
BLUES BARDS

The biggest single influence on all modern music is the American jazz which had its beginnings in the blues of the old South. And these blues had their roots in Africa—the rhythmic chants which accompanied many of the daily tasks and the communal songs sung around the evening fire relating events of the day or stories of the historic past. Africans, brought to America as slaves in the agricultural South, improvised songs to relieve the monotony of their day and "hollered" in the fields to ease the strain of their work. From these came the railroad songs of the section gang, steamboat songs of the levee workers, and prison songs of the chain gang. With emancipation and mobility came the songs of "movin' on," transient sex, lost love and loneliness, all expressed in the restrained emotionalism of a suffering, uprooted, and well-oppressed people.

The first professional blues shouters were probably the men who, in the early 1900's, wandered through the South, earning bed and board by singing on the street corners and in the bars. Among these early bluesmen were Charley Patton, Son House, Skip James, "Bukka" White, Huddie "Leadbelly" Ledbetter, Big Bill Broonzy and Mississippi John Hurt. But the best known and the most extensively recorded was Blind Lemon Jefferson.

Lemon Jefferson was born in the summer of 1897 on a small farm outside Couchman, Texas, the youngest of seven children. Because he was blind, he began singing for money in the town of Wortham before he was fifteen. By the age of twenty he was singing for parties and dances throughout Freestone County. Sometimes he would have an accompanist, but more often "it would be just him, sitting there playing and singing all night."

The first blues singers moaned a single story on a single theme, sometimes accompanied by a battered guitar and the spontaneous rhythmic shouts of the audience. Gradually a definite song style emerged: three line stanzas that stated a problem, repeated it, then carried it forward with hope, resignation, or ironic humor. As an example:

Laid down las' night tired as I could be.
Yes, I laid down las' night just as tired
    as I could be.
'Tween cotton pickin' and women, not much
    left of me.

Lemon's voice had a startling intensity, ". . . a desolate, lost sound, tinged with loneliness, with the restless guitar moving below it as though searching for a phrase to end its incessant movement." During the early twenties the recording industry discovered the popularity of the blues and in 1925 brought Lemon from Dallas to Chicago for the first of the many recording sessions he was to do for Paramount until his death four years later. There had been earlier recordings by bluesmen—Ed Andrews, Daddy Stovepipe, Papa Charlie Jackson—but Lemon's distinctive style had the greatest influence on such later artists as Sonny Terry, Muddy Waters, Joe Turner, T-Bone Walker and the famous Josh White.

There is some confusion over Lemon's death, but the story with most credence is that he was found frozen to death in a Chicago street one February morning in 1929. He left behind him a legacy of more than eighty records, which not only tell a folk story of America's early history but clearly illustrate the pentatonic scale, rhythmic combinations, harmonies, dissonance, and twelve-bar progression which grew out of the vocals and tribal music of Africa.

Charters, Samuel, *The Bluesmen* (New York, Oak Publications, 1967); Charters, Samuel, *The Country Blues* (New York, 1959), pp. 57, 60; Keepnews, Orin, *Pictorial History of Jazz* (New York, Crown Publishers, 1961), pp. 69, 79.

Harry T. Burleigh (1866-194[)

SINGER, COMPOSER, ARRANGER

NEGRO
SPIRITUALS

Arranged for Solo Voice by

H. T. BURLEIGH

Ain't Goin' to Study War No Mo'
Balm in Gilead
Behold That Star
By An' By
Couldn't Hear Nobody Pray
De Blin' Man Stood on De Road An' Cried
De Gospel Train
Deep River
Didn't My Lord Deliver Daniel
Don't Be Weary Traveler
Don't You Weep When I'm Gone
Ev'ry Time I Feel the Spirit
Give Me Jesus.
Go Down in De Lonesome Valley
Go Down Moses
Go Tell It On De Mountains
Hard Trials
Hear de Lambs a-Cryin'
Heav'n Heav'n
He's De Same Today
I Don't Feel No-Ways Tired
I Got A Home In A-Dat Rock
I Know De Lord's Laid His Hands On Me
I Stood On De Ribber Ob Jerdon

I've Been In De Storm So Long
I Want To Be Ready
John's Gone Down On De Island
Joshua Fit De Battle Ob Jericho
Let Us Cheer The Weary Traveler
Little David Play on Your Harp
My Lord What A Morning
My Way's Cloudy
Nobody Knows De Trouble I've Se[
Oh Didn't It Rain
Oh Wasn't Dat a Wide Ribber
Oh Peter Go Ring Dem Bells
O Rocks Don't Fall On Me
• Ride on King Jesus
Sinner Please Doan Let Dis Harves[
Sometimes I Feel Like A Motherless
Stan' Still Jordan
Steal Away
Swing Low, Sweet Chariot
'Tis Me O Lord
Wade In De Water
Weepin' Mary
Were You There
You May Bury Me in De Eas'

The small boy stood in the snow outside the Russell home for hours, hoping to hear the pianist, Rafael Joseffy, when he played for the drawing room packed with guests. The Russells employed his mothers as a maid, and Burleigh had often accompanied her to work and heard snatches of good music whenever the Russells decided to present famous artists in their Erie, Pennsylvania home. Young Harry almost forgot about the cold, the wet and the snow as he listened to the music floating out of the windows. When the music ended, Harry hurried home, late, hungry and cold.

Mrs. Burleigh told her employer that young Harry was ill of exposure whereupon Mrs. Russell gave the Erie High School lad a job as a doorman to admit the guests—and to hear and see what was going on at her parties. Thus Harry T. Burleigh became acquainted with good music and began the contacts that were to bring him fame in later years.

When not attending school or working in Erie hotels, young Burleigh trained and sang with Negro choirs and choral groups. In 1892 he won a scholarship to the National Conservatory and began his formal training in music. Here he studied under such men as Christian Fritsche, Robin Goldmark and John White. Here also he met Anton Dvorak who was teaching there at the time. He

and Dvorak became good friends. Many evenings the[could be found together, the Hungarian composer and t[young Negro singer. Burleigh would sing spirituals f[Dvorak and in turn would be permitted to copy mus[from the composer's manuscripts.

In 1894, over a large field of trained competitor[Burleigh won the job of baritone soloist at the ultra-ric[ultra-fashionable St. George Episcopal Church in Ne[York. The parishioners were divided over his being er[ployed but the majority of them supported him. In 190[Burleigh was selected baritone soloist at Temple Emmanu[in New York, one of the nation's wealthiest synagogues. [kept both posts for over a quarter century. His splendi[voice even took him before King Edward VII in a com[mand performance.

Burleigh's greatest artistic ambition was the arrang[ment of the spirituals for use in concert halls. Today man[of the old familiar spirituals presented by leading con[cert singers carry the notation "Arranged by Harry [Burleigh." He also composed art songs such as *In th[Wood of Finvara, The Prayer* and *Ethiopia Salutin[the Colors.* His song cycles include *Down by the Se[* and *Who's Dat Yonder.*

In 1917 Harry T. Burleigh was given the Spingar[Award for distinguished contributions to the progress [the Negro in music. He died in 1949.

Maud Cuney-Hare, *Negro Musicians and Their Music* (Washington, D.[1936), pp. 323-329.

Nathaniel Dett (1882-1943)

COMPOSER

JUBA

R. NATHANIEL DETT

Non Troppo Allegro ♩:120-144

mf *non legato*

Nathaniel Dett made significant contributions to America's musical heritage with his compositions and arrangements. Throughout his long career Dett insisted on the dignity of the Negro spiritual. His compositions encompass both racial and non-racial themes.

Especially popular are his works *Oh Holy Lord* and *Listen To The Lambs* which are performed by many choral groups throughout the country. Dett's better known compositions for the piano are *The Magnolia Suite*, *The Enchantment Suite, In the Bottoms*, and the motet *Chariot Jubilee*. His opera, *The Ordering of Moses*, was performed in the forties by the National Negro Company and presented at Carnegie Hall in 1951. It was recorded by the Voice of America for broadcasting overseas.

In addition to his compositions and arrangements, Dett was a highly successful choral leader. Beginning with his organization of the Musical Arts Society in 1919 at Hampton Institute, Dett raised the Hampton Institute Choir to international eminence. In 1930 under his leadership the Hampton choir made a tour of seven European countries and received great critical praise. Prior to his success at Hampton, Dett had been summoned to his home town of Drummondsville, Ontario to organize and lead a 100-voice all-white choral group in the celebration of music week in 1924. Dett also developed excellent choral groups at Lane College in Jackson, Tennessee and at Lincoln Institute (now Lincoln University) in Jefferson City, Missouri.

Born in 1882, Nathaniel Dett decided on a career in music early in life. From 1901 to 1903 he attended the Oliver Willis Halsted Conservatory and received the degree of bachelor of music from Oberlin College in 1908. He continued his studies at the American Conservatory of Music in Chicago, at Columbia University and the University of Pennsylvania. Dett first achieved wide notice while at Harvard where, as a student in 1920, he won the Bowdoin Prize for an essay, "The Emancipation of Negro Music," and the Francis Boott Prize for motets on a Negro motive.

Maud Cuney-Hare, *Negro Musicians and Their Music* (Washington, D.C., 1936), pp. 336-339; Margaret Just Butcher, *The Negro in American Culture* (New York, 1957), Mentor Edition, pp. 74-75.

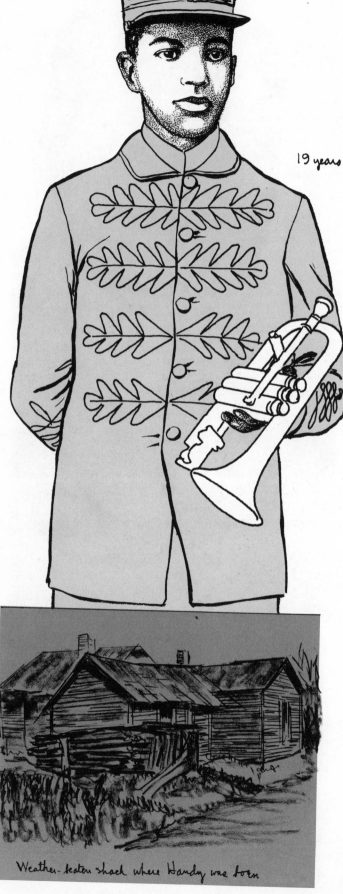

19 years old, Hampton Cornet Band, Evansville, Indiana

Weather-beaten shack where Handy was born

W. C. Handy (1873-1958)

"THE FATHER OF THE BLUES"

The story of the blues is the story of the life of W. Handy, often called the "father of the blues." Farm hand washerwomen, wood cutters, railroad laborers, and rous abouts for years had lightened their daily rounds wit secular songs of love, of despair, of hope and longin Unlike the spirituals, the blues are about the relation ships between men and women on this earth.

W. C. Handy, in a sense, was the first to bring thes secular songs to the larger world. Many other traine musicians had heard the blues and dismissed them as th rude and bawdy music of the oppressed. The music them was interesting but somehow too blunt and coarse be taken seriously. W. C. Handy himself felt this way u til one night while leading a group called Maharas' Ban he chanced to hear some musically illiterate country pe formers move an audience with the not-quite-respectabl blues songs and music.

Handy, too, was moved and that very night hurrie home to write the *Memphis Blues*. He followed this wit the *Beale Street Blues* and finally the classic *St. Lou Blues*. The tremendous public response to Handy's blue soon made him an internationally known figure. Deem Taylor and Walter Damrosch, musical luminaries, led th way with their praise of him. Handy soon played his blue before high society and even royalty.

W. C. Handy was born in Florence, Alabama, in 187 While his mother felt that his large ears indicated mus cal aptitude, his father strongly objected to the boy showing any interest in the "sinful" music of the fields an streets. Handy learned the rudiments of music in th local school for Negroes in Florence. By the time h reached his teens he was arranging choral parts for churc groups. He left home when he was eighteen years old an decided to strike out alone. He sang and played his wa from Florence to Chicago with the Lauzetta Quartet. H then worked his way back down to St. Louis, Missouri, bu found little opportunity to make a living from his music In St. Louis Handy was so poor that he had to sleep o the levee and to depend upon his wits for food. In hi wanderings Handy passed through many towns where Negro was not welcome after sundown. He summed u these experiences in the famous line, "I hate to see th evening sun go down."

During these early days, Handy was so eager to hea good music that he once took a job as a janitor in Hender

amp issued May 17, 1969

n, Kentucky in order to hear an excellent German chorus
one hundred voices as he swept the rehearsal hall.
andy did not neglect his own music and from time to
me would play with small bands and minstrel groups;
e cornet and the trumpet were his favorite instruments.
By the turn of the century, Handy's fortunes had im-
oved to the point that he was invited to Alabama A & M
llege to serve as director of music. He remained here for
ly two years and returned to the road where he could
ake more money and possess a freedom not usually
und on college campuses.

He wrote his *Memphis Blues* in 1909, and his fame be-
n to spread after the tune was used in a political cam-
ign. He decided to make Memphis his headquarters
d opened up the offices of the Pace and Handy Music
mpany. The company skyrocketed to success within a
ar, for among the many compositions Handy turned out
r the company was the *St. Louis Blues* which was an
stant success. The earlier fame of his *Memphis Blues*
as such that the Handy organization could send out up-
ards of eighty men each night to play dance engagements
different parts of Tennessee and the surrounding areas.
The "big" song was of course the *St. Louis Blues* which
as netting W. C. Handy $25,000 yearly by 1940. The com-
ser of the blues did not stop with just the above-named
nes but wrote over sixty others. Nor was his work limited
the blues. He is the composer of *Aframerican Hymn,*
ue Destiny* (a symphonic piece) and over 150 other
mpositions, both sacred and secular.

In 1928 William Christopher Handy sponsored and con-
cted a sixty-voice chorus and a thirty-piece orchestra at
rnegie Hall in a musical history of the Negro. In this
rformance during the height of the "Negro Renaissance"
re "Fats" Waller, J. Rosamond Johnson and other dis-
guished Negro musicians.

By 1930, Handy's name was a household word. The
ues were regarded as a legitimate part of the country's
usical heritage. In 1931 the city of Memphis, Tennessee
med a park after Handy. Sixteen years later a huge
eatre in Memphis bore his name. In Florence, Alabama,
ands the W. C. Handy School.

W. C. Handy died in 1958, but his contributions to
usic live on as a part of America's musical heritage.

C. Handy, *The Father of the Blues* (New York, 1941); *Current Biography,*
1, pp. 361-362.

Statue of Handy in Handy Park, Memphis, Tennessee

William Grant Still

(1895-   )

MODERN COMPOSER

However, his great interest was music and after three years, he withdrew from Wilberforce without taking a degree. Only in his early twenties at the time, Still became a drifter. For a short time he worked as an office boy for W. C. Handy in Tennessee and played in Handy's band. During all of his wandering, Still never lost the desire to compose.

A small inheritance enabled William Still to attend the Oberlin Conservatory of Music in Ohio. Later grants made it possible for him to go to the New England Conservatory of Music. He began the serious study of composition under George Chadwick and the famed Edgar Varese. Combining the musical heritage of Europe with his own Afro-American background, Still began to produce music for songs, ballets, symphonies and operas.

Some of his better known songs are *Breath of a Rose, Levee Land* and the beautiful *Kaintuck*. Among his ballet compositions are *Sahdji* and *La Guiablesse* which was performed in Indianapolis, Indiana. His better known symphonies are *Afro-American Symphony, Africa* and *Symphony in G minor. Blue Steel* and *Troubled Island* are among his more popular operatic compositions.

William Grant Still has received numerous awards and honors. Extended Guggenheim and Rosenwald fellowships freed him for creative activity during the early part of his formal career. He won the Harmon Award for his contributions to music in 1927. For his *Troubled Island* he was cited by the National Association for American Composers and Conductors for a distinguished contribution to American music. He has had numerous commissions from the Columbia Broadcasting Company, the New York World's Fair (1935), and several other cities for special occasions. He has received honorary degrees from a number of institutions, including Wilberforce and Oberlin. His works are now a part of America's musical treasure.

Edwin R. Embree, *13 Against the Odds* (New York, 1944), pp. 197-210. Richard Bardolph, *The Negro Vanguard* (New York, 1961), paperback, pp. 221-222.

The night William Grant Still stood before the Los Angeles Philharmonic Orchestra in 1936 and conducted one of his own compositions marked the first time an American Negro had ever led a major orchestra in the performance of serious music. This occasion was also a hight point in the life of Still who had played honky-tonks and dives in the Deep South, in Ohio and New York. The occasional "gig" (musical engagement), the catch-as-catch-can combos and bands, the orchestra pits of musical revues were all behind him.

The route from his native Woodville, Mississippi to the Philharmonic contained many detours and by-ways. His parents had sent him to Wilberforce to study medicine.

William L. Dawson

(1898-   )

COMPOSER-ARRANGER

Taking high rank among creators of American music is William Levi Dawson, the eminent composer whose works have brought pleasure to thousands of music lovers. The beauty of his music shines through such experiences as not being allowed to take part in one of his own graduation exercises in 1927 because of his color, and having to secure special permission to attend a concert featuring his work in Birmingham, Alabama, for the same reasons.

Born in Anniston, Alabama in 1898, William Dawson ran away from home to attend Tuskegee Institute. At Tuskegee he landed a job caring for the instruments of the institute band and learned to play most of them. After finishing Tuskegee in 1921, he attended Washburn College, Topeka, Kansas, the Institute of Fine Arts, Kansas City, Missouri and later he went to Chicago, Illinois to continue his studies in composition and orchestration. At the Chicago Musical College he studied under Felix Borowski, and at the American Conservatory he studied with Adolph Weidig. At the same time he earned his living playing in Windy City bands, training Negro church choirs and occasionally playing the trombone with the Chicago Civic Orchestra as its only Negro member during that time.

Among his compositions are *I Couldn't Hear Nobody Pray*, and *Talk About a Child That Do Love Jesus, Here 'Tis One*. His most notable symphonic work is *Negro Folk Symphony No. 1*. Its world premiere was at Carnegie Hall under conductor Leopold Stokowski in 1934. For many years, William Dawson was director of music at Tuskegee Institute. With his compositions and arrangements, he made the Tuskegee Institute Choir one of the nation's best. Following his retirement from active direction of the choir in 1955, Dawson was sent to Spain by the U. S. State Department to train Spanish choral groups in the singing of Negro spirituals.

Dawson has a deep and abiding love for spirituals. To their natural beauty he has added the discipline and training of the devoted professional.

Maud Cuney-Hare, *Negro Musicians and Their Music* (Washington, 1936); Who's Who in Colored America, 1950, p. 145.

Paul Robeson (1898-)

A BARITONE TO REMEMBER

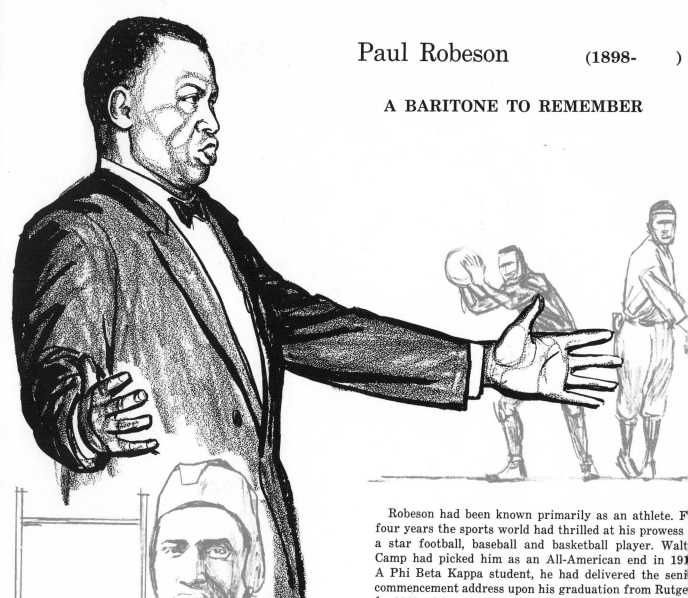

One night on the stage of Greenwich Village Theatre in April, 1925, during the height of the "Negro Renaissance," a huge black giant of a man threw back his head and sang:

> Go down Moses
> Way down in Egypt's lan'
> An' tell ol' Pharaoh
> To let——my——people——go!
> Let my people——go!

This majestic spiritual was followed by others, among them being "Sometimes I Feel Like a Motherless Child," and "Joshua Fit the Battle of Jericho." The packed hall resounded with praise and applause as the concert ended. The singer was Paul Robeson, who had never taken a singing lesson in his life.

Robeson had been known primarily as an athlete. F four years the sports world had thrilled at his prowess a star football, baseball and basketball player. Walt Camp had picked him as an All-American end in 191 A Phi Beta Kappa student, he had delivered the seni commencement address upon his graduation from Rutge in 1919. After Rutgers, Robeson had gone on to t Columbia University Law School to earn a law degr by 1923.

At the suggestion of his wife Eslanda Goode, who he had married in 1921, Robeson decided to try actin His first part was that of a cross-bearer in a Harlem YMC production of *Simon the Cyrenian*. After seeing him this amateur production, Eugene O'Neill tried unsucces fully to give him the lead role of *Emperor Jones*. In 19: Robeson had played with Margaret Wycherly in *Voodo* When he later essayed the role of the porter in *Emper Jones* his potentialities as a singer were first noticed. *A* an actor, he achieved wide recognition for his work *All God's Chillun*.

After Robeson's Greenwich concert his future as singer was assured. In 1926 he repeated his earlier triump by singing to a full house at New York Town Hall. F then followed this with appearances in Boston, Philade phia and Baltimore. In the same year he went abroa repeating his American successes on a larger scale. Alte nating between America and Europe, Robeson was polished performer by 1929. On May 19, 1930 he playe the role of the jealous Moor in *Othello* at London's Savo

182

Uta Hagen and Averell Harris co-starred with Robeson in the Theater Guild production of Othello

Theatre. Of his performance, the *London Morning Post* declared that "there has been no 'Othello' on our stage, certainly for forty years, to compare with his dignity, simplicity and true passion."

In between concert tours of Europe, Robeson appeared in O'Neill's *The Hairy Ape* and *Stevedore* (by Paul Peters and George Sklar), an important play showing the Negro's awareness of the larger economic issues of the thirties. Robeson also appeared on the screen in early productions of *Emperor Jones, Showboat, Jericho, King Solomon's Mines* and *Saunders of the River*.

On the legitimate stage Robeson is best known for his work in the American production of *Othello*, first playing the Moor in 1934 and again in 1943. In the latter production, Robeson perhaps achieved his greatest fame. He played opposite Uta Hagen's "Desdemona" and Jose Ferrer's "Iago." Critics were unrestrained in their praise. Opening on October 19, 1943, *Othello* ran for 296 performances before it closed on July 1, 1944. The *New York Sun's* drama critic exclaimed that Paul Robeson was "the first Negro of modern times to appear in a New York production," and added that "he gives a giant's stature and remarkable clarity and vitality to his role."

Robeson has been popular as a recording artist, having over 300 disks to his credit. He has studied nine languages, including Chinese and Russian. He has been able to sing to and speak with people of many different nationalities in their native tongues.

From his early youth as a poor minister's son in his native Princeton, New Jersey, Paul Robeson had a deep sympathy for the social underdog. His political views swung to favor Russia. In his admiration of that country, he sent his only son there to be educated. He himself has been to Russia many times, and since the late forties, has spent much of his time there and elsewhere. Naturally his career has gone in eclipse in America. A writer once declared that it is "one of the extravagances of the theatre that Paul Robeson is not active in it." Perhaps the same could be said of a society which so embittered Robeson that he felt it necessary to leave it.

Shirley Graham, *Paul Robeson; Citizen of the World*, New York, 1946; Edwin Embree, *Thirteen Against the Odds*, New York, 1946, pp. 243-261.

Roland Hayes
(1887-   )

GOD'S OWN TENOR

Born in Georgia in 1887, Roland Hayes seemed destined for the fate of many a gifted but rudderless artist. Of his early years, the cultivated, mild-mannered Hayes has said, "It was as natural for me to sing as to breathe." By chance he was invited to hear some recordings by the great tenor Enrico Caruso, and from this moment on Roland Hayes was determined to become a professional singer.

Eventually making his way to Fisk University, it was perhaps inevitable that Hayes joined the famed Fisk Jubilee Singers. On a trip to Boston, Massachusetts as a member of the Jubilee Singers, Hayes decided to give up Fisk and to secure competent training for his voice. Supporting himself with a variety of random jobs, he began the serious study of voice and by 1916 felt ready for a concert tour. He received very little encouragement as Negro concert artists were not yet in demand. Concert managers felt that his desire to become a concert performer was noble but naive. Hayes undertook his own management and succeeded far beyond the expectations of the professionals.

After several seasons of touring in America, Hayes decided to go to Europe to enhance his professional career. Shortly after his arrival in England, he was commanded to sing before the King of England, George V. This command performance helped to secure his reputation and for the next fifteen years the concert managers who had rejected him earlier were proudly presenting "Roland Hayes in Concert" in America as well as abroad. Once financially successful, Hayes followed a policy of low-cost admissions so that the poor of all races could hear him.

Despite many unpleasant experiences as a pioneer, Roland Hayes has never lost his belief in the essential goodness in man. He believes that social progress may take many avenues. The elevation of the hearts of men through song is one of them. When Roland Hayes received the first Amistad Award for contributing creatively to the improvement of human relations, Virgil Thomson, himself an outstanding musical composer and critic, said to him, "You do the human race honor to exist."

For almost half a century, Roland Hayes has taken the world for his stage and has never lacked an audience. Blessed with a superb voice, he sang his way from a window-sash factory in Chattanooga, Tennessee to the chandeliered halls of Buckingham Palace. Illiterate peasants of the Deep South and musical sophisticates of the world have been touched by the voice of the man who has been called the "greatest tenor ever born in America."

"Roland Hayes: A Lifetime on the Concert Stage," *Ebony* (September 1946), pp. 26-46; McKinley Helm, *"Angel Mo' and Her Son: Roland Hayes* (Boston, 1942).

Dean Dixon
(1915-   )

CONDUCTOR INTERNATIONAL

He was born in Harlem in 1915. He speaks Swedish, French and German but he interprets the international language of classical music with a skill, insight and sensitivity which have made him one of Europe's busiest conductors. Conducting has been his joy and his life. Yet, Dean Dixon left America in 1949 because he could not find a regular post as a symphony conductor despite his admittedly great talents.

Before taking over the Hessian Radio Symphony of Frankfort, Germany in 1962, Dean Dixon had been the conductor of the Goteborg Symphony in Sweden for nearly a decade. To the Swedish orchestra he imparted a technical finesse and a melodic quality which brought it wide acclaim. He also introduced many American works to Europe, especially the compositions of William Grant Still and Gordon Parks.

Dean Dixon is known in Europe far beyond the borders of Sweden and Germany. He has conducted nearly every major symphony orchestra in Europe including those of Austria, Italy and Israel.

Recently he conducted orchestras on opposite sides of the globe in the same year. For three months of the year, he conducted the Sydney (Australia) Symphony Orchestra. For five months, he was chief conductor and general music director of the Frankfort Radio Symphony.

Born of West Indian parents in New York, Dixon learned to read music and the alphabet at about the same time. When his legs were almost too short to climb the stairs, his mother would take him to Carnegie Hall. He played the violin in the DeWitt Clinton High School band and after graduation, organized an amateur interracial orchestra in the Harlem YMCA.

Dixon received very little encouragement when he decided to become a symphony conductor, especially at a time when Negro instrumentalists could not find permanent employment. Nevertheless his ability was so great that he led the New York Chamber Orchestra when he was twenty-five and still a student of conducting at the Juilliard School of Music in New York.

After completing his Juilliard studies under Albert Stoessel in 1939, Dean Dixon began an uncertain career as a guest conductor, leading such groups as the New York Philharmonic Orchestra, the NBC Symphony Orchestra and the Boston Symphony. In 1948 he received the $1,000 Alice M. Ditson Award as the outstanding music conductor of the year. He received several awards for his work in encouraging an interest in music among young people.

However none of the many honors and awards could take the place of a regular podium for this gifted conductor who left America nearly fifteen years ago. Dean Dixon still dreams of returning to the land of his birth, "leading my own symphony."

Arna Bontemps, *We Have Tomorrow* (Boston, 1945), pp. 46-58; *Who's Who in Colored America, 1950*, p. 157; "An American Abroad." *Time* (May 4, 1962), p. 48.

Louis "Satchmo" Armstrong
(1900- 1972)

THE JAZZ AMBASSADOR

When Louis Armstrong was sent to the Waif's Home for Boys for discharging a pistol in the streets of New Orleans, Louisiana, he had no idea that twenty years later he would appear before the King and Queen of England in a command performance. Then a poverty stricken urchin of thirteen, he could play no instrument save a home-made guitar. Louis Armstrong's casual interest in music was cultivated by the bandmaster of the Waif's Home. There the round-faced youth with the wide open eyes learned to play the cornet and bugle so well that he was leading the band before his release eighteen months later.

While supporting himself by selling newspapers and working in a dairy, Armstrong began loitering around the places where his idol Joe "King" Oliver was appearing with Kid Ory's band. "King" Oliver taught Armstrong to play the trumpet and when he left for Chicago in 1917, Louis Armstrong took his place in Ory's band. Armstrong experienced his first long journey away from New Orleans when he accompanied Kid Ory's group on a 2,000-mile cruise up and down the Mississippi in 1921-22.

In 1922 Armstrong took the Mississippi northward to Chicago to join his trumpet mentor, "King" Oliver, who was then appearing at the Royal Palm Gardens. Two years later Armstrong headed for New York and worked with Fletcher Henderson's orchestra, but returned to Chicago in 1925. In 1926 he joined Erskine Tate at the old Vendome Theater. Earl Hines, the pianist in Tate's orchestra at the time, and the boys doubled nights at the Sunset Cafe. Louis' name went up in lights—"World's Greatest Trumpeter." Following his success, he organized his own group, "Louis Armstrong and His Hot Five."

After a series of profitable engagements in Chicago Armstrong returned to New York to a spot called Connie's Inn and had a highly successful run. He left Connie's Inn and became a star of the musical *Hot Chocolates* where he first introduced *Ain't Misbehavin'*.

In 1933 Armstrong made his first trip abroad and toured France, Italy, Switzerland, Norway, Holland, and England. In 1934 he appeared before England's King George VI in the first of several command performances. During most of his stay abroad, the former New Orleans waif made his home at la rue de l'Auvergne in Paris.

Following his return from Europe in 1936, Armstrong made his motion picture debut in *Pennies from Heaven*. In the next few years he appeared in *Everyday's a Holiday*, *Going Places*, and *Cabin in the Sky*. His recording career dates from the middle twenties, and many of his records are collectors' items.

Since these early days Louis Armstrong's trumpet has been heard in many parts of the world, including Africa. His virtuosity on the trumpet and influence on early jazz earned him a secure place in the annals of popular music.

Louis Armstrong, *Satchmo: My Life in New Orleans* (New York, 1954).
Louis Armstrong, *Horn of Plenty* (New York, 1947).

Duke Ellington
(1899-   )
THE MAESTRO

Whenever music is discussed, by layman or professional, young or old, jazz fan or classicist, in any part of the world, the name Duke Ellington is quite likely to be mentioned. Such is the reputation and musical accomplishment of this maestro. He has achieved practically every musical honor imaginable, from popularity polls and hit records to sell-out, standing-room-only crowds at Carnegie Hall. His plaques and trophies, dating back to 1940, would completely fill a room. To date he has written over 1,000 tunes, and the amazing part of his fabulous career is that it seems not to have reached its peak—his musical creativity is ever expanding, continuously growing.

The "Duke" was born Edward Kennedy Ellington on April 29, 1899, in Washington, D.C. He earned the nickname "Duke" in school for his somewhat flashy clothes: he was always "duked out." Like most truly creative people, the Duke evinced his talent early. Although he hated to practice, he was playing the piano at seven. He composed his first piece, *The Soda Fountain Rag*, at seventeen, and at eighteen was playing professionally.

At twenty-four he hit Broadway with his own band, the Washingtonians; at twenty-eight he was booked into the Cotton Club, where his nation-wide fame began; at thirty-four he played for royalty in London and toured Europe as a concert artist; at thirty-nine he gave one of the first college jazz concerts at Colgate University; at forty he made a second triumphal European tour, giving twenty-eight performances in twenty-eight days; at forty-four he performed the first of his many concerts at Carnegie Hall; at forty-five he added Chicago's Opera House and San Francisco's Philharmonic Hall to his list of "firsts"; and he celebrated his seventieth birthday as a guest of President Nixon at a "swinging" birthday party in the East Room of the White House.

National recognition of his musical superiority dates back to 1940 when he won honors in a nation-wide poll. Since then, there has hardly been a single year in which he has not won similar honors in comparable polls. He has been hailed by such outstanding names in serious music, as Lauritz Melchior, Stokowski, Reiner and Deems Taylor. He was the first living artist to sponsor a scholarship fund to the Juilliard School of Music.

Ellington has evidenced creative talent, as well as interest, in serious music, also. His more ambitious musical scores include *Black, Brown and Beige,* a tone poem of the history of the American Negro; *Perfume Suite,* and his musical salute to the Negro entitled *My People.*

His popular song classics include: *Mood Indigo, Solitude, The A Train, Caravan, Sophisticated Lady,* and hundreds of others whose appeal, like their originator, has not been dated by the passing years. In recent years, he has developed a number of "jazz masses" which have been performed in some of the leading churches in America.

Peter Gammond (ed.), *Duke Ellington: His Life and Music* (New York, 1958).

Marian Anderson
(1902)

THIS CENTURY'S CONTRALTO

When Marion Anderson finished her audition, Mr Borghetti sat motionless. Tears were streaming down his cheeks. Miss Anderson's church had raised money for her first year's fees and Mr. Borghetti was so impressed by her voice that he taught her an additional year without cost.

After several years of private study Miss Anderson resumed her tours of southern colleges and, in 1925, she felt that she was ready for a Town Hall concert. The concert was a failure and the young, novice singer was on the brink of despair. But in 1926 she sang at a Spingarn Award dinner for Roland Hayes and took a renewed interest in her own career.

In 1927 Miss Anderson entered a competition with 300 other young singers and won first prize which consisted of a contract for concert tours. This led to an appearance with the New York Philharmonic Orchestra. Finding her concert opportunities limited, Marian Anderson went to Europe in 1929 and made her continental debut in Germany. Returning to America, she continued her training and touring. In 1933-35 she spent two years in Europe with the aid of fellowships and sang for the crowned heads of Sweden, Norway, Denmark, and England. She also came under the management of the impresario, Sol Hurok, and the praise of Arturo Toscanini who declared that hers was a voice "heard only once in a hundred years."

Within three years after her return, Marian Anderson was one of America's leading contraltos. Her recordings were a staple of the Columbia recording company. Her concerts were generally sell-outs. With Franz Rupp Marian Anderson criss-crossed the Americas. By 1941 she was one of America's highest paid concert artists.

Her standing was so high in 1939 that when the Daughters of the American Revolution denied her the use of Constitution Hall, a national scandal was created. Deems Taylor, Walter Damrosch, and other musical leaders expressed their disapproval of the DAR. Mrs. Eleanor Roosevelt resigned from this organization. As though in disapproval of the DAR, 75,000 people gathered before Marian Anderson on the steps of the Lincoln Memorial as she sang on Easter Sunday morning in 1943.

Marian Anderson was awarded the Spingarn Medal and the $10,000 Bok Award in 1939. Other awards and distinctions came her way. She was the first Negro to sing at the Metropolitan Opera. In 1957 she toured the Orient, and in India moved tens of thousands with her music.

Without a doubt Marian Anderson, through her music and her regal behavior, has contributed greatly to the success of other Negroes on either side of the footlights.

When she stood before the famous music teacher, Giuseppe Borghetti, the church recitals, the amateur cantatas and oratorios, the timid tours south, and the tutoring of good friends were all behind her. Auditioning for a professional career, she was a stately young woman with a serene face. Her outward calm and dusky complexion seemed almost a part of the gathering twilight as she started to sing:

> Deep river . . . My home is over Jordan.
> Deep river . . . Lord, I want to cross over
> Into camp ground.

Marian Anderson, *My Lord, What a Morning; An Autobiography* (New York, 1956); Kosti Vehanen, *Marian Anderson; A Portrait* (New York, 1941).

Ulysses Kay (1917-   ) IN A CLASSICAL VEIN

Ulysses Kay ranks high among the serious black composers of today. He has produced superb works for voice, groups, chamber ensembles and full orchestra. Awards for his work include a Gershwin Memorial Prize for his *A Short Overture;* first prize from Broadcast Music, Inc. for *Suite for an Orchestra;* and an American Broadcasting Company prize for *Of New Horizons.* Kay's *Triptych* has been described as evidence of a "masterful composer." Classical status was predicted for *Alleluia.* His *Serenade for Orchestra* has been called a "symphony of remarkable eloquence, energy and integrity." Kay wrote *The Boor,* an opera after Anton Chekhov. Commissioned by the Koussevitzky Music Foundation, *The Boor* has been praised as revealing a "Mussorgskyan flair for a speech-like melorhythmic line."

The creative talents of Ulysses Kay have been recognized by the following awards: a Ditson Fellowship for study at Columbia University, a Julius Rosenwald Fellowship, a Ford Foundation grant, grants from the American Academy of Arts and Letters and the National Institute of Arts and Letters, a Fulbright scholarship to Italy, and a Prix de Rome for residence at the American Academy at Rome. Kay was selected to be a part of a cultural exchange with Russia, the other Americans so chosen being Roy Harris, Peter Mennin and Roger Sessions.

In addition to his formal works, Kay has composed background music for documentary films such as *The Quiet Ones, New York: City Magic,* and two television documentaries for the Twentieth Century series on CBS— *FDR: Third Term to Pearl Harbor* and *Submarine.*

Ulysses Kay was born in Tucson, Arizona in 1917. He attended the public schools of Tucson and is a graduate of the University of Arizona. In 1938 he left Arizona for New York and entered the Eastman School of Music at the University of Rochester to earn the M.A. degree in music. He also studied at Yale and the Berkshire Music Center. Following these experiences, Kay was drafted for military service. In the Navy he continued to compose and arrange.

Upon his discharge, Ulysses Kay returned to his first love, creating such works as *Concerto for Orchestra* (1948), *Sinfonia in E* (1959) and *Suite from the Ballet Danse Calina.* Kay's *Cantata, Phoebus, Arise* (1959) evoked much praise. It was described as a "vigorous, lyrical and in many ways attractive work."

Ulysses Kay (New York, 1962) pamphlet, p. 2; New York Times (May 18, 1959); Nicolas Slonimsky, *American Composer's Alliance Bulletin* (Fall, 1957).

Leontyne Price (1927-   )

PRIMA DONNA

Following Marian Anderson as the reigning bronze diva, Leontyne Price has been at the center of the stage in American grand opera. She once declared that "since I first began to train as a singer, my goal and ambition has been to sing at the Metropolitan Opera in New York." She not only made her debut at the Old Metropolitan Opera building in 1961, but also officially opened the new Metropolitan in the Lincoln Center complex in 1966.

Leontyne Price has had a star-spangled career that includes triumphant appearances as "Bess" in the famous State-Department-sponsored European tour of *Porgy and Bess* (1952-1954). In 1955 Miss Price appeared in Puccini's *Tosca*, Mozart's *Magic Flute* (1956), Poulenc's *Dialogues of the Carmelites*, and Mozart's *Don Giovanni* (1960). When, in 1961, she made her debut at the Met in *Il Trovatore* by Giuseppe Verdi, Miss Price was given an ovation that lasted forty-two minutes for her stunning portrayal of "Leonore." This was followed by excellent performances as "Cio-Cio San" in *Madame Butterfly*, "Donna Anna" in *Don Giovanni* and "Liu" in *Turandot*. Miss Price launched the 1961-1962 season of the Met in the role of "Minnie" in *La Fanciulla del West* (Girl of the Golden West) by Puccini.

She has appeared in the role of "Aida" at the Vienna State Opera, and has performed this role in Yugoslavia, Belgium and Italy. In the latter country, at Milan, Miss Price had to sing without rehearsal but still won the bravos of a hypercritical audience. She has recorded songs in the major languages of Europe as well as the spirituals of her native South.

Mary Leontyne Price was born on February 10, 1927 in Laurel, Mississippi. Her parents, James and Kate Price, reared her in the black Puritan tradition of religion and church. Her Sundays were spent with choirs and choruses, both as singer and pianist. After completing high school in Laurel, Miss Price went to Central State College in Wilberforce, Ohio. There she was encouraged by the then president Charles Wesley, among others, to secure additional training.

Paul Robeson was among those who assisted in raising funds for her. Finally Miss Price was offered a tuition scholarship to the Juilliard School of Music in New York. Mrs. Elizabeth Chisholm, a banker's wife in Laurel, Mississippi, supplied additional funds for her living expenses. While a student at Juilliard, Leontyne Price appeared as "Mistress Ford" in *Falstaff* opposite her future husband William Warfield, the great baritone. From *Falstaff*, Miss Price was assigned by Virgil Thompson to the role of "Saint Cecelia" in his *Four Saints in Three Acts*.

Whenever Miss Price performs at the Metropolitan Opera, the event is regarded as major news, not because she is a black woman, but because of her artistry. She takes her work seriously. Perhaps the greatest example of the care with which she approaches a role is seen in the fact that she practiced the part of "Cleopatra" for one solid year before the curtain rose in the first opera to grace the new Metropolitan Opera house.

Price, Leontyne, *"Current Biography,"* (1961); *Ebony* (December, 1966), pp. 184-192; *Newsweek* (September 19, 1966), pp. 70-79.

XII VISUAL ART

Every Eye a Witness

Removed from his native Africa and shackled as a slave to a plow and hoe in America, the African was henceforth and forever divorced from his native artistry and culture. The creative sculpture, metalwork, weaving and pottery of his native Africa were no longer his to pursue in the new land.

Thus, the Negro as a group was denied creative expression for more than a century, and it was not until the planters and merchants of the South grew rich and began to ornament their mansions and buildings that his artistic talents were employed. When given the opportunity, he proved to be a fine carpenter, cabinet maker, wood carver, blacksmith, and harness maker. In New Orleans, where he worked as a blacksmith fashioning the beautiful wrought iron grilles that decorate the balconies and balustrades of the finest homes and buildings, his artistry may be seen today. There is little doubt that the handicraft was a carryover from his ancestral Africa.

Skill in slaves was sought and encouraged among the prosperous slave holders, who recognized that a skilled slave was worth more as a worker or when sold.

Throughout the pioneer days and up to the industrial revolution in America the nation afforded little encouragement to the artists in the plastic and graphic arts. Individuals who amassed fortunes and began to acquire art, patronized the European artists. It was not until about 1870 that the American artists began to gain recognition. Before this, however, we find that Robert Duncanson, an Ohio Negro, had painted *Blue Hole* in 1851, which is now in the collection of the Cincinnati Art Museum. Duncanson had studied in Canada, England, and Scotland. The London Art Journal in 1866 credited him with being one of the outstanding landscapists of his day. About 1870, in Providence, Rhode Island, Edward Bannister, a painter of great talent, organized the Providence Art Club in his home. This was the first American art club and he was the only Negro member. It is still that city's leading art club.

Later, around 1876, Edmonia Lewis, who was born in Boston in 1854 of mixed parentage (Negro and Indian), came to prominence as the first Negro sculptor. Henry O. Tanner, at the turn of the century, was establishing an international reputation as a painter of religious subjects in Paris. He taught and influenced two younger painters of his day, William Harper and Edouard Scott, who became renowned after the turn of the century. A second woman sculptor, Meta Warrick Fuller, became noted for her "power and originality."

Negro artists up to this time avoided Negro subject matter in their work. Duncanson and Bannister who were landscape painters employed the style of the European masters of their day. Scott's early work showed the influence of Tanner, with whom he studied in Paris. However, during his stay in Haiti the local color of lush green foliage and rich brown skin-tones found their way into his canvases. Harper's surroundings dictated a native interpretation of his experiences into his works.

May Howard Jackson (1897) was one of the first Negro artists to break with tradition and turn to "frank and deliberate racialism." She possessed a deep feeling and love for Negro types, and sculpted portraits of many important Negroes.

Before 1940 the number of professional Negro artists were few. Outstanding among these were Aaron Douglas, William Farrow, Charles Dawson, Archibald Motley, Laura Waring, Palmer Hayden, Hale Woodruff, Albert Smith, William H. Johnson, James L. Wells, Sargent Johnson, Malvin Gray Johnson, Augusta Savage, James A. Porter, Richmond Barthé, Selma Burke, Ellis Wilson, and Charles Alston.

It would be a gross oversight not to include the creative genius of the great architect, Paul R. Williams, and the talented cartoonist, E. Simms Campbell, in the allied arts.

With the establishment of the Federal Art Projects, Works Progress Administration, America witnessed a surge of creative talent. Financed by government funds, people with artistic talent were put to work as writers, actors, musicians, and plastic and graphic artists. These projects not only encouraged talented artists, but brought about a new cultural vista in America.

Perhaps the greatest beneficiaries of this program were the black artists who were for the first time gainfully employed in the arts. In Chicago and New York, young Negro artists who had come from all over the nation to these metropolitan centers in the hope of developing their artistic talents, found the answer to their quest in the art projects. Of the two cities, Chicago produced more professional artists in all of the allied arts.

To name only a few, there were Richard Wright, Arna Bontemps, Gwendolyn Brooks, Katherine Dunham, Frank Neal, Charles Sebree, David P. Ross, Eldzier Cortor, William Carter, Charles White, Sinclair Drake, Horace Cayton, Willard Motley, and Bernard Goss.

New York and the East produced its fair share of professional artists, also. Included among these, in addition to those previously mentioned, are: Marlin Smith, Jacob Lawrence, Robert Blackburn, Donald Reid, Ernie Crichlow, Elton Fax, Ellis Wilson, Zell Ingram, Wilbert Warren, Laura Wheeler Waring, Robert Pious, Lois Mailou Jones, Wilmer Jennings, Alice Elizabeth Catlett, Allan Rohan Crite, and Frederic Flemister of Georgia.

Among the younger contemporaries who have gained recognition, there are Richard Hunt, John Arterberry, Clarence Brisco, Lawrence A. Jones, Jack Jordan, Leon Leonard, Jimmie Mosely, Hayward Oubre, Harper T. Phillips, Gregory Ridley, Hobie Williams, Hughie Lee-Smith, Geraldine McCullough, Frank Wyley, and Romare Bearden.

Alain Locke, *Negro Art: Past and Present* (Washington, D.C., 1936); Alain Locke, *The Negro in Art* (Washington, D.C. 1940); Cedric Dover, *American Negro Art* (New York, 1957); James A. Porter, *Modern Negro Art* (New York, 1943).

Robert Duncanson (1821-1871)

EARLY AMERICAN ARTIST

Robert Duncanson has been called the most accomplished American Negro painter of the 1840's and 50's. His most productive years were between 1840 and 1865. A native of Cincinnati, Ohio, Duncanson was the son of a transplanted Scotsman and a Negro woman. His youth was hard and unpleasant, although little or none of this is reflected in his landscapes, murals or portraits. He began sketching in his teens and before he was twenty had excited the admiration of prominent artists in and around Cincinnati.

In 1840 the Freedmen's Aid Society of Ohio collected funds to send him to Glasgow, Scotland, for formal training, where he remained for three years.

Duncanson executed many portraits of leading citizens in Cincinnati. His *William Carey* may be seen at the Ohio Military Institute; his *Nicholas Longworth* hangs in the Ohio Mechanics Institute. Although Duncanson's forte was landscape painting, he was a competent muralist and painter of the American West. In 1860 the *London Art Journal* named Duncanson as one of the outstanding landscape painters in an era when such painting was in vogue.

His pictures were exhibited in the United States, England and Scotland. He often took themes from Shakespeare and Tennyson and entitled some of his work *The Trial of Shakespeare* and *The Lotus Eaters*.

While abroad, Duncanson met Alfred Lord Tennyson and enjoyed the patronage of the Earl of Essex. One of his paintings was secured for Windsor Castle. Duncanson's famous *Trial of Shakespeare* is still in Cincinnati, after having been initially presented to the Douglass Center in Toledo. Another of his paintings, *Blue Hole*, is owned by the Cincinnati Art Museum. Unfortunately most of Duncanson's paintings have become lost or destroyed over the years.

Duncanson returned from his last trip abroad in 1860 and is believed to have died in a Detroit, Michigan hospital eleven years later.

James A. Porter, *Modern Negro Art* (New York, 1943), p. 46; Alain Locke, *Negro Art: Past and Present* (Washington, 1936), pp. 18-20; *Negro Yearbook, 1947* (Tuskegee, 1947), p. 413. *Dictionary of American Artists: 1564-1860*, edited by George C. Grace and David Wallace (New Haven, Yale University Press, 1957), gives Duncanson's birth and death dates as 1837 and 1872 respectively, p. 193.

Edward M. Bannister
(1828-1901)
LANDSCAPE PAINTER

One day in 1867 Edward M. Bannister became enraged by a *New York Herald* article which flatly declared that "the Negro seems to have an appreciation of Art while being manifestly unable to produce it." He had a right to be angry, for he had been sketching since he was ten years old, had taken private instruction from Dr. William Runner, an able teacher of Art Anatomy in Boston, and had studied art at Lowell Institute in Boston where he was ostracized by white artists.

Life had not been easy for Bannister. He was of mixed parentage and had been orphaned while quite young. Born in Nova Scotia, Bannister had supported himself with a variety of menial jobs: cooking on a coastal vessel, sweeping the floor in a Boston barbershop, serving as a man-of-all-work at different times. At no time did he despair of his painting and in every spare moment took out his paints and brushes. The *Herald* fired his determination to make a career as an artist.

Although he had a small reputation in Boston, Bannister moved to Providence, Rhode Island in 1870. Within six years his painting gained for him an entry in the Centennial Exhibition held in Philadelphia in 1876. His painting *Under the Oaks* took the Gold Medal. A revolt of the other entrants occurred when the judges wanted to "reconsider" the Gold Medal Award after discovering that

Bannister was a Negro. The white competitors insisted that the decision stand and Bannister walked off with the prize. *Under the Oaks* was sold for $1500 during that same year.

After the Centennial Exhibition, Bannister's reputation continued to grow and the commissions freed him from odd jobs. It is likely that he made a rather good living as a painter for one account of his life states that he could be seen sailing his yacht on Narragansett Bay and Newport Harbor studying the clouds and the sky. He produced a large number of landscapes, most of which possess a gentle arcadian quality and carry such titles as *By the Brook* and *Landscape*. Today some of his work may be found in the collections of the Providence Art Club, the Rhode Island School of Design, the Howard University Art Gallery and the John Hope Collection at Atlanta University.

Edward Bannister was one of the seven charter members of the famed Providence Art Club which was incorporated in 1870. During his life he was widely recognized as one of America's more competent landscapists who happened to be Negro. He died in Providence in 1901.

Cedric Dover, *Negro American Art* (New York, 1960), pp. 26-27; Alain Locke, *The Negro in Art* (Washington, D.C., 1940), p. 130.

Henry Ossawa Tanner
(1859-1937)

PAINTER OF RELIGIOUS SUBJECTS

One day a small boy in Pittsburgh, Pennsylvania stood watching a painter at work. From pots and tubes the painter took all kinds of colors and on the easel before him a recognizable figure took shape. To the thirteen-year-old boy, Henry O. Tanner, it seemed almost magical the way the dead pigments and oils were transformed into a representation of life. Inspired by the creation of the painter, Henry decided then and there that he was going to be a painter. He had no idea of the trials and tribulations facing an artist, especially a Negro artist in 1872. So Henry set out to become an artist.

He studied earnestly and his skill grew. Finally he felt confident enough to submit some of his drawings to publishers in New York, but most of his work was returned. Some drawings he never saw again. Eventually he sold a painting for $40.00, and later one brought him $80.00. Tanner grew to manhood and began to travel. He secured a position as an instructor at Clark University in Atlanta. He learned photography and, between it and his art, earned a modest living. He sold one photograph for $15.00 and considered he had gotten a good price for clicking a shutter. But to his surprise, the same photo was re-sold for $250.00 in Philadelphia.

Tanner continued to develop his skill and to grow in confidence. In the 1890's the French Impressionists were creating a stir in Europe, and those who aspired to become great painters went there to study. Fired by the idea of going to Rome to study, Tanner worked hard preparing for a major exhibit in Cleveland at which he hoped to raise enough money for his trip. His show was well attended, but he sold not a single painting. His talent was recognized by Bishop and Mrs. Joseph C. Hartzell, who decided to support him by purchasing his entire collection.

Tanner sailed for Rome. The trip was to be something of a grand tour, with stops in Liverpool, London and Paris. However, he got no farther than Paris, for it was to him the perfect place to work and study. Here he met many of the great artists of the day. Benjamin Constant, the famous landscape artist, admired Tanner's work and encouraged him. After five years in the "City of Light," he had developed a technique and individual style. He had taken a special interest in religious subjects.

Sketch of detail from Tanner's "Daniel in the Lion's Den"

In 1896 his famous painting *Daniel in the Lion's Den* won him major honors. His *Resurrection of Lazarus* stunned the artistic world and was purchased by the French government. Following this, honors came one after the other. His work won the Salon Medal in 1897 and again in 1907. The Louisiana Purchase Prize was awarded him in 1904. In Philadelphia he received the Lippincott Prize in 1900. The Art Institute in Chicago awarded him the Harris Prize of $500 in 1906.

Today his paintings are regarded as a successful combination of deep religious fervor and high artistic technique, somewhat in the manner of the master painters of the Renaissance.

Benjamin Brawley, *The Negro Genius* (New York, 1940). Alain Locke, *The Negro In Art* (Washington, 1940), p.134.

Edmonia Lewis

(1845-1890?)

PIONEER WOMAN SCULPTOR

Sketch of bust of Henry Peck

also did a bust of Henry Wadsworth Longfellow for the Harvard College Library.

Miss Lewis first exhibited her work in Boston in 1864. At this exhibition her sculptured portrait of Colonel Robert Shaw, the martyred leader of the all-Negro Massachusetts Fifty-fourth Regiment, evoked such a favorable reaction that she was able to travel to Rome to study, with the proceeds from the sale of copies of it. As her skill and fame grew, Miss Lewis exhibited her work in Chicago in 1870, in Rome in 1871, and at the Centennial Celebration in Philadelphia in 1876.

Born in Albany, New York of mixed Negro-Indian parentage, Miss Lewis was first reared by her mother's tribe, then placed in an orphanage and finally adopted by an abolitionist family. She was sent to Oberlin College in 1865. During her three years there her talent for modeling was noticed by William Lloyd Garrison who brought her to the attention of Edmund Brackett, a prominent sculptor in Boston, Massachusetts. Under his guidance, she began her career.

Resembling an East Indian in physical appearance, Miss Lewis possessed "an appealing intensity and forthrightness." In Rome she was an exotic sight, wearing mannish garb and hacking directly from marble the images she had created in her mind. Most of her adult career was spent in Italy. Sometime during her later years she returned to America. However, the vogue of neo-classicism was passing. Edmonia Lewis also passed from public notice, and her last years were so obscure that art historians can only surmise that she died in 1890.

Edmonia Lewis was the first American Negro woman sculptor to achieve distinction in a field generally dominated by men. Riding the crest of the neoclassical revival in the 1870's, she attracted wide notice in artistic circles. Miss Lewis did portrait busts of a number of the prominent figures of her era, including Abraham Lincoln, Wendell Phillips, Charles Sumner and John Brown.

Miss Lewis also executed a large number of complete figures and groups: *Hagar*, depicting a biblical theme; and *Hiawatha*, *The Marriage of Hiawatha*, and *The Departure of Hiawatha*, on the famous Indian legend, are among her better works. Though less technically accomplished than her bust of Charles Sumner, for example, a figure group called *Forever Free* aroused the greatest general interest. This particular group shows a Negro couple, just out of slavery, becoming aware of the fact that they are no longer in bondage. (*Forever Free* was made for the Harriet Hunt Mausoleum in Cambridge, Massachusetts.) She

Cedric Dover, *American Negro Art* (New York, 1960), pp. 27-28; Alain Locke, *The Negro in Art* (Washington, D.C., 1940), pp. 133-134; Margaret Just Butcher, *The Negro in American Culture* (New York, 1957), Mentor Edition, pp. 170-171; James A. Porter, *Modern Negro Art* (New York, 1943), pp. 57-63.

Horace Pippin

(1888-1946)

MODERN PRIMITIVE

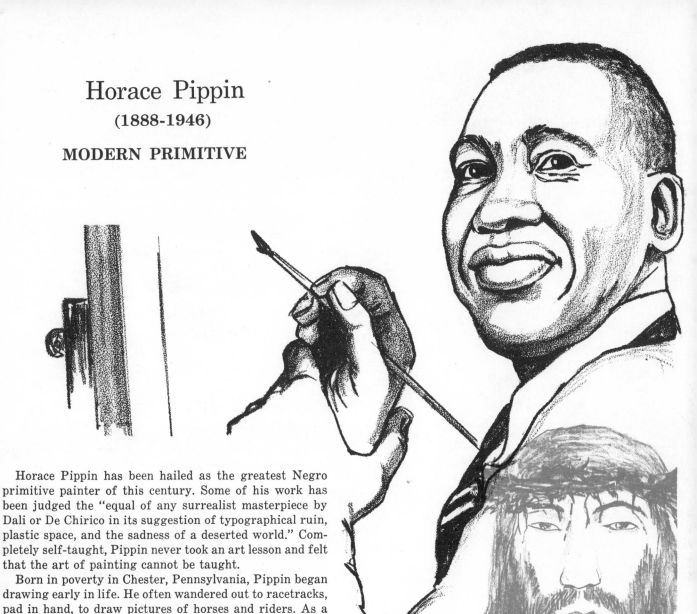

Sketch of detail from painting "Christ"

Horace Pippin has been hailed as the greatest Negro primitive painter of this century. Some of his work has been judged the "equal of any surrealist masterpiece by Dali or De Chirico in its suggestion of typographical ruin, plastic space, and the sadness of a deserted world." Completely self-taught, Pippin never took an art lesson and felt that the art of painting cannot be taught.

Born in poverty in Chester, Pennsylvania, Pippin began drawing early in life. He often wandered out to racetracks, pad in hand, to draw pictures of horses and riders. As a child he moved to Goshen, New York with his parents. His formal education ended with grammar school and he began a series of routine jobs as a hotel porter, molder, and junk dealer. His passion for art was so strong that he often sought jobs in warehouses where paintings were stored, in order to touch the paint and to study the way different artists did their work.

In 1917 Pippin entered the army and served overseas until severly wounded. He received the Croix de Guerre and the Purple Heart and was discharged in 1918. Returning to America, he married in 1920 and settled down in Westchester, New York. Supported by his disability checks and his wife's earnings, Pippin could not still his desire to paint. His war wounds made it impossible for him to raise his arm above his shoulder and his first efforts at serious painting required him to place a wooden panel in his lap, draw his outlines with a hot poker and then apply the house paint he used for oils.

Not until 1931 did Pippin recover sufficiently to try his skill on canvas. His first picture was three years in the making and he labeled it *The End of the War; Starting Home.* Then he executed another picture called *Shell Holes and Observation Balloon, Champagne Sector,* which received very high praise.

Through the efforts of friends, Pippin had his first one-man show at the Westchester Community Art Center in 1937. By 1938 he had developed to the point that four of his paintings were exhibited at the Museum of Modern Art in a show entitled "Masters of Modern Painting." Two years later he had a one-man show in New York which was a huge success. This success was repeated in Chicago and Philadelphia. His *Cabin in the Cotton* won fourth Honorable Mention in 1944, and two years later his *Milkman of Goshen* won the J. Henry Scheidt Memorial Prize, one of the major awards of the Pennsylvania Academy of Fine Arts.

Current Biography, 1945, pp. 470-472; *The Americana Annual, 1947,* p. 566; James A. Porter, *Modern Negro Art* (New York, 1943), p. 149.

Malvin Gray Johnson
(1896-1934)

SYMBOLIC ABSTRACTIONIST

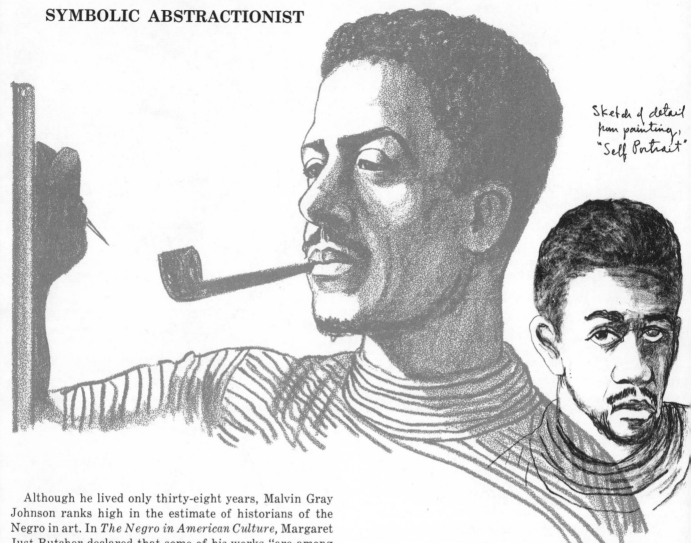

Sketch of detail from painting, "Self Portrait"

Although he lived only thirty-eight years, Malvin Gray Johnson ranks high in the estimate of historians of the Negro in art. In *The Negro in American Culture*, Margaret Just Butcher declared that some of his works "are among the most significant commentaries on the American Negro scene." Alain Locke felt that Johnson caught better than most artists the sardonic humor and mystical pathos in the moods of the Negro. James Porter, seeing Johnson as a maturing experimentalist, wrote that Johnson's later work was stated in "terse, pregnant patches of color."

In the interpretative paintings such as *Swing Low, Sweet Chariot* and *Roll, Jordan, Roll,* Johnson attempted to treat the spirituals in terms of abstract symbolism. These and similar works were regarded as technical advances in the handling of Negro thematic material. During the last years of his life, Johnson turned to genre subjects, painting a brilliant series of watercolors of urban and rural Negroes. *Dixie Madonna, Ruby, Brothers, Red Road* and *Convict Labor,* works from his final period, are believed to be typical of his best efforts.

Johnson's work was shown in several of the Harmon Exhibits in 1929 and the early thirties. In 1931 the Anderson Gallery displayed some of his work, and, in 1932, several of his paintings were hung in the Salon of America. He won the Otto H. Kahn prize for painting in 1929.

Born in 1896, Malvin Gray Johnson was a native of Greensboro, North Carolina where he grew up in dire poverty. He managed to get to New York where he studied at the New York Academy of Design. Along with many other artists, he worked on the Federal Arts Project during the Depression. During the last few months of his life, he went to Brightwood, Virginia, the locale of his last and finest watercolors and paintings.

Johnson was deeply interested in the technical problems of painting. Lighting, composition and, above all, form held a deep fascination for him. This is evident in his interpretations of the spirituals, particularly where he tries to convey the awe and majesty of the nobler slave and sorrow songs. In his genre painting, Johnson even rose above form in an effort to convey the quality of the lives of his people on this earth.

Margaret Just Butcher, *The Negro in American Culture* (New York, 1957), Mentor Edition, p. 186.; Alain Locke, *Negro Art: Past and Present* (Washington, D.C. 1936), pp. 73-75; James A. Porter, "Malvin Gray Johnson, Artist," *Opportunity*, XIII (April, 1935), pp. 117-118; James A. Porter, *Modern Negro Art* (New York, 1943), pp. 122-123.

Richmond Barthé
(1901-)

REALISTIC SCULPTOR

ketch of bust,
West Indian Girl"

Richmond Barthé recently declared that "all of my life have been interested in trying to capture the spiritual quality I see and feel in people, and I feel that the human figure as God made it, is the best means of expressing this spirit in man." Since he began his quest more than two score years ago, Barthé has built up a body of work which places him in the front ranks of modern sculptors. In America he is represented in the Metropolitan Museum of Modern Art, New York City; the Hackley Museum at Oberlin College; Pennsylvania Academy of Fine Arts; Philadelphia Museum; Atlanta University; the Art Institute of Chicago, to name a few. Barthé's works may be seen in collections in England, Germany, France, Africa, Canada, the Virgin Islands and Haiti.

Barthé has been a Rosenwald and a Guggenheim Fellow. He was a recipient of awards for interracial justice, and citations from the American Academy of Arts and Letters. In 1945 he was presented the Audubon Artists Gold Medal, and the Haitian government commissioned him to do two special monuments in 1950.

Richmond Barthé has done both heroic and miniature sculpture, but there is general agreement that he excels in executing small works. Exquisitely graceful pieces such as *The Harmonica Player, Shoeshine Boy, Boxer*, or *Black Narcissus* show the sculptor at his best. His pieces such as *Mother and Son, Blackberry Woman*, and *African Boy Dancing* are likewise excellent examples of the work of this distinguished sculptor.

Born in St. Louis, Mississippi, the artist spent his early youth in New Orleans. He left school at the age of fourteen, took a job as a houseboy and handyman, and spent every available free moment drawing. After unsuccessfully trying to enter art schools in the South, he was aided and encouraged by friends of the Catholic church in getting to Chicago, where in 1924 he entered the Art Institute with the intention of becoming a painter.

He found employment at a small cafe as a busboy where he worked for four years during his study at the Institute. His paintings came to the attention of Dr. Charles Maceo Thompson, a patron of the arts and sponsor of many of the talented young Negro artists. Barthé had a flattering style as a portrait painter and Dr. Thompson was influential in securing him many profitable commissions among the Negroes of means in the city.

At the suggestion of an instructor who recognized the direction of Barthé's greater talent, he turned to sculpture. So skilled was he that within two years, he was able to present a one-man show of his work. Within the following year, he was awarded a Rosenwald Fellowship (1931). His first commissioned work was a bust of Toussaint L'Ouverture.

Since these early years, the artist has received many important commissions and awards, making it unnecessary for him to depend on anything other than his work as a sculptor for his livelihood. As a sculptor, a teacher and lecturer, Barthé has contributed to the advancement of the Negro and the progress of art.

James A. Porter, *Modern Negro Art* (New York, 1943), pp. 136-137; *Who's Who in Colored America, 1950*, p. 23; Richard Bardolph. *The Negro Vanguard* (1961), Vintage Edition, pp. 245-247.

Jacob Lawrence
(1917-   )

PAINTER:
CONTEMPORARY PRIMITIVE

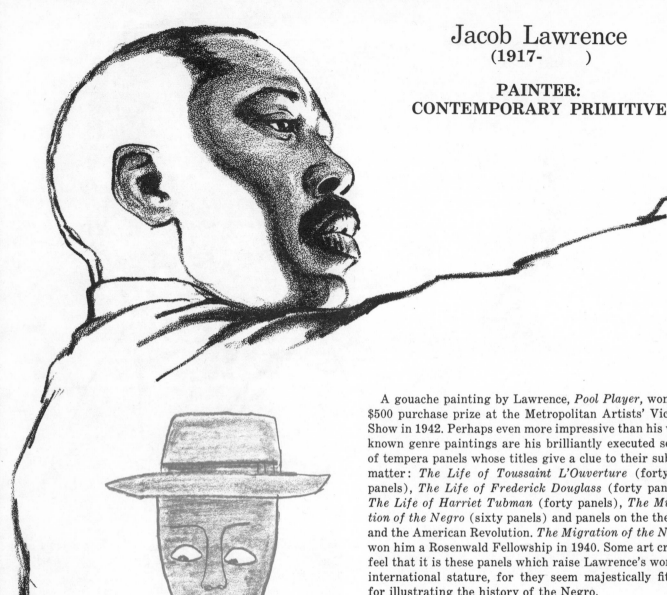

Sketch in the style of Lawrence

A gouache painting by Lawrence, *Pool Player*, won the $500 purchase prize at the Metropolitan Artists' Victory Show in 1942. Perhaps even more impressive than his well-known genre paintings are his brilliantly executed series of tempera panels whose titles give a clue to their subject matter: *The Life of Toussaint L'Ouverture* (forty-one panels), *The Life of Frederick Douglass* (forty panels), *The Life of Harriet Tubman* (forty panels), *The Migration of the Negro* (sixty panels) and panels on the theatre and the American Revolution. *The Migration of the Negro* won him a Rosenwald Fellowship in 1940. Some art critics feel that it is these panels which raise Lawrence's work to international stature, for they seem majestically fitting for illustrating the history of the Negro.

Jacob Lawrence was born in Atlantic City, New Jersey in 1917. The product of a broken family, he was shunted between his mother and foster parents. When his mother, a domestic, finally took him to New York to live, the two of them found living quarters near a settlement house which greatly encouraged the study of arts and crafts. Charles Alston, an able painter and a member of the settlement house staff, encouraged the boy with his early drawing and painting.

Jacob Lawrence is regarded primarily as a sophisticated primitive painter, although he studied at the Harlem Workshop and the American Artists School in New York during the thirties. His formal education was obtained in the Philadelphia and New York public schools.

With the exception of interruptions due to illness, Jacob Lawrence has devoted his adult years to expressing his version of the Negro's experience in America. Though not as prolific as he was during the thirties and forties, Lawrence is still producing exceedingly powerful work. His genre pictures and his series on historical events appear to have earned him a lasting place in American art.

Long regarded as one of the most significant painters in America, Jacob Lawrence stands high in the history of the Negro in art. His angular, seemingly two-dimensional world of ordinary Negroes doing ordinary things is familiar to all who profess to be abreast of the development of American art history. Equally well-known are Lawrence's magnificent series of panels devoted to personalities and events in Negro history.

Jacob Lawrence's paintings have been shown as far west as the Detroit Museum and as far south as Dillard and Fisk universities. He is represented in private collections and in many of the leading art galleries, including the Whitney Museum, the Phillips Memorial Gallery, the Howard University Gallery of Fine Art and the Worcester (Mass.) Art Museum.

James A. Porter, *Modern Negro Art* (New York, 1943), pp. 151-152; *Who' Who in Colored America, 1950*, p. 332.

Marion Perkins
(1908-1961)

SCULPTOR

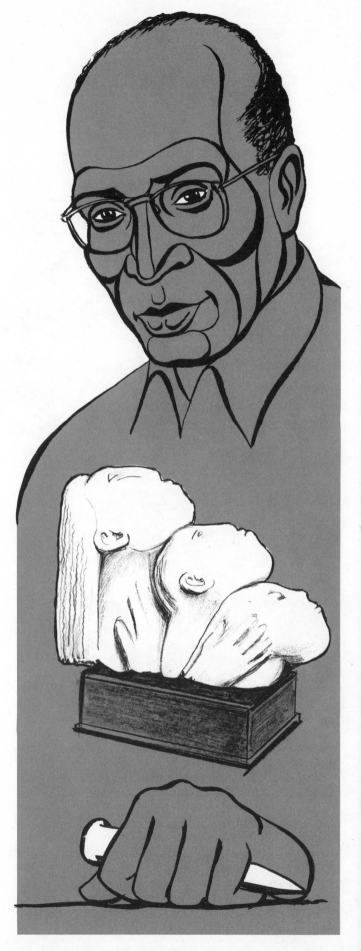

During the Depression of the thirties, Marion Perkins sold papers at a newsstand on Chicago's South Side. In his free moments at the stand he busied himself whittling on bars of soap, usually before a curious group of youngsters eagerly waiting to see just what form would evolve from his skilled fingers.

One day Peter Pollack, then director of the Community Art Center Division of the Illinois Art Project (W.P.A.), chanced upon Perkins and immediately recognized his creative talent. Pollack introduced Perkins to Si Gordon, a sculptor, who at the time was teaching at the South Side Community Art Center. Si Gordon took a special interest in Marion Perkins, and taught him to model in clay, make plaster molds and casts, and eventually to chisel stone.

Perkins worked hard, as if driven by some unseen force. He labored as though he sensed that he had a limited time in which to complete his work. One might see him carting huge stones which he collected from demolished buildings, and later witness the transformation of those stones into sensitive works of art.

Working as he did, it was not long before Perkins began to earn a place for himself as a sculptor of merit. His work earned the recognition of the Rosenwald Foundation, and he received prizes and purchase awards. His *Man of Sorrow* won the Art Institute of Chicago sculpture purchase prize in 1951. Of all his achievements, he considered teaching at Jackson State Teachers College his most rewarding experience, although it was for a short time. He found that the college lacked sufficient equipment and materials to provide art education, and so he returned to Chicago and devoted his attention to securing funds and materials for the students at Jackson State.

Before Marion Perkins died on December 17, 1961, his works had been exhibited in many of the principal museums and galleries throughout the United States and Europe. He inspired his friends to the extent that they established the Marion Perkins Memorial Foundation, which has as its purpose the support of Jackson State Teachers College and other worthy schools in the area of art education.

Based on data supplied by Toussaint Perkins, son of Marion Perkins, Chicago, Ill., 1963.

Charles White
(1918-   )

MODERN PAINTER

Sketch of detail from
"There Were No Crops This Year"

As a poor boy living in the slums of Chicago's South Side, Charles had but one ambition: to become an artist. His mother's window shades were his first canvases; his first art schools were the buildings and lots surrounding him. At the age of fifteen he began exhibiting his drawings and paintings in empty stores, in churches, in vacant lots, anywhere that people would stop and look. Finally, he managed to study at the Art Institute of Chicago. When the Illinois Art Project, WPA, put artists to work in Chicago, Charles White was gainfully employed on the easel project. Here he was provided materials and complete freedom to work as he chose. He quickly won a Rosenwald Fellowship, a John Hay Whitney Fellowship, and a National Institute of Arts and Letters grant. He was an artist-in-residence at Howard University.

In spite of many tempting commercial offers, White has remained true to "art for art's sake." He feels that an artist, particularly an artist who is also a Negro, has a social responsibility, and that the demands of art and society are not necessarily in conflict. He says, "I look to life and to my people as the fountainhead of challenging ideas and monumental concepts. I look to the bright new world coming; as I face a blank canvas, it is with such thoughts that I, an American Negro, turn to the business at hand—Art."

Possessing the richness, power, and moving simplicity of the spirituals, the graphic art and paintings of Charles White have won him the honor and recognition of being one of America's foremost modern contemporary artists. The titles of many of his works are taken directly from the spirituals: *More On Up A Little Higher*, depicting a woman with her palms stretched heavenward; *Take My Mother Home*, a young man with one hand raised in benediction; and another, *Mary, Don't You Weep*, illustrates two women in sorrow. These and other representational works have a force, vitality and humanity absent from much of the modern art.

White's work demonstrates a technical virtuosity and universality of feeling that finds a ready market for everything he produces. He has had many, many one-man shows. His works may be seen in the collections of the Library of Congress, the Whitney Museum of American Art, Long Beach (California) Museum of Art, the Barnett Aden Gallery in Washington, D.C., at Atlanta University, Tuskegee Institute, Howard University and the Deutsche Akademi, Berlin, Germany. He is represented in private collections in France, England, Canada, Switzerland, Italy, Africa, India and Japan.

Janice Lovoos, *American Artist: Anniversary Issue* (June, 1962), pp. 9-102, 118-120; Hoyt W. Fuller, "Charles White, Artist," *Negro Digest* (July, 1963), pp. 40-45.

Charles H. Alston (1907-   )

FAMED MURALIST

Sketch of large painting.
"Black Man and Woman"

The greatest cultural advancement in the history of our nation was made during the years of the federally funded Works Progress Administration. During the years of 1937-1941, thousands of artists, writers, actors, musicians, and allied craftsmen were gainfully employed. Although many of those employed were professionals out of work, the majority were students and amateurs. Charles H. Alston was one of the professionals.

Alston was born in Charlotte, North Carolina in 1907 and moved to New York while a boy. He received his Master of Arts degree from Columbia University in 1931 and served as an art instructor at the Harlem Art Center and the Harlem Art Workshop prior to working on the WPA. When he came to work on the New York Art Project, a department of the WPA, he brought with him a background of formal education and teaching experience. His talents and ability he shared with the promising amateurs and students with whom he worked in Harlem.

Alston has earned distinction as an easel and mural painter, sculptor, and illustrator. He was awarded the Arthur Wesley Dow Fellowship, Columbia University; the Rosenwald Fellowship in Painting, 1939-1940 and 1940-1941; and a National Institute of Arts and Letters Grant in 1958. His paintings won first prize at the Atlanta University Annual Exhibit in 1941; first prize at the Dillard University Annual Exhibit in 1942; and the Joe and Emily Lowe Award in 1960. His impressive murals "Primitive Medicine" and "Modern Medicine" adorn the walls of the Harlem Hospital. Others are on the walls of the

Golden State Insurance Company in Los Angeles, the Abraham Lincoln High School in Brooklyn, and the City College of New York. He also designed and executed panels and murals for the Hall of Forestry in the Museum of Natural History. He recently completed a mosaic mural on the theme of "Man on the Threshold of Space" at the Harriet Tubman School in Manhattan, New York, and a mural for the new Hall of Invertebrate Biology at the Museum of Natural History.

In 1958 he was one of the three U.S. representatives of the Museum of Modern Art and the State Department at the Children's Creative Center at the Brussels World Fair. He is a member of the National Society of Mural Painters. In 1967 he was named to the Advisory Board of the National Council of the Arts. Alston is a member of the faculty of City College of New York (1968). His works are in the collections of the Metropolitan Museum of Art, the Whitney Museum, International Business Machines, and others. Some of the magazines in which his illustrations have appeared are *Fortune, Red Book, Collier's, The New Yorker* and *Mademoiselle*.

Dover, Cedric, *American Negro Art* (London, Studio, 1960); Locke, Alain, *Negro Art: Past and Present* (Washington, D.C., Associates in Negro Folk Education, 1936).

Geraldine McCullough (1922-   )

PAINTER-SCULPTOR

The interesting thing about Mrs. McCullough winning the top prize at the Academy that year is the fact that this annual exhibit is one to which only established artists are "invited" to enter their works. Geraldine McCullough entered the competition without an invitation—and won. The honor brought her national acclaim and invitations to lecture and exhibit. Featured articles appeared in *Time, Ebony* and *Chicago* magazines. She made radio and television programs, including "To Tell the Truth," " The Artist and Psychology," "Our People," and "The Voice of America" show. In 1966 she was invited to Russia as a distinguished guest artist of the Soviet government, during which time she visited Moscow, Leningrad, Azerbaidzhan, and Prague.

Geraldine McCullough is a native of Maywood, a suburb of Chicago, where she was born December 1, 1922. Much preparation, work and experience preceded the honors bestowed upon her. She graduated from the Art Institute in 1948 and received her master's in Art Education in 1955 from the Art Institute. As a student there, she was awarded the John D. Steindecker Scholarship and the Memorial Scholarship, and won a Figure Painting citation. After teaching at Wendell Phillips High School for 14 years, she accepted an art professorship at Rosary College, River Forest, Illinois. She won honors as a painter and exhibited in national galleries, winning first a Purchase Award in 1959, and a first prize in 1961 at the annual Art Exhibit of Atlanta University, in addition to other awards in painting.

Turning to welded sculpture, after being encouraged by Richard Hunt and Rudolph Seno, masters of the art, she devoted her full talent to creating in metal. Her husband, Lester McCullough, taught her to weld and later helped her to handle the heavy metal objects and to crate her works for shipping. She made her debut as a sculptor at the Century of Negro Progress Exposition held in Chicago in 1963. She was represented in exhibits as a painter and sculptor until her "one man show" at the Ontario East Gallery in March, 1967. Here the true versatility and genius of her sculpture won the praise of top critics.

The artist has a strong social conviction that is so evident in her paintings and sculpture. One sees in her work, as she states it, "the universal struggle of people, their wrestling with adversity, their eventual triumph, and the perfection that resulted from their struggle."

When viewing the work of Geraldine McCullough, one is impressed by the power and strength so evident in her creations. It is impossible to conceive that the artist is a delicate and soft-spoken woman, just slightly more than five feet tall. Her sculpture titled *Phoenix,* which was awarded the George D. Widener Memorial Gold Medal for the "most meritorious work" in sculpture at the 159th annual exhibition of the Pennsylvania Academy of Fine Arts in 1964, was a welded steel and copper abstraction of 250 pounds of solid metals.

Who's Who of American Women 1968-69 (Chicago-A.N. Marquis Co., 1968).

Richard H. Hunt (1935-   )   MASTER OF METALS

In March, 1963, the noted art critic Hilton Kramer wrote that Richard H. Hunt was "one of the most gifted and assured artists working in the direct open form medium . . and I mean not only in his own country, but anywhere in the world." The direct-metal open-form medium is especially demanding of artists, for they must combine a mastery of metal working techniques with a talent for artistic creation and expression. Before and since the cautious Hilton Kramer evaluated his work, Richard H. Hunt has been important in the world of art. Many other equally competent critics have lavished praise upon the quiet, boyish-looking artist who works not with paint, brush and canvas, but with blow-torch, hammer and metal.

The creations of Richard Hunt stand in modernistic splendor in public and private collections throughout the nation. Carrying titles such as *Linear Spatial Form*, *Branching Construction*, and *Standing Forms*, Hunt's messages in metal have placed him in the vanguard of modern art. His works have been exhibited on many occasions and in many places, including the Carnegie International at Pittsburgh, the Museum of Modern Art, the Alan Gallery and the Whitney Museum in New York City, the Albright Gallery in Buffalo, the Art Institute of Chicago, the World Festival of Negro Art in Senegal, and the National Museum, Tel Aviv, Israel. Hunt has won a number of important prizes, including the Frank A. Logan Medal (1956, 1961-1962), the Paul Palmer Prize (1957) a James Nelson Raymond Travelling Fellowship (1957), a Guggenheim Fellowship (1962-1963), and a Ford Foundation Fellowship (1965).

A son of a barber, Richard Howard Hunt was born in Chicago, Illinois on September 12, 1935. He began the serious study of sculpture under the noted Nelli Bar when only fifteen years of age and won his first major prize when he was twenty-one. He studied at the University of Chicago (1953-1955) and received the B.A.E. certificate from the Art Institute of Chicago in 1957. He did further study in Italy, France, Spain and England. He taught at the Art Institute of Chicago (1960-1961), University of Illinois (1960-1962) and Chouinard Art School, Los Angeles (1964-1965). With the exception of teaching and a period of military service, Richard Hunt has devoted himself full-time to the production of his avant-garde masterpieces, which can be found in the permanent collections of art museums in Chicago, Cleveland, New York, Buffalo, Milwaukee and Israel.

Unlike the usual hush of a painter's studio, Hunt's working quarters resound to the sound of the hammer and the clash of metal as his work takes shape. In size, his work, which he refuses to call abstract or representative, ranges up to twelve feet in height and two or three feet in width. Not only the metal, but the spaces surrounding it are regarded as part of the complete work. His sculpture has been hailed as the work of a master whose artistry belies his comparative youth. Of his early development, Richard Hunt has said, "I must work fast. Any artist, particularly a Negro, has a responsibility to locate the truth."

Hilton Kramer, "Art," *Nation* (March 23, 1963), pp. 255-256. *Time*, (December 1, 1967), pp. 96-99; *Who's Who in America* (1964-65), p. 983; *Ebony* (April 1969), pp. 31-41.

Sketch of "Pyramidal Construction"

E. Simms Campbell
(1908-   )
CARTOONIST

During the thirties and forties, the symbols of sophisticated humor included cartoons whose situations revolved around an Arabian potentate and his scantily-clad harem of tantalizing blondes, brunettes and red-heads, or the contrasting attitudes toward the fair sex of the blasé business tycoon and the baffled young newlywed. In a syndicated cartoon series appearing in hundreds of newspapers, in ads for some of the nation's leading manufacturers, and in *Esquire* magazine could be found drawings and illustrations signed "E. Simms Campbell."

This artist's work captivated millions, including fellow artists. Few knew that E. Simms Campbell was Elmer Simms Campbell, the most successful Negro commercial artist of that time.

Little publicity has been given the fact that Campbell has illustrated children's books and exhibited paintings of a serious nature, good enough to merit an Honorable Mention. Most readers are unaware of the fact that he attracted national attention in 1926 with his cartoon commemorating Armistice Day in which he summed up the debt we all owe those who died in World War I; or his prize-winning cartoon of the tax grabbers which appeared before he was thirty years of age.

A native of St. Louis, Missouri, E. Simms Campbell attended Chicago's Englewood High School (where he was editorial cartoonist for the school paper) and the Chicago Art Institute. He broke into commercial art in his home town of St. Louis where he was told that it was a waste of time for a Negro in his youth to try to make a living in commercial art. Confident in his own ability, Campbell went to New York. With the help of other cartoonists, he began free-lancing. *Esquire* quickly spotted his talent and signed him to a long-term contract. Advertising agencies sought his talents and, in some years, he was turning out over 500 finished cartoons of high quality each year.

When the new men's magazine, *Playboy*, made its appearance in the mid 1950's, Campbell enjoyed the distinction of having his cartoons appear in competing publications.

Campbell's skill has earned him a place in *Current Biography*, *We Have Tomorrow*, *Who's Who* and other biographical works. So sophisticated is his work that the changing taste and style in journalism have failed to outdate it. In a highly competitive and specialized field of commercial art, Campbell ranks with the best. He and his wife now make their home in Switzerland. With the vigor of a beginning artist, he continues to meet the heavy demands of his syndicate and magazine contracts.

Arna Bontemps, *We Have Tomorrow* (Boston 1945), pp. 1-14.

Gordon Roger Parks
(1912-   )

MASTER OF THE CAMERA

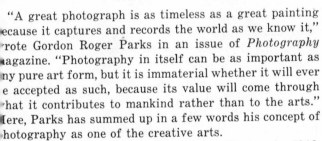
etch of photo from "Life" Harlem gang leader story

"A great photograph is as timeless as a great painting ecause it captures and records the world as we know it," rote Gordon Roger Parks in an issue of *Photography* agazine. "Photography in itself can be as important as ny pure art form, but it is immaterial whether it will ever e accepted as such, because its value will come through hat it contributes to mankind rather than to the arts." Iere, Parks has summed up in a few words his concept of hotography as one of the creative arts.

Born on a small farm in Ft. Scott, Kansas in 1912, Fordon Parks migrated to St. Paul, Minnesota in his teens. After leaving high school he worked as a waiter, lumberack, piano player, band leader and semi-professional basetball player. In 1937 he chose photography as a career. Ie moved to Chicago where he was inspired and influenced hrough his association with the artists of the South Side Community Art Center. Here he was provided a darkroom n which to work, and eventually given a one-man exhibit by David P. Ross, director of the gallery. As a result of his show he won a Rosenwald Fellowship, the first awarded or photography, and went to the Farm Security Administration unit directed by Roy Stryker. After a year there, ne joined Elmer Davis in the OWI's Overseas Division.

Parks rejoined Stryker in 1945 as a member of a sevenman photographic team which made documentaries for Standard Oil of New Jersey. In 1949 he was engaged by *Life* magazine as a staff photographer. Some of his imortant assignments with *Life* were stories on a Harlem gang leader, segregation in the South, crime in the United

States, and on the plight of an underprivileged Brazilian boy named Flavio. He wrote and directed a documentary film on Flavio.

Gordon Parks is acclaimed one of the most versatile photographers working today, ". . . he slips easily from rugged and often raw photo journalism to lush settings of fashion or the drama and emotion of the theater." The A.S.M.P. named him, "Magazine Photographer of the Year" in 1961, and he received the Newhouse Award in photography from Syracuse University. He won honors in the Art Directors show and the News Pictures of the Year competition.

As a *Life* photographer, Parks has had assignments in every part of the world. He was assigned to the European staff of *Life* and together with his wife, two sons and daughter lived in Paris for more than a year.

Parks considers himself a "week-end composer." He has written several musical compositions, including First Concerto for Piano and Orchestra, which was performed in 1953, and three piano sonatas, performed at Philadelphia in 1955. His written works include a book on photography, a novel, *The Learning Tree*, published in the fall of 1963 and *A Choice of Weapons*, a finely wrought autobiography which appeared in 1966. In 1968, he published *Photos and Poems* and commenced the filming of *The Learning Tree* for Warner Brothers-Seven Arts.

Life Magazine, 1963; *Photography* Magazine, 1963; Personal association with the Editor, 1940-1963; Gerald Moore, "Suddenly Doors Open Up," *Life* (November 15, 1968) : 123-124.

PUBLISHER'S NOTE

Every American has a stake in the present and future welfare of our nation, and it behooves us individually and collectively to do that which is in our power to improve the conditions of life in all areas.

In our area of specialized education we publish African-American materials which shed increasing light on the role of black Americans and their African ancestors in the history and culture of our nation and the world. Our efforts have been rewarded and have enabled us to produce new materials in an area where they are vitally needed.

The second edition of GREAT NEGROES, *Past and Present*, published in 1964, has been one of the most widely used supplementary textbooks for the introduction of African-American history and culture at the junior high and secondary school levels.

Comparison of this third edition with the second edition will reveal revisions in the content of some of the repeated material, as well as changes in dates and spellings. This is due in part to the availability of a greater amount of data as well as time to resolve conflicting data. While we attempted to at least mention the hundreds of individuals contributing to black history, it was obviously possible to include only representative complete biographies. Thus, lesser-known individuals in rarely-mentioned fields were sometimes included in preference to more famous personalities in more publicized fields. Many sport, entertainment and political figures were slighted in order to balance the book with black pioneers in the less glamorous but equally important fields such as church and fraternal organization, education, and the arts.

We publish three portfolios of display pictures which are used extensively in the lower grades, and which adorn the walls of schools and libraries across the nation. In 1968 we issued *The Meeting*, a one-act play based on our multi-ethnic American heritage, written by Peggy Orsborn for grades 7 through 12. This, too, has been well received in educational institutions throughout the country.

New publications in our schedule for immediate and future production include primary materials (readers, poems, plays, and puzzles for grades K through 6), a two-volume Afro-American art history, and several more portfolios of study prints covering contributors to the arts, science, business, and government. Study guides will be made available to aid the teacher in utilizing most of our materials.

In answer to many requests for a comprehensive guide to the teaching of Black History, we are now producing a teachers' guide which will correlate GREAT NEGROES, *Past and Present* with United States history.

Anyone desiring to receive literature on our new releases will be placed on our regular mailing list. We welcome all ideas, suggestions, and criticisms which will contribute to the improvement of our materials. We regret we cannot assume responsibility for unsolicited materials.

AFRO-AM PUBLISHING COMPANY, INC.
CHICAGO, ILLINOIS

BIBLIOGRAPHY

OUR AFRICAN HERITAGE

Davidson, Basil. *The Lost Cities of Africa.* Boston: Little, Brown & Co., 1959.

Graves, Anna Melissa. *Africa: The Wonder and the Glory.* Baltimore, 1961.

Owens, William A. *Slave Mutiny: The Revolt on the Schooner Amistad.* New York: John Day Co., 1953.

Ritter, E. A. *Shaka Zulu: The Rise of the Zulu Empire.* New York: G. P. Putnam's Sons, 1955.

Shaw, Flora L. *A Tropical Dependency: An Outline of the Ancient History of the Western Souden with an Account of the Modern Settlement of North Nigeria.* London, 1905.

EARLY AMERICAN HISTORY

Boston, City of. *A Memorial of Crispus Attucks, Samuel Maverick, James Caldwell, Samuel Gray and Patrick Carr.* Boston, 1889.

Bradford, Sarah. *Harriet Tubman: The Moses of Her People.* New York: Corinth Books, 1961.

Breyfogle, William. *Make Free: The Story of the Underground Railroad.* New York: J. B. Lippincott Co., 1958.

Douglass, Frederick. *Narrative of the Life of Frederick Douglass, an American Slave.* Hartford: Miller, 1845.

Douglass, Frederick. *Narrative of the Life of Frederick Douglass, an American Slave.* Edited by Benjamin Quarles. Cambridge, Mass.: Harvard University Press, Belknap Press, 1960.

Drewry, William J. *Slave Insurrections in Virginia 1830-1865.* Washington: Neale Co., 1900.

Litwack, Leon. *North of Slavery: The Negro in the Free States, 1790-1860.* Chicago: University of Chicago Press, 1961.

McElhiney, Edna. *Historical St. Charles Missouri.* St. Louis, 1967.

Morris, Saurian. *A Sketch of the Life of Benjamin Banneker: Own Notes Taken in 1836.* Baltimore: Maryland Historical Society, 1854.

Nell, William C. *The Colored Patriots of the American Revolution.* Boston, 1855.

Pauli, Hertha E. *Her Name was Sojourner Truth.* New York: Appleton-Century-Crofts, 1962.

Quarles, Benjamin. *The Negro in the American Revolution.* Chapel Hill: University of North Carolina Press, 1961.

Sherwood, H. N. *Paul Cuffe.* Washington, D.C.: Association for the Study of Negro Life and History, 1923.

Stampp, Kenneth. *The Peculiar Institution; Slavery in the Ante-Bellum South.* New York: Alfred A. Knopf, 1956.

Sterling, Dorothy. *Freedom Train: The Story of Harriet Tubman.* New York: Doubleday & Co., 1954.

Vandercook, John. *Black Majesty: The Life of Christophe, King of Haiti.* New York: Harper & Brothers, 1928.

Williams, George W. *History of the Negro Race in America from 1619 to 1880.* 2 vols. New York: G. P. Putnam's Sons, 1882.

FROM THE CIVIL WAR FORWARD

Cornish, Dudley Taylor. *The Sable Arm; Negro Troops in the Union Army, 1861-1865.* New York: Longmans, Green & Co., 1956.

Franklin, John Hope. *Reconstruction After the Civil War.* Chicago: University of Chicago Press, 1961.

Meier, August. *Negro Thought in America, 1880-1915: Racial Ideologies in the Age of Booker T. Washington.* Ann Arbor: University of Michigan Press, 1963.

Simmons, William J. *Men of Mark: Eminent, Progressive and Rising.* Cleveland: George M. Rewell, 1887.

Sterling, Dorothy. *Captain of the Planter: The Story of Robert Smalls.* New York: Doubleday & Co., 1958.

SCIENCE and INDUSTRY

Buckler, Helen. *Doctor Dan: Pioneer in American Surgery.* Boston: Little, Brown & Co., 1954.

Henson, Matthew A. *A Negro Explorer at the North Pole.* New York: Stokes, 1912.

Robinson, Bradley. *Dark Companion.* New York: R. M. McBride Co., 1947.

Taylor, Julius H., ed. *The Negro in Science.* Baltimore: Morgan State College Press, 1955.

BUSINESS PIONEERS

Andrews, Robert McCants. *John Merrick: A Biographical Sketch.* Durham, N.C.: Seeman Printery, 1920.

Harris, Abram. *The Negro as Capitalist: A Study of Banking and Business among American Negroes.* Philadelphia: American Academy of Political and Social Science, 1936.

Oak, Vishnu V. *The Negro's Adventure in General Business.* Yellow Springs, Ohio: Antioch Press, 1949.

Ottley, Roi. *The Lonely Warrior: The Life and Times of Robert S. Abbott.* Chicago: Henry Regnery Co., 1955.

Penn, I. Garland. *The Afro-American Press and Editors.* Springfield, Mass.: Willey and Co., 1891.

Pierce, Joseph. *Negro Business and Business Education: Their Present and Prospective Development.* Harper & Brothers, 1947.

RELIGION

Foley, Albert S. *God's Men of Color: The Colored Catholic Priests of the United States, 1854-1954.* New York: Farrar, Straus & Young, 1955.

Lincoln, Charles Eric. *The Black Muslims in America.* Boston: Beacon Press, 1961.

Woodson, Carter G. *The History of the Negro Church.* Washington, D.C.: Associated Publishers, 1945.

LEADERS and SPOKESMEN

Bennett, Lerone. *What Manner of Man: A Biography of Martin Luther King, Jr.* 3rd rev. ed. Chicago: Johnson Publishing Co., 1968.

Brazeal, Brailsford R. *The Brotherhood of Sleeping Car Porters: Its Origin and Development.* New York: Harper & Brothers, 1946.

Cannon, Poppy. *A Gentle Knight: My Husband, Walter White.* New York: Rinehart & Co., 1956.

Cronon, Edmund D. *Black Moses: The Story of Marcus Garvey and the Universal Negro Improvement Association.* Madison: University of Wisconsin Press, 1955.

Hughes, Langston. *Fight for Freedom: The Story of the NAACP.* New York: Berkley Publishing Corp., 1962.

King, Martin Luther. *Stride Toward Freedom: The Montgomery Story.* New York: Ballantine Books, 1960.

Lewinson, Paul. *Race, Class and Party: A History of Negro Suffrage and White Politics in the South.* New York: Oxford University Press, 1932.

Malcolm X. *The Autobiography of Malcolm X.* Edited by Arthur Haley. New York: Grove Press, 1965.

Malcolm X. *Malcolm X Speaks: Selected Speeches and Statements.* Edited by George Breitman. New York: Grove Press, 1965.

Peare, Catherine O. *Mary McLeod Bethune.* New York: Vanguard Press, 1951.

Reddick, Lawrence Dunbar. *Crusader Without Violence: A Biography of Martin Luther King, Jr.* New York: Harper & Brothers, 1959.

Terrell, Mary Church. *A Colored Woman in a White World.* Washington, D.C.: Ransdell, 1940.

Torrence, Frederic Ridgely. *The Story of John Hope.* New York: Macmillan Co., 1948.

White, Walter. *A Man Called White, The Autobiography of Walter White.* New York: Viking Press, 1948.

Yates, Elizabeth. *Howard Thurman: Portrait of a Practical Dreamer.* New York: John Day Co., 1964.

BIBLIOGRAPHY

EDUCATION

Broderick, Francis L. *W. E. B. Du Bois: Negro Leader in a Time of Crisis*. Stanford, Calif.: Stanford University Press, 1959.

Range, Willard. *The Rise and Progress of Negro Colleges in Georgia: 1865-1949*. Athens, Ga.: University of Georgia Press, 1951.

Bone, Robert. *The Negro Novel in America*. New Haven: Yale University Press, 1958.

Brawley, Benjamin. *Paul Laurence Dunbar, Poet of his People*. Chapel Hill: University of North Carolina Press, 1936.

Brooks, Gwendolyn. *The Bean Eaters*. New York: Harper & Row Publishers, 1960.

Chesnutt, Helen M. *Charles Waddell Chesnutt: Pioneer of the Color Line*. Chapel Hill: University of North Carolina Press, 1962.

Cross, Samuel H. and Simmons, Ernest J. *Alexander Pushkin, 1799-1837: His Life and Literary Heritage*. Washington, D.C.: American-Russian Institute, 1937.

Cunningham, Virginia. *Paul Laurence Dunbar and his Song*. New York: Dodd, Mead & Co., 1947.

Dreer, Herman. *American Literature by Negro Authors*. New York: Macmillan Co., 1950.

Ethridge, James M. *Contemporary Authors*. 2 vols. Detroit: Gale Research Co., 1962.

Gloster, Hugh Morris. *Negro Voices in American Fiction*. Chapel Hill: University of North Carolina Press, 1948.

Johnson, James Weldon. *Along This Way*. New York: Viking Press, 1933.

THE THEATRE

Bond, Frederick W. *The Negro and the Drama: The Direct and Indirect Contribution Which the American Negro Has Made to Drama and the Legitimate Stage, with the Underlying Conditions Responsible*. Washington, D.C.: Associated Publishers, 1940.

Dunham, Katherine. *A Touch of Innocence*. New York: Harcourt, Brace & Co., 1959.

Graham, Shirley. *Paul Robeson, Citizen of the World*. New York: Julian Messner, 1946.

Isaacs, Edith J. R. *The Negro in the American Theatre*. New York: Theatre Arts, 1947.

Waters, Ethel and Samuels, Charles. *His Eye is on the Sparrow*. New York: Doubleday & Co., 1951.

MUSIC

Anderson, Marian, *My Lord, What a Morning; An Autobiography*, New York: Viking Press, 1956.

Armstrong, Louis. *Satchmo: My Life in New Orleans*. New York: Prentice-Hall, 1954.

Daly, John Jay. *A Song in His Heart*. Philadelphia: John C. Winston Co., 1951.

Ewen, David, ed. *Popular American Composers, from Revolutionary Times to the Present*. New York: H. W. Wilson Co., 1962.

Gammond, Peter, ed. *Duke Ellington: His Life and Music*. New York: Roy Publishers, 1958.

Goffin, Robert. *Horn of Plenty: The Story of Louis Armstrong*. Translated by James F. Bezou. New York: Allen, Towne & Heath, 1947.

Hare, Maud. *Negro Musicians and Their Music*. Washington, D.C.: Associated Publishers, 1936.

Helm, MacKinley. *Angel Mo' and Her Son, Roland Hayes*. Boston: Little, Brown & Co., 1942.

Sayers, W. C. Berwick. *Samuel Coleridge-Taylor, Musician: His Life and Letters*. New York: Cassell and Co., 1915.

Stearns, Marshall W. *The Story of Jazz*. New York: New American Library, 1958.

Vehanen, Kosti. *Marian Anderson; A Portrait*. New York: McGraw-Hill Book Co., 1941.

THE VISUAL ARTS

Dover, Cedric. *American Negro Art*. Greenwich, Conn.: New York Graphic Society, 1960.

Locke, Alain L., ed. *The Negro in Art: A Pictorial Record of the Negro Artist and of the Negro Theme in Art*. Washington, D.C.: Associates in Negro Folk Education, 1940.

Porter, James. *Modern Negro Art*. New York: Dryden Press, 1943.

GENERAL HISTORY and BIOGRAPHY

Aptheker, Herbert, ed. *A Documentary History of the Negro People in the United States*. 2 vols. New York: Citadel Press, 1951.

Baldwin, James. *Notes of a Native Son*. Boston: Beacon Press, 1955.

Bennett, Lerone, Jr. *Before the Mayflower: A History of the Negro in America, 1619-1962*. Chicago: Johnson Publishing Co., 1962.

Bontemps, Arna. *One Hundred Years of Negro Freedom*. New York: Dodd, Mead & Co., 1961.

Bontemps, Arna. *We Have Tomorrow*. Boston: Houghton Mifflin Co., 1945.

Brawley, Benjamin. *Negro Builders and Heroes*. Chapel Hill: University of North Carolina Press, 1937.

Brawley, Benjamin. *The Negro Genius*. New York: Dodd, Mead & Co., 1937.

Brawley, Benjamin. *A Short History of the American Negro*. 3d rev. ed. New York: Macmillan Co., 1931.

Brown, Sterling et al. *The Negro Caravan*. New York: Dryden Press, 1941.

Bullock, Ralph. *In Spite of Handicaps*. New York: Association Press, 1927.

Butcher, Margaret Just. *The Negro in American Culture*. New York: New American Library, 1957.

Commons, John et al. *A Documentary History of American Industrial Society*. Vol. 9. 2d ed. New York: Russell & Russell, 1958.

Du Bois, W. E. B. *The Souls of Black Folk: Essays and Sketches*. New York: Blue Heron Press, 1953.

Essien-Udom, Essien Udosen. *Black Nationalism: A Search for an Identity in America*. Chicago: University of Chicago Press, 1962.

Fleming, Beatrice and Pryde, Marion. *Distinguished Negroes Abroad*. Washington, D.C.: Associated Publishers, 1946.

Franklin, John Hope. *From Slavery to Freedom: A History of American Negroes*. 2d ed. New York: Alfred A. Knopf, 1961.

Isaacs, Harold. *The New World of American Negroes*. New York: John Day Co., 1963.

Johnson, James Weldon. *Black Manhattan*. New York: Alfred A. Knopf, 1930.

Locke, Alain L. *The New Negro: An Interpretation*. New York: Albert & Charles Boni, 1925.

Ottley, Roi. *New World A-Coming; Inside Black America*. New York: Houghton Mifflin Co., 1943.

Ovington, Mary White. *Portraits in Color*. New York: Viking Press, 1927.

Ploski, Harry A. and Brown, Roscoe C. Jr., eds. *The Negro Almanac*. New York: Bellwether Publishing Co., 1967.

Richardson, Ben Albert. *Great American Negroes*. New York: Thomas Y. Crowell Co., 1945.

Rogers, Joel Augustus. *World's Great Men of Color, 3,000 B.C. to 1946 A.D.* 2 vols. New York: J. A. Rogers, 1946-47.

Schulte Nordholt, Jan Willem. *The People That Walk in Darkness*. New York: Ballantine Books, 1960.

Voorhis, Harold Van Buren. *Negro Masonry in the United States*. New York: Harry Emmerson, 1940.

Wesley, Charles H. *Negro Labor in the United States, 1850-1925*. New York: Vanguard Press, 1927.

Woodson, Carter G. *The Negro in Our History*. 7th ed. Washington, D.C.; Associated Publishers, 1941.

INDEX